A BITTER REVOLUTION

THE MAKING OF THE MODERN WORLD

This group of narrative histories focuses on key moments and events in the twentieth century to explore their wider significance for the development of the modern world.

PUBLISHED:

The Fall of France: The Nazi Invasion of 1940, Julian Jackson
A Bitter Revolution: China's Struggle with the Modern World, Rana Mitter

FORTHCOMING:

The Vietnam Wars: A Global History, Mark Bradley
Algeria: The Undeclared War, Martin Evans
The Burning of Louvain, Alan Kramer

SERIES ADVISERS:

PROFESSOR CHRIS BAYLY, University of Cambridge
PROFESSOR RICHARD J. EVANS, University of Cambridge
PROFESSOR PAUL PRESTON, London School of Economics
PROFESSOR DAVID REYNOLDS, University of Cambridge
PROFESSOR MEGAN VAUGHAN, University of Cambridge

A BITTER REVOLUTION

*China's Struggle with
the Modern World*

RANA MITTER

OXFORD
UNIVERSITY PRESS

OXFORD
UNIVERSITY PRESS

Great Clarendon Street, Oxford OX2 6DP

Oxford University Press is a department of the University of Oxford.
It furthers the University's objective of excellence in research, scholarship,
and education by publishing worldwide in

Oxford New York

Auckland Bangkok Buenos Aires Cape Town Chennai
Dar es Salaam Delhi Hong Kong Istanbul Karachi Kolkata
Kuala Lumpur Madrid Melbourne Mexico City Mumbai Nairobi
São Paulo Shanghai Taipei Tokyo Toronto

Oxford is a registered trade mark of Oxford University Press
in the UK and in certain other countries

Published in the United States
by Oxford University Press Inc., New York

© Rana Mitter, 2004

The moral rights of the author have been asserted

Database right Oxford University Press (maker)

First published 2004

British Library Cataloguing in Publication Data

Data available

Library of Congress Cataloging in Publication Data

Mitter, Rana, 1969–
A bitter revolution : China's struggle with the modern world / Rana Mitter.
p. cm.
Includes bibliographical references and index.
ISBN 0–19–280341–7
1. China—History—20th century. 2. China—Politics and government—20th century.
I. Title: China's struggle with the modern world. II. Title.
DS774.M55 2004
951.06—dc22 2004041561
ISBN 0–19–280341–7

1 3 5 7 9 10 8 6 4 2

Typeset in Janson
by RefineCatch Limited, Bungay, Suffolk
Printed and bound in Great Britain by
Biddles Ltd, King's Lynn, Norfolk

'Didn't you say, as we were going through those streets, "They never greet me, they hate me?" Well, you're a clever man, you ought to know that those children don't hate you at all – it's just that they've got nothing to eat.'

'I think they hate me,' [the priest] told me, slowly, 'because they've abandoned their belief in God.'

Ödön von Horváth, *The Age of the Fish* (1939)
[orig. *Jugend ohne Gott*, tr. R. Wills Thomas]

For Pamina

Contents

PART II: AFTERSHOCK

Preface

Chairman Mao, more than a quarter-century after his death, probably remains the one Chinese name generally well known in the west. From there onwards, the map has a lot of blank spaces. Despite this, I felt it was possible, and worthwhile, to try to write a book explaining how and why so much of contemporary Chinese politics and culture is heavily shaped by what happened in the early twentieth century. This book would not be a survey obliged to deal with every single aspect of modern Chinese history (and end up very long as a result), nor would it be a piece of very specialized scholarship, of the type essential to those working in the academic field but often inaccessible to those outside it. I hoped it would be possible to integrate the political, cultural, and social history of China, and give some idea of how the places where people lived, loved, and worked affected how they thought and behaved. I also felt it important to showcase some of the new directions taken by writing on Chinese history, politics, and literature in the last few decades, particularly as China itself has become much more accessible to researchers.

I hope that this book will act as a useful interpretation of modern Chinese history and politics, and show how the two are linked. It is a cliché, but nonetheless true, that one cannot fully understand what is going on in China today if one does not understand what happened there in the past. Anyone who reads a newspaper will see that Chinese politicians are acutely conscious of their own history. The Communist leadership greeted the return of Hong Kong in 1997 as the ending of 150 years of imperialist aggression in China; the 1989 Tian'anmen Square demonstrators compared themselves with students who had protested in that same spot 70 years previously. This book starts with one brief moment in Chinese history, a demonstration in Beijing on 4 May 1919, goes on to look at the cultural and social turmoil that surrounded that event, and argues that the ghosts of what happened that day are visible, often in very strange and unexpected ways, in the development of modern China. This book does not use the rise to power of the Communist Party as the central narrative. Instead, it argues for a more diverse way of looking at what Chinese politics was in the past, and what it might be again. The Communists are very important, but they are not the whole story. For those who are visiting or studying China in the early years of the new millennium, I hope that this will be a stimulating way to think about this immensely important country.

The book has also had to come to terms with the often rather closed-off nature of Chinese studies: things that need careful explanation to even well-informed readers often seem obvious to experts. For those who study China, names such as the May Fourth Movement, Lu Xun, or *Heshang* are well known. Yet I hope that some of the lesser-heard voices that are presented here may be of interest even to those who know China and its twentieth century well. I also hope that this attempt, even if tentative, to downplay the Communist revolution of 1949, which for so long acted as a gaping divide between 'history' and 'contemporary politics' in the China field, may be useful, and that it may be productive to look at China's twentieth century through the continuities, as well as changes, that run across the decades. Finally, those familiar with Chinese politics know that it is a commonplace that the 'spirit of May Fourth' has remained tremendously important in China since the events of 1919: this book attempts actively to trace *how* and *why* that 'spirit' has remained so significant.

It will be clear from the endnotes that I am heavily indebted to many outstanding scholars and their books and articles. It is a sign of the vibrancy in the field of modern Chinese studies that this book could not have been written in this form just ten or fifteen years ago, as so many of the most pathbreaking studies have appeared within that period. I would like to acknowledge here my immense gratitude to the authors of the array of stimulating works on which I have drawn.

Finally, I must thank a number of people who have been essential to the completion of this book. First, my thanks to Chris Bayly for so generously suggesting that it would be a good idea to write a book of this sort, and for making its publication possible. Various readers took time from their very busy schedules to read through the manuscript at various stages of completion and made immensely helpful comments: Robert Bickers, Enrico Flossmann, Euan Graham, Nancy Kelley, and Eddy U. I have also benefited immensely from conversations with and helpful suggestions from many people, including Iris Chang, Glen Dudbridge, David Faure, Henrietta Harrison, Simon Kuper, Deep Lahiri-Choudhury, Frank Pieke, Steve Smith, and Hans van de Ven. Red Chan exercised particular ingenuity in obtaining a rare copy of *Heshang*. I am also most grateful to the Press's anonymous readers for their thoughtful comments. Although all these readers saved me from many mistakes, all errors and misinterpretations remain entirely my responsibility.

I am particularly in the debt of David Helliwell, librarian of the Chinese collection at the Bodleian Library, Oxford, and Minh Chung, librarian at the Institute for Chinese Studies, Oxford, both of whom were cheerful and resourceful well beyond the call of duty in response to my requests for obscure books and CD-ROMs.

At Oxford University Press, I benefited greatly from the professionalism and good humour of Katharine Reeve and Emily Jolliffe. I am also grateful to Catherine Clarke, who dealt with the project in its initial phase.

Finally, I have unrepayable debts to my parents, Partha and Swasti, my sister Pamina, and to Katharine, all of whom not only read the manuscript, but provided love and support throughout its writing.

Rana Mitter
Oxford
September 2003

List of Illustrations

Chronology

1842:   Treaty of Nanjing is signed after the end of the first Opium War between China and Britain: Hong Kong is ceded, treaty ports including Shanghai opened up to trade

1856–64: Taiping civil war convulses much of central China

1881:   Lu Xun (original name Zhou Shuren) born

1895:   Zou Taofen (original name Zou Enrun)

1898:   Reform movement at court, thwarted by conservative backlash; and Du Zhongyuan born

1900:   Boxer War: western powers unite to defeat Qing dynasty forces

1904:   Ding Ling (original name Jiang Bingzhi) born

1911:   Revolution overthrows Qing dynasty

1912:   Republic of China is formally established; Republican period lasts 1912–49; Yuan Shikai becomes president

1915:   Yuan Shikai attempts to become emperor and restore Confucian government; Chen Duxiu and other intellectuals form New Culture Movement in response

1916:   Yuan Shikai dies

1917:   China enters World War I

1918:   Lu Xun publishes *Diary of a Madman*

1919:   Paris Peace Conference denies return of German colonies to China; patriotic students demonstrate at Tian'anmen in Beijing on 4 May and end by attacking and burning government minister Cao Rulin's house

1925:   May Thirtieth Incident in Shanghai

1926:   Zou Taofen becomes editor of *Life* magazine

1926–7:   Northern Expedition by united front of Nationalists and Communists

1927:   Ding Ling publishes *The Diary of Miss Sophie*; Nationalists turn on former Communist allies in Shanghai, ending united front

1928:   Nationalist government under Chiang Kaishek is established, with its capital at Nanjing

1931:   Manchuria invaded by the Japanese; Hu Yepin, Ding Ling's lover, is arrested and executed for Communist activities; Du Zhongyuan becomes a regular writer for *Life* magazine

1933:   *Life* closed down by Nationalist government; Zou Taofen flees abroad

1934:   Du Zhongyuan becomes editor of *New Life* magazine

1935:   Du Zhongyuan is imprisoned for anti-Japanese subversion

1936:   Zou Taofen active in National Salvation Movement, agitating against Japanese aggression; Du Zhongyuan is released from prison; Lu Xun dies; Ding Ling escapes to Communist base area in northwest China; Nationalists and Communists agree united front against Japanese

1937:   War of Resistance against Japan breaks out; Du Zhongyuan becomes war reporter, then moves to become head of Xinjiang Academy in Urumqi; Nationalists move capital to Wuhan, accompanied by Zou Taofen; Nanjing Massacre of Chinese civilians by Japanese troops

1938:   Nationalist capital moves to Chongqing, accompanied by Zou Taofen

1940–4:   Zou Taofen aligns with Communists, moves around China on propaganda work

1941:   Du Zhongyuan arrested by militarist leader of Xinjiang

1941–3:   Ding Ling subjected to increasing criticism by Communist leaders

1944:   Zou Taofen dies of cancer in Shanghai; Du Zhongyuan executed in prison

1945:   War of Resistance against Japan ends

1946–9:   Civil War between Nationalists and Communists ends with Communist victory

1957:   Hundred Flowers Movement, followed by Anti-Rightist campaign; Ding Ling exiled

1958–62:   Great Leap Forward collectivization campaign and famine

1966–9:   Initial phase of Cultural Revolution

1969–76:   Second phase of Cultural Revolution

1972:   US President Richard Nixon visits China

1976:   Arrest of 'Gang of Four' (Cultural Revolution leadership group)

1978:   Ascendancy of Deng Xiaoping: Four Modernizations and economic reform programmes endorsed

1985:   Publication of Bo Yang's *The Ugly Chinaman*

1986:   Ding Ling dies

1988:   Broadcast of television documentary *Heshang*

1989:   Tian'anmen Square occupied by students' and workers' demonstration; negotiations fail, end in bloodshed on 3–4 June; Jiang Zemin picked as 'core' of new Communist leadership

1992:   Jiang Zemin confirmed as core of new leadership

1996:   Publication of *China Can Say No*

1997:   Deng Xiaoping dies; handover of Hong Kong from Britain to China

2002:   Leadership passes from Jiang Zemin to Hu Jintao

Pronunciation, Transliterations, and Names

Chinese and Japanese names are given throughout in East Asian style, that is, with the surname first and the personal name second. So Mao Zedong's surname was Mao, and his personal name Zedong.

This book mostly uses the now standard Pinyin system of transliterating Chinese words. Most letters resemble their English pronunciations, although readers who want to pronounce the names with full accuracy may wish to consult a guide to the Chinese language. The following sounds, however, are not obvious:

> 'q' is pronounced 'ch' (therefore 'Qing' is pronounced 'ching')
>
> 'x' is pronounced 'sh' (therefore 'Xiaoping' is pronounced 'Shiao-ping')
>
> 'c' is pronounced 'ts' (therefore 'Cai' is pronounced 'tsai')
>
> 'chi', 'zhi', 'shi', 'si', 'zi', 'ci', and 'ri' are pronounced as if the final 'i' sound is almost an 'r', so 'chr', 'zhr', 'shr', and so forth.

In most cases, I have used Pinyin to transliterate names: therefore, I have used Mao Zedong rather than Mao Tse-tung. There are two major exceptions. One is for names that are better known under an alternative transliteration, for example Chiang Kaishek, Sun Yatsen. Another is where the name appears in an original source in a different spelling. In those cases, I have given the Pinyin form in square brackets: so 'Lu Hsun [Lu Xun]', or 'Tu Chung-yuan [Du Zhongyuan]'.

Older books use a transliteration system known as Wade-Giles, which, unfortunately, has rather different rules from Pinyin. Any volume of the *Cambridge History of China* (see Guide to Further Reading) contains a guide to reading Chinese names in this system.

Finally, a note on Beijing and its changing names. China's capital has always been known as 'Beijing' (meaning northern capital) in Mandarin (standard) Chinese. The name 'Peking' emerged as a western approximation, which then found widespread usage outside China, and this is how the city was known to foreigners in the early twentieth century. In 1928, the Nationalist government moved the capital of China to Nanjing (then known in the west as 'Nanking'), and renamed the former capital 'Beiping' (northern peace), although at the time it was usually known in the west as 'Peiping'. In 1949, the new Communist government moved the capital back and once again named it Beijing. The government continued to refer to the city as 'Peking' until the 1970s, when it indicated that it would prefer foreigners to use the name 'Beijing' instead. I have done so here, with one exception. The main university in Beijing found fame in the early twentieth century under the name 'Peking University' and has specified in recent years that it does not wish to be known as 'Beijing University'. I have followed that convention.

The thing to remember, in case of emergency, is that Beijing, Peking, Beiping, and Peiping are all the same city. If this name-changing seems complex, you have grasped something of the nature of the debate about identities that has so convulsed modern China.

PART I

Shock

1

FLASHPOINT: 4 MAY 1919

The Making of a New China

An observer standing by the back wall of an old, attractive house in a back alleyway in Beijing, late in the afternoon of 4 May 1919, would have glimpsed an unusual sight. Sounds of shouting and smashing furniture were emerging from inside the house, which appeared to have been taken over by an enthusiastic group of young people bent on destruction. A man suddenly appeared and jumped over the back wall – one source later suggested that he showed 'rare agility', and another claimed that he was wearing a uniform borrowed from a policeman – and landed awkwardly in the street. He was then picked up by attendants and rushed away from the scene.[1]

The man who had leaped so nimbly was Cao Rulin, minister of communications in the government of the Republic of China, and it was his house that was being so comprehensively destroyed. The attackers were students from Beijing's top colleges and universities. Earlier that day, some 3,000 students had gathered in front of the Tian'anmen, the Gate of Heavenly Peace which fronts the Forbidden City complex in the centre of the Chinese capital. The students, from 13 different colleges in the city, had listened to speeches protesting the shameful settlement that China had been forced to accept at the Paris Peace Conference which had ended World War I. Under the terms of the Versailles Treaty, the former German colonies on Chinese territory were not to be given back to China, but would instead be handed over to another imperialist power, Japan. By two o'clock, the students had had enough of speeches. Carrying placards, they started to march towards Beijing's diplomatic quarter, demanding justice for China in the international arena. As the students became more heated, they moved on to the house of Cao Rulin, who was regarded as being close politically to the Japanese. After destroying much of the interior of the house, and assaulting visitors whom they found there, some of the demonstrators then set fire to it. At this development, the police moved in, and 32 of the protestors were arrested.[2]

This sequence of events, which lasted just a few hours, gave rise to a legend. The date of the demonstration, May Fourth, became famous across China. Without the controversial, elusive, infuriating 'May Fourth Movement', and the closely related but wider 'New Culture Movement', twentieth-century Chinese history would be completely different. Yet the movement is still only sketchily known about or understood outside the world of China specialists, and even the Chinese themselves are locked in combat to this day about the 'real' meaning of the heady events and new trends of the early twentieth century. This book examines the different facets of this movement and suggests that its legacy, in varied forms, underpins the whole history of twentieth-century China.

At the time, it was not immediately clear that the events of 4 May 1919 would have such lasting effects. Yet the demonstrations did not emerge spontaneously, but were planned as a powerful political gesture by students angry with a Chinese government they felt had betrayed the interests of the country. Why, then, did the gathering at the Tian'anmen gate and the subsequent destruction of Minister Cao's house take place?

The trigger had come just a few days previously. On 30 April, news came from Paris, where the Peace Conference had been negotiating on the question of how China should be treated. Educated Chinese such as the students at Peking University had been watching events in Europe carefully, and had good reason to expect that the Versailles settlement would be a turning point for China's efforts to establish the legitimacy of the new Republic, founded just seven years previously. The government of the Republic did not consist of popular leaders with a mandate, but was rather the product of a seemingly unstoppable series of intrigues between militarist leaders with their

own armies and civilian elites with power over finance and governance. Nonetheless, the governments did employ skilled, often
western-educated diplomats who had high hopes of using the Great
War in Europe as a means of bolstering China's position in the world.
In 1917, Chinese Prime Minister Duan Qirui's government decided to
let China for the first time enter an international conflict voluntarily,
and the Beijing government declared its support for the Allies.
Although no Chinese soldier fought in combat, some 96,000 were
sent as labourers to the Western Front in Europe, and around 2,000
died there. Such a substantial contribution, China's patriots felt,
would surely result in an appropriate reward: in particular, the return
of the ports of Jiaozhou and Qingdao, and part of Shandong province
in northern China, all of which had been German colonies. As
Germany was to be stripped of its colonies under the Versailles
Treaty, China could expect to regain the territories it had lost so
unwillingly in the scramble for imperial possessions in China which
had marked the late nineteenth century.

But the message from Paris was bleak. China would not regain its
territory, and the formerly German areas would instead be handed
over to Japan. It emerged that the deal with China was not the only
one made by the Allies in 1917. They had also approached Japan,
which had agreed to assist the Allies in the Pacific in return for
territories in China after the war. The United States, which had
entered the war late, was not party to this agreement, and President
Woodrow Wilson was at first sympathetic to Chinese protests at Paris
with regard to this fait accompli, but when persuaded that the offer
to Japan was binding in international law, regretfully declined to
intervene against Britain, France, and Italy. Wilson made his position
public on 30 April 1919.

Chinese nationalists were outraged. And they took full advantage
of the globalized world which China had been forced into entering
after its disastrous defeat in the Opium Wars of the 1840s. The news
from Paris, thanks to the introduction of telegraphy and newspapers
into China, could be transmitted and published within hours, rather
than months. Nor were the Chinese themselves confined to China.
There had been a large ethnic Chinese diaspora within Asia for

centuries, and this had expanded into the western world in the nineteenth century: as the west forced itself into China, so China engaged with the west. The Chinese labourers on the Western Front had not been their only compatriots in France. There were also many Chinese students, largely from the educated elites, in Paris. When they heard about the humiliating terms of the Treaty, they surrounded the hotel where the Chinese delegates to the Peace Conference were staying and physically prevented them from signing the Treaty. But the most lasting legacy of the Allies' snub to China would be in the capital city on 4 May 1919, when the students made their protest at the heart of China's capital, the Tian'anmen gate.

The events of 'May Fourth' became well known quickly. However, there were very different interpretations of what they meant. Many of those who participated went on to shape modern China, and looked back on the events of May Fourth as part of their own political and spiritual journeys. One such figure was Luo Jialun, a 22-year-old student at Peking University who coined the term 'May Fourth Movement' in a journal article published just a few weeks after the demonstrations. Luo would go on to become President of Qinghua, one of China's top universities. In an oral memoir set down in 1931, Luo remembered the chain of events that led to the demonstrations on that hot Sunday in May. The previous evening, students had gathered at the Qinghua campus to plan a demonstration against the settlement at the Paris Peace Conference. Feelings ran high, so much so that one student threatened publicly to rebuke the Chinese government by killing himself with a knife which he had brought to the meeting. In the face of this anger, a demonstration which had been planned for the following Wednesday, 7 May, was abandoned in favour of action the very next day, Sunday 4 May. The students hastily cashed in a savings account to buy cloth and bamboo sticks to make banners, drawing on the help of the student calligraphy and art groups at Peking University to write the slogans, and soon had 3,000 banners ready.

The tactics of the demonstration were not invented on the spot. There was a wide range of international examples that educated Chinese of the period could now draw upon, a real change from the preceding centuries when foreign political ideas were rarely considered by Chinese thinkers. 'In March and April of that year, the Koreans had carried out an unarmed revolution [against the Japanese colonial occupiers] which greatly inspired all of us,' Luo recalled, and there was also the example of the 'revolutionary tide everywhere after the European war [World War I]'. Furthermore, the students of 1919 were acutely conscious of the need to let the outside world know about their rage. 'On the morning of the second day, we prepared some English-language statements to present to the embassies of various foreign countries.'[3] (This planning foreshadowed events exactly 70 years later, on 4 May 1989. On that date, student demonstrators in the same location, now expanded and renamed Tian'anmen Square, would make sure that their demands were written on placards in English to catch the eye of international television crews.) Certainly, foreign reporters did not miss their cues in 1919. One journalist, Rodney Gilbert, described the demonstration as 'a sort of pacific Korean protest, undoubtedly inspired by the reports of Korean methods, in which all classes of Chinese have been taking the clearest interest'.[4]

The meeting at the Tian'anmen gate (not at that time located in a square) started at 1 p.m. on Sunday 4 May. The city police came in a little beforehand, demanding that the demonstrators disperse, but were ignored. After speeches from some of the student leaders, the 3,000 or so demonstrators moved off. They went first to the Legation quarter, where foreign diplomats in Beijing were stationed, but after being moved on by the police, the increasingly angry crowd decided instead to gather at the house of Cao Rulin, the minister of communications, who had been judged one of the 'national traitors' who had sold out Chinese economic and political sovereignty to Japan. Yet even a foreign reporter who was not sympathetic to the demonstrators noted: 'There was no shouting and no cheering, and their appearance, after a long tramp in the hot dust and sun, was anything but sinister.' This made him more surprised at what happened next: 'They came to Hatamen Street . . . advanced quietly down the hutung [alleyway] to the little side street in which Tsao Ju-lin [Cao Rulin] resides, came to his big double doors – and then went mad.'[5]

Peking. Hata-men Street

1. **Hatamen Street in Beijing around 1925.**
The house of communications minister Cao Rulin was in one of the small alleys that led off Hatamen Street. On 4 May 1919, an anti-imperialist demonstration by Beijing college students ended up forcing entry to Cao's house and setting it on fire.

Luo Jialun did not describe the events which followed in terms of madness, but he acknowledged that they were violent:

Cao Rulin's house was a big residence in the style favoured by the former Manchu imperial family. When we got to the front gate of his house, the front door was already locked, and there was a group of . . . armed police standing in front. Everybody reached the front door and started cursing the 'traitor to the country.' At first people threw their banners on the roof, then someone smashed a window at the side, and everybody climbed in. I saw with my own eyes that the first people to go in were a Peking University student . . . who was studying natural science and a student . . . from a college of advanced engineering.[6]

A small group rushed in after these two, and opened the front door from inside, allowing the rest of the demonstrators to come in. The police protecting Cao were now outnumbered, and the minister himself decided that it was time to make himself scarce. 'As we were breaking in,' Luo said, 'Cao Rulin changed into a policeman's uniform, melted into the crowd of police, and jumped over the back wall.' A later report said that he had 'landed with a badly injured leg in another street, where he was picked up and taken to the sanctuary of a foreign hotel'.[7] Less swift was Zhang Zongxiang, the former Chinese minister to Japan, who had been visiting Cao that day along with a Japanese guest, and was now caught by the angry crowd. The Japanese visitor was pelted with eggs obtained from a nearby grocery store, but Zhang was not to be let off so easily. The crowd

. . . tore apart an old iron bed, and used the legs of this iron bed to beat him up, so that Zhang really was covered in scars that looked like fish-scales all over his body. Everybody thought that he had actually been killed. Cao's ornaments, his antiques . . . all of them were just smashed to pieces, and the many perfume bottles in his wife and daughter's rooms all were broken into shards on the floor. The smell of the perfume wafted everywhere.[8]

The demonstrators were not yet satisfied. Luo recalled that he saw a group of students with matches, and suspected that they had had something more than peaceful demonstration on their mind from the start. 'If they hadn't intended to [set the house on fire] beforehand,'

9

he asked, 'why had they brought quite so many matches along with them?'[9] As the house went up in flames, the police regrouped and made some arrests, although the majority of the demonstrators sensed that this was the right moment to disappear and melted away into the backstreets.

Foreign observers were dismayed at the day's events. For a while it was thought that Zhang Zongxiang had been killed, so serious were his wounds, although he did recover and lived on for several decades. The *North China Daily News*, the most prominent journalistic voice of the British settler community in China, described the day's happenings as 'The Peking Riot'. Its editorial chided the Chinese government for allowing this sort of disturbance to take place:

The Peking government has again displayed its weakness, this time by releasing on bail the Chinese students who were arrested in connexion with the burning of Tsao Ju-lin's house and the murder of the minister to Tokio [who had not, in fact, died]. It is not improbable that the young men who were taken into custody were merely onlookers or less culpable demonstrators. Nevertheless their release . . . cannot but stimulate these young men to further acts of rowdyism, if not of violence. Students in other cities are holding demonstrations . . . and the bad example of the authorities in the Capital may lead to excesses in the provinces.[10]

For the students and their supporters, the day had a very different significance. No longer would the Chinese be willing to allow 'national traitors' to carve up the country between the various imperial powers who wanted to colonize it. Xu Deheng was one of the most prominent of the demonstrators, a student at Peking University aged 29. He was one of those who was arrested and held for a few days after the burning of Cao's house. Years later, as a high official in the People's Republic of China, he would declare that 'the most important characteristic of the May Fourth movement was that it was when the Chinese revolution became a fellow-combatant in the world proletarian revolution.'[11] Although this sweeping view of May Fourth's significance is shaped by hindsight, even on the day itself, Xu had written a poem declaring that the events had been carried out 'to purge clean the shame from Chinese hearts and minds'. 'In ferreting out traitors we've spared no cost', he wrote. 'We'd do anything to save China.'[12] In practice, Xu and his fellow-prisoners spent just a few days locked up, as powerful figures, including the President of Peking University, intervened with the authorities to secure their release.

The events of May Fourth showed certain significant characteristics. First, the prime movers behind the demonstration were young students, most of them men, in their twenties. Second, the events were stimulated by developments far outside Chinese territory, shaped by practices learned from the outside world, and were in part carried out so as to catch the attentions of that wider world. Third, the day's events were violent. The violence was perhaps not premeditated, but the nature of the language and the politics which surrounded the demonstrations had made it easy to translate words into action. The combination of these factors – youth, internationalism, and violence – would shape not just the day of the demonstrations, but much of the path taken by twentieth-century China.

The location of the demonstration was also significant. Within weeks, news of the May Fourth events led to demonstrations, protests, and boycotts all across China's cities, Shanghai, Hangzhou, and Harbin among them. Yet the Beijing demonstrations which began at the Tian'anmen gate retained a particular significance and prestige, and the date 4 May 1919 has a cultural resonance for educated Chinese that has lasted for the best part of a century. It was no coincidence that students and workers were gathered before the same gate 70 years later on 4 May 1989, their occupation of the square then cut short on the night of 4 June, a month later. A year earlier, in 1988, a prophetic television series, *Heshang* [River Elegy], had warned: 'It is as if many things in China ought to start afresh from May Fourth.'[13] It is not just one date that was so important; the date sums up a time, an atmosphere and an energy that have such potency that they inform Chinese politics today, so much so that the Chinese government put up new memorials to May Fourth 1919 at the turn of the new millennium.

2. Demonstration in Canton by students and others against imperialism, 1925.
The May Fourth demonstrations by Beijing students were just one part of a wider movement against foreign imperialism and internal political chaos in the 1910s and 1920s. Students were particularly active in the movement, but radicalized workers and middle-class nationalists played a significant role.

Why was May Fourth Important?

The atmosphere and political mood that emerged around 1919 are at the centre of a set of ideas that has shaped China's momentous twentieth century. This phenomenon is known as the May Fourth Movement. This book looks at slices of time – broadly speaking, the 1920s, the 1940s, the 1960s, the 1980s, and the turn of the millennium. The societies described in each of these periods are very different, considering that each is only 20 years from the next. In the 1920s, China had only recently seen the 2,000-year-old imperial system collapse, and a fragmented series of militarist governments competed with the imperial powers for control over China's resources. Twenty years later, China was in the midst of a devastating world war which killed tens of millions of its citizens. Forty years later, China had undergone the horrors of the war against Japan and the victory of the Communists only to descend into the bizarre, seemingly anarchic world of Mao Zedong's Cultural Revolution. And 60 years after the May Fourth events, the Communist Party, while still in charge, now sanctioned domestic reform and a more tolerant and welcoming attitude towards influence from outside, although the tensions within society led to the showdown at Tian'anmen Square in 1989. As that confrontation fades into history, it is still unclear what China is becoming. Its contradictions include being a state that is communist in name but now more like a corporatist, semi-capitalist state in reality, fuelled by nationalism but also a desire to be seen as a responsible member of international society, and by the hope that the economy will continue to bring prosperity.

Yet these very different Chinese realities over a century reflect a set of ideas that runs like a thread through the many governments and systems that have shaped modern China. These ideas are at the centre of the May Fourth experience, as are the thinkers behind them. In the 1920s, those thinkers included Zou Taofen, Chen Duxiu, Ding Ling, and Lu Xun. In the 1980s, among the important figures were Su Xiaokang, Chen Ziming, and Li Zehou. The later generation did not know their predecessors in person, yet the idea of May Fourth runs through their lives and thoughts, a common thread passed from one generation to another.

There are important reasons why the May Fourth Movement has been the subject of historical and political controversy for nearly a century. Those reasons are embedded in the political development of China. Later, we will trace that development in more detail, but for the moment, an outline is as follows. The impact of western imperialism in China from the 1840s onwards helped to stimulate internal collapse of the ruling Qing dynasty. A revolution deposed the last emperor, and a Chinese republic was declared in 1912. However, the Republic proved unstable, and until 1928 was ruled by a succession of militarist leaders, many of whom controlled only parts of China at any one time. In the early 1920s, the two major political parties, the Nationalist Party (also known as the Kuomintang or KMT) and

Communist Party (known as the Chinese Communist Party or CCP) both became prominent. At first they were allies, particularly during the period of cooperation from 1923 to 1927 coordinated by the Comintern. However, after 1927, the Nationalists managed to declare a unified government based at Nanjing, and purged their Communist allies. The two parties were then bitter enemies, with the partial exception of the period of World War II when they were in uneasy alliance against Japan. The Nationalists grew weaker as the CCP grew stronger, and finally the civil war between them ended with the victory of the CCP in 1949 and the forced departure of the Nationalists to the island of Taiwan. The period from 1949 to 1976 in which Mao was paramount leader in China saw massive social change and redistribution of land and privileges, but also the chaotic campaigns of which the Cultural Revolution was perhaps the most destructive. Mao's eventual successor, Deng Xiaoping, spent much of the 1980s converting China from a command economy with a controlled employment and welfare system to one that responded more to market pressures, but also chipped away at the guaranteed livelihood that Mao's China had provided. The 1990s onwards have seen China continue its reforms towards a marketized system, as well as coping with the post-Cold War world where ideological differences have been less important in international relations.

Since the rise of the CCP and the ultimate defeat of the Nationalists, perhaps the most visible narrative in modern Chinese history, was heavily influenced by the events of the 1910s and 1920s, the 'May Fourth Movement' and the era that produced it have been discussed fiercely by historians of China since the events that gave it its name. Points of dispute have included who the members of the movement were, its chronology, and even whether it really existed at all.

A standard definition of the movement might well describe it in this way: it was a period from the mid-1910s to the late 1920s or early 1930s when a group of Chinese thinkers felt that something was holding their country back from combating evils such as imperialism and warlordism, even though the old imperial Qing dynasty had been overthrown and a republic established. The answer these thinkers came up with was that traditional Chinese culture, based on the philosophy of Confucius, was largely to blame. This ancient form of hierarchical thinking, they felt, was responsible for the callous treatment of the poor, the persistence of patriarchal oppression of women, and the inability to create a modern nation state.

Later in the book, the topic of Confucianism and its influence will be dealt with in much greater detail. However, to understand what the May Fourth Movement and the generation that created the New Culture were reacting against, it is important to understand the basic tenets of Confucian thought.

Confucianism was at the basis of Chinese government and society for some 2,000 years. It is not easily defined by any one set of books or teachings, nor is it a religion, although it has a spiritual dimension. Rather, it is an understanding of how society should be ordered, including behaviour and action both on earth and in the other world. It originated with the teachings of Confucius (551–479 BCE), a travelling philosopher and teacher who lived during a period when China was a collection of rival and warring states. Confucius was disturbed by the violence and lack of morality that he saw around him, and spent his life trying, not very successfully, to persuade rulers to employ him as an adviser on reform. As with Socrates, the only record we have of Confucius's thoughts are recollections by his disciples, recorded in a collection known as the *Analects* [Lunyu]. Reading these, certain themes emerge. The single most important element in organizing society, Confucius suggested, was *li*, a term usually translated as 'ritual'. However, he did not have in mind the formal and repetitive sort of actions that the term implies in English. Instead, he used the term to indicate certain acceptable and morally correct forms of behaviour that would enable people to show their best qualities. These qualities were expressed in terms which are known in China to this day as 'Confucian' values, *ren*, *yi*, *xiao*, and *zhong* among them – although again, the English translations as 'benevolence', 'propriety', 'filial piety', and 'loyalty', respectively, give a rather Victorian and musty air to what was supposed to be a rich cultural repertoire. 'Order' became an important element in a society that followed 'ritual' correctly; not just being orderly, but also arranging things in the right order and creating stability by doing so.

The purpose of 'order' was not to oppress people, but rather to allow moral and ethical behaviour (*de*) to flourish.

Confucius argued that an ordered and morally correct society would be able to refrain from the use of force. Violence and coercion were deviant and unwelcome, in Confucius's view. Instead, the morally correct person would aim to become a *junzi*, a phrase translated sometimes as 'gentleman' or 'person of integrity'. For society to remain stable, it was also important that correct hierarchies were maintained: servants should obey masters, subjects obey rulers, children obey parents, and women obey men. The qualities of obligation, loyalty, and filial piety were tied into this understanding. However, if a person in authority, whether a ruler, master, or parent, abused his power, then he would also be in violation of the norms of what was right and correct. The idea of the family was vitally important to Confucius. This was true at the most basic level, with parents and children, and was extended by analogy to the level of state; the king stood in a parental relationship to his subjects. The emphasis on family also meant that individualism and putting oneself forward in a brash way was frowned upon as somehow selfish and petty. In addition, Confucian thought did not respect the urge to make money and seek profit. Long after Confucius's death, when China had been unified into one state, the development of Confucian thought gave the emperor a partial role in the ordering of society. He was considered to be the fulcrum connecting the spiritual world of heaven to the earthly realm, and as such, was central to the hierarchy that underpinned the Chinese empire.

Confucius did not deny the existence of spirits, but his teachings concentrated on the material world. Ancient China developed other religious traditions that were more overtly fixed on the world of gods and supernatural phenomena, including Daoism, and, after its introduction in the second century CE, Buddhism. These were not mutually exclusive belief systems, but coexisted, and it would have been quite normal for people to participate in rites and ceremonies that came from a variety of religious and philosophical backgrounds. This syncretic mixture shaped the lively political and spiritual life of pre-modern China.[14]

Political rulers from the Han dynasty onwards (220 BCE–221 CE) drew upon Confucianism. It was a highly attractive way of thought, since it provided an ethical basis for a strong and stable government. Yet the practice of government, which was often based on the need or desire for force, violence, and conquest, meant that Confucius's precepts on avoidance of force, or the need for mutual obligation between superiors and inferiors, could not always be followed. Therefore, political philosophers over the centuries adapted Confucian thought to make it more compatible with the realities of statecraft, often retaining harsh and coercive laws while using a rhetoric of persuasion and loyalty. However, the basic tenets that underpinned Confucius's ideas remained engrained in Chinese minds at all levels of society: the imperial family and the poorest farmers alike believed in the importance of family and obligation to one's parents (hence the dread in Chinese society of dying without any children to cherish one's memory) and in the importance of maintaining government that was regarded as benevolent and therefore legitimate.

Nonetheless, China was frequently shaken by instability, even when Confucianism was strong. Peasant uprisings were frequent across the ages, although the successful ones were given retrospective justification, as it was assumed that they had been justifiable revolts against cruel rulers who had broken the Confucian social contract. The most violent challenge to Confucian values, though, was the introduction of two western systems of thought in the nineteenth century: capitalist modernity and Christianity. Part I of this book, and Chapter 4 in particular, goes into detail about how these systems of thought clashed and co-existed in the twentieth century. But put simply, the arrival of the western imperialists and their thought was a catalyst for many Chinese to look again at their own society and assess its faults. Too many people were poor, yet did not rise up against their fate. Women were oppressed – physically, by having their feet bound painfully small, and psychologically, by being treated as social inferiors and being deprived of education. More widely, the Chinese state was clearly in trouble: western barbarians were able to come and invade with impunity. Where did the fault lie for this crisis?

For the most radical thinkers, the only rational response was to declare that Confucian thought had been all-pervasive in China, and therefore Confucian thought was responsible for the country's present crisis. For these critics, all aspects of China's Confucian past were pernicious and corrupting, and must be exterminated from Chinese society and culture before the country could truly be saved. As a result, these activists revolutionized the Chinese language, abandoning the old classical written form for a vernacular language, thought about new political systems, and threw off social conventions on traditional relations between men and women. It was a movement particularly associated with young, urban patriots, hence its association with the demonstrations on 4 May 1919. Yet that one day was only a symbol of a much wider change in Chinese society. For that reason, the term 'New Culture Movement' is often used almost interchangeably with 'May Fourth Movement' in writing about the era. In fact, the two are not identical. The 'New Culture' idea emerged in significant part as a protest by elite groups shocked at a particular event: the attempts by the new Republican President, Yuan Shikai, in 1915–16 to restore Confucianism as the basis of the country's political system and, as part of this, to have himself declared emperor. However, the term 'new culture' can be used more widely. When the Chinese thought about their identities, understandings, assumptions, systems of shared comprehension, that whole amorphous web which defines 'culture', the May Fourth era stands out as a period of change which was innovative and irreversible.[15]

The terms 'May Fourth Movement' and 'New Culture Movement' were not invented by historians after the fact. Both titles were created at the time by participants in the movements themselves, yet this did not prevent them becoming potent.[16] The advocates of change outlined their aims as bringing 'science' and 'democracy' to China. Perhaps the single most important organization that emerged from the movement was the Chinese Communist Party, founded in 1921. In retrospect, the Party itself would stress over and over again that the May Fourth Movement, with its questioning of how China could be made modern, had found the answer to its own question located in the victory of Mao in 1949.

18

There is no absolute agreement on how long the May Fourth era lasted, and many books offer confident but differing verdicts on this: 1917–23, 1915–25, and other variations. What seems fair to say is that the movement was not active before the 1911 Revolution, and had faded by the time war with Japan broke out in 1937. It also seems reasonable to say that it started and ended a little after and before these dates, respectively. More precise dating is difficult, and also misses the point, because so much of what made the movement important was not specific events, but atmosphere and mood.

Every generation of scholars finds its own meaning in the May Fourth Movement. One of the earliest and still most important books in English on the topic was Chow Tse-tsung's *The May Fourth Movement*. First published in 1960, Chow was himself a junior participant in the movement (Mao Zedong had attended Chow's school, 15 years previously), and his book's careful examination of the differing interpretations of the movement by such varied groups as the Communists, Nationalists, traditionalists, and westerners still repays reading. Chow's own conclusions were that 'The May Fourth Movement was actually a combined intellectual and socio-political movement to achieve national independence, the emancipation of the individual, and a just society by the modernization of China'. He argued that the movement sought to do this by 'attacking tradition and by re-evaluating attitudes and practices in the light of modern western civilization, the essence of which they thought to be science and democracy. The basic spirit of the movement, therefore, was to jettison tradition and create a new, modern civilization to "save China" '.[17] Later studies moved the focus away from the intellectual ferment in Beijing and looked to other cities, for instance Joseph Chen's work on Shanghai, where popular protest and the labour movement had more effect than they had done in the capital. A significant reassessment of the movement was Lin Yu-sheng's *The Crisis of Chinese Consciousness* (1979). This argued that the single-minded iconoclasm of the most radical May Fourth opponents of Confucianism was, ironically, shaped by the uncompromising morality of Confucianism itself.[18] More recently, the effect of the movement in cities outside Beijing and Shanghai has been examined in much more detail, in works such as Wen-hsin Yeh's study of the rise of communism in Hangzhou, and James Carter's consideration of its effects in the far northeastern city of Harbin.[19]

In addition to a geographical spread in examinations of the movement, terms such as 'modernization', 'tradition', 'science', and 'democracy' also came under the spotlight in the following decades. A powerful re-examination of the May Fourth Movement's legacy was Vera Schwarcz's *The Chinese Enlightenment* in 1986. This made a crucial distinction between the older May Fourth generation, including figures such as the author Lu Xun and the founder of the CCP, Chen Duxiu, who had an unremitting hostility towards China's Confucian tradition, and a younger generation who were willing to adapt, rather than reject, aspects of China's past in their quest to 'save' it in the present.[20] Even now, academic interest in the topic shows no signs of waning; a group of scholars produced a major reassessment of the movement in 2002.[21] Although not so much work on the movement has been aimed at the non-specialist reader, Jonathan Spence's *The Gate of Heavenly Peace: The Chinese and their Revolution, 1895–1980* (1981) provides an incisive account on the grand scale of the lives of a generation of May Fourth writers and thinkers as their lives were changed by war and revolution.[22]

There has also been new thinking in China itself on the movement. Although most recent Chinese writing on May Fourth and the New Culture Movement is not accessible in English, it is important to know that there has been a lively interest in contemporary China in the history of the early twentieth century. Academic work, which for many decades was dominated by the need to follow the political orthodoxy of the Communist Party, has now been given more freedom to explore other aspects of the era. Books both popular and academic pour out on everyday life, thought, politics, and society in the Republican era. The era of May Fourth has come into popular consciousness as China tries to define its contemporary identity.[23]

What, then, is important to understand in trying to assess the May Fourth Movement and the New Culture at the turn of a new century? Why is this set of events from the early part of the previous century still so potent that the Chinese government would install new memorials to it in the centre of their capital city in 2002? And why does it matter to our understanding of what 'modern' China means?

Going back to the May Fourth Movement is important in an era in which China has seen the abandonment of Maoism at home and the collapse of the Cold War order abroad. Under these circumstances, the idea that Communist China was the logical endpoint of the country's early twentieth-century quest for modernity is less convincing than it might have been in the 1950s or 1960s. Looking again at the May Fourth period, the time when Chinese Communism emerged, and seeing what alternative paths China might have taken, has a great deal of significance for understanding the variety of political possibilities in China today.

But it is important to understand that the May Fourth experience is a very elusive one. For instance, there is a lively debate about whether the 'May Fourth Movement' was quite as spontaneous as many observers later declared. One historian has examined the question of when the term itself emerged, and declared: 'The May Fourth movement did not end up with this name. It had it before it started.'[24] This 'canonization' of the idea led to it being taken up by various groups, including the CCP and the Nationalists, either as an object of veneration or of vilification. But the 'May Fourth' that they talked about had little to do with any events on the ground in the early years of the Chinese Republic.

Some are happy to suggest that the May Fourth Movement existed, but want to question its 'uniqueness' as a crucible of iconoclastic, modern thought in China. Recent work has reassessed the last years of the Manchu Qing dynasty which ruled China, arguing that the last decade of the nineteenth and first decade of the twentieth century were not the last throes of a decadent, dying imperial regime doomed to fail. The 'Hundred Days of Reform' in 1898, which we will encounter shortly, saw a short-lived flowering of highly progressive reformist thought that made use of Chinese indigenous belief systems such as Confucianism rather than rejecting them. Although a countercoup by the Dowager Empress Cixi put an end to the reforms, their legacy lived on into the next century. Yet reformers

21

did not have to wait two decades after 1898 for the May Fourth Movement to turn up to justify their demands for change. After the disaster of the 1900 Boxer War against the imperialist powers, which saw the Qing government defeated and humiliated by having to pay crippling reparations, the dynasty itself realized that it would have to change. The first decade of the twentieth century saw significant reform in Chinese public life, including the establishment of local assemblies, chambers of commerce, and academies, all with government encouragement.[25] Students also studied in Japan in ever-greater numbers, bringing their new-found knowledge back with them. By this stage, the sudden reverse in policy was too late for many of the students, merchants, and secret societies who were now dedicated to revolutionary overthrow of the Qing dynasty rather than constitutional reform alongside it. But the change in China's public culture during the era of the 'New Governance' (*Xinzheng*) reforms was remarkable, and it can be argued that a real 'enlightenment' in Chinese thought took place. The most symbolic action was the abolition in 1905 of the traditional examination system, the point of entry for the civil service for a millennium, replaced by tests in 'western learning'. We have to venture into the realms of counterfactual history to work out whether the Qing could have survived if it had reformed more quickly or carried out its policies slightly differently. But the idea that the late Qing was essentially a time of inevitable decline and moribund thought on governance and society is misleading. People started thinking in innovative ways before the Republic had been established in 1912, let alone before the student demonstrations of 1919.

So the May Fourth period did not spring up from nowhere. But it was significant, and significantly different from what came before and after. Despite its efforts at reform, the Qing dynasty *did* fall, and the Republican society that followed it *was* new in important ways, from the type of clothes people wore to the way in which they related to symbols of the nation such as memorials and flags.[26] The 'May Fourth' era has become legendary in Chinese memory to the extent that in later years it has indeed become endangered by becoming a sort of brand name within which different political groups can include any events or strands of thought that are useful to them. When we go back to the reality of that period in the early Republic, between World War I and the crisis over the Japanese invasion of Manchuria in the early 1930s, we can identify changes and ideas that were real at the time to many of the participants, people who did not think of themselves simply as pawns in a wider game of political manoeuvring, but people whose everyday existence – where they worked, ate, studied – was a bewildering mixture of old and new. Many people living in that period *did* see the era at the time as something new and different. The May Fourth era reflected much that was innovative, often brought in from the west, though, as we will see, showing an interest in sources as varied as Japan, Turkey, India, and Eastern Europe as well. It also reflected continuity with the past: Confucius was forgotten or condemned only by the most radical of that era, while others put the spin of modernity on the venerable sage to help them make sense of the new world.

The May Fourth era represented, then, a distinct break from the late Qing empire and the era of the Nationalist government in the 1930s, which was cut short by war. It took place during a period when the world, weary after the Great War, turned its face outward and celebrated internationalism. This was an era when, however slowly, the global tide started to turn against imperialism. It did not seem to do so to the Chinese at the time, for the western powers appeared hypocritical in their advocacy of self-determination for nations while they steadfastly held on to their large territorial possessions. Yet the age of empire was drawing to a close. It was also a time when the cosmopolitan city came of age in an era of globalized culture, in Shanghai in particular. All these elements came together for one short period, and while aspects of everything I have listed appeared both before and after that time, the May Fourth period marked a unique combination of all of them: a sense of real and impending crisis; a combination of a plurality of competing ideas aimed at 'saving the nation', and an audience ready to receive, welcome, contest, and adapt these ideas. In that way, the era remains unique to date in the history of mainland China, although liberalization in Taiwan at the end of the twentieth century has given rise to a situation in some ways quite similar, but, as I will suggest in the final chapter, for rather different reasons.

The fact that 'May Fourth' did become a phrase or set of images that meant different things to different people suggests that something about it continued to resonate in Chinese intellectual and political life long after the events themselves, in the way that 'the Sixties', that vaguely defined term, still captures a wealth of images, often contradictory, for many in the west. Clearly the meaning of 'May Fourth' changed according to who used it. It had a very different significance for the CCP leadership and for the students in Tian'anmen Square in 1989, both of whom claimed ownership of the legacy of the 'real' May Fourth and of terms such as 'democracy' which were associated with it.[27] But the fact that it was 'May Fourth' that they both chose to fight over in 1989, icons of 'May Fourth' such as the writer Lu Xun that the Cultural Revolution had tried to claim for a very different sort of China a quarter of a century before, and 'May Fourth' that the Nationalist leader Chiang Kaishek had attacked a quarter of a century before that suggests that for all these very different people and movements, the idea of May Fourth had, and continues to have, a symbolic significance over a century not shared, for instance, by the May Thirtieth Incident of 1925 or the National Salvation Movement in 1936, both of which were also important demonstrations against imperialism.

This book follows one set of people and their ideas, the 'May Fourth' generation and their 'New Culture' in the early twentieth century, over the course of some 80 years. But these people are a very particular section of Chinese society. In all the periods, they have tended to be the best-educated, most cosmopolitan urban-dwellers. What makes them interesting is their fascination with the foreign, the unfamiliar, the bizarre, but by definition this makes them less than typical. The cities on which I concentrate, Beijing and Shanghai, were often different from many of the smaller and more inward-looking cities of the interior. The largest area that remains in the shadows in the story told here is what the pre-eminent sociologist of Republican China, Fei Xiaotong, called 'China of the native soil' (*Xiangtu Zhongguo*), the vast rural hinterland which contained the overwhelming majority of China's population in the early twentieth century, as it does today.[28] This is a book about urban ideas. However, for much of the twentieth century, the growing dominance of the countryside in Chinese politics, culminating in the rural revolution of the CCP, meant that the cities, at least for a while, became subject to policies that tried to downgrade their importance in comparison to the prominence they had had in the earlier part of the century. Yet in a real sense, Mao's turn towards rural politics was shaped by the May Fourth Movement as well. His increasing hostility towards the cities and the educated classes, expressed most violently in the Cultural Revolution of the 1960s, was fuelled by his conviction that many of the systems of thought that appeared in early twentieth-century China did not get to grips with the reality of rural poverty. In addition, he was angered by the often high-handed tendency of Chinese urban intellectuals to extrapolate from their own experience to assume that they knew what was best for the population at large.

Yet the cities remained a source of fascination even under Mao, and were always an essential part of defining what it was that made China modern. Ideas of the city were important even for the rural-dwellers who knew it only in their imaginations. At the beginning of the twenty-first century, when millions of rural migrants flood illegally to the cities, and large parts of China's international self-image are tied up with the Olympic Games in Beijing in 2008 and the World Expo in Shanghai in 2010, it is hard to argue that the cities do not have a vital role to play in the mind of China, even for those who do not live in them.

The rest of the book will map the larger contours of change and continuity in the way that May Fourth thinking changed China over the decades. Where people lived, ate, drank, and went on dates will be of as much concern to understanding the context of particular strains of thought as a detailed analysis of how various political, philosophical, or literary factions disputed with each other. Yet to understand the period, it is important first to ask what it was that drove China to the point where the demonstrators came together in the movement of 1919. The answers lie in the decades that preceded that explosive event.

The Fall of the Chinese Empire

A novel published in 1830, Li Ruzhen's *Flowers in the Mirror*, deals with the lives of upper-class Chinese, one of whom, Duo the Helmsman, firmly states 'The fact of the matter is that our China must be regarded as the root of all other countries.'[29] Although the author could not know it, *Flowers in the Mirror* was written in the very last days of the period when China could be utterly self-confident about its own culture. When the novel was written, China did not just believe that her own civilization was superior to that of any other country; she knew it for an indisputable fact. Chinese technology, after all, had invented printing, gunpowder, and ceramics centuries before they had appeared in the west; the government was organized by a bureaucracy chosen, to a certain extent, on merit through written examinations; and its ethical system, based on the teachings of Confucius, told its people that their way of life and thought was the best that there could be.

China can trace its culture in an unbroken line to societies that emerged some 4,000 years ago. Written Chinese characters used today look very similar to those that emerged in the third century BCE. The same century saw the first unification of the warring kingdoms scattered around the North China plain. The first Emperor of China who ruled over those unified states called his dynasty 'Qin' (pronounced *chin*), from which the word 'China' originates. And although the Qin Emperor spent just a few decades on the imperial throne, the unified empire he had established lasted, albeit in slightly different forms, for the next 2,000 years. Dynasties rose and fell: the early Han, when China's first historical classics were composed; the medieval Tang, which saw the flowering of perhaps China's finest poetry; and the Song, marked by a new commercial culture that saw roads and canals expand all across China. Science and the arts flourished, and government developed into a sophisticated system of control run by bureaucrats who were chosen by competitive examination. China was self-confident but not self-contained: culture from central Asian and northern Tungusic civilizations was absorbed willingly on occasion, by force on others. The wonders of the Chinese civilization were reported back to the west by travellers: Marco Polo's famous (though possibly fraudulent) account calls the southern city of Hangzhou 'Without doubt the finest and most splendid city in the world'. Although China, like all societies, went through periods of war and decline, a new dynasty always emerged to bring the society back to a new peak of splendour.[30]

But in the mid-nineteenth century, this changed. China began to fall apart for a variety of reasons: revolutions from within; a growing dissatisfied underclass who resented the wealth of the ruling classes; and, in addition, a violent catalyst, the attacks by the western imperial powers, determined to open China up to trade.

Since 1644, the Chinese empire had been under the control of the Qing dynasty, whose leaders were not ethnically Chinese but Manchus, a nomadic warrior people from a region to the northeast of the main Chinese landmass. This region became known in the west as Manchuria. In the seventeenth century, the native Chinese dynasty, the Ming, had lost its grip on rule, and proved no match for the agile Manchu invaders. Having taken over China, for much of the eighteenth and nineteenth centuries, the Manchu rulers undertook military campaigns which expanded their territories into one of the world's great land empires. Over the years, they brought under their control areas as far away as Central Asia and Tibet. Yet the Manchu emperors were sensitive to the charge that although they had conquered China's territory, their subjects considered them to be uncouth barbarians unfitted to rule over the oldest civilization in the world. So the Manchu emperors followed two policies at once. On the one hand, they showed that they were in tune with traditional Chinese culture. They wrote their imperial orders in elegant classical Chinese script, and painted and wrote poetry in the long-honoured style of the Chinese literary scholars. Kangxi, one of the greatest of the Qing rulers, sponsored the publication of a massive new encyclopedia, intended to define knowledge on all aspects of Chinese tradition and society. However, the Manchus also kept themselves carefully separated as an ethnic group, with clearly different customs from the majority ethnic Chinese population (known as the 'Han'), and with the privileges that an occupying power expected to enjoy.[31]

The balance between the rulers and ruled lasted throughout the eighteenth century, a time when China thrived under its alien but naturalized ruling dynasty. Although there were pockets of resistance by some who regarded the Manchus as invaders, the majority of China's elites and masses seemed to have little resentment at Qing rule. Meanwhile, China's population doubled from 150 million to 300 million. The population grew stronger as it ate crops such as maize and potatoes newly imported from the New World; better still, these crops grew in barren soil where rice and wheat did not, enabling settlers to move for the first time to remote regions in the west and the north, and claim them for China. Health and welfare improved under the Qing, with a complex system of disaster relief and surveys of public health undertaken by the government at central and local level. Perhaps the most striking aspect of the development of preventative medicine was the widespread use of inoculation against smallpox, a century before it became widespread in the west, although unlike in Europe, the serum developed by the Chinese doctors was not injected but blown up the patient's nose.[32]

But beneath the prosperity were darker signs. Young, poor men found it harder and harder to find wives, partly because of female infanticide, and also because richer men took several wives at once to show off their prosperity; this created a discontented, unstable underclass. While crops grew well in many areas, in others they failed, causing famine, or else were washed away by disastrous floods. Social unrest could be seen in the wave of uprisings that swept across China from the mid-eighteenth century onwards. Some were small-scale, like the 'sorcery scare' of 1768 which saw hundreds of people in the coastal province of Anhui convinced that sorcerers were stalking the land, turning victims into zombies who would do their bidding. Others were much harder to suppress, such as the Wang Lun rebellion of 1774, in which a mendicant martial-arts expert led thousands of followers who were convinced that his special Buddhist powers made them invulnerable to weapons; the rebellion was put down only with massive bloodshed. In addition, China's sheer size became a problem. The Qing dynasty's massively successful territorial expansion had brought it military glory, but it also made it easier for people to disappear to a new life, avoiding obligations such as paying taxes. Slowly the Qing dynasty's finances began to weaken as their revenues became too small to maintain their overstretched empire.[33]

So China was showing signs of breakdown even when the first foreigners arrived from the west demanding trade. But at first, the Son of Heaven, as the Chinese Emperor was always known, could afford to send the foreigners away empty-handed. In 1793, the British sent an ambassador, Lord Macartney, at the head of a large delegation which was to negotiate with the emperor to allow trade to open up with Britain. The Emperor sent him off almost immediately with a polite but firm dismissal. Looking at the machines and tools which Macartney had brought from the west, the Emperor told him: 'We have never valued ingenious articles, nor do we have the slightest need of your country's manufactures.' The British, however, were not to be put off that easily, and they had a tool to force their way into the China market, a new, and astoundingly popular product: opium. Opium had been known but relatively little used in China before the early nineteenth century, as it tended to be an exclusive, luxury product. However, its popularity suddenly grew after 1800. As the British East India Company grew more and more opium poppies in India, they looked to expand the market for their product. They soon found that there were eager customers in China. At all levels of society, people smoked opium; rich court officials bored by their sedentary lives, or urban workers whose daily drudgery of hauling large loads from place to place, could be eased by opium's pain-killing effects.[34] By the 1820s, there were around a million regular users of the drug in China. The sale was highly profitable for the British, but it provoked the anger of the Chinese imperial court. The Emperor made it clear that this pernicious substance, nick-named 'the foreign mud' or 'the black smoke' by the Chinese, had to be dealt with. In 1836, the Emperor declared that it had 'pervaded the country with its baneful influence'.[35]

After toying with the idea of legalizing opium, in 1839 the court demanded that the British cease all trade in the drug. They sent a special 'Opium Commissioner' named Lin Zexu, who besieged the

British opium factories in the southern city of Canton until they agreed to hand over the drugs. Lin then arranged for the raw opium to be flushed out to sea, and sent a stern letter to Queen Victoria, in which he advised her to tell her countrymen not to deal in opium, but to stick to trading in goods such as 'tea and rhubarb' (Lin was convinced that the latter was essential to the health of Europeans). As far as Lin was concerned, the dispute was over. But this was not the end of the matter. The British Prime Minister, Lord Palmerston, regarded the seizure of the opium by the Chinese as an act of war against the British Crown, and authorized warships to go to China and force the Chinese to retract the 'injuries inflicted by Chinese authorities upon British subjects resident in China'. The 'Opium War' of 1839–42 followed, with superior British technology literally outgunning anything the Chinese defenders could offer. In 1842, the Chinese had to sign the humiliating Treaty of Nanjing, whereby they agreed to open ports to British trade, pay compensation for the destroyed opium, and hand over the island of Hong Kong to Britain 'in perpetuity'. Among the 'treaty ports' set up in this way was the small port town of Shanghai. This was the beginning of what the Chinese even now refer to as the 'century of humiliation', the period when China's foreign and domestic policy was largely decided not by the Chinese government or people, but by foreign occupiers.

For the British had breached the Chinese wall, but there were plenty of other powers waiting to rush in. The Chinese had chosen the worst moment to fall behind in military technology; the late nineteenth century saw a huge scramble for empire in Asia and Africa, with European powers ranging from Britain, France, and Russia to smaller players such as Belgium and Sweden all looking for their share of the spoils. This was a time of scientific and pseudo-scientific triumphalism in the west, and perhaps the most powerful of all ideas was Social Darwinism, the perversion of Darwin's idea of natural selection by sociologists such as the Briton Herbert Spencer. Spencer had argued that races and nations were in competition, just as species were, and those races that did not come out on top of the evolutionary battle were doomed to become slave races, or worse still, disappear completely.

Although Social Darwinism is now recognized as racist pseudo-science, in the late nineteenth century it was a powerful idea in Europe, and it caught on rapidly in one of China's neighbouring states – Japan. Before the mid-nineteenth century, Japan had had a very different history from China. Christian missionaries from Europe had arrived in Japan in the sixteenth century, and the Japanese regents, or shogun, became worried that the new faith might catch on in Japan and destroy the traditional religions of Buddhism and Shinto, undermining social stability. So around 1600, the shogun took the radical step of closing off Japan to the outside world almost entirely. Japanese citizens might not leave the country on pain of death, and only a few foreigners, mostly Dutch and Chinese, were allowed to trade with Japan via a small trading post in the harbour of the city of Nagasaki. Japan turned inwards, and for 250 years its rulers had no intention of allowing any foreign contacts to develop. But as in China, the mid-nineteenth century saw western powers refusing to accept 'No' for an answer to their requests for trade and diplomatic relations. In the case of Japan, it was not Britain but the United States who forced the issue. In 1853, US Commodore Matthew Perry sailed a fleet of gunships into Tokyo Bay, and gave the shogun an ultimatum to accept his demand that Japan should open its ports to US ships, or else be prepared for war. The shogun had to accept, but his capitulation in the face of the foreigners destroyed his prestige utterly. Two feudal clans hatched a conspiracy, and began to undermine the shogun; in 1868, he was overthrown to make way for a new regime.

This coup, known as the Meiji Restoration, ushered in a complete change of policy in Japan. The new leaders, including men such as Yamagata Aritomo and Ito Hirobumi, saw the dreadful fate that had overtaken China during the Opium Wars, and resolved that Japan must resist the west at all costs. The way they did this was a crash programme of modernization, introducing into Japan a whole range of reforms at breakneck speed: a new western-style constitution, a massive conscripted army, universal compulsory schooling, and, above all, modern technology and weapons. At the same time, western political ideas, including nationalism, Social Darwinism,

Christianity, and democracy, flooded in, as books on these topics were eagerly translated into Japanese from the original English, French, or German. There were native bestsellers too, such as the writer Fukuzawa Yukichi's book *Conditions in the West*, which quickly became a million-copy seller, no mean feat in nineteenth-century Japan. The result of all the reforms was perhaps the quickest and most total transformation of any society in history. In 1853, Japan had been a feudal, agricultural country in danger of being taken over by western powers. By 1895, it was a rapidly growing industrial power, with a modern political system and the highest literacy rate in Asia. Significantly, it also had colonies of its own. From being a country in danger of being colonized itself, Japan had managed to become the latest great imperial power on earth.[36]

This never happened in China. There are several reasons why not, including a much greater level of social unrest and the sheer size of the country. However, an important reason was the lack of direction from the top. The continued, if precarious, survival of the Qing may have hurt China's chances of rapid reform, as the 70 years after the Opium War saw a constant battle between the conservative and reformist factions at court, with the former generally on top until late in the dynasty's history. While the conservatives were willing to allow a certain level of reform in the area of technology or industry, their efforts were ambivalent. However, the imperialist powers met less opposition to their plans to expand than they might have expected. Efforts such as the 'self-strengthening' movement of the 1860s saw attempts to develop western technology in China in the context of Confucian reforms. Yet the revolutionary nationalist Sun Yatsen wrote to the prominent official Li Hongzhang in 1893, pointing out that Japan 'opened her country for western trade later than we did . . . yet in only a short period her success in strengthening herself has been enormously impressive . . . Here lies the reason why we in China have not achieved much; public opinion and entrenched ideas simply will not allow it'.[37]

By 1900, the foreign presence in China was inescapable; whole areas such as Hong Kong and the centre of Shanghai were ruled by the British, the French controlled areas of Yunnan, in the southwest, and even where they did not have formal control, foreigners were granted special legal and trade rights anywhere on Chinese soil. Shanghai, in particular, was now well on its rise to become a world trading entrepôt and was without doubt the major city of East Asia. Yet this was in large part because of the special rights granted to foreigners, which were as great, if not a greater, source of anger among the Chinese than the outright colonization of places such as Hong Kong. Under these 'extraterritoriality' rules, foreigners from countries such as Britain and the US could not be prosecuted under Chinese law for most offences committed in China. They had instead to be tried in a special expatriate western court, whose western judges were suspected (understandably if not always justly) of being biased against the Chinese. (No wonder that among many Chinese, feelings toward Germans warmed considerably when they later lost their extraterritorial rights in China after their defeat in World War I.) The injustice of extraterritoriality was most strongly symbolized in a notorious sign reading 'NO DOGS OR CHINESE' which was said to have been placed outside a British-run public park in Shanghai. The sign itself was an urban legend, and never actually existed, but the attitudes it reflected were real and everyday experiences for many Chinese people.[38] As well as having its authority eaten away by the foreigners, the Qing also suffered from internal rebellions. The Taiping Uprising of 1856–64 was one of the bloodiest civil wars in history, with hundreds of thousands of Chinese following Hong Xiuquan, a half-mad visionary who claimed to be the younger brother of Jesus sent to save China from the Manchu 'devils' who ruled it. The Qing rulers put the Taiping down, but at tremendous cost to their own power. Then there was the Boxer Uprising of 1900. This was a peasant rebellion, dedicated to supporting the Manchus and expelling the foreigners, and the Qing gambled for high stakes by backing the rebellion and declaring war against the foreign powers. The strategy backfired as the imperialists joined forces (the first ever multinational armed intervention), put down the rebellion, and forced the Qing to pay massive indemnities in retribution. All these factors gave added force among the elite to a newly introduced ideology from Europe: nationalism. Thinkers such as Yan Fu argued that it was the constitution of Britain and France as modern nation-states, with their people educated to think of themselves as citizens not subjects, rather than an empire built on Confucian ritual, that had enabled them to prosper and conquer in the new world order.[39]

The relationship between China and Japan during the late nineteenth century gave many people in both countries pause for thought. For China's weakness and Japan's rise to strength were utter reversals of the traditional order in East Asia. Over the centuries, Japan, like Korea and much of Southeast Asia, had drawn heavily on Chinese culture in religion, architecture, literature; even the Japanese writing system was borrowed from China's. Now, suddenly and bizarrely for both sides, it was Japan that had won out and China that was being defeated in the region. This led to a curious mix of cultural deference towards China's past and racism towards its present. Fukuzawa Yukichi, who had praised westernization so lavishly in the nineteenth century, justified Japan's drive to conquer colonies and leave China behind: 'Intimacy with bad friends will necessarily give us a bad reputation. From the bottom of my heart I reject such friendship in East Asia.'[40]

Whatever the Japanese claims for altruism, however, Japanese politicians were as caught up in the same Social Darwinist rush to 'conquer or be conquered' as the western powers, and they had set their eyes early on two neighbouring territories that they feared would be taken over by western powers who wished to cut Japan down to size. One of those territories was Korea, which Japan had begun to annexe in the 1880s. It won even more secure control after defeating the Chinese for possession of the Korean peninsula in the Sino-Japanese War of 1894–5. The other was Manchuria. If Russia had control over the Sea of Japan, politicians in Tokyo thought, might it not soon decide to invade Japan? Negotiations between the two sides broke down, and in 1904 war broke out. The western world was stunned as Japan, the upstart Asian power, battered the Russian fleet, launched a massive campaign on the territory of Manchuria, and won a surprise victory. Russia was forced to concede its gains in the southern part of Manchuria, although it retained railway rights in the northern half. It was notable that neither side, throughout the war, had asked the

Chinese government, on whose soil the war was taking place, what they thought. It was proof that China's destiny now lay in the hands of foreigners who bore her little goodwill.

The late Qing did see attempts at reform. In 1898, the Guangxu Emperor proved willing to consider wide-ranging technological, constitutional, and social changes, although the reforms were cut off after a mere three months when the conservative faction at court launched a counter-coup against him. Ironically, the failure of the Boxer Uprising against the foreign presence just two years later forced many of the same conservatives into changing their minds from 1902 onwards, with 'New Government' (*Xinzheng*) reforms leading to changes such as the institution of more representative local government and the abolition of the centuries-old examinations in classical literature for entry to the bureaucracy.[41]

Uneasy Birth: The Chinese Republic

Despite its reforms, the first decade of the twentieth century was marked by yet more crises for the Qing, including attempts at revolution, some led by the Cantonese political activist Sun Yatsen, and ever-increasing demands from the foreign powers for concessions and territory. The end came unexpectedly, though. An uprising in Wuchang, in the southwest of China, started a local rebellion in late 1911 which sparked off uprisings against the dynasty by army commanders and the newly empowered middle classes. The Qing lost its grip on power, and the last emperor, the five-year-old Puyi, abdicated to make way for a republic. The first president, the revolutionary leader Sun Yatsen, was forced to resign after just six weeks to make way for Yuan Shikai, a conservative leader with strong armed forces behind him. Yuan nipped China's fledgling democracy in the bud. China had developed its first political party, the Nationalists (or Kuomintang), led by Sun Yatsen, which had won a large number of parliamentary seats in China's first (and last) free and open general election in 1912. But Song Jiaoren, the brilliant young politician tipped as the Nationalist prime minister, was gunned down at Shanghai railway station as he was about to board the train to Beijing to start negotiations with President Yuan Shikai. Agents of Yuan were strongly suspected of having arranged the killing. In the chaos that followed, Yuan outlawed the Nationalist Party and forced Sun Yatsen and his followers into exile, while taking more and more power for himself. He eventually tried to restore Confucianism to its former position of authority in public discourse, and even attempted to have himself crowned emperor, though he was forced to step back from this decision after local militarist rulers around China made it clear they would not permit it.[42] It was his attempt at a Confucian coup that provoked radical thinkers to promote the idea that what China needed was a 'new culture'.

Yuan died of uraemia in 1916, and China then split into several regions, all under the control of military leaders ('warlords') who engaged in endless battles trying to take over the whole of China, without lasting success. For the next decade, China had no strong central ruler at all.[43] China's lack of unity during this period had serious consequences for the country's future. The foreign powers, seeing that they could play China's rivals for power off against one another, took to stirring the China pot with gusto. The British, French, Americans, and, above all, the Japanese began to make rival claims and demands on China. World War I provided a temporary distraction for the western powers, but this gave the Japanese an advantage in pushing for concessions. In 1915, the Japanese government put forward 'Twenty-One Demands' to Yuan Shikai's government, demanding huge economic and commercial rights throughout Chinese territory, as well as the right to station Japanese police in north China. In 1917, the Japanese made a secret deal with Britain and France to transfer German colonies in China to Japanese control if the Allies won. This led to the confrontation of 4 May 1919.

The ideas of nationalism which had developed among a small elite exposed to European thought in the late nineteenth century had by now spread to many of the urban youth, who for the first time realized that their future lay in the modern, globalized world, utterly different from the old Confucian one that lay in ruins. As part of China's effort to understand the west, students were sent to Europe and America to study; their exposure to foreign countries only served to strengthen their nationalist consciousness.[44] So in 1919, hundreds of Chinese students in Paris surrounded the hotel where the Chinese delegates to the Versailles Conference were staying, making sure that they were physically unable to step out and sign the treaty. And in Beijing, 3,000 young students gathered in Tian'anmen Square on 4 May 1919, and marched through the city, demonstrating to show their disgust with the Chinese government's capitulation to imperialism.

For the Versailles humiliation was just the latest in a string of defeats for China. First the Opium Wars had forced China to open up its doors to invading traders in narcotics who had the temerity to bring their religion of salvation along with the opium. Then the war against Japan, for so long China's cultural inferior, had ended with defeat at sea in 1895, and the cession of the island of Taiwan to the Japanese. Just a decade later, in 1904–5, the Chinese could not stop the Russians and the Japanese fighting over Manchuria, a piece of Chinese territory. And now Versailles showed that the west's supposed desire for international justice and order was yet another sham, with the Japanese acting like old-style imperialists. Many of China's youth turned to nationalism, or in some cases Marxism, for salvation. Li Dazhao, one of the founders of the Chinese Communist Party, declared in 1918: 'The victory of Bolshevism is the victory of the new spirit of enlightenment that all mankind can share in the twentieth century.'[45]

In China and Japan, the ideas of an Asian brotherhood united against the west gained serious weight among those who thought about the ways in which their countries should develop. Pan-Asianism is now a largely forgotten concept, but before World War II it took powerful hold among many people in Asia, particularly those living in countries colonized by the west. Pan-Asianism started as a philosophical movement that believed that the nations of Asia had a spiritual quality absent in the materialist west. Although western nations might have more powerful technology and financial might, the power of spirituality resided first and foremost in Asia. The movement united thinkers from all over Asia, although ironically it was inspired by an American, Ernest Fenollosa, who emigrated to teach at Tokyo

University in 1878 and made it his mission to alert the Japanese to their own cultural past, which he felt they were neglecting in the rush to westernization. His first disciple, Okakura Kakuzô, enthusiastically took up these ideas, declaring that 'Asia is one', and further noting that Asia was 'the source of our inspiration', but 'the expenditure of thought involved in synthesizing the different elements of Asiatic culture has given to Japanese art and culture a freedom and virility unknown to India and China'. In other words, it was Japan's task, or rather its sacred duty, to awaken the rest of Asia to its destiny.[46]

This was largely because Social Darwinism had become powerful at that time. In both China and Japan, with the increasing spread of the great western empires, it seemed that it was eat or be eaten in the battle of the nations. The real turning point was the Russo-Japanese War of 1904–5. Once Japan had shown that it really could beat a European nation, it was clear to many Chinese that they had to pay attention to what Japan had done if they wanted to be in the same position. Important in developing this kind of cooperation was the *Tôa Dôbunkai*, the Society for East Asian Common Cultures, which was started by the prominent pan-Asian Japanese politician Konoye Atsumarô, and joined by young Chinese modernizers such as the pioneering journalist Liang Qichao and Kang Youwei, a prominent and progressive adviser to the Chinese emperor.

This Japanese influence was very relevant, even for staunch Chinese nationalists such as Sun Yatsen. When Yuan Shikai seized control of the new republic, Sun fled to Japan. In 1916 Sun returned to regather his shattered Nationalist Party in the southern city of Canton. During a speech given in Shanghai that year, Sun declared: 'If we want the Republic to be solid, we must first build its foundation. We need not look abroad for this foundation; we should seek it in the hearts of all the people of the nation.'[47] Yet the future of Sun's project looked bleak at that point.

However, two major developments then took place. First, Sun was now totally disillusioned with the western powers who talked about peace and justice but seemed intent on carving China up yet further. Then, he was unable to persuade the Japanese to back him, though he made several attempts to get them to do so. So he turned to the new power on the world scene who seemed to promise a new and fairer world: Soviet Russia. Having instigated a revolution and won a bloody civil war, the Bolsheviks began to turn their attention to revolutions abroad. In 1923, with encouragement from the Soviet agent Borodin, Sun Yatsen's Nationalists and the fledgling Chinese Communist Party united their forces and started to train the National Revolutionary Army, a force intended to seize all China from the hands of the militarists and unite the country under one leader. Two men stood out particularly at the Military Academy set up by the USSR in Canton. One was a young Communist in charge of propaganda named Zhou Enlai. The other was a young military tactician named Chiang Kaishek. Both would have a powerful part to play in the shaping of twentieth-century China. Many years later, Zhou Enlai would become Prime Minister of Communist China. But in 1925, after Sun Yatsen's death from cancer, it was Chiang Kaishek who came to prominence first. He used his influence in the National Revolutionary Army to gain control of the Nationalist Party, and in 1926 he began to lead his forces, with the Nationalists and Communists working together, in a campaign to conquer China. In fact, the army only managed fully to conquer the populous provinces of the east coast, their campaign ending near the cities of Nanjing and Shanghai. One of the prime threats to Chiang's advance was neutralized when he coordinated the massacre of his Communist allies in Shanghai in April 1927, followed by the purge of an attempted uprising in Canton in December of the same year. Chiang also persuaded, cajoled, and bribed various warlords elsewhere in China into accepting his authority, and in 1928 he proclaimed himself the head of new National Government of China, with its capital based at Nanjing (known in the west at that time as Nanking). He would rule there for the next ten years, until war with the Japanese forced him to retreat in 1937. However, behind the façade of national unity, Chiang's government was an uneasy affair, desperately balancing rivals for power against each other: provincial warlords, the Communists, and the Japanese.[48]

There has been a tendency, in looking at the wider sweep of Chinese history before Mao's victory in 1949, to regard the period after the 1911 revolution as a desolate era of lost opportunities. In many ways, though, the period was intellectually and socially one of the most promising and exciting in Chinese history. The rest of the book examines in detail how the May Fourth era and the 'New Culture', lived both in the mind and on the streets by elite and ordinary Chinese alike, have reverberated through Chinese history ever since the heady days of 1919, when the student demonstrators and their generation turned their thoughts to 'saving the nation'.

'Revolution,' the great Chinese writer Lu Xun once observed, 'is a bitter thing'. China has experienced a great deal of pain in its search for a modern identity, and its revolutions over the twentieth century – 1911, 1927, 1949 – have brought great suffering in their wake. Yet the story of China in that century is also of ideas that, for a time, brought joyful, transformative change, and may yet do so again. The May Fourth era was the crucible of many of those changes. It is impossible to understand how thoroughly this society of over a billion people was changed in the course of a hundred short years without returning to examine the experience and possibilities of that short period of promise in the early twentieth century.

2

A TALE OF TWO CITIES

Beijing, Shanghai, and the May Fourth Generation

'Youth,' wrote the radical activist Chen Duxiu in 1915, 'is like early spring, like the rising sun, like trees and grass in bud, like a newly sharpened blade. It is the most valuable period of life.'[1] To be young and living in the city in China during the early years of the Republic, the period when Chen was writing, was to grow up in a dangerous yet deeply exciting time. For this generation, space opened up. This could be as individual as the opportunity to walk around freely given to young women whose feet were no longer bound; as local as the new places such as public parks, schools, cinemas, department stores, and factories which had not existed a generation before; and as global as the modernizing, imperialist, capitalist world that had forced itself on China but was also open for exploration by the Chinese.

In short, this chapter is about the excitement, the arrogance, and the uncertainty of being young at the dawn of Chinese modernity. To understand the ideas that changed China during this period, it is essential to understand the places and the people associated with those ideas. This chapter examines the atmosphere in Beijing and Shanghai in the interwar period, and then takes a closer look at some of the individuals and groups who lived in those cities. For the cities were essential to China's development of a modern identity.

It was a very particular type of modernity which the new Chinese Republic encountered. Within a few years of the Republic's birth in 1912, China had to deal with global powers exhausted by the destruction of World War I. China itself had, of course, been a participant in the war, an event leading to the betrayal and disillusionment that caused the 1919 May Fourth demonstrations in Beijing. In Europe, though, there was a strong sense that the promise of progress of the Victorian era had been destroyed in the killing fields of the World War. Ideas that undermined rationality and grand, romantic views of the future jostled with the now tarnished idea that scientific, clinical modernity was an unalloyed good that could show the way forward for the world. Science was mustard gas as well as Marconi radios or medicine. The great powers, regardless of which side they had fought on, struggled to recover a lost pre-war idyll.[2]

Europe's wartime agony and the culture of often forced frivolity that supplanted it was visible every day in China through the continuing imperialist presence. British veterans such as Maurice Tinkler, unable to find work at home in Lancashire after coming home from the Western Front, shipped out to Shanghai in 1919 as new recruits of the Shanghai Municipal Police, which kept law and order in the International Settlement. 'Shanghai is the best city I have seen and will leave any English town 100 years behind', he marvelled on arrival. 'It is the most cosmopolitan city of the world bar none and the finest city of the Far East.'[3] In the French Concession, marks of the European war could be seen everywhere, with major boulevards renamed Avenues Joffre and Foch after the victorious generals. Throughout the city, the newest American and European-style culture could be seen: fast cars, jazz bars, and advertisements for exciting new consumer products such as RCA gramophones and Golden Dragon cigarettes (for opium was not the only addictive drug that was mass-marketed in China; so was nicotine). The treaty port cities, and in particular Shanghai, created a particular type of imperial modernity that sometimes seemed to suspend the reality that the cities were squarely in Chinese territory, inhabited mostly by Chinese. Yet outward-looking aspects of that modernity were explored by Chinese too, such as the writer Shi Zhecun, who wandered around the bookstores of the International Settlement and the coffee shops of the French Concession, living a Parisian Left Bank lifestyle at one remove.

The world the Great War had made was part of China's Republican experience, for Chinese as well as foreigners. From the White

Russians in exile in Shanghai from the Soviet government brought to power by the collapse of the Czarist empire to the associations of Chinese labour veterans of the European front, the world of war came to China just as China had gone to the war. The May Fourth era itself was part of that changed world. It was in China's cities where the new thinking developed, and in particular in Beijing and Shanghai.

Beijing: Intellectual Centre of the Movement

If a present-day visitor to Beijing wanted to retrace the path that Luo Jialun and his fellow-students took during the demonstration described at the start of this book, she or he would see little of the city as it was in 1919. But not everything has gone.

Starting in what is now Tian'anmen Square, you can walk through the Forbidden City in Beijing across a string of enclosures where emperors once held court. The yellow roof tiles and deep red buildings are still preserved as a monument to the grandeur of China's imperial past. As you come out of the complex, you may see a Starbucks coffee stand, a symbol of how far global capitalism has reached. Walk across the moat at the back, cross the road, and walk right for about fifteen minutes. The avenue becomes less green and more cluttered with undistinguished buildings, mostly shops. The name of the street changes: it is now Wusi Dajie – 'May Fourth Avenue'. Near a major crossroads, you can see a large gateway giving onto a large, redbrick building three storeys high, fronted by a court-yard. There is a stone canopy with four large pillars protecting the entrance from the elements. The notice at the front describes it as 'The Museum of the New Culture Movement'. If you go in, you can see several large, whitewashed rooms with blackboards set at the front, and in the middle glass cases full of photographs of young, mostly smiling, men and women.

In the early decades of the twentieth century, this building was the main part of Peking University.[4] Known as the 'old red building', this particular structure was left behind after the Communist victory in 1949, as the University moved in the 1950s to its current, much larger site, in the far northwest of Beijing. The building was then used as a set of offices, closed to the public, until the turn of the millennium, when it was refurbished, and opened in 2002 as a museum, with the teaching rooms repainted and preserved as they were in the 1910s and 1920s. For those who know modern Chinese history, the figures who spent time at the University are famous ghosts indeed. In particular, those who shaped the Chinese Communist Party (CCP), one of the most powerful political organizations in history, were here. Mao Zedong was an assistant in the library, under the head librarian Li Dazhao, one of the co-founders of the Party, along with Chen Duxiu, who became the dean of humanities. It was this university's students who were also at the heart of the demonstrations on 4 May 1919.

Come out of the museum and keep walking along Wusi Dajie until you get to the top of Wangfujing Street. Turn right and walk south. Now Beijing's most prestigious shopping street, lined with Japanese department stores and branches of McDonald's, Wangfujing was known as Morrison Street in the early twentieth century, and was even then famous as a place for luxurious living. At the bottom, turn right, and walk for about fifteen minutes, and you will come right round again to the front of the Forbidden City, which looks onto Tian'anmen Square. The Square is a concrete giant, about a kilo-metre in each direction, built in the early 1950s. It can hold a million people, and has done so, at Mao Zedong's orders in 1966 during the mass political rallies of the Cultural Revolution, and again in 1989, this time in defiance of the orders of the Communist Party. Like most of Beijing's wide boulevards and grey, boxlike buildings, the square is an expression of architecture as faceless power: designed for mass rallies, not so friendly to individual human beings. Little of this was there in the early twentieth century, with the exception of the Tian'anmen itself, the Gate of Heavenly Peace which fronts the Forbidden City complex and is now located at the north end of the square, conveniently flanked by its new guardians, two metro stations, one to the west, one to the east. It was in front of the gate that the students gathered on 4 May 1919.

Beijing was the first centre of the May Fourth Movement. It had been made the capital during the Ming dynasty, some 500 years before, and had the walls and towers of a typical Chinese city, although as in most cities, these fell victim to war or city planners in the course of the twentieth century. The government remained under the control of battling warlord factions through much of the period from 1911 to 1928. Liberalism and openness were therefore in short supply.

'Few cities in China in the 1920s', writes the historian David Strand, 'looked so traditional and Chinese and at the same time harboured the essentials of modern and Western urban life'.[5] Yet it was a city in crisis, lacking the self-confidence that would mark Shanghai during the same era. For most of the period after 1916, Beijing was a capital in name rather than reality, and after 1928 not even that. The death of President Yuan Shikai in 1916 led to over a decade of conflict between rival militarist rulers, and although the seizure of Beijing as a national capital was a goal for many of these rulers, few of them controlled more than a restricted area of China while claiming countrywide authority. Eventually, in 1928, the victory of the Nationalists' Northern Expedition under Chiang Kaishek led to a new government being declared with its capital at Nanjing. Beijing, meaning literally 'Northern Capital', was renamed Beiping (transliterated at the time as Peiping), the name it retained for the period until 1949 when the victorious Communists renamed it Beijing and restored its status as the capital.

But even as it became shabbier and its infrastructure was neglected through the 1910s and 1920s, the city retained much of its imperial splendour. The city had been laid out with the magnificent, if brooding Forbidden City, the former imperial palace, at its centre, accessed through the Tian'anmen gate. The two main parts of the city, the Inner City to the north and the Outer City to the south, were surrounded by high grey walls of earth and brick, torn down in the early Maoist era. (Very few Chinese cities have large parts of their old walls left, Xi'an and Pingyao in Shanxi being among them.) Yet the modernization that arrived in so many Chinese cities – such as Shanghai, Tianjin, and Guangzhou – was to be seen in Beijing as well, in the form of sewage pipes, telephones, and eventually trams. The roads were asphalted, but only in part, because traditional mule-drawn carts could not cope with hard roads. Unlike Shanghai, the city did not become industrialized in a major way during this period. Therefore, the industrial working class, who would become the basis of a powerful labour movement in Shanghai in the 1920s, particularly after the foundation of the Communist Party, were not so much of a factor in Beijing, although rickshaw pullers and craft guild members provided the basis for protest against militarist politics and exploitative conditions.[6] Foreigners were not officially involved with Beijing's city administration as they were in Shanghai, but the foreign presence was considerable nonetheless: diplomats were stationed in the capital, naturally, and they were joined by missionaries and traders. Exotic birds could be spotted, such as Bertrand Russell, who wrote his book *The Problem of China* (1922) as a result of a period as visiting professor of politics at Peking University.

The University was a reminder that, even at a time when much of the city appeared to be going to seed as the republican experience soured, there were oases of excellence. Peking University was the geographical and spiritual centre of the new thinking. This institution had been set up in 1898 as part of the reform movement of that year, when it was known as the Imperial University. It had had a very uncertain beginning, as many at the imperial court were unhappy about the institutionalization of western thought in the Chinese curriculum. After the revolution of 1911, the reformer Yan Fu, who had been the first translator of Mill and Spencer into Chinese, was made President of the University, and while he only lasted a few months, he insisted on standards of academic rigour which led to a series of significant faculty hirings. Among those who joined the teaching staff in the next couple of years were Chen Duxiu and Li Dazhao, later to become the founders of the Chinese Communist Party, and Hu Shi, one of the most prominent literary reformers in modern China. Most notably, in 1916 a new University President, Cai Yuanpei, was appointed, whose period in control was to prove crucial not just for the University's reputation, but for the whole May Fourth era. Cai was a brilliant scholar who had flourished in the late Qing dynasty, then gone to Germany for further study, and returned to China as an advocate of modernized education, or in his own phrase, 'education for a worldview'.[7] Cai's most notable policy was the encouragement of genuine academic freedom. This enabled younger scholars such as Li Dazhao, who personally disagreed with Cai Yuanpei's Confucian morality, to publish and advocate alternative ideas.

The University's most famous building was located very centrally, near the back wall of the Forbidden City and near Beihai Park. The 'old red building' was one of the landmarks that would always be recalled by former students of 'Beida' (as the university was known in abbreviated Chinese form), long after the campus had been moved, first during the war against Japan, then as a result of post-1949 expansion.

The somewhat Bohemian air that pervaded the university area was not lost on its students. The writer Zhu Haitao wrote that in 'China's Latin Quarter', countless students lived packed into tiny apartment blocks, with the ground outside studded with tables, chairs, wash-stands, and so on. 'Eating at Beida was casual [*ziyou*]', Zhu noted. 'It was convenient, cheap, and tasty, so everyone just got what he wanted.'

He explained:

You could eat in any way you wanted to. There were some people who were not used to this when they enjoyed it for the first time, especially people who were too used to a regulated, collective life, and they were a bit like people who lived underground and then came out . . . into the light of 500 electric lights, and were a bit startled . . . I myself had gone through ten years of strict missionary school life. Especially in the two years before [coming to] Beida, when we heard the gong, we ate . . . When we came here, there was none of that at all, no gongs, bells, calls . . . the call of your stomach was the only thing that called you to eat . . . In other schools, this was impossible.[8]

This *ziyou* (free, casual, almost licentious) attitude towards eating was unusual in a society in which regular meals were a cultural obsession in the face of the threat of drought, flood, and famine. But the term *ziyou* was also an indicator of the atmosphere that emerged more widely in the reconsideration of Confucian norms that the New Culture Movement unleashed. It was used not only for food, but also for a new concept of 'free love' (*ziyou ai*). The element *zi* in *ziyou* also implied a new way for the Chinese to think about their conception of the self. Confucian thought had not been enthusiastic about pushing the individual self forward: to do so was to offend against dictates of proper modesty and the need to adhere to a more collective sense of good. Now, as part of the impact of western thought, which included ideas of the modern, autonomous self, the Chinese were encouraged to celebrate individual identity.

A general air of anarchic possibility perhaps flowed from the institution of the University itself:

The nicest thing [about being at Peking University] was searching out teachers. The doors of the university were open to anybody who wanted to come in . . . If you wanted to, you could go and hear any teacher's class, and absolutely nobody would come in and ask you whether you were a Beida student or not, nobody would come . . . and want you to pay money as a listening-in fee for a class, and the most marvellous thing was that all Beida professors had this generous attitude . . . so not only could you listen in, but when you'd listened, you could go up to the professors and ask about difficult or doubtful parts . . . So I've described the most valuable atmosphere of the 'Latin Quarter' – a generous spirit of scholarship that did not calculate profit.[9]

The premodern Confucian tendency to value scholarship over monetary gain is evident in Zhu's comments. But not everyone was quite as reverent towards Peking University, nor was formal enrolment quite as easy as slipping in and out of classes at the 'old red building'. At that time, Zhu reminisced, only some 300 students applying to Beida and its prestigious rival, Qinghua, might get in from some 3,000 applicants. A popular saying had it that when one took entrance examinations, it was *xiong* (ferocious), but when one got in, one could *song* (slack off), and when one graduated, one's belly would be *kong* (empty).[10]

Generational collaboration and conflict marked the short years of the May Fourth era, when intellectual debates were largely carried out through journals such as *New Youth* (the most radical in its hatred of Confucianism) and *New Tide* (more moderate, although its key contributors were generally younger than *New Youth*'s). Later, we will examine in more detail some of the ideas about which they enthused. But when doing so, it is important to keep in mind the influence of the close-knit, challenging, hothouse atmosphere of the Peking University campus: students who lived together acted together as well. The same atmosphere at the same institution, although by then in a geographically different spot, would have a similar effect in the demonstrations of 1989 that would lead to the Tian'anmen tragedy.

Shanghai: China's Modern Challenge

Beijing's rival, Shanghai, was a very different sort of place. An outward-looking colonial city, it thinks now, as it did in the early twentieth century, not of the parochial task of upstaging its rival cities in China, but rather of ranking itself with New York, Paris, or Tokyo as one of the great cities of the world. Some of the most central parts of Shanghai's architecture have survived much better than the monuments of the capital. The view that a visitor would see today on Shanghai's famous waterfront, the Bund, is very similar to the vista in 1920, consisting of pompous buildings that housed landmarks such as the Hongkong and Shanghai Bank. The major shopping thoroughfare that leads off the Bund, Nanjing Road, has rather different businesses lining it today: Ajinomoto Noodles, the Sofitel Hotel, and McDonald's again. But its mix of bright lights, advertising, and unashamed consumerism would not surprise anyone who knew the street in the 1920s. If you were to cross from the Bund to the other side of the creek, the Pudong area, which was mostly muddy flats covered in warehouses before 1990, you would find it now a science-fiction metropolis of skyscrapers, complete with a twenty-first-century magnetic levitation train to the new airport.

For practical reasons, Shanghai attained greater significance for many of the May Fourth generation from the early 1920s. The vicious competition between military ruling factions in Beijing led to ever greater political instability and the persecution of political radicals. In addition, the more outward-looking and relatively politically tolerant atmosphere of Shanghai appealed to many, along with the commercial opportunities for publishing and distributing the new thought which poured from their pens.

Shanghai was a legendary city for all classes and nations; the Briton Maurice Tinkler was not alone in his awe. 'Making whoopee' was the crude but not inaccurate way in which a guidebook of the 1930s summed up the nightlife of Shanghai for rich foreign visitors.[11] A character in a short story by the writer Ding Ling, a peasant seeking his fortune, says, 'Shanghai's a big place, not like where we come from. Lots of people with plenty of money. It'll be easy making a living there.'[12] For people around the globe, from world travellers to the poorest Chinese, Shanghai had a reputation for trashy verve befitting a polyglot bastard child of imperialism.

The city in its modern form was the product of the Opium Wars, a treaty port in which the western powers and, later, the Japanese provided a more obvious face for the imperialist presence in China than in a city such as Beijing. The city was physically divided into different sectors: most of the city was under Chinese rule, but along the waterfront of the Huangpu River sat the International Settlement, run by a Municipal Council dominated by the British, and to the west, the French Concession. The latter two areas were in effect colonies within Shanghai, with borders and guards to police travel between them, although, as in Cold War Berlin before the Wall went up, people did in fact go back and forth between the areas of the city for work and recreation. Even in the 'foreign' concessions, the Chinese made up more than 90 per cent of the population.

This forced encounter with imperialism was simultaneously galling and seductive for the May Fourth generation. Chinese were frequently on the end of racist attitudes and abuse from the British, French, Americans, and Japanese who made up the bulk of the foreigners whom they encountered. Events such as the May Thirtieth Movement of 1925 showed how clashes could spiral. After the shooting of 11 Chinese workers during a demonstration against the owners of a Japanese mill by the Shanghai Municipal Police (many of whose squad were Chinese), there were widespread boycotts of foreign businesses and street demonstrations against imperialist aggression. Both the Nationalists and the CCP received valuable momentum from public anger at the May Thirtieth killings, which spread far beyond the city itself. Professors at Peking University declared on 9 June 1925 that:

The tragedy which has taken place in the International Settlement of Shanghai has filled the Chinese nation with horror and indignation...some Chinese students, who were merely young boys and girls, paraded as a manifestation of protest in the streets of Shanghai on May 30 last...Would any right-minded person regard these boys and girls as rioters and treat them with bullets and rounds of machine guns?[13]

Even when confrontation was not as violent as this, everyday reality made it clear that Shanghai was a society deeply divided by hardened European ideas of race, often expressed by the places where Chinese could not go and the roles they could not play. The public gardens on the Bund, the famous waterfront, were not open to the Chinese until 1928, with the exception of 'servants in attendance upon foreigners'.[14] Interracial marriages or even relationships were heavily frowned upon. All this rankled more in Shanghai than in Beijing precisely because of the seeming cosmopolitanism of the 'world city' which Shanghai had become. The British settler community invented the term 'Shanghailand' to express the idea that the tripartite city was somehow Other, not a part of China, not a colony, but a pseudo-country perhaps best described as a state of mind. And it is clear that this idea, if not the term, was also shared by many Chinese. For many Chinese in Shanghai, their primary identity continued to be derived from their places of native birth, rather than from their newly adopted city.[15] Nonetheless, it is hardly surprising that Chinese nationalism developed so strongly in Shanghai, where the most confrontational aspects of imperialism were visible and rubbed in wherever either foreigners or Chinese walked, worked, or lived.

Yet the cosmopolitanism of the city, though tainted by the hierarchy of race, was not an illusion either. Architecture is one area in which this became apparent. True, the most visible architectural highlight, the Bund, was rooted in a parochial vision of Britishness, a mishmash bringing to mind the buildings of Manchester or other outposts of empire such as Calcutta, with few Chinese elements. Yet other parts of the cityscape looked to the future and inspired foreigner and Chinese alike with their visions of a young city in a hurry. Skyscrapers appeared in Shanghai earlier than anywhere else in China, along with the neon lights which the novelist Mao Dun incorporated on the first page of his novel *Midnight* to give the flavour of Shanghai in what he called a 'Romance of China in 1930'. Near the start of the novel, one character, an old man being driven through the centre of the city in a '1930-model Citroen' is increasingly startled by what he sees:

A snake-like stream of black monsters, each with a pair of blinding lights for eyes, their horns blaring, bore down upon him, nearer and nearer!... He felt as if his head were spinning and his eyes swam before a kaleidoscope of red, yellow, green, black, shiny, square, cylindrical, leaping, dancing shapes, while his ears rang in a pandemonium of honking, hooting and jarring till his heart was in his mouth ... [Looking out of the window, his eyes] fell straight away upon a half-naked young woman sitting up in a rickshaw, fashionably dressed in a transparent, sleeveless voile blouse, displaying her bare legs and thighs. The old man thought for one horrible moment that she had nothing else on.[16]

The impact of all these new sensations is too much for the old man, who has a stroke and dies at the climax of chapter 1. For some, however, the stimulation of the city was what made it unique. The writer Shi Zhecun, one of the most notable modernists of the 1930s, recalled how important the bookstores of Fuzhou Road, full of the latest European and American writing, had been to him as he developed his personal style. This was not just a world of bookstores, but also teahouses, stationery stores, and even brothels which made up a whole literary demi-monde. Literary figures might head to the bookstores of the big Chinese presses in Shanghai, the Commercial Press and the Zhonghua, and then to the import stores, Kelly and Walsh or the Sino-American Bookstore, a wealth that could stand comparison with bookshop paradises such as Charing Cross Road in London. For others, it was the smaller innovations, such as the café culture of (where else?) the French Concession which enabled them to inject an idea of European cosmopolitanism into their lives even when they had never set foot outside China. The essayist Zhang Ruogu was caught up in the literary world's 'coffeehouse craze' in the 1920s, spending time at favoured haunts such as Sullivan's coffee shop, Constantine's Russian café, and the Balkan Milk Store. He wrote, '. . . I spent practically all my leisure time in the cafés on Avenue Joffre . . . Come late afternoon, all of us would gather . . . and as we drank the strong and fragrant coffee to enhance our fun, we would gently talk our hearts out'.[17]

Education was also part of the Shanghai experience. Although Peking University had the greatest prestige of any institution in China, Shanghai also had education at all levels and for all classes. St John's University in Shanghai, founded in 1879, educated the children of the local elite, and became the most prominent Chinese Christian university in China in the 1920s. In contrast, Shanghai University, founded in 1922, had a more radical reputation, with Communist luminaries such as Qu Qiubai (a future Party leader) and Deng Zhongxia on the faculty. Learning English became an important skill in college, as textbooks for so many of the new western subjects were only available in that language. Yet as a total proportion of the population, university students were a very small minority. In 1934, there were fewer than 28,000 students registered at universities and colleges across all of China. Throughout this time, most of them attended institutions in three cities: Beijing, Shanghai, and Nanjing.[18]

In general, the Chinese who lived the most 'modern' lives were an elite. The working classes did not spend their time drinking coffee or browsing through English-language books. The poorest might live in shanty-towns of dilapidated reed huts or even boats, or a straw shack. The better-off might aspire to the crowded backstreet alleyway houses known as *shikumen*.[19] But even for those who did not share the life of the educated May Fourth generation, the modernity and internationalism of Shanghai was there every time they passed an advertisement for powdered Momilk or a Hollywood movie in the street, a Sikh policeman brought in by the British in the International Settlement, an elegant villa in the French Concession, or a marble British bank. Shanghai placed its contradictions squarely in the view of all its residents.

People: The May Fourth Generation

What sort of people lived in the cities and were makers of the New Culture experience? The answer is that the movement was the product of hundreds, if not thousands, of lives and voices. I have highlighted a few figures in particular because each of them expresses something central about the movement: its questioning of Chinese culture and its ability to deal with modernity, its ability to use commercialism and mass media to get its message across, and its struggle to reconcile nationalism with issues of gender and class. These are people with very different careers. Zou Taofen was a journalist and media entrepreneur; Du Zhongyuan a businessman and political activist; and Ding Ling and Lu Xun were among the most prominent literary figures of their day. They were not 'typical' May Fourth figures, because their commitment and their driven energy for their particular causes would have made them unusual in any society. But they give us a clear picture of the many facets of the era, and their writings and legacy will recur throughout the story told here of China's twentieth century.

One factor that does unite these four figures is that they were, or ended up, broadly on the left wing of politics. Yet, with the implicit or explicit understanding of 'progress' that underpinned the New Culture, this is perhaps unsurprising. What is notable is how far that rather vague label of 'left' included such a wide variety of attitudes and ideas. These are lives of contradiction. Another thing that the May Fourth generation had in common was that they knew that there were no easy answers in China's quest to find a modern identity. Here, then, are some of the people who made their lives in May Fourth Beijing and Shanghai.

Zou Taofen

Even now in China, he is often referred to just as 'Taofen'. A little north of the top of Wangfujing, one of the more upmarket shopping streets in central Beijing, there is a branch of the Sanlian Bookstore named after him, and whose parent company he helped to found. His collected essays and selections of his works remain in

3. Zou Taofen.
Zou Taofen was the most prominent example of how writers in the new commercial print culture centred on Shanghai could create a popular media persona. His 'Readers' Mailbox' advice column helped propel *Life* magazine to record sales.

print. In the 1930s, he was a great inspiration to radical Marxist youth.[20] Yet, so far, Zou Taofen (1895–1944), originally named Zou Enrun, has not received his full due as a central figure of the New Culture era. This may be because his activities during the 1920s took place in Shanghai, not Beijing. Or perhaps it is because those activities were not much concerned with the development of Marxist thought that occupied his contemporaries Chen Duxiu and Mao Zedong; when Zou did turn to Marxism in the 1930s, his previous activities were viewed (not least by himself) as a dilettante and irrelevant deviation from the really important issue of class struggle.

Yet to ignore Zou Taofen's influence in the 1920s is to ignore a figure who both shaped the New Culture era and who reflected the many changes it made to China. Through Zou's writings, hundreds of thousands, possibly millions, of men and women read about the changes in society and were given new ways to think about those changes. Through him, the 'new culture' became comprehensible as part of their lives.

Zou Taofen was born to a Fujianese local elite family in decline. His family lived on a mixture of his father's undependable income and charity. Zou remembered that his and his two siblings' 'clothes and shoes were all made by my mother herself. She often received orders from outside the family to make women's clothes for festivals, so she was always very busy'.[21] When Zou was 12 years old, his mother died. Yet he managed to gain entry to St John's University, one of the most exclusive missionary universities in Shanghai, although he had to do a variety of jobs to pay his tuition and keep. He used his time at college to develop a thirst for reading widely in English, and after graduation in 1921, his education opened a series of white-collar jobs for him. The major change that would shape his life came in 1926, when he was asked to take over the editorship of a small-circulation journal named *Life Weekly* [*Shenghuo zhoukan*; I will refer to it simply as *Life*]. The journal had been founded by the Chinese Society for Vocational Education, which had been set up by local notables in Shanghai and the surrounding Jiangnan area in 1913. The Society's aim was to encourage 'vocational youth', primarily young men who wanted to move up into a lower middle-class professional stratum of society and feared most of all being pushed down into the labouring classes. Zou understood these readers. Although he had managed to obtain a full university education, a rare privilege indeed at the time, he recognized the difficulties of trying to educate oneself at the same time as needing to make a living.[22] As we will see in this and the next chapter, Zou turned out to be one of those legendary editors who found out just what made their readerships laugh, cry, and, most importantly, come back the following week for more. In numerical terms, *Life* expanded from a circulation in 1926 of some 2,000, mostly given away free, to some 40,000 just three years later, with a doubling to perhaps 80,000 on the eve of the outbreak of the Manchurian crisis in 1931, and a record 200,000 by the time the magazine was shut down by Chiang Kaishek's Nationalist government in 1933.[23] At a time when each copy may have been read by between three and ten readers, this suggests a very significant circulation of ideas.

What a factual account of Zou's life and times does not convey, however, is the sheer zest and enthusiasm with which he absorbed the wealth of new ideas about culture and politics which were flooding into China. As we will see, when thinking about how China could rescue itself from its current crisis, he brought up political thinkers as far apart as Gandhi and Kemal (Atatürk), business entrepreneurs such as George Eastman (the founder of Kodak) and Thomas Edison (discussed further in Chapter 3), and scientists and thinkers such as Louis Pasteur, Marie Curie, and Albert Einstein. Nor were these superficial portraits; many of them stretched over weeks as serials, and Zou came back to some particularly significant figures such as Gandhi many times over the years. Yet he did not restrict himself to consideration of abstract politics. His concern for his readers as real, troubled individuals led him to become an advice columnist, giving him a further opportunity to become known simply as 'Taofen' to a generation of young women and men coming of age in a time of opportunity and uncertainty.

Lu Xun

When a Chinese person is asked who was the foremost figure of the May Fourth era, or the greatest writer in modern China, they are as likely as not to mention Lu Xun. Lu Xun (1881–1936), the pen name of the writer Zhou Shuren, has practically become a patron saint in the People's Republic of China. One can visit his old residences in Beijing and Shanghai, which are preserved as shrines, his pens and bed left behind as relics. Lu Xun himself would have been appalled at this: one of his explicit last wishes was that people should 'Do nothing in the way of commemoration' after his death.[24] Lu Xun's beatification was engineered in part by the League of Left-Wing Writers, a CCP-oriented literary organization of the 1930s, to portray him as a leftist writer who wrote on behalf of the masses. However, this

4. Lu Xun as a young man.
Lu Xun was one of the most important literary figures in the May Fourth era.
His sardonic, uncompromising condemnation of China's Confucian past was
inspiring to many of the writers and politicians who emerged in the May
Fourth era.

picture hides the reality of a much more complex, sardonic, and even
at times nihilistic writer.

Lu Xun was born in Shaoxing in Zhejiang province. He grew up in
a low-level elite family, and although he was given the traditional
training in the Confucian classics that constituted the path to an
official position in the bureaucracy, his father was an invalid and an
opium addict, leading to the family's slow impoverishment. Poverty
forced Lu Xun to turn to the cheaper but less respectable westernized education which was then available in China, and, when aged 21,
he went to Japan to train in medicine. Yet in the years leading up to
his departure, Lu Xun had also been deeply impressed by the huge
increase in foreign fiction appearing in translation in China. In particular, he became convinced that fiction was a powerful way to alert
the country to the political crisis it faced; this idea was influenced by
the wave of 'reform fiction' during Japan's Meiji Restoration, which
had itself drawn on writers such as Disraeli and Bulwer-Lytton.
However, Lu Xun's medical training was brought to a halt shortly

after the outbreak of the Russo-Japanese War, which took place largely on Chinese territory, in 1904. It was not the war that prevented him studying. Rather, in his own account, it was an incident in class:

I have no idea what improved methods are now used to teach microbiology, but in those days we were shown lantern slides of microbes; and if the lecture ended early, the instructors might show slides of natural scenes or news to fill up the time. Since this was during the Russo-Japanese War, there were many war slides, and I had to join in the clapping and cheering in the lecture hall along with the other students. It was a long time since I had seen any compatriots, but one day I saw a newsreel slide of a number of Chinese, one of them bound ... They were all sturdy fellows but looked completely apathetic ... The one with his hands bound was a spy working for the Russians who was to be beheaded by the Japanese military as a warning to others, while the Chinese beside him had come to enjoy the spectacle.

Before the term was over I had left for Tokyo, because this slide convinced me that medical science was not so important after all. The people of a weak and backward country, however strong they might be, could only serve to be made examples of or as witnesses of such futile spectacles; and it was not necessarily deplorable if many of them died of illness. The most important thing, therefore, was to change their spirit; and since at that time I felt that literature was the best means to this end, I decided to promote a literary movement.[25]

This passage sums up much of what makes Lu Xun stand out in the largely sentimental, romantic, and sometimes kitsch world of modern Chinese literature: it is unsentimental and self-deprecating, but also filled with a genuine passion for 'saving' the Chinese nation. Yet it also shows the slightly chilling nature of Lu Xun's vision in its throwaway comment that 'it was not necessarily deplorable if many of them died of illness'. It is possible that Lu Xun did not mean this literally. Nonetheless, it is unsurprising, perhaps, that he started life as a trainee doctor: throughout his life, the tone he adopted was reminiscent in some way of a grizzled physician who continues to dole out pills and potions while becoming ever more cynical about the inability of his patients to learn from their errors. Throughout his writing career, Lu Xun offered a humanistic vision, but it was a weary, pessimistic one, very different from the brassy optimism or multicoloured tragedy that informed the literary and political romantics of the left and right.

Lu Xun's first attempts to save the nation through a redemptive literary movement were not an outstanding success. Of his first print run of 1,500 volumes of his short stories, around 40 copies were actually sold. Furthermore, despite his increasing disillusionment with traditional Chinese society, a disillusionment fuelled by the impoverished background from which he had arisen, he took part in a traditional arranged marriage. He continued to think about questions of culture and politics. One of his most suggestive pieces is 'On the Power of Mara Poetry' (1908), which identified the Buddhist god of destruction and rebellion, Mara, with poets who had rebelled against their own societies, such as the Hungarian Sandor Petöfi and the Pole Adam Mickiewicz.[26] Lu Xun's 'Mara' piece, inspired by Nietzsche and Ibsen, exalts the individual over the mass, but it is hardly a call for democracy: the mass of the people, he argued, are simply too inclined to conform under pressure to be able to offer any kind of way forward. This attitude was not dissimilar to the late Qing reformers, who despaired of the 'people' whom they were attempting to educate in the ways of constitutional reform; and there are echoes of it in the more elitist arguments used by some of the students in Tian'anmen Square in 1989.

It was only after 1915, when writing for the magazine *New Youth* [*Xin qingnian*], founded by Chen Duxiu, that Lu Xun began to make his mark. His finest short stories, such as 'Kong Yiji', 'Diary of a Madman', and 'My Old Home', appeared in this journal over the next few years. *New Youth* was a particularly significant publication, as it was also the showcase for the emerging Marxist thought of Chen Duxiu, Li Dazhao, and others who would go on to found the Chinese Communist Party.

During the height of the May Fourth Movement, the fact that Lu Xun was already coming up to 40 years old gave him an edge of experience and cynicism that prevented him sharing in the high hopes of the younger generation. Yet the May Fourth Movement and his name remain closely linked in the Chinese imagination to this day.

5. Ding Ling as a young woman.
Ding Ling's writing dealt frankly with female sexuality. Her most famous
character, 'Miss Sophie', was a self-tormenting figure who found herself unable
fully to express the longings she felt for the man she loved. Later in her life,
Ding Ling would be condemned by the Communists for the 'bourgeois'
concerns of her heroine.

Ding Ling

Ding Ling (1905–86) is probably the best-known woman writer of
twentieth-century China, and, like Lu Xun, she has become a figure
in the pantheon of May Fourth. Yet her determination to act on the
promise of that era, and particularly the opportunities for freedom
for women, meant that she ran into frequent, serious trouble, both
with the Nationalist government, which executed her lover Hu

Yepin, and the Communist Party, for which she worked over decades and which both fulfilled and betrayed her.

Ding Ling, the pseudonym of Jiang Bingzhi, was born into a moderately well-off landowning family in Anfu, Hunan province. Her father died when she was still a child, and she was deeply influenced by her mother, who left the family home to seek a modern education and succeeded in becoming a schoolteacher. Ding Ling, as a result of this influence, became precociously radical and enrolled at Shanghai University, an institution with a free-thinking, mostly left-wing faculty. She then moved to Beijing, where she attended Lu Xun's classes, among others, and began to live in *ziyou* style with a young man, Hu Yepin. Both Hu and Ding Ling were aspirant writers, but her career soon far outshone his. In 1927, her first story, 'Meng Ke', the tale of a wide-eyed young rural girl who eventually becomes a Shanghai movie star but loses her innocence along the way, was a major success, leading to the publication the next year of perhaps her best-known piece, 'The Diary of Miss Sophie'. This told the tale of a neurotic 'modern' young woman, who mentally tortures the people closest to her, and who is racked by self-loathing in the midst of a changing society which she embraces and yet dreads. Yet Hu and Ding Ling were still living in genteel poverty: even critically successful fiction did not bring in much cash.

In 1930, the couple's lives changed radically. They had moved to Shanghai, where Hu Yepin joined the Communist Party, and while Ding Ling was kept in the dark about many of his activities, she could see that he was involved in any number of clandestine meetings and attempts to overthrow the Nationalist government, which had savagely purged its Communist allies in 1927. In January 1931, Ding Ling heard that Hu had been arrested at one of his secret meetings. The Shanghai Municipal Police had been tipped off about the gathering, which took place within the International Settlement, and Hu and the others captured that night were handed over to the Nationalist government's police shortly afterwards. Frantic attempts to free him through appeals and bribes came to nothing: on the night of 7 February, Hu was executed by firing squad, along with 22 comrades. Ding Ling later wrote the story 'A Certain Night', a fictionalized account of

Hu's death which portrayed him as a martyr for the Communist cause, and which saw her own entry into the Party in 1932. Her despair is summed up in the story's last line: 'When will it be light?'[27]

Du Zhongyuan

Du Zhongyuan (1898–1944) made up for the short length of his life by the number of different roles he managed to squeeze into it. Journalist, political activist, businessman, porcelain enthusiast, inveterate traveller: for a brief period in the 1930s, he was one of the best-known journalistic voices in China. His greatest moment of fame came during the National Salvation movement of that era, when nationalist activists (in some cases in association with the Communist Party) lobbied Chiang Kaishek to change his policy of non-resistance to the increasing Japanese encroachment into North China. Between around 1930 and 1937, Du became one of the most prominent anti-Japanese, pro-resistance voices in China. He was given the platform of his mentor Zou Taofen's mass-circulation publications, *Life* and its successors, and benefited from their readerships, which may well have reached 1.5 to 2 million at their peak.

Du's outlook was heavily shaped by growing up in the imperial melting-pot that was Manchuria in the early twentieth century, and he was certainly not born as a sophisticate or cosmopolitan. He grew up in an impoverished village in Huaide county in Fengtian province, and was then sponsored by local elites to attend school and then college in Shenyang. He returned to Huaide to teach English in 1917, but the influence of the New Culture Movement on him had been strong during his college days, and he was inspired by the National Products Movement, which believed in encouraging people to buy Chinese rather than foreign goods, to move from teaching into business.[28] He was particularly keen to set up rival business enterprises to those run by the Japanese, particularly the South Manchurian Railway (SMR) Company in the northeast. He later stated that porcelain, one of the products perhaps most archetypally associated with China, must be developed as a native product, regaining market share from the cheap Japanese imports that dominated the market. He scraped together investment to set up his first factory just outside Shenyang,

6. Du Zhongyuan (back row, middle) with friends in Wuhan.
Du Zhongyuan was a successful entrepreneur in his native Manchuria before
the Japanese invasion of 1931. Forced into exile in Shanghai, he became a fierce
voice of protest against Japanese imperialism. He was imprisoned in 1935 for
publishing a newspaper column so controversial that it provoked a diplomatic
incident.

and by the late 1920s he was a prominent local businessman and
official of the provincial Chamber of Commerce. From 1928 to 1931,
the militarist ruler of Manchuria, Zhang Xueliang, included Du in
the group of prominent young nationalists around him who were
charged both with spreading propaganda against the Japanese presence in the region and with developing locally sponsored modernization projects in areas such as transport, education, and broadcasting.
During this time, Du also got to know Zou Taofen, already by then a
well-known journalist in Shanghai, and he started writing regularly

for Zou's *Life* magazine. This would stand him in good stead in the 1930s as he tried to use his journalism to rally the nation against what he saw as the greatest threat facing it: the menace of Japanese aggression.

Subcultures

These four people, of course, cannot represent anything like the whole of the May Fourth generation. There were large numbers of subcultures, each with their own set of concerns and cliques. Two particular groups are worth mentioning here, if only to give a flavour of the wide range of thought that May Fourth opened up.

One subculture which would have lasting significance was that of the young leftist radicals, many of whom would go on in 1921 to found the Chinese Communist Party. Yet in the early years of the Republic, many of them were excited thinkers who had not yet come to a decision about how they would 'save China'. It was some time before they even decided that they would be Marxists. One of the most significant was Chen Duxiu (1879–1942), a well-known radical academic who founded the magazine *New Youth*, and in doing so provided the most concrete forum for the New Culture Movement and its rejection of the Confucian past. It was in this journal that Chen put forward the slogan which has been associated ever since with May Fourth: what China needed, he argued, was 'Mr Science' and 'Mr Democracy'. At the time, these terms were still in flux. Chen understood 'science' as a concrete, positivistic concept that could stand in stark opposition to Confucianism, and 'democracy' had the implication of a search for a new morality, rather than just a political system. Chen, like so many other thinkers of the time, was heavily influenced by Social Darwinist ideas, which seemed to him to explain the process through which China had become so fatally weakened.

Peking University was highly significant in crystallizing Chen's thought and his ability to act on it, and, as discussed earlier in this chapter, the foundation of the Communist Party is closely linked to developments at the University in this period. Chen Duxiu and Li Dazhao (1889–1927), the party's co-founders, were respectively dean of humanities and head librarian under Cai Yuanpei's presidency, and they used the intellectual freedoms afforded by Cai's pluralist regime to argue the case for a Marxist solution to China's problems. The betrayal at Versailles which had angered their students now pushed Chen and Li towards Marxism, which they explored in *New Youth* and other journals in 1919–20. Other young radicals joined them, dissatisfied with the seeming collapse of stability and moral politics, and they met together in 'study societies' where theories of reform could be discussed. It would take much of the 1920s, the influence of the Soviet Comintern, and a radical change in political circumstances before the organized, disciplined CCP that the world later knew would appear.[29]

The founder member of the CCP who would go on to global fame was a young man from Hunan named Mao Zedong (1893–1976). Mao would later become the chairman of the Communist Party and the dominant leader in China for over a quarter of a century. Early in his life, he had rebelled against his father, a well-off farmer whom Mao deeply resented, and had moved to the city of Changsha around the time of the 1911 revolution. While there, he read widely in western as well as Chinese politics and philosophy, and became involved in a discussion group, the New Citizen Study Society. Mao became steadily more disillusioned by the breakdown of politics in the early Republic, and in 1920 declared that only a 'Russian-style revolution' could save China. At this time, Mao decided to move to Beijing, and although he was not a student at the university, he became actively involved in the study society convened by Li Dazhao, while working for Li as an assistant librarian.[30]

Not all the reformers turned to Marxism. Hu Shi (1891–1962), who had studied at Cornell and Columbia universities, joined the Peking University faculty and became a close friend and collaborator of Chen Duxiu's. They agreed in particular about the need for China to adopt a more accessible form of the written language to promote mass literacy. Yet Hu was not enticed by the attractions of Marxism's wide-ranging explanations, and wrote a famous set of articles entitled 'Problems and -isms' in 1919, in which he criticized those who 'don't study the standard of living of the ricksha coolie but rant instead about socialism; . . . don't study the ways in which women can be emancipated . . . but instead . . . rave about wife-sharing and free love'.[31] Hu Shi was a liberal who would eventually move to the right politically, but at this time, he was an active member of the close, if sometimes fractious, political world that centred on the University.

Another subculture was formed by the writers of fiction. 'May Fourth literature' has become a recognized, almost clichéd term in the discussion of modern Chinese writing. Lu Xun and Ding Ling are among its best-known figures, despite the major differences in their writing style. But there was also what the critic Leo Lee has called the 'romantic generation'. This included Xu Zhimo, Guo Moruo, and Mao Dun, whose works explode with individualistic energy. Rival literary factions were a constant feature of the era, with groups quarrelling with each other, often in the most bitter terms, in small-circulation journals.[32]

The intellectual differences between these groups and people were fiercely argued. But it is important to remember what held them together. All of them gravitated to Beijing or Shanghai, many of them spending time in both cities through the 1920s. All would have been familiar with the very different atmospheres of the two places. They would have wandered through the crowded backstreets near Coal Hill, behind the Forbidden City, or beyond the Qianmen gate in the centre of the city, buying snacks and spending endless hours in teahouses laughing, shouting, and arguing. Or else they would have been spending anxious moments getting in the manuscripts of the articles on the latest political or philosophical wonder – whether a reflection on Romantic poetry or a condemnation of patriarchal oppression of women – to the printers for the next edition of one of the ever-proliferating journals. Many of these people knew each other, and would continue contact throughout the century – those who survived it, anyway.

The spread of discontent during the 1989 Tian'anmen uprising in Beijing has been attributed in part to 'campus ecology' – lots of like-minded young men and women, based at universities in a small area of a major city.[33] The 'ecology' of everyday life also explains a great deal about the New Culture generation. It explains how and why they reacted to May Fourth, and why its effects stayed with them for so long afterwards, when the cityscapes and atmospheres in Beijing and Shanghai that had produced those effects had long since disappeared under the impact of war and revolution.

3

EXPERIMENTS IN HAPPINESS

Life and Love in New Culture China

Not every person's natural intelligence or strength is equal. But if each person develops his mind towards service and morality . . . so as to contribute to the mass of humanity, then he can be regarded as equal. That is *real* equality.[1]

Zou Taofen wrote this in an essay on the subject 'What is equality?' in 1927. Along with a host of other new concepts that entered Chinese thinking in the late Qing and early Republic, the theory of 'equality' was not always easy to put into practice, and Zou's genius was in managing to explain such terms to his army of readers. People seemed self-conscious of living in 'new times', and the word 'new' was used by radical thinkers over and over again to emphasize that their time, the early twentieth century, was qualitatively different from everything that had gone before. However, this was not just empty rhetoric. At all levels of society, it became clear that the introduction of new ways of thought and living, and the influx of larger numbers of foreigners than had ever been seen before, was changing China forever. In a very short number of years, many of the fixed certainties of Chinese life were changed utterly: how people worked, what they read and wrote, and perhaps most importantly, how people related to one another – men and women, politicians and citizens, old and young, Chinese and foreign. Not everyone rejected the old Confucian hierarchies, but few could carry on everyday existence without admitting that the world in which those hierarchies had emerged had disappeared in little more than half a century since the arrival of western imperialism. There was a change in culture – 'culture' in the sense of a system of mutual understandings, a society whose parts make sense in the context of each other, but which appears alien to those who have not been initiated into it. To understand 'Chinese culture' in the May Fourth era now meant that one had to cope with the reality of foreign ideas and goods, the new confidence of youth who would formerly have been deferential to the elderly, and of women who would have previously bowed down to men. The individual self, previously regarded as something to be downplayed in favour of a more collective identity, was now celebrated instead. These changes, initially condemned as foreign intrusions, were now part of being Chinese, and made up a 'new culture'. The May Fourth demonstrations and the political demands that accompanied them were emblematic of that culture, but it spread far more widely than just the world of high politics.

For Chinese men and women in the New Culture era had jobs constructing the fine buildings that were a product of the capitalist, imperialist culture; they spent endless hours on factory lines, spinning cotton, at the mercy of rude and violent supervisors, in constant danger of being maimed or killed by unsafe and rickety equipment; and they wandered into parks, chatting with friends and keeping half an eye out for any decent-looking members of the opposite sex. The world of the workplace and the world of private life were both changed by the political and social revolution that came to China in the early twentieth century.

New Classes, New Opportunities

The rise of an industrial working class was one of the most notable features of the arrival of western capitalist modernity to China. One historian has assessed the number of workers, including employees in transportation, handicrafts, factories, and the service sector, as being over 500,000 in Shanghai, the most industrialized city in China, by 1919.[2] The presence of this class would allow the Communist Party, founded in 1921, to make significant organizational advances in the

7. A tank patrols in the French Concession, Shanghai, around 1927.
Tensions were high as the Northern Expedition of united Nationalist and
Communist forces marched on Shanghai. The foreign powers prepared to be
attacked, but Chiang Kaishek decided against provoking them.

1920s, particularly after its alliance with the Nationalist Party of
Sun Yatsen. However, this class had already begun to find its own
sense of identity in the previous decades. From early in the century,
these workers organized and protested or went on strike against
intolerable working conditions, or took part in boycotts of foreign
goods as a protest against western and Japanese imperialism.[3] Other
groups also emerged and developed during this period. Professional
workers – teachers, doctors, lawyers – trained and carved out status
for themselves. Another class, who perhaps judged themselves a
shade below the professionals but above the working classes, was the
group known at the time as the *xiao shimin*, sometimes translated as
'petty urbanites'. Small shopkeepers, clerks, and office workers, these
members of a self-defined 'respectable' lower middle class were often
just a few steps away from economic disaster and descent into the
feared world of the lumpen poor. All these groups were, of course,

miles away from the world of the genuinely rich, the factory-owners and entrepreneurs.[4]

In all these groups, a notable feature was the rise of women workers. Some working-class occupations, such as dock work and construction, were the preserve of men, but in other areas, such as the cotton mills, women workers were in the great majority. Among professionals, too, women lawyers and teachers emerged for the first time. However, the entry of women into the working sphere was a major social shift. The structures that underpinned Confucian society gave women very little space to become autonomous workers or social actors in their own right. In the most physical sense, they were tied to the home by their bound feet, and it was only in the late nineteenth century that footbinding was phased out (though it continued in some rural areas into the Republican era).[5] More widely, patriarchal structures made the idea of women seeking their own professions somehow unseemly. Women had not, prior to the twentieth century, been universally forbidden from entering traditionally male spheres: for instance, local elite families in certain parts of China had for centuries encouraged female education. But the wider spread of education and opportunities for women emerged in the late Qing and early Republic, as the concept of the 'New Woman' began to emerge. It was an elite idea; New Women did not become factory workers, but instead sought professional status, which might in aspiration be journalism or law but in reality was more likely to be work in an office. Still, the spirit of the age gave women, like men, a chance to dream. Zhu Su'e, who would become one of China's first women lawyers, remembered that, when she refused to have her feet bound by her mother, who then said that Zhu would never find a husband, she replied: 'Fine! If I can't be married out, that will be fine . . . I will support myself.' And her family proved less narrow-minded than she had feared, allowing her to go to law school.[6] Zou Taofen, as ever a maker as well as mirror of current mores, had included among his role models for his lower middle-class readers the scientist Marie Curie, along with Einstein and Pasteur.[7] But for most of his readers, a high-school education was a dream, and university education a fantasy.

For factory workers, conditions were harsh, but also provided a chance to make friends and enjoy the odd entertainment. The historian Emily Honig has reconstructed the working day of women in the Shanghai cotton mills. The factory whistle would sound at 5.30 a.m., and at the gates, one could see 'women hobbling on bound feet, women wearing cloth shoes, and women wearing high heels ... old women with buns and young women with braids, short bobbed hair or even a permanent wave'. The working day was heavily regulated, with even toilet breaks run on a quota system. The work itself was heavy and destructive: Yu Rong, a worker whose job it was to place silk cocoons into cauldrons of boiling water, found that 'our hands would swell up every night. So we would go to the medicine store and buy an ointment. We would put that on and wrap up our hands. They would hurt and hurt at night.' Even the women's weekly rest day would probably be taken up with family duties. Yet there was sometimes an opportunity to slip out and enjoy street theatre or operas. Mill-worker Chen Zhaodi remembered that when she needed time out, 'I would not tell my family where I was going. My mother-in-law would never have let me go. I just went secretly.'[8]

Another profoundly important and symbolic change in the May Fourth era was the new stress on youth. 'Youth' had become a catchword in many of the liberation movements of the late nineteenth and early twentieth centuries in Europe, among them Young Ireland and the Young Turks. The destruction of much of Europe's youth in World War I led to an even greater focus on the virility and power of the young on the part of the new Soviet and fascist regimes, which started to shape their ideologies in the wake of the conflict. In China, too, the overturning of Confucian norms of veneration for the old meant that the young were now given opportunities to explore the modern world and their individual selves in an unprecedented way. One of the most prominent articles, written in 1915 at the start of the New Culture Movement by Chen Duxiu, was entitled 'Call to Youth', and was published in his own journal, the symbolically entitled *New Youth*.

But even during this great inversion of pre-existing values, aspects of the old norms were visible. In the old Confucian world, students had traditionally been given a certain amount of leeway to express criticism of those in authority. Education conferred not just knowledge, but moral weight as well. The division between high school and university students was not as well defined as in the west, and therefore many of the great student demonstrations of the era actually involved children in their mid-teens, with all the determination, exuberance, and irresponsibility that that implies. (Those qualities would come to light in sinister fashion during the Cultural Revolution half a century later: see Chapter 6.) In the May Fourth era, this indulgence towards the young continued even when the students took part in activities which Confucian thought frowned upon, such as the violent beating of Zhang Zongxiang and burning of Cao Rulin's house during the 1919 May Fourth demonstration. Even the students who were detained afterwards were released after the President of Peking University interceded for them, and the authorities also showed their understanding of the special status students had by agreeing to their release. (Although there was far less violence in the 1989 demonstrations in Tian'anmen Square, a similar double standard operated then: the students who were arrested were generally treated much more leniently than the workers' leaders who had also been instrumental in organizing the demonstrations.)

Many aspects of everyday life for all classes stayed constant or similar to what had come before. Chinese religious practice, which had underpinned so much of life for centuries, no longer provided a chain that led from the emperor all the way down to the ordinary farmer or villager. Yet people continued to worship at temples, respect ancestral shrines, and also take part in periodic waves of enthusiasm for Buddhist or Taoist folk religion – often to the rage of modernizing nationalists who felt that religion, which they termed 'superstition', was yet another 'feudal' aspect of a China that should be left behind.[9] However, there was no doubt that the very structure of Chinese society, particularly in the cities, had changed irretrievably, and it was generally the young who found themselves able to take up the opportunities that had opened up. For the first, and perhaps the last time, there were no older role models in China who could tell them what to expect or how to behave in the new world.

8. City policemen in Beijing, around 1919.
The militarist Chinese governments of the early Republic were on constant watch against threats to their unstable rule. The police were used to try to prevent protests such as the one on 4 May 1919. Confrontations between demonstrators and police could often become violent.

With conventional veneration for age being overturned in favour of a cult of youth, this was an intoxicating time for many. This explains why the role of someone like Zou Taofen, setting himself up as an advice columnist, was so important to this generation, who had so few places to turn in their quest to understand the changes in society.

Print, Commerce, and Culture

The interaction between technology, language, and culture was a large part of what made the New Culture so new. The era brought together the technical possibility of mass-market publication of periodicals and newspapers with linguistic reforms that popularized a simpler, easier language in which the published material could be read even by people who were not highly literate.

The arrival of print technology had led, in the late Qing, to the emergence of western-style newspapers which appeared initially in the treaty ports. The first such newspaper, *Shenbao*, was edited by the Englishman Ernest Major in the International Settlement of Shanghai, but it was soon followed by many others: by 1912, there were some 500 daily newspapers in China, and over 600 by 1928, with Shanghai and Beijing boasting around 40 to 50 each.[10] Print culture helped to shape Shanghai modernity in particular.[11] The intensely commercial rivalry between the papers led to various innovations, of which supplements containing new fiction were among the most important. Along with daily newspapers came weekly and monthly periodicals. These could be specialized, dealing with particular political or literary debates or quarrels. Others had wider circulations, such as *Life* or the *Fiction Monthly* [*Xiaoshuo yuebao*]. Mass fiction took off as well. As in nineteenth-century England and America, popular novels were often issued in serial form in the weeklies or monthlies before being reissued as books in their own right. This was big business: one of the bestselling authors of the era, Zhang Henshui, managed to extend the circulation of *Xinwen bao*, the newspaper that serialized his most famous novel, *Fate in Tears and Laughter* (1929), to around 150,000.[12]

These magazines helped to shape minds far beyond the cities in which they were produced. Zhu Su'e, who grew up in the small city of Changzhou, remembered in an interview with the historian Wang Zheng: 'I learned the world *nüquan* [women's rights] from reading new magazines after the May Fourth movement . . . I decided to leave home to study so that nobody could control me. That is how I came to Shanghai in the fall of 1919 – all because those magazines made me feel Changzhou was a small place, and I wanted to see the big world.'[13]

The fact that such a large readership was available was in significant part due to one particular strand of the New Culture: language reform. Radical thinkers such as Hu Shi argued that part of China's inability to abandon the Confucian past was caused by the fact that the traditional classical style of writing was still used for most 'respectable' purposes such as composing official government documents. Hu regretted that the vernacular style of writing, which was much closer to the spoken language and therefore easier for most people to learn, was still largely restricted to 'vulgar' forms such as popular plays or sensational novels. In fact, the situation was more complex than this rather black-and-white portrayal of language usage would suggest, and simplified written forms were already used more widely than Hu admitted.[14] But it remains the case that one of the greatest victories of the New Culture Movement was the official embrace and popularization of vernacular written Chinese within less than two decades. In a sense, it is a tribute to how quickly the language reformers' ideas caught on that the classical language, so long the mainstay of official Chinese culture, became a secondary, and after 1949, largely ignored cultural resource in China.[15] The spread of written vernacular Chinese was aided in large part by the ever-greater availability of mass publishing; and mass publishing, in turn, was stimulated by the spread of a language which made it easier for readers to access written material. The cultural changes of the era were strongly shaped by the permanent shift in the linguistic resources in which they were expressed, even if that victory was not as total as the May Fourth legend would later suggest.

Love, Labour, and Liberty

Perhaps it is in the area of the new possibilities for love that the May Fourth era really belonged to the young. Of course, there were many older people who found new spouses and lovers in the turmoil of those years, but this was the generation that had the first and fullest chance to think about the end of the extended family and arranged marriages, and explore romance (a concept originally translated phonetically as *luo-man-ti-ke*) and, more daringly, ideas of more anarchic 'free love'. It was not for nothing that the Nationalists, when they turned to cultural conservatism, attacked the Communists with the slogan 'property in common, wives in common'. (The Chinese term for 'Communist', *gongchan*, literally translates as 'common property'.) The association of spouse-swapping with Marxist dialectics and land redistribution, while not entirely fair, is a good indication of the daring nature of the ideas which the era had thrown up.

As with many other cultural understandings of the period, the idea of 'romance' and 'love' in the westernized 'Romantic' sense of being individualistic, passionate, and self-centred was created in large part in the Chinese mind through western templates which were then adapted.[16] Romantic solipsism was also the basis for one of the first pieces of modern fiction by a woman to achieve fame in China. 'Miss Sophie's Diary' [*Shafei nushi de riji*], by Ding Ling, was published in 1928. It was not Ding Ling's first published success, but it is in retrospect perhaps her best-remembered story. Even the name of the protagonist is symbolic. 'Sophie' (or 'Shafei' in the Chinese transliteration) is clearly a westernized name, and it furthermore brings to mind the Russian anarchist revolutionary Sofia Perovskaya, who had been an inspiration to many of the Chinese revolutionaries and anarchists of the late Qing. Yet the story's protagonist is not politically committed; rather the reverse. The narrative is fairly static, covering Sophie's diary entries from December to March. Sophie is suffering from tuberculosis (another western romantic theme), and lives alone in a small room. She is attended by various friends, including a would-be boyfriend named Wei, whom she simultaneously leads on and tortures mentally by refusing to respond to his gestures of affection. When he weeps, Sophie replies: ' "Save your tears," I said, "and don't think I'm weak like other women who can't resist a tear. If you want to cry, go back home to cry. Tears get me down." ' Yet the story also suggests that Sophie's capriciousness is a product of the difficulty of dealing with the concept of 'love' which faced all Chinese youth (urban, cosmopolitan youth, anyway) at that time:

These days young people like talking about 'love' whenever they're together. Even though I may know a little about it I can't really explain it when it comes down to it. I think I know perfectly well about those little movements that men and women make together. Perhaps it's just because I know about those movements that I'm so confused about 'love' ... that I'm suspicious of what the world calls 'love' and of the love I've received.[17]

The story also deals with sexual longing in a way that had not been publicly discussed before: 'I can't control the surges of wild emotion, and I lie on this bed of nails of passion, which drive themselves into me whichever way I turn. Then I seem to be in a cauldron of oil ... as my whole body is scalded.' Her fantasies also show the cosmopolitanism of the era. Speaking of the man whom she adores from afar, she says: 'I dreamt of a man with the manner of a mediaeval European knight. Anyone who's seen Ling Jishi will realize how appropriate the comparison is. He combines it with the special gentleness of the East.'

Sophie eventually decides, in a fit of self-loathing, to leave Beijing and go south 'to waste what's left of my life where nobody knows me'.[18] In later years, Ding Ling would join the Communist Party, and during the 'rectifications' of the 1940s, and in the crackdowns on 'bourgeois thought' of the early People's Republic, 'Miss Sophie' was one of the characters brought back to haunt her by angry commissars, who disapproved of what they saw as the character's individualism and self-obsession. Ding Ling was herself radicalized by the execution of her lover, Hu Yepin, by the Nationalist government in 1931. Ding Ling herself moved to writing more ideologically committed, though still in some ways ambivalent, fiction, and in later years seemed to have some doubts about the solipsistic way in which she had portrayed Sophie.[19] Yet she had created a character who summed up many of the complications of an era when individual desires came into conflict with a still-evolving cultural framework.

But Sophie was fictional. Were there real Sophies? How did women and men deal with the reality of the new freedoms that had emerged with the Republic?

Ask Taofen!

As with so many other questions, freedom was in large part a question of social class. If one were among the tiny elite who won entrance to the prestigious halls of Peking University, then, as the writer Zhu Haitao recalled, there were opportunities to carve out new and unsupervised ways to live:

If you wanted to live in college, you could (though you had to have a way to get a room). If you wanted to live in a house, you could. If you wanted to live with a lover in an apartment block, you could. If you wanted to eat rice, you could. If you just wanted to eat cold snacks, you could . . . And if you wanted to go to classes, you could. If you didn't want to go to classes, you didn't have to. If you wanted to go to classes you liked and not go to ones you didn't, then that was absolutely fine! In other words, everything was as you liked it [*suiyi*].[20]

But for the vast majority even of the increasingly literate lower middle class and working classes, even school-level education was still a privilege, particularly for women, and college-level education was rare indeed. The still-developing boundaries of the new environments for work and leisure which the emergence of capitalist, imperialist modernity had brought to China were not yet clear. However, the majority of city-dwellers in Beijing or Shanghai were less able to throw off all the weight of past conventions and customs, even if they had wanted to. One window we have into the way in which they tried to puzzle out the way that they should behave in the transition between the old and new worlds is the lively 'Readers' Mailbox' [*Duzhe xinxiang*] section of *Life* magazine, where editor-publisher Zou Taofen took on the role of advice columnist to puzzled young women and men who wrote to ask him about the new mores.[21]

The letters cover a wide range of topics, but a recurring theme for readers of both sexes was that they found it hard to know the new boundaries, particularly when the worlds of work and love overlapped. Take a letter from 1931. You Mei, a 19-year-old, had joined an office the previous year. 'This was the first time I had worked somewhere else, especially together with men, and I couldn't help but feel timid and shy.' But with an elderly mother at home to support, she had no choice. At first, things went fine, and You Mei's colleagues were helpful and made her feel comfortable. But then one senior colleague started to become rather too helpful. He asked her out, and started sending her ardent letters. As You Mei was already betrothed to somebody, she tried to discourage him discreetly, not wanting to cause either one of them embarrassment in the workplace. 'I'm in a situation where I don't know what to do,' she wrote, 'I don't even want to look at him – I can only deal with it by faking illness or stupidity.' Yet he continued to come over and chat to her at closing time, arranged work details so that the two of them were working together, or used his influence to release You Mei from less desirable tasks. 'How I wish I could escape this pit of torment! But I can't find a good position – that is, in a different place, it would [still] be difficult to avoid this sort of problem, and who will support my old mother and our household expenses?' She concluded: 'Sir! If I can maintain my current attitude and [show] not the tiniest bit of feeling toward him, will there be any problem for my reputation or status? I don't have much experience, so can I ask you . . . to find a good way to deal with this situation?'[22]

A letter on a similar issue, but this time from a man, was published in the same year. Cai Zhiji wrote in on behalf of a colleague of his who was an English teacher at a college. The English teacher had written a note (in English) to Miss Wang, a student in his class, suggesting that they should have a liaison. Miss Wang promptly took the note to the principal. If she wasn't interested, asked the writer, couldn't Miss Wang have just ignored the letter? Wasn't it rude and rash of her to have done what she did? A follow-up letter came in the next edition, from a fellow female student of Miss Wang's, Zhu Min, who disagreed strongly with the previous writer. Using the type of scientific metaphor which flavoured the period, she declared:

If you want to know whether seeking love is a serious matter or not, then you definitely can't skimp on attempts, and should look upon it as doing an experiment, turning the other party into your experimental sample. Success in the experiment would be unexpected happiness; failure would be unhappiness, but not unexpected.[23]

The rosy-eyed view of scientific experiment, teamed in the May Fourth mindset with 'democracy' as a panacea for China's crisis, was a common one at the time, encouraged by Chen Duxiu's widely circulated call for 'Mr Science and Mr Democracy' to save China. Yet even in this scientific spirit, it was important to stick to proper morality (*daode*). The school, Zhu Min explained, was coeducational, but in fact there was little mixing between girls and boys, and even less between staff and pupils of the opposite sex. Now,

Mr Zhang was a newly-arrived English teacher this term ... During that time, aside from [Miss Wang] nodding her head in the English class when her name [was called], and him seeing her face, there was no contact or conversation between them, and naturally no way for him to know anything about any aspect of her. They had no deep acquaintance, no mutual contact, but because he saw Miss Wang play the leading role in the play during the twentieth anniversary celebrations of the school, which won much applause from the audience, ... Mr Zhang wrote a love-seeking letter to Miss Wang. Now, may I ask, is this a reasonable and appropriate way of seeking love?[24]

No, Zhu Min concluded, it was not. Miss Wang was quite right to let the principal know about this.

The point of the 'Readers' Mailbox' was not just for readers to air their problems, but to let Zou Taofen give them the benefit of his advice. His answers were generally liberal-minded, but they were tinged by a realistic pessimism. To You Mei, he pointed out first of all,

A girl who's betrothed should not have to avoid friends of the opposite sex. The important thing is to be careful as to whether the friend you are making is a righteous person, whether or not he is a person of upright character ... Getting close to male colleagues is not in itself a bad thing, if it is done with cooperation and respect. But if they do not know how to behave with dignity, then this is a very dangerous place to be, and for the sake of your whole life's happiness, it's best that you make definite plans to leave.

It may be, Zou went on, that You Mei's suitor did not realize that she was betrothed, and had only honourable, if unprofessional, intentions towards her. But 'perhaps he already has a wife, and sees you as a toy'.

At any rate, 'you should honestly let him know [about your betrothal], explaining that being friends is fine, but you don't want to go outside the zone of friendship'. If he still refused to hear the message, though, Miss You would seriously have to think about leaving. 'I can't hide,' said Zou gloomily, 'that you've got something of a crisis, in that you've settled a marriage, and if your bridegroom-to-be hears about this, perhaps this could raise further complications and cause a lot of vexation for you.'[25]

It was not that Zou approved of the patriarchy, although he still reflected many of its assumptions. Rather, he felt he should tell his readers that they could not yet escape its effects, regardless of the kind of new-style lives they were living. It was unfair that You Mei, and not her harasser, would have to move; but it would be a greater economic disaster to lose her 'reputation' and her fiancé along with it. Zou acknowledged that some people would attack him for claiming that much of the talk of more open relations between men and women was in fact a 'false mask' for predatory men: 'perhaps you will curse my thought as being behind the times'. Yet,

on the men's side, they can take advantage of the opportunity of open social relations between men and women so as to advance their selfish desires, and the happiness through her whole life of the woman who is sacrificed does not come into the consideration of this sort of selfish man out for his own advantage.

In short, 'I positively advocate men and women interacting socially,' but 'if we want men and women openly to relate socially, then men must seriously respect these two conditions toward women; first, they must pay attention to the happiness that she expects for her whole life; second, they must respect her free will.'[26] The historian Wen-hsin Yeh has pointed out that Zou's attitude towards love was clear: 'Do not seek happiness at the expense of others. Do not send false signals during courtship. Always take full responsibility for what you have done.'[27]

One reader's letter from 1930 shows the limitations which Zou felt, in practice, still applied to women in this new world:

The evening of the day before yesterday, my sister and I, along with a couple of fellow-suffering girlfriends, who had recently graduated, went for a walk together in the park along the Bund. Because all our feet were exhausted, we found a bit of grass (because all the deckchairs were already taken). We sat down and talked about our happy life at school, and how sad it was to have graduated, but we hadn't been there more than twenty minutes when we wanted to get up and go. But there wasn't the tiniest path to let us go; we had been surrounded on all four sides by nasty men. Ah! Ya! Young and scared as I was, I couldn't help crying out. My two girlfriends comforted me, saying: 'Don't be afraid, see how it goes, let's just sit here a while.' As we didn't want to go yet, we kept sitting there, but soon, we could hear them, one saying, 'What a lovely scent!' . . . (In fact, we weren't wearing any scents or powders, it was just their fabrication.) When we'd heard a lot of inappropriate banter, and couldn't bear any more, we replied to them in a warning tone: 'It's not too late to keep your dignity!' 'If any foreigners see you, won't you look like fools to them? Won't you be causing bad luck to the country?' 'Ah! This really makes me sigh!'[28]

Finally, the exasperated and slightly scared young women burst through the cordon of young men and went to sit somewhere quieter. But within ten minutes, their persecutors had returned to haunt them. 'What's more, this time, we couldn't understand their conversation, as these were boys somewhat older than us who were able to speak English.' The ladies finally made a run for it, only to find that they were being chased, and were saved only by meeting a group of friends, after which they were able to get safely home.

'Wise sir,' Miss Zhu quizzed Taofen,

I am a young and ignorant girl . . . Were these men's brains really filled with any [sense]? . . . Our admonitions spurred them on, and everything [we said] just stimulated them more. In discussing their education, it was as if they wanted to raise themselves above our level, and they could even speak English! Surely their families, their schools, all had taught them that one's behaviour should not be unreasonable? Or was it their intention to make friends with us? (Because people have been saying that men and women are now equal, what does it *mean* to make friends?)[29]

Sexual harassment, to use an anachronistic phrase, was not invented in China during the May Fourth era. Crowds thronging public places (not generally parks, which did not exist as public

9. The Bund, Shanghai, around 1930.
Until 1941, this waterfront street stood in the middle of the British-dominated International Settlement. The city's foreign concessions had an ambivalent role, simultaneously rubbing in the imperialist domination of China's greatest seaport, but also providing a picture of technological modernity seductive to many Chinese.

spaces until the nineteenth century) are recorded throughout Chinese history. But this account is very much part of the New Culture experience. For a start, before the advent of mass literacy and modern periodical publishing, a concept such as the 'Readers' Mailbox' would not have been practical. But Miss Zhu's attempt to get to grips with what had happened in the park was suffused with the misunderstandings that the new culture had brought in its wake. First, there was the mantra that 'men and women are now equal'. Yet it was not clear what form that this equality was supposed to take. Would the young men harassing Miss Zhu and her friends have said that 'free love' meant that they now had the right to woo as they wished, without constraints? It is Miss Zhu herself, after all, who puts forward this explanation for their boorish behaviour. Perhaps she thought that they had been reading too much about Miss Sophie's unrequited longings and hoped to save other young women from her fate. Also, progressive bandwagons in modern China, as elsewhere, have always had various fellow-travellers who take on the label without sharing the agenda. For many young men, no doubt the idea of 'new women' who could be treated like men (rather a different thing from equality, of course) was a powerful piece of fantasy. A rather gentler, but indicative example of this was a story by Ding Ling's lover, Hu Yepin, entitled 'Living Together', in which a peasant woman living in the CCP-controlled Jiangxi base area leaves her husband of several years, and starts living with another man instead; the husband acquiesces without any fuss.[30] Hu's story was a fiction taken to an extreme, of course: but in general, cultural norms and boundaries of understanding about what post-Confucian relations between urban men and women should be like were in flux during this period.

The other cultural change that emerges from this letter is the importance of the foreign. First, the park itself is significant: the park along the Bund in Shanghai was the Shanghai Municipal Gardens, located in the International Settlement, which was run by a colonial Municipal Council, mainly British. Until 1928, the park had not admitted Chinese, so it was a new and sweet experience for Miss Zhu and her friends actually to go there, as well as a small victory over imperialism and racism. It also explains why they thought that it might be effective to admonish the young men by asking them to consider what foreigners would think if they could see them. The idea that such behaviour would give strength to European scorn for the Chinese was clearly powerful. The reverse side of this is the detail that on their second attempt to 'make friends', the men tried to show that they were a cut above the girls by speaking English. The supposed dash of sophistication that came from this not particularly casual dropping of their linguistic ability backfired here, of course: Miss Zhu sensibly thought that such well-educated boys should know how to behave better. Students at any time in Chinese history, after all, might well be patriotic, politically engaged, and with their minds on higher things. However, in the 1920s as in the 1980s, they were also capable of being boorish and foolish.

Zou Taofen's reply reflects the limited options which he felt were available. 'This situation,' he fumed, 'is nothing but hooligan behaviour, and if some of them had the appearance of students, their behaviour still runs along the same path as hooligans.' He observed that this kind of behaviour does not just take place in parks, or just in China, though in other countries, 'society and the police' would stop it.

But in China, this group of shameless types . . . dares to call themselves by the name of 'new people,' as with what Miss Zhu has cited as this brazen [justification that] 'Men and women are equal,' and so on, which is an example of this . . . To take oppressive behaviour towards women and call it equality, where is the 'fairness' in this?[31]

He then told Miss Zhu not to give these layabouts the benefit of the doubt just because of their education. However, his solution was hardly a very feminist one, although perhaps a practical one in the circumstances: he proposed that women should make sure they had a male escort (the word 'escort' appears in English type in the Chinese text) in all unsafe places.

It is clear that the pious declarations of 'female liberation' which reformers of the era put forward led to real difficulties in practice. Without citing it, Zou's replies continually echoed the argument of one of Lu Xun's most famous essays, inspired by a reading of Ibsen's *A Doll's House*. In the play, the protagonist, Nora, ends up leaving her husband and family after realizing that she will never have any status in her own right until she does. Lu Xun's essay, however, asked: 'What happens after Nora leaves home?', and it was clear that the answer was bleak, at least when applied to China as it was in the early twentieth century. Without major change in the patriarchal structures of Chinese society, Lu Xun argued, it was not nearly enough for an individual woman to declare herself 'free'. Reality would deny her that freedom. Zou also declared that one aspect of that freedom, women's education, was becoming more widespread, with more opportunities for women to find jobs and to mix with men in open society. This was all most welcome. But during this time of transition, he went on, 'the defeat of the old views is not sufficient [in] people's minds, and a new morality has not yet been nurtured'. There would inevitably be people sacrificed along the way, he warned, and the most important thing was to make sure that those sacrifices were as minimal as possible. His advice both to You Mei and to Cai Zhiji was similar: men should respect women's free will, and women should be aware that the devastating pace of change on the surface of Chinese society did not mean that the underlying structures had yet shifted all that much. Sometimes this led Zou into moral relativism. The new relaxation on 'making friends' between the sexes did not mean that men should use this to pressure women into 'what ordinary people would call "keeping a mistress," for a forced mistress is much more blameworthy than having a mistress by mutual consent'.[32]

The phenomenon was hardly restricted to China, of course. The 'free love' of American youth culture in the mid-1960s gave way by the end of the decade to a women's liberation movement that wondered whether giving young men the freedom to sleep with a plethora of women was necessarily an advance from the stultification and hypocrisy of the 1950s. As we will see, the experience of the young women in the May Fourth era was echoed in the 1980s. In the former case, people were groping to find a 'new morality' after escaping the confines of the Confucian social norms. In the 1980s, it was the equally sexually prurient and hierarchical Cultural Revolution that people sought to overcome. But in both cases, the transition period was as difficult as Zou had warned.

The tone of the letters from these correspondents are typical of the May Fourth era in one respect: they are full of anxiety. But in another sense, the anxiety of the *producers* of the New Culture was not the same as the anxiety of its *consumers*. The New Culture radicals were worried about China being held back from entering the modern world, and resented old customs and ways of thinking that prevented China's progression. Young men and women reading *Life* were also concerned about finding ways to take up new opportunities in work and love: yet it was not *just* the burden of old customs holding China back that was the major problem for them. Rather, their anxiety was tied to their struggle in trying to deal with a changing and unpredictable new world. For them, the neon lights, the new sexual mores and gender relations, the urge to save China, were all worrying, and not necessarily inspirational. The extent of this anxiety is suggested by the kind of writing that sold best during this period. It was not in fact what would become the 'classic' texts of the May Fourth era: Lu Xun, Ding Ling, Mao Dun. Instead, the best-selling literature of the time was an escapist fiction known as 'Mandarin Duck and Butterfly' writing, named after traditional Chinese symbols of eternal love. The topics of these novels were usually stories of star-crossed lovers, hair-raising escapades, or comic vignettes. They were intended to entertain rather than to stretch the reader.

Much of this writing has not lasted, partly because it has been shut out of the approved canon of 'great books' created by the influence of May Fourth, and partly because much of it is repetitive and unengaging. Yet there are some works that stand out, and one of those is Zhang Henshui's *Fate in Tears and Laughter* [*Tixiao yinyuan*]. The novel has a long and picaresque plot.[33] One of its notable features, however, is the two women who are rivals for the affections of the hero, Fan Jiashu. One of them, Shen Fengxi, is a traditional Chinese street-entertainer. The other, Helena Ho (He Lina), is the westernized daughter of a bureaucrat, who insists that Fan call her 'Miss Ho' in English. Helena is something of a figure of fun in the novel, and it is clear that Zhang Henshui was creating a sort of sly complicity with his readership, who were intended to laugh at this humorous portrayal of a Chinese girl who took on not just western manners, but even a western name. 'Miss Sophie' was intended as a figure of romantic tragedy; 'Miss Helena' was the butt of a joke. Miss Helena, of course, was also created by a man, Miss Sophie by a woman, but the romantic comedy of *Fate in Tears* was aimed at women as well as men.

The social background of these readers is important to understand the appeal of writings such as *Fate in Tears* or the 'Readers' Mailbox'. These readers were the 'petty urbanites', the urban lower middle class, scrabbling for respectability. They were often internal migrants from China's smaller inland towns who had come to Shanghai, and now had a precarious respectability as small merchants, clerks, or teachers. In a country with no government support network, and where they might be separated from traditional family networks located back in the provinces, they dreaded any sudden changes that might lead to them losing their jobs and falling into the awful commonality of 'the masses'. For them, literature mocking the more obvious aspects of modernity and modern living was a source of comfort. Rather than feeling like bumpkins or fools for not embracing the more frightening aspects of modernity, this fiction told them, it was permissible to laugh at the excesses of foolish behaviour that modern living caused in its most ardent advocates. The political activist Du Zhongyuan, writing in the mid-1930s for this same audience, once sought a shorthand way to sum up the silliness of young radicals he had met in his own youth. He did it by describing them as sporting an exotic, laughable style of dress, wearing 'swallowtail beards and foreign leather shoes'.[34] Du's readers, people such as Miss Zhu, the young woman who was harassed in the park, were aware of the new possibilities open to them; but in those opportunities there was also the scent of danger.

The May Fourth Entrepreneur

The May Fourth era was about being radical, but that radicalism could take many forms. One of the most potentially powerful new role models was the idea of the entrepreneur, who used learning from abroad to make a fortune. Lu Xun had written of how his mother had wept when she heard he wanted to go to Japan and study medicine: 'That she cried was only natural, for at that time the proper thing was to study the classics and take the official examinations. Anyone who studied "foreign subjects" was a social outcast...'[35] Lu Xun, of course, abandoned his scientific training to write fiction after his epiphany in Japan. But similar sentiments were expressed by two other writers, Du Zhongyuan and Zou Taofen, both of whom engaged with entrepreneurialism, but in rather different ways.

The 1920s saw Zou Taofen become one of the first media moguls in modern China as editor and publisher of *Life*. Zou was very much a figure of the May Fourth era, just 26 years old at the time of the 1919 student demonstrations in Beijing. However, it was in Shanghai that he was to make his name. Rather than the agonized introspection of the literary and philosophical circles centred on Peking University, Zou and his associates breathed the commercial air of Shanghai and made a rather different sort of May Fourth for themselves. Zou's cosmopolitanism cannot be doubted, but even though this insatiably curious young man had such a wide variety of role models to offer his readers, it was the business geniuses who seemed to have won his heart. As with other aspects of the New Culture, the idea of patriotic entrepreneurs was not new in the 1920s. Zhang Jian of Nantong, near Shanghai, was just one of the late Qing businessmen who combined the new industrial culture with a social and political agenda, becoming one of the largest cotton mill owners as well as a prominent figure in public life in the late nineteenth century.[36] During that era, there was a lively debate about the extent to which China needed to industrialize and encourage the growth of capitalism, and this discussion became more widespread in the twentieth century. Yet there was still something of a cultural prejudice against this particular path to modernity in the May Fourth era. Therefore, Zou took the opportunity to proselytize for entrepreneurship, and to give publicity to the foreign mentors who he felt could show the way forward for China.

In June 1926, Zou wrote a three-part feature on the life and achievements of the American inventor Thomas A. Edison, who had just turned 80. The morals drawn from his life were designed to encourage readers to be inspired to hard work and entrepreneurship. 'There were many occasions,' noted Zou of Edison, 'that he did eighteen hours' work a day over seven days': many ordinary people, he went on, would have had to live over a hundred years or more to match his energy. 'So how is Edison doing now? Does he want to stop work and relax? No! No! He still has a lot of things he wants to invent to benefit the world . . . This man really deserves the title, "The most useful old man in the world".'[37] Edison's life story is related for the edification of readers: this was a poor young man who spent his last dollar on a ticket from Boston to New York, and who worked his way up from the bottom. When asked if he would change anything in his life, he replied: 'I wouldn't want to change my life of struggle', for without struggling, there would have been less chance of his ultimate success.

This was a man whose image fitted the philosophical currents shaping China's New Culture. This last idea of 'struggle' has overtones of the Social Darwinism which had become so prevalent in the preceding decades in China. Other May Fourth themes emerge in these writings. Zou notes that journalists found it hard to get Edison to tell his life story, 'because his whole spirit is focused on "now," and he simply hasn't time to spend efforts on the past'. Edison was cast as a true hero of the New Culture, which gave little reverence to history.

The altruistic elements of the New Culture are also here, reflected in the reporting of Edison's observation that 'money was not the primary goal of carrying out an enterprise'. In fact, this was not such a 'new' element, since it reflected in part the morality derived from Confucian embarrassment about profit as an end in itself. Merchants and commercial culture had generally not received much official praise or support in the past centuries, with a few exceptions such as the Yuan dynasty (1179–1268) which was established by Mongols rather than ethnic Chinese. Indeed, the philosophy of Mencius, one of the most influential of the early Confucians, starts with a king asking Mencius, 'How can your advice profit my kingdom?' to which the philosopher replies: 'Why must your majesty speak of profit?' This remained, and has remained, one of the greatest problems of congruence between western modernity and Confucianism in its premodern form. The industrialized, capitalist growth that underpins the modern idea of the progressive society is dependent on economic expansion and therefore profit, even if it does not always praise it explicitly. It has therefore been a continuing challenge to find a way to adapt the Confucian world-view, which starts by condemning profit as small-minded, egotistical, and petty, and making it explicitly compatible with the reality of a globalized world that is underpinned by capitalism. (The 'Asian values' debates of the 1990s, when Chinese and other Asian leaders attempted to define their own economic growth as somehow being a Confucian enterprise, were ingenious, if contorted attempts to square this circle.) In the 1920s, the solution for the most radical May Fourth thinkers was to declare that Confucian thought was outmoded anyway and that westernized modernity was therefore the only way forward for China. But for Zou Taofen, who wanted to preserve aspects of Confucianism while embracing the more tempting aspects of modernity, other, more thoughtful solutions had to be found. And in this case, Thomas Edison's personal wealth gained through his inventions was downplayed in favour of his argument that an invention's value to humankind was the true indicator of its worth.

If the tales Zou told bear a striking resemblance to late Victorian self-help stories, or the archetypal Horatio Alger stories of young men making good, then that is no accident. Self-help tales owed a considerable debt to the Japanese 'reform fiction' of the late nineteenth century. In the rush for westernization and modernization after 1868, the Victorian work ethic, expressed through writers such as Samuel Smiles, with their advocacy of self-help, by which deserving young men could pull themselves up by their bootstraps, became extremely popular.[38] These books were then widely translated and introduced into China. As in Japan, though, part of the reason for promoting this sort of story was the perceived need to overcome the Confucian scorn toward the merchant classes. While China had had a commercial revolution as early as the Song dynasty (960–1276), the reaction of Lu Xun's mother to his decision not to follow the path of traditional official life shows that attachment to the old ideas of what was a respectable profession still held strong.

Saving the Nation, Making a Profit

Zou was a successful entrepreneur in his chosen field of publishing. For the most part, though, he did not portray himself as a role model for others. One of his friends and star columnists did, however. During the May Fourth era, Du Zhongyuan turned his nationalistic instincts toward setting up his own business as a means of 'saving the nation'. The story of one man was used to show how one small enterprise, in this case a porcelain factory in the remote region of Manchuria, could be used as a symbol to millions of readers of what the New Culture could achieve for the nation as a whole. In doing so, it aimed to suggest that there was no necessary conflict between making private profit and contributing to a collective goal of saving the country from the dangers that menaced it.

In a set of articles in *Life*, Du Zhongyuan used his own life story as an example, telling the readers how he had come to enter the porcelain business. It was an Edison-like tale of struggle against the odds, and of the challenge, as well as the burden, of imperialism. In 1915, Du remembered, there had been mass boycotts of Japanese goods because of the Twenty-One Demands (a set of notoriously harsh diplomatic and trade demands on China by the Japanese government), yet the anti-Japanese anger had dissipated because, in Du's opinion, his 'Chinese compatriots [were] like a tray of scattered sand, unable to keep up more than a five-minute enthusiasm'.

There was a linked commercial reason. Du's arguments were part of a wider phenomenon, the National Products Movement, which encouraged consumers to buy Chinese goods over foreign ones. However, the unstated reality was that most Chinese bought imported goods, rather than those made in China, when they were given a choice: imported goods were generally cheaper and better-made, often because dumping had destroyed the indigenous Chinese market. The appeal to buy national goods was powerful at times of heightened popular feeling, as at the time of the Twenty-One Demands or the May Fourth demonstrations, but at other times, other more basic economic considerations controlled buyers' impulses, and they tended to purchase cheaper foreign-made goods.[39]

So Du set his mind to producing goods that would both be popular and help to restore China's status: 'I clung to the hope of promoting business enterprises so that I could save China.' However, 'any one individual can only make his own contribution to his utmost ability, so when wishing to use enterprise to save the country . . . I wanted to choose a business that would be what China needed, but would also exercise me to the utmost.'[40]

It was in Japan, that menacing yet tempting source of Asian modernity, that his inspiration lay. Du had always had a fascination with porcelain. This product had become known in the west as 'china', so associated with its country of origin was it, but by the early twentieth century, control of the industry, at least in Manchuria, had slipped largely out of Chinese hands. 'Porcelain was invented in China,' said Du,

and in Tang and Song dynasty times, the Japanese repeatedly sent people to China to study it . . . but in the last hundred years, all sorts of countries have used the fierce advance of technology to discover all sorts of technological manufactures . . . Therefore, these Chinese national products . . . suffered a steep fall in the tables recording numbers sold, to the point where this country's market was filled with foreign goods.[41]

How should he respond? Du recalled:

By chance one day I read in a porcelain industry journal an article about the Dahua porcelain company which the Japanese were building at Dalian, and I was very excited. The gist of this article was that the Dalian Mantetsu company had set up a central experimentation office and each year spent a tremendous sum of money to . . . invite specialized talents from all over [Japan] to research and do trials on all sorts of agricultural, mining, forestry, husbandry and fishery matters in Mongolia and Manchuria . . . If the specialized research had any results, then they would put together capital and set up a factory for manufacture.[42]

This venture capitalism had certainly paid off in the porcelain business, Du reflected. The Japanese had investigated which sticky clay soils were best for raw materials, which of the places where the soil was abundant were well-linked to transport facilities, and how the factory and kilns would be set up. 'Finally, they put together the capital to put the whole plan into practice, step by step.'

'When I read this essay,' Du continued, 'I thought that this company . . . with its encouragement and coaching of all sorts of enterprises, was the opposite of China's sloppy and confused way of letting the days pass, letting our precious resources be utterly plundered. This made me sigh very deeply.'[43] Japanese porcelain, he went on, had achieved a reputation as 'cheap but high quality'. How could China compete? Once again, it was Japan that gave Du the chance to move ahead. He was one of the students chosen by the Fengtian provincial government in 1916 to study technology in Japan:

When we got to Japan, the thing I noticed most was that it was impossible to find in their country a single piece of unused waste land, or a bit of unnavigable waterway, or an uneducated or unskilled person, and everywhere, I noticed the level of development of industry and commerce. I considered that we should certainly feel hatred for the Japanese invasion of China, but we should absolutely take their creative and hardworking spirit as a model.[44]

The next few years saw Du immersed in study in the ceramic technology department of the Tokyo Industrial College. In 1923, he came home, and immediately had to start looking for capital to help him set up his dream of a porcelain factory. Yet his aspirations did not please everyone he met:

The feeling in the past in China was that if a foreign student came home from abroad, no matter what he'd studied, his many relatives and friends always hoped that he'd become an official! At the very least, they'd hope you'd become head of some agency, and when I returned home at that time, there were people hoping this of me, constantly asking straight out, quite rudely. I had made up my mind, and just smiled at them. But I definitely had difficulties.[45]

Lu Xun, of course, had had his mother in tears when he abandoned the path to officialdom in favour of western studies in the late Qing; even by the early Republic, that mentality had not been fully transformed. Du found that his quest for venture capital was frustrating, with few people willing to back his idea. Nor, he pointed out, did the provincial government do much to follow up on the skills that they had paid for their scholarship students to learn in Japan. At the time, the Northeast was run by Zhang Zuolin, a militarist leader known for his enthusiasm for unending wars of conquest and lack of interest in infrastructural development, so perhaps it is unsurprising that Du found little official backing for his ideas.[46] So Du decided that rather than leaping straight to manufacturing porcelain, which would involve an investment of millions of yuan, he would start with a brickworks, which would need just several tens of thousands and which would produce items that could easily be sold. There was another reason for starting with bricks:

Ordinary people often believe that students [i.e. people who have been to modern colleges] only live the good life and never do any real graft. A brick business would be seen by people with ordinary levels of knowledge as a humbling and difficult thing to do. I wanted to prove that we students could also bear difficulties, and were willing to do a difficult business which ordinary people scorned.

The attitudes of May Fourth youth, in their contradictions, shine out in this statement. On the one hand, Du was eager to prove that the agenda of 'national salvation' was for real, and that like Edison and the other great inventors who studded *Life*'s pages, he was not only willing to work hard, but to do so for reasons which were for the greater glory of the nation or humankind, not merely for grubby profit. On the other, the openly stated distinction between 'ordinary people' with 'ordinary levels of knowledge', as opposed to the educated students, was a blatant statement of the division which education, even though it was now modern rather than classical, seemed to create even among Chinese who wanted to unite the nation. (It was this continued attitude of *de haut en bas* that angered Mao Zedong so much, leading him to demand a literature much more oriented towards the masses in his 1942 'Talks on Art and Literature', and, towards the end of his life, stimulated his enthusiasm for the supposedly anti-hierarchical Cultural Revolution.) In the later 1930s, when he became a much better-known journalist and a more committed leftist, Du specialized in writing in a way that blurred, rather than emphasized, the difference between himself and the 'ordinary people'.[47]

Eventually, thanks to a loan from a friend who had been a fellow-student in Japan, Du was able to set up his first brickworks in the north part of Shenyang. His relatives and friends continued to bemoan his choice of career, and even the 'ordinary people' whom he wanted to impress did not seem so much admiring as contemptuous of this educated fellow who was now messing around with dirt and clay. 'I had never really dreamed of this when I was a student', Du admitted. But he always stuck to the maxim, 'If I don't go down into hell, who else is going to go down into hell?' The business slowly built up, however, and in turn attracted more and more funds, meaning that they could upgrade to high-quality German Hoffmann kilns. Eventually, 'The Japanese couldn't monopolize the new-style bricks and tiles which were needed for buildings all over Liaoning province and thus we snatched over 200,000 yuan from the hands of the Japanese.'

Yet the brickworks was not what Du had dreamed of. 'The goal I had imagined,' he reminded the reader, 'was porcelain.' But this was a more demanding task than making bricks and tiles: it needed more capital, more specialized materials such as clays, and also much more highly trained workers. To find his staff, Du ultimately had to poach workers who had been trained by the Japanese and were now employed in their factory at Dalian. The initial products of Du's porcelain factory, he admitted, were not much good, but they improved rapidly, and by 1929, they produced over 3 million items, rising to 10 million by 1931, making a profit of over a million yuan.

Following the style of his editor, Zou Taofen, Du ended his account with a moral, a very Confucian conclusion to his tale and one that prevented it from looking like mere self-aggrandizement:

Although I've struggled for eight years, and am still engaged in the struggle, any success I have had, however small, has been the result of praise from society and help from all quarters . . . This is an extremely good opportunity to develop National Products, and I am willing to work with like-minded people to improve China's porcelain industry, to struggle strongly in competition with foreigners, and to lessen the strength of foreigners in the porcelain industry in China.[48]

Du's tale, like those Zou put forward weekly in *Life*, was a thoughtful alternative to what often appeared a self-indulgent May Fourth mentality which concentrated only on the self. But it is important to note its limitations as well. Du's nationalistic tone was undoubtedly sincere, but he did not offer clear, wide-ranging solutions to how businesses of the type he described might cope with the much wider issues that China faced at the time, including widespread rural poverty and seemingly endless civil conflict. In addition, the vision of entrepreneurship that Du put forward is implicitly a male one, with no suggestion that the economic energies of the 'new woman' might also be harnessed for the nation. In contrast, this was not an omission that would plague his successors in the 1980s.

End of an Era?

When did the May Fourth era, the world of possibility opened up by the New Culture, end? There is a good case for various end-points: for instance, the May Thirtieth anti-imperialist uprisings of 1925, because these marked the rise of the Nationalists and the Communists in their united front; or else the establishment of the Nationalist government under Chiang Kaishek at Nanjing in 1928. A useful way to think about it, however, is not in terms of a specific date, but of a time when the atmosphere changed significantly. As the 1920s moved into the 1930s, the values and lifestyles of experimentation, internationalism, and reassessment of the past, infused by an atmosphere and language of possibility and progress, slowly faded.

Why did the change come, and how would it have been noticed? The May Fourth era cannot be conveniently divided in the way that a parallel era such as the Weimar Republic in Germany can: the German empire ended sharply, if not neatly, in 1919, and the Nazi era which began in 1933 marked an equally obvious break with the Weimar past. A better comparison here is the western experience of 'the Sixties', which does not refer to the period 1960–9, but rather to a time and place not easily captured by precise dates. Even at the end of the 'long Sixties', when the oil shock of 1973 put paid to the prosperity which had fuelled economic development since World War II, values and everyday experience did not change overnight in western society.

For the May Fourth generation in China, two major changes come to mind. First, in the 1910s and 1920s, the ever-present threat of foreign imperialism had been tempered, however grudgingly, by the internationalist spirit of the times, marked by Woodrow Wilson's idealism and the establishment of the League of Nations. In the 1930s, this changed: the threat of invasion from Japan became a constant, repeated theme for Zou Taofen, Du Zhongyuan, and writers such as Lao She and even the populist Zhang Henshui. Then, the Chinese economy, which had been showing reasonable signs of growth up to the early 1930s, became subject to the great world depression, and China was struck by mass urban unemployment and rural agricultural crisis.[49]

In retrospect, the year in which the change occurred may well have been 1931. The most notorious incident in that year was the occupation of Manchuria, the northeastern provinces of China, by the Japanese Kwantung Army, which had had a semi-colonial presence there since 1905. Worried by the growing tide of Chinese nationalism, and with Japanese politics sliding away from democracy and crushed by the economic depression, the Japanese stepped up military adventurism in China. The year also saw turmoil within Chiang Kaishek's Nationalist Party, leading to his temporary resignation (he returned to power in early 1932). Meanwhile, the Yangtze River flooded, drowning millions and destroying harvests.

Yet none of these events changed China overnight. Peking University carried on educating students. Shanghai's lower middle class went on reading Zou Taofen and Du Zhongyuan's publications, although the two authors became increasingly vulnerable to Chiang Kaishek's censors. Women continued to find independent work, and entrepreneurs continued to build up businesses. The invasion of Manchuria was, at least for a while, considered a great blow to the national honour, and demonstrations filled the streets about it; but in the end, for people living in Shanghai and even in Beijing, Manchuria was a very long way off, and there were more immediate problems nearer home to deal with.[50] A much more obvious change would come in 1937, with the outbreak of full-scale war with Japan. Both Beijing and Shanghai would be occupied within months, leading to a mass exodus by the May Fourth generation to exile in the remote inland cities of Chongqing, Kunming, or Yan'an.

The people who lived through this era saw China in a period of change, yet there were many directions in which that change could have led. Du Zhongyuan's story is a May Fourth one just as much as Lu Xun's. A faith in science and technology, linked with ideas of national salvation and reform, seemed to many to provide a way forward out of China's crisis. The era was also obsessed with the purifying qualities of difficulty and struggle. The retrospective glow which the CCP has cast on collective values simultaneously down-graded the experiences of entrepreneurs and capitalists in general as exploitative and in league with the imperialist powers, until the 1980s, when they were praised once again during Deng Xiaoping's economic reforms. Yet the CCP's criticisms of alternative paths to their own were surely unfair: the option exemplified by Du in the 1920s was not sufficient to answer all the vast problems in China, yet that did not make it valueless either. The young woman who wrote to Zou Taofen to chide the lascivious teacher mentioned that the search for love should be treated as an 'experiment'. The nature of the era's cultural change was that it carried out different 'experiments in happiness', not just in personal relationships but in all aspects of life, while the opportunity was there to do so. As politics changed in the 1930s, and the door that had brought the outside world to China began to close, so the opportunities to experiment became fewer and fewer.

4

GOODBYE CONFUCIUS

New Culture, New Politics

Although the May Fourth Movement broke out in May 1919, its original causes emerged before May Fourth itself, as a result of China's social situation and the First World War . . . In June 1916, [president of the Republic] Yuan Shikai, who had spent 83 days as [self-declared] emperor, died. After Yuan died, all sorts of people who had fled the country because they opposed Yuan returned home, and the worlds of Chinese politics, thought and education, which had been moribund, livened up from then on.[1]

Xu Deheng's retrospective musing on the origins of May Fourth and the New Culture Movement was not quite accurate in detail: several important events in its development, including the foundation of *New Youth*, the journal edited by Chen Duxiu, had happened before Yuan Shikai's death. But on the big picture, he was quite correct. May Fourth, as an era, was not just about 4 May 1919, and politics and thought certainly 'livened up' during it. The questions people asked were about politics in the widest sense. 'China's social situation' included poverty, famine, and internal warfare. The legacy of 'the First World War' included the question of how China would deal with imperialism, and reflected the reality that China could not shut itself off from the rest of the world. Xu had been one of the original participants in the May Fourth demonstrations, and had been arrested and held for a few days after the arson attack on minister Cao Rulin's house. His summary of the causes of that day's events reflects these new realities, which were understood by large numbers of Chinese. The students who had demonstrated were among the most prominent of those who shared this realization, but lower middle-class shopkeepers who lived in cities full of advertisements for the fruits of international capitalism (American movies, Swedish matches) and ordinary labourers who had been sent to the Western Front in France, or who had relatives who had been and returned, also started to think of themselves as part of a global society, and their understanding of politics changed accordingly. This chapter looks at the new ways in which thinkers analysed and presented the new political realities. It is a story that is sometimes complex, but that complexity reflects the rich and exciting range of possibilities that were, paradoxically, nurtured by the very instability of China's government at the time. Among the questions that arose were: How far can the old Confucian norms be abandoned or adapted? What can we take from western political thought, and what should we oppose? Are the experiences of other non-western societies relevant for us? And for some, though not all: Are Marxism and the Soviet Union useful examples for China to follow?

For a long time, the story of Chinese politics in the twentieth century has generally been regarded as equivalent to the story of the rise of the Communist Party to power. Yet it is important to remember that the Communist story is remarkable partly because its beginnings in the 1910s and 1920s were so unpromising, and because it won out against what was, for a time at least, a wide range of political options. The May Fourth Movement has become a touchstone for the Chinese Communist Party. The New Culture era was the birthplace of Chinese nationalism and communism, and in the Party's view, its logical result was the communist revolution, a quarter of a century later. The need to secure official memory of May Fourth meant that subversive, alternative interpretations (such as the 1989 Tian'anmen demonstrations) were particularly worrying to the Party. Even those who are not necessarily sympathetic to the CCP sometimes assume that there was some sort of inevitability about the political path that China took between 1911 and 1949, with the Republican period as an anomalous period of darkness ended by 'liberation', a phrase still commonly used to refer to the Communist revolution of 1949.

This is a pity, for several reasons. The first reason is that this interpretation suggests a seemingly logical conclusion to China's twentieth-century history, whereas the disillusionment in present-day China with much of Mao's record suggests that the Chinese experience from 1949 to 1976 was a detour in China's historical path: an epoch-making detour, but a detour nonetheless. The second reason is that the communist-dominated version of Chinese history obscures the rich variety of political alternatives which the May Fourth era brought forward. There were many different ideas put forward to 'save the nation'. Communism was the thread of thought which would ultimately win out, but in the early twentieth century, there were Chinese interested in anarchism, guild socialism (a bottom-up form of socialism that argued, unlike Marxism, that class struggle was unnecessary), feminism, fascism, and liberalism, to name but a few.[2]

The period is also important because it forced an argument about how China should deal with its Confucian past. Again, the retrospective version of the story is that the May Fourth period 'enlightened' the Chinese people into rejecting the oppressive, patriarchal web of Confucian culture wholesale, freeing them to embrace western political thought and the CCP in particular. Yet it is clear only the most radical of the May Fourth generation advocated complete and utter rejection of Confucianism, and that for many others, it was important to salvage or adapt China's past while coping with the new reality of the present.

Another great theme of modern Chinese history, the rise of nationalism, has sometimes been obscured under the dominant Communist narrative. Often, the rise of Communism and nationalist ideas fuelled by anti-imperialism in general and the coming war against Japan from the 1930s have been treated as aspects of the same phenomenon. Yet it is misleading and unfair to characterize nationalism as simply a second fiddle to the all-important rise of Communism. In particular, the Nationalist (Kuomintang) government of Chiang Kaishek (1929–49) gets short shrift in histories that take the rise of Communism as the most important story of mid-twentieth-century China. The Nationalists have been dismissed as corrupt, brutal, and incompetent. All these epithets were true, in many instances. However, the Nationalists were also a genuinely ideological party with a patriotic agenda, and Chiang Kaishek was throughout his life every bit as strong an anti-imperialist as Mao Zedong. Most of the intellectual assumptions of the May Fourth generation were shared by Communists, Nationalists, and those of other or no party affiliation: these included patriotism, Social Darwinism, and a fixation on 'modernizing' China, however that term was defined. On the issue of class divisions and class warfare, of course, the CCP had their own distinctive position, but this was not, at the time, as all-encompassing a difference as it later became. And in the early years of the fledgling CCP, 1923–7, the two parties were locked in a united front that meant it was sometimes hard to distinguish between their policies.

The party to 'win' in the initial aftermath of May Fourth was not the Communist Party, but that of the Nationalists, who set up their government in Nanjing in 1928. Just as 1960s America was the period of Nixon's victory and the Goldwater boom as much as it was the time of hippies and anti-Vietnam demonstrations, so May Fourth cannot simply be interpreted as a time when 'progressive' forces won out over 'conservatives', in the arena of thought, let alone governance.[3]

In addition, the attention usually given to the two big political parties of the era, the Nationalists and the Communists, can be misleading when we consider the way in which politics became popularized during this period. Ordinary Chinese did not, for the most part, identify with political parties in the way that mass populations did in the west over the decades of the late nineteenth and early twentieth centuries. In the US, Andrew Jackson's presidency had popularized politics in the mid-nineteenth century; in Britain, the Conservative Party under Disraeli had used the Primrose League to increase participation in the Victorian era as the franchise expanded; and in Germany in the same era, the new Social Democratic Party had brought political participation to the working classes. This type of mass identification with parties was far less evident in China. Even though parliaments and assemblies existed in China during the Republic, they rarely expressed popular will directed through political parties, as did happen to a significant degree in Japan, or even India after Gandhi promoted the idea of a mass-membership Congress Party.[4] Yet this was also a period when a large proportion of the population did become politically aware. Some aspects of that awareness were in fact directed through party political structures. Notably, industrial labour movements in Shanghai and Guangzhou in the 1920s came under significant Communist influence. Nonetheless, for most of the 1920s, the changing governments in Beijing had little to do with the political aspirations or ideologies of either the parties or the wider population, and even when Chiang Kaishek established his National government at Nanjing in 1928, having first purged his former Communist allies, his regime realized that their victory had been primarily military, and that they would have to inculcate their political agenda from the top down, rather than relying on a non-existent swell of popular support.

But if most people did not identify with *party* politics, how can one say that a significant proportion of the population became politically informed? In the cities, the press, that great engine of the New Culture in all its forms, was a powerful source of political information. For instance, as noted in Chapter 2, Zou Taofen's *Life* magazine took off from small beginnings in 1925 to become the best-selling journal in China, with perhaps 1.5 million readers by the 1930s. Zou himself started off as a liberal influenced by the ideas of the American philosopher John Dewey, although he would later become a Marxist.[5] His political agenda can easily be discerned from looking at the type of articles he published in *Life*. The inspirational articles about personal entrepreneurialism mentioned above reflect the liberal individualism which inspired him, and which had been influenced by the self-improvement craze of late nineteenth-century Japan. Zou's entrepreneurialism, like that of his friend Du Zhongyuan, was expressed in terms of the values of May Fourth: science, modernization, and nationalism.

To many Chinese, their country, which just a few decades before had been one of the world's great land empires, now seemed to have split into fragments, ruled by avaricious militarists and under attack from foreign invaders. Yet from this seeming chaos would come the

10. **George Bernard Shaw with Chinese students, 1933.**
During the May Fourth era, Chinese thinkers were enormously enthusiastic about intellectual influences from the outside world. Foreign writers such as Shaw, the British philosopher Bertrand Russell, and the Indian poet Rabindranath Tagore gave lectures to large audiences.

most important threads of cultural and political thinking which would still be shaping China nearly a century later. Chaos produced disorder and disillusionment, but it also opened up new ways of thinking and a profoundly different understanding of what it meant to be Chinese. This chapter looks at the various ways in which the thinkers of the May Fourth era tried to get to grips with China's crisis and the ever-present legacy of its Confucian past.

Iconoclasm

The single adjective most associated with the May Fourth Movement is 'iconoclastic'. The writing and actions of the time are marked by an unwillingness to accept the norms and assumptions of the Confucian culture, which was deemed to have failed China. One such norm was the traditional veneration of old age and wisdom in Chinese culture, which was of course challenged by the very title of the journal that Chen Duxiu founded in 1915, *New Youth*. In one of the first articles he published in it, 'Call to Youth', Chen declared: 'The function of youth in society is the same as that of a fresh and vital cell in a human body.'[6] Linked to this new enthusiasm for youth was the idea of 'newness'. Since the late Qing, the word 'new' (*xin*) had been used to describe the 'new life', 'new citizen', and 'new civilization' that a modern China was to produce. The western consciousness of a linear flow of time had also begun to make a significant impact on Chinese society. This encouraged many thinkers, including Chen Duxiu, to propose that China had entered a 'new epoch', a very different and profound time which ought to be perceived as significantly different from the 'old' society.[7]

The stress on youth was linked with a new interest in a modern projection of the self, which took pride in individual and autonomous identity. It is notable that many of the writings, both fiction and fact, that appear in this book are first-person accounts of experiences and feelings. To produce this sort of account, putting the individual self firmly in the foreground, rather than modestly claiming anonymity or a reluctance to put oneself forward, was also a significant cultural change, and out of keeping with the Confucian norms of how one should talk about oneself in a public forum.[8]

The iconoclastic urge was also notable in the May Fourth generation's rejection of the patriarchal treatment of Chinese women. In 1918, Lu Xun published an essay in *New Youth* entitled 'My Views on Chastity', which condemned the traditional insistence that women remain chaste, whereas men were not required to be so: 'These women are to be pitied. Trapped for no good reason by tradition and numbers, they are sacrificed to no good purpose . . . We must do away with all the stupidity and tyranny that create and relish the sufferings of others.'[9] 'Moderation' was another Confucian virtue which the May Fourth radicals rejected. Too often, Lu Xun argued, 'moderation' was merely a codeword for tolerance of abuse and turning a blind eye to corruption. Mao Zedong wrote an essay in 1917 which also took issue with the Confucian ideal of sage, calm, and moderate action, and instead demanded that the Chinese people learn 'to charge on horseback amid the clash of arms and to be ever victorious; to shake the mountains by one's cries'.[10] One can see Mao's enthusiasm for revolution in his earliest utterances.

The most famous example of the May Fourth radicals' desire to root out all aspects of China's Confucian culture is Lu Xun's short story 'Diary of a Madman' (1918), which is included in his collection *Call to Arms [Nahan]*. It is largely on these stories that his reputation as China's finest modern fiction writer rests, and there is no doubt about their literary quality. However, this story's power derives from its uncompromising anger with Confucianism. The unnamed narrator of the story slips into madness, and as he does so, becomes convinced that his fellow-Chinese are all cannibals. 'It has only just dawned on me,' he declares, 'that all these years I have been living in a place where for four thousand years human flesh has been eaten.' 'They eat human beings,' he worries, 'so they may eat me.' He tries to look up the history of cannibalism in a book of Chinese history, but all he finds in the book are the two phrases 'Confucian virtue and morality' and 'eat people'. Finally convinced that 'I may have eaten several pieces of my sister's flesh unwittingly', he begs in the last lines of the story: 'Perhaps there are still children who haven't eaten men?

Save the children ...'[11] In Chinese history, cannibalism has been one of the most powerful images of a society whose values have lost all morality, and for Lu Xun to assault the entire basis of Chinese governance and society using this metaphor was a powerful indictment indeed.

The uncompromising nature of Lu Xun's abhorrence of the past, along with that of figures such as Chen Duxiu and Mao Zedong, stemmed from their own experience of the crisis which China faced in the early twentieth century. Yet there is a disturbingly extreme tone to their writings as well. The message not to tolerate 'moderation' could be seen as a warning against compromise with evil, but could also encourage a single-minded reluctance to grant tolerance to alternative views. The shrill denunciations of Confucian culture may have been partly fuelled by the real sense of self-doubt and, at times, self-loathing that marked the May Fourth generation. One of the most famous short story collections of the era is Yu Dafu's 'Sinking', whose title refers to a psychological feeling of uncertainty, 'the clash between soul and flesh'.[12] Or there was Sophie, the antiheroine of Ding Ling's short story: 'I pray[ed] that other women wouldn't be like me ... falling into a vast misery from which I'll never be able to extricate myself.'[13] This ungroundedness seemed to infect the whole May Fourth generation. It seems that those who shouted loudest were perhaps those most unsure of where they stood.

Goodbye Confucius?

Yet there were other ways to deal with the feeling of having lost one's bearings. There was a great deal of thinking not just about culture from abroad, but also about China's own political and philosophical traditions. Zou Taofen, for instance, came to startlingly different conclusions from Lu Xun, arguing that Confucianism could be adapted and changed to fit the requirements of the modern world.

One of the victories, retrospectively, of the most radical part of the May Fourth Movement, the iconoclastic anti-Confucians, was that they managed to portray China after 1915 as a place where most sensible people quickly saw the light of the New Culture and threw off the shackles of the old thinking. And it is genuinely remarkable how quickly a world-view that had shaped not only the huge Chinese empire but much of the surrounding region for more than two millennia withered so swiftly under the impact of modernity. Modernity was a powerful influence in China, of course, but so it was also in India, the Middle East, Japan, Korea, and Southeast Asia. These societies all produced indigenous, hybrid interpretations of what 'modernity' meant that pushed aside artificial distinctions between what was 'traditional' and 'modern'. Gandhi's thought or the development of politicized Islamism showed ways in which modern nationalist ideologies could incorporate world-views not derived from western thought. Japan and Korea incorporated Buddhism, Shinto, and also Confucianism into a modernized ideology which contributed to those states' development of nationalism. Chinese politics did not do so, not because it was impossible to find a modernized Confucianism, but because the two political parties who would go on to fight for control of China's destiny in the century, although bitterly divided, shared one crucial characteristic: both the Nationalists and the Communists were secular and drew on western political models in their intellectual derivations and assumptions (even though the Nationalists later made attempts, such as the New Life Movement of the 1930s, to start recycling Confucian language). Secularism did not necessarily mean being anti-religious – although the Communists were hostile to religion *per se*, the New Life Movement did approve of and authorize recognized religions within China, differentiating them from cults and superstition – but it did make a point of separating the spiritual world from the material and political sphere.

So Confucianism undoubtedly came under assault and buckled under the impact of modernity in China. But the extent of its demise, as well as the speed with which that demise happened, has been exaggerated. In the form in which it existed before the great crises of the nineteenth century, the broad tenets of the Confucian world-view were fundamentally challenged by foreign invasion. These tenets include a belief in spiritual and cosmic harmony, in which the Chinese Emperor played a pivotal role. The Confucian world-view believed in stability as an absolute overriding good for the state, to be maintained through *li*, the intricate and complex system of ritual behaviour which defined what it was to be human. The word 'ritual' is itself an unsatisfactory way to translate what was a far more all-encompassing system of understanding of both hierarchy and mutual obligation. China was assaulted in the nineteenth century by two thought-systems from the west which undermined these assumptions. Modernity, in its many incarnations (Social Darwinism, liberalism, imperialism, capitalism, socialism), made assumptions that were clearly at odds with Confucianism. The modern mindset was concerned with dynamic growth rather than orderly stasis. It made assumptions that were less hierarchical than those of Confucianism, but also lessened social obligations from one group or individual towards another. The other thought-system was Christianity, whose influence, particularly as filtered through the radicalism of the Taiping movement, should not be underestimated. It was not just a religion, but also a dynamic, and non-hierarchical alternative to the Confucian world-view, though this time with a very strong ethic of mutual obligation, as well as a spiritual dimension.[14] Like modernity, this put it in powerful tension with Confucianism. It is no surprise that many of the social reformers and revolutionaries of the early twentieth century, such as Sun Yatsen and the agricultural reformer James Yen, were either Christians or at least given a missionary education.

Anti-Confucianism was, in the twentieth century, really about the need to break down the complex network of social relations that was encompassed in the concept of *li*. This was what made the most radical language of the New Culture seem so exhilarating to many, and echoes of this desire to break down *li* can be seen as late as the Cultural Revolution of the 1960s. Anti-Confucians such as Lu Xun, Mao Zedong, or Hu Shi argued that Confucianism was a prison which forced hierarchies on the vulnerable, such as women and the poor. Yet to argue this, they resorted in part to caricature. Confucian thought-systems were shared by politicians and courtiers in power in the late nineteenth century who seemed unable to lift China out of its crisis. But immediate social and political problems in the Qing court were to blame for the most pressing causes of social breakdown. Furthermore, there were Confucian ways to reform, such as the moral revival and encouragement of technology that the late Qing reformer Zeng Guofan offered. Hierarchical oppression without acknowledging any social obligations, which was what anti-Confucians accused the dominant system of practising, was not supposed to be the driving force of Confucianism, even if it seemed to be the practice of the Qing government at that particular historical moment.

But although the radical anti-Confucians, and particularly the CCP, became the dominant voices in the story of China's twentieth century as it was later interpreted, their position was strongly contested at the time. The legacy and world-view of two millennia, although they were challenged, were far too long-standing simply to disappear overnight, however much Lu Xun or Chen Duxiu might want them to do so.

For Zou Taofen too, as we will see, Confucianism was a source of political thought to be adapted, not abandoned. There is a space to be found between the radical May Fourth argument that the twentieth century saw the death of Confucianism, which was finally found to be past its sell-by date, and the argument, still sometimes heard today, that China has remained a Confucian state and culture, that Chiang Kaishek and Mao were simply returning to the Dragon Throne, and that the hierarchies of premodern China are preserved largely intact. For Confucianism did not stay the same in the twentieth century, any more than something called 'Christianity' was the same system of beliefs and world-views in 1700 or 2000 that it was in 1100 or 500. The spiritual element of Confucianism, in terms of the balance between heaven and earth, has been a far less major element in its twentieth-century incarnation everywhere, including in Japan, Taiwan, Korea, and other societies where it has not been formally persecuted; and it was always a spiritually somewhat pragmatic system anyway, with Buddhism, Daoism, and folk religion often fulfilling needs for more mystical and irrational elements in society.

However, the framework of mutual obligation, ethical behaviour, ritual, stability as a good in its own right, and disdain for commerce and profit remains important in a belief-system that contrasts with the underlying assumptions of modernity. It was much of this structure that the early Communists chose to throw off; hence the exhilaration of one of the early Communists, Cai Hesen, when he discovered Leninism not just as a system of control but as a justification of the very un-Confucian idea that one can do evil to bring about a greater good.[15] This does not mean that one cannot find a way to justify, say, making a profit on sales in Confucian language, and Zou Taofen and Du Zhongyuan's writings effectively do just this, but it has always been clear that Confucian thought must justify profit as part of a wider social good. In the same way, Zou's admiration for Thomas Edison was expressed not in terms of his great personal fortune, but rather because he was 'the world's most useful old man'. This ethic is reflected in Zou Taofen's comment that Edison's first intention in developing movies was not to provide a frivolous leisure item, but instead something that could be used for educational purposes. This was a very Confucian justification, as was the background tale told of Edison bringing himself up from poverty through hard studying.[16]

However, it is not possible simply to separate out and isolate the constituent parts of a system of thought, like a chromatogram separating out the dyes in ink. Confucianism, like Islamism, has inevitably been shaped by global modernity, because the twentieth century, for all societies that were not wholly isolated, was an era when modernity had an impact on all significant political and cultural movements, even when those movements rejected it. Some aspects of the premodern Confucian world-view did not survive the mid-nineteenth century. How, after all, could the belief that the person of the emperor was the fulcrum of a spiritual harmony between heaven and earth survive in a China where there was no emperor? Yet assumptions which are clearly Confucian in their origins survived well into the New Culture Movement and beyond.

Some of the applications of Confucian thought in the 1920s and 1930s were inadvertent or perhaps slightly ironic. For instance, the senior CCP leader Liu Shaoqi made use of Confucian thought in his book *How to Be a Good Communist*. Furthermore, as we will see later, in the early 1930s, the Nationalist government of Chiang Kaishek started advocating a return to Confucian values, urging that the state rather than the emperor should be the object of loyalty. Chiang promoted the New Life Movement, initiated in 1934, which advocated a 'secular and rational Confucianism' which 'constituted a uniquely Chinese "spirit" compatible with modernity and shared by all Chinese'.[17] The movement was not ultimately successful in its attempts to mobilize China, as its formal prescriptions, including not spitting in the street and queuing up in an orderly fashion, came over as trivial in comparison with the much larger issues of national coherence which dogged twentieth-century China. But the idea behind it, that 'personal cultivation' (*xiushen*) by the individual would contribute to a healthy society and country owed a great deal to Confucian thinking, as well as being influenced by western ideas of Social Darwinism. Nor did the New Life Movement come out of thin air. Throughout the 1920s, various thinkers had argued that it was possible to provide an adaptation of Confucian values which would be compatible with a secular (but not anti-religious) Chinese modernity. In 1927, before Chiang Kaishek had even come to power, Zou Taofen had put forward an argument that Confucian values could be reinterpreted to give China prestige in the new internationalized world:

The most important part of China's innate morality is *zhongxiao, xinyi, ren'ai* and *heping* [loyalty and filiality, trust and righteousness, benevolent love, peace and stability]. Some people have misunderstood, and considered that whereas in the monarchical era, there was loyalty, now in the republican era there is no loyalty. But why isn't loyalty to the country [*guo*] counted as loyalty? In fact, with regard to these several good moralities, we should not only preserve them, but also develop and expand them, and solidify our national base. Aside from our innate morality, there is also our innate wisdom [*zhishi*]. We ought to recover this, and honestly and sincerely cultivate [*xiushen*] principles of ordering the family and regulating the country. This is the most precious item of the innate wisdom of China . . . If foreigners see that China cannot govern the country, then they will come and exercise joint control over it [*gongguan*].[18]

In part, Zou went on to argue, it was individual behaviour such as spitting on the ground and not cleaning one's teeth properly that created a moral deficit which prevented the country as a whole from taking its rightful place in international society. These connections

115

between the individual and the country at large would underpin the New Life Movement just a few years later, and would even make their way into the People's Republic (see Chapter 8).

This sort of attempt to popularize modernized Confucianism was attacked by some May Fourth thinkers, who claimed that Chiang Kaishek wanted to take China back to its oppressive, hierarchical past. Hu Shi, although he was never enticed by Marxism as his contemporaries Chen Duxiu and Li Dazhao were, nonetheless felt obliged to speak out in 1933 during a series of public lectures in the United States against Chiang's seeming return to Confucianism, and against those who advocated a return to 'traditional culture'. Hu declared that this was a 'most fashionable expression of a reactionary mood prevalent today'.[19] Yet the opponents of this revived Confucianism were to some extent creating a monster that did not exist. Even though he used Confucian language, Chiang's policy was still an essentially secular project based on an assumption that industrial modernization and nationalism were the bases for the development of China. Chiang had not turned himself into an emperor or god to be worshipped. The New Life Movement did not contain an integrated religious dimension, although it praised Taoism and Buddhism as aspects of China's ancient culture, and was tolerant of worship as long as it did not take extravagant or superstitious forms. The Movement and Chiang's regime could be justifiably attacked for being dictatorial and unimaginative in the face of China's political crisis. But it did not challenge the drive to secular modernity. It was, rather, an attempt to *create* it.

To see how far Chiang might have gone in creating a non-secular political system, one needed only to look at what was happening at the same time in Japan. In that country, the political usage of religious practice within a modern state showed how far Confucianism could have been pushed. The Kyoto School is probably the most famous group of political thinkers in early twentieth-century Japan. It became notorious for the role it had in justifying Japan's increasing militarization and aggression against its neighbours in the 1930s, as many of its thinkers provided a religious and philosophical justification for Japan's aggression in East Asia, casting it in terms of a sacred mission to liberate Japan and its neighbours from corrupting western influence. One of the most notable thinkers linked with the Kyoto School, the philosopher Nishida Kitarô, was heavily influenced by western thinkers such as Hegel, but was also strongly committed to Zen Buddhism, as well as the Confucian norms that had influenced premodern Japan after their introduction from China.[20] In Nishida, and in many other Japanese thinkers of this period, there was an active mystical and proudly irrational dimension which was far less evident in China. Chiang Kaishek was attacked by radical and progressive Chinese thinkers in the 1930s for trying to take China back to what they saw as the past. Ironically, Japanese politicians attacked him at the same time for being too similar in his secular nationalism to groups such as the Communists. In terms of Chiang's political grounding and the meaning he ascribed to Confucianism, the Japanese may have been more accurate in their accusations.

Confucianism, then, did not simply disappear, however much its iconoclastic opponents might have wished it to do so. Yet it is clear that terms such as 'nationalism', 'science', and 'democracy' became widespread in May Fourth China. Next, we must examine how and why they did so.

爱国主义　科学　民主主义

China's Road to Nationalism

The major strand of modern thought that took form in China in the late nineteenth and early twentieth centuries was nationalism. As the assumptions of modernity began to replace Confucian thinking about how the state should be organized, Chinese thinkers recognized that the 'nation' had been an important political concept in the west, and considered its possibilities carefully.

What was nationalism in China, and why did it take the form that it did? Nationalism in China was an ideological creation that emerged largely in reaction to the perceived inadequacies of a political identity that was based on Confucianism. As we have seen, not all Chinese thinkers believed that Confucianism needed to be wholly abandoned. But even its supporters saw that it would have to be adapted to take account of the modern world which had impacted on

China so violently. The assumptions of the Confucian world-view in the premodern era – stasis, the need for order, hierarchy, ritual, mutual obligation, the downplaying of the individual self – came into conflict with the assumptions of nationalism as developed in the west in the context of capitalist, imperialist modernity – ideas of progress, rationality, scientific categorization, hostility to hierarchy, and the downplaying of premodern ideas of mutual obligation in favour of individualism, which held that the modern self was a positive and productive idea. Yet, despite the alien nature of the concept, Chinese thinkers quickly saw that the nation-state had become the dominant political form in global politics, and that they would have to think through its implications for their own country. A 'nation', a political form based on the idea of equal citizenship, was a foreign concept, yet it quickly became clear that it was a powerful and potentially useful one. These thinkers also understood that nation-states were a product of western modernity, and that modernity had more than one form. Therefore, the further question emerged: not just how to make China modern, but what type of modern China should they aim for?

A wide variety of proposals for nation-building was put forward by thinkers of the late nineteenth and early twentieth centuries. They were a relatively small elite who had access to books and ideas from the west and Japan, yet they sought to create a model for the nation which would enable them to mobilize all of China's vast population. They differed widely in their proposals for how to do this. For some, influenced by Victorian pseudo-biology, a supposedly objective definition of the Chinese 'race' became an essential defining characteristic to decide who could be members of a Chinese nation. This type of racial nationalism became much sharper in the very late Qing when the main target of the revolutionaries was the ethnically separate Manchus who ruled the dynasty. For others, creating equal citizens, as opposed to subjects of the emperor, was the defining characteristic of a nation, and writers such as the late Qing polymath Liang Qichao developed and popularized ideas of the 'New Citizen', a Chinese who would be committed to this new way of thinking about being identified as Chinese.[21]

After the 1911 revolution, though, there was a change in emphasis. Anti-Manchu racial nationalism lost its potency after the Qing dynasty had ended, and internal conflict and imperialist attack from outside seemed to be more pressing concerns for the new state. Consequently, certain models of nationhood tended to dominate in the minds of most of the thinkers who became prominent during this period, which we now associate with the May Fourth Movement. For instance, nationalism of this era tends to share a centralized, as opposed to federal, vision of China, an understandable development at a time when it appeared that China might be carved up by the various great powers.[22] In addition, there is an overwhelming emphasis on mass political participation and scientific and technical rationality as ways to achieve 'national salvation' (jiuguo), that is, to unite China and make it strong and prosperous. These two concerns are summed up in Chen Duxiu's formulation that what China needed was 'Mr Science' and 'Mr Democracy'. 'Science and democracy' have been associated with the May Fourth period ever since, and are promoted today by many Chinese reformers who argue that they are still valid as a solution to the country's problems. These terms have become so natural in China that they are sometimes uttered without thought. However, their wide adoption in the May Fourth era suggests that reformers made an active choice to pursue a version of nationalism which was dominated by a vision of modernity primarily derived from Enlightenment assumptions about 'science'. This was something that, in contrast, their neighbours in Japan did not so unequivocally embrace. Why was this choice attractive to the May Fourth generation of Chinese?

To answer this, it is necessary to turn briefly to the source of rhetoric on 'science' as a panacea, the European Enlightenment. The Enlightenment, emerging in the seventeenth century and reaching its zenith in the eighteenth, 'led to the conviction that reason could uncover the rules that underlay the apparent chaos of both the human and the material world'.[23] Its advocates were seized with the conviction that 'rationality' and a scientific mindset were sufficient to unlock the ordering of the world and its societies, and this world-view had a profound effect on the rise of scientific modernity in western society. This idea of science as a sort of analytical searchlight was highly influential in shaping not only ideas about the natural world, but also the analysis of socially constructed ideas such nations, races, and classes. In Europe, the eighteenth and nineteenth centuries saw reactions against this sometimes uncritical confidence in scientific rationality. Romanticism, in particular, was a reaction to what its followers saw as the dry, passionless mastery of reason, and instead embraced passion, irrationality, the supernatural, and even ideas of madness and death.[24] Romantics praised the cult of the hero, an individual, often self-obsessed, who nonetheless achieves great things through the force of his own will.

The ideology of nationalism, like many other ideologies, was created in the west as part of the era of modernity.[25] When examining the history of China and Japan, one of the most important developments that has been analysed is the two countries' trajectory from 'tradition' to 'modernity', and the part that the development of nationalism played in that move: how did these two neighbours progress from the old world to the new, and why did Japan seem to have done so more successfully than China? This is still a valid question, even though the division between 'tradition' and 'modernity' has been questioned as it has become clear that aspects of the past remain embedded in the present, and the two concepts cannot be so easily separated. However, relatively little attention has been paid to the way in which China's and Japan's dominant political thinkers chose different types of modernity to cope with the world into which the western gunboats had thrust them. For in the May Fourth era, there was more than one version of modernity available in the global market of ideas.

First, the world contained two major types of 'Enlightenment modernity'. Liberal democracy and Communism both laid claim to ideas of secularism and rationality (Communism adopting an aggressively anti-religious stance). Both also advocated 'democracy', although their definitions of the term were very different indeed, and both approved of the scientific world-view (Communism in particular, as it derived its strength from the supposedly 'scientific' basis of Marxism). Then there was a third type of modernity, this time one

120

that claimed to reject Enlightenment assumptions but shared many of them in practice. Nazism and Italian fascism claimed to reject 'bourgeois' values such as democracy, capitalism, and ideas of secular, rational progress. Nonetheless, they can be meaningfully termed ideologies of modernity, because they so explicitly used Enlightenment modernity as a convenient foil against which to oppose themselves and employed the tools of modern state-building, such as creating political status based on mass citizenship (although this was denied to groups judged enemies of the 'nation'). Furthermore, states such as Nazi Germany whose rhetoric rejected industrial capitalism and claimed to yearn after an agrarian past when their countries were peopled by a pure-blooded racial stock, in fact took full advantage of the same techniques and industries as states whose rhetoric embraced the scientific world-view. The fascist and ultranationalist states, supposed enemies of modernity, nonetheless delighted in scientific and technological progress (such as *Autobahn* roads and *Messerschmitt* aircraft in Germany), as well as pseudo-scientific ideas of 'race'. This type of 'anti-modern modernity' needs to be distinguished from thought-systems such as pre-twentieth-century Confucianism. That type of Confucianism was not anti-modern, or a reaction against modernity. It was just non-modern: it was based on a completely different set of assumptions.

Chinese and Japanese thinkers used different ingredients from these various recipes for modernity. There were few Chinese fascists, for instance. They did exist, and in the 1930s Chiang Kaishek even explored some of the mobilization techniques of the European fascist states, whose ability to unite their nations he had admired.[26] But the mainstream rhetoric from most prominent Chinese nationalists was taken from Enlightenment modernity, and used the language of science, technological progress, and democratic politics. Mao Zedong and Chiang Kaishek had rather different ideas about what those concepts meant, so much so that they ended up at war with each other for two decades, but they started from the same premise that China needed to be 'modern'. In contrast, Japanese nationalism was always more mystical and romanticist, which led it in the more avowedly anti-western direction that it took in the 1930s. For many thinkers in

Japan, science and democracy might have been useful as tools of development, but they could be cast off if they did not serve some spiritual essence of what it meant to be 'Japanese'. The modern, individualized 'self' also came under attack in Japan, just as it did under the collective values of fascist Europe. As Japan became more obsessed with a spiritual mission to 'liberate' Asia (the practical effect of which was usually to invade and terrorize its neighbours), the Enlightenment model fell so far out of favour that one famous Japanese conference held during the war was entitled 'Overcoming modernity'. But no major Chinese leader ever rejected the idea that China should become 'modern', although there were deadly disputes about the path needed to get there. Romanticism was not absent from the Chinese nationalist project (Mao Zedong, for one, was highly shaped by it), but it tended to cloak itself more in seemingly rational ideas of progress. The dedication to an Enlightenment model also led many Chinese nationalist thinkers to make an unnecessary assumption that western thought was always universally valid.[27] In contrast, few Japanese thinkers or writers, even those who were glad to learn from the west, showed such ardent enthusiasm as the May Fourth radicals in China for rejecting their own past.

Why, though, was the Enlightenment language of 'science and democracy' so much more dominant in China than Japan at this time? No one reason can be found, but various factors may have played a role. First, in the late nineteenth century, Chinese intellectuals were more exposed to British, French, and American thought, all countries where Enlightenment values held strong. Japanese thinkers were exposed to all of these, but also had more contact with Germany and German romanticism in the same period. Then, China and Japan were in different global positions in the May Fourth era. Japan was now a significant power with an empire of its own, and was able to use those achievements as evidence to its own people of some indefinable but vital Japanese spirit of superiority. In the same period, China was still under pressure from imperialism and felt itself to be a victim. Therefore practical solutions that seemed to be promised by scientific progress and democratic reform may have seemed more suitable than mystical reflections on the primordial essence of Chineseness. Additionally, the intellectual traditions of both countries had differed. China had been a great bureaucratic empire for centuries, run on a system of examinations and assessments of merit for officials, and meticulous textual criticism (*kaozheng*) had been part of the classical training. The Confucian penchant for order had also infused the culture with a desire for careful arrangement and categorization. This may have made the critical and scientific Enlightenment mindset a less awkward fit than it might at first have seemed. Japan also had its own tradition of textual criticism and investigation, of course. But promotion in its political system had not depended on dedication to bureaucratic scholarship; military prowess or landed wealth had been more important. In addition, the influence of religious systems of thought such as Zen and Nichiren Buddhism had been much greater in Japan. These varieties of Buddhism delighted in paradox and the flouting of rationality as a means of gaining 'enlightenment' in the Buddhist sense (*satori*). True enlightenment also demanded not just the de-emphasis of the self, in good Confucian style, but its submission and ultimate destruction. These strands of thinking provided a grounding much more favourable to European concepts of irrationality when they arrived in East Asia in the late nineteenth century.

Nationalism, then, was one of the most prominent political products of China's encounter with modernity. In one form or another, the conception of nationhood and its attached ideology, nationalism, is at the centre of most of the politics of the May Fourth era. The approaches to nationalism differed from thinker to thinker, party to party, but the idea, developed from contact with western political thought, that a Chinese nation existed, and that it was in crisis, proved a constant theme for the May Fourth generation.

Internationalism, Cosmopolitanism, and Nationalism

Nationalism, however, was shaped in the May Fourth era by the outside world. For what, in retrospect, seems clear is that in the 1920s, China was still wide open to a universe of influence from the world outside. To understand the politics of Communism and nationalism, and the people involved, we need to know more about rather nebulous, but very important, political and cultural phenomena which also shaped the May Fourth generation: internationalism and cosmopolitanism.

'Nothing mattered more', says the historian William Kirby, referring to China's encounter with the world in the Republican era.[28] Every aspect of life, he suggests, was affected by the international climate. This was certainly true with respect to diplomatic and military policy, of course. But it was also true for Chinese society, culture, and thought, even in places many miles away from the nearest foreigner. To try to understand China in the May Fourth era without understanding it as part of an international culture removes a large part of what made it so distinctive.

For it is a mistake to think of China as a society simply buffeted by imperialist and capitalist forces from outside, which it was powerless to resist. China was not simply a country which passively encountered the forces of modernity. Instead, it made those forces its own, adapting them in creative and often surprising ways to suit its own unique circumstances.

For mainland China, the Republican period is generally considered to have lasted from 1912 to 1949. That period, though, also coincided with a particular era of global political change. Although that 'interwar' period is generally defined rather uncomfortably in terms of the two dreadful conflicts which sandwiched it, it can also usefully be seen as the short age of the League of Nations. The first decade or so was the age of the great international agreements, such as the Locarno and Washington Treaties, and a sunnier, more cooperative outlook in international society, fuelled by a willingness for the League to work as an alternative to the carnage of World War I. The 1930s, known to the Japanese as 'the valley of darkness' (*kurai tanima*) and called by W. H. Auden the 'low, dishonest decade', marked the League's failure, exacerbated by the world economic depression, with the rise of Hitler, Mussolini, and Japanese militarism. These generalizations also hide many complications, for the seeds of the second decade were planted in the first, but they also express wider realities about the global atmosphere which China had to deal with during its short and turbulent Republican era.

The League is generally associated with US President Woodrow Wilson, who saw it as a means of taming the warlike *Realpolitik* of the old European world. Wilson also disapproved of the large European empires, and his embracing of the 'self-determination of peoples' led to a wholesale reconstruction of much of central and eastern Europe as well as the Middle East, which had been under the German, Austro-Hungarian, and Ottoman empires. New nation-states such as Czechoslovakia, Yugoslavia, and Hungary appeared on the map. Also visible was a reconstituted Poland, last sighted before its partition in 1795 and now apparent once more, although in a rather different position, sitting where much of pre-war Germany had previously been. The Allied empires of Britain and France were not, of course, dismantled, but even now, they were put on notice. Neither country attempted to seize new colonies pure and simple. Instead, blown by the Wilsonian breeze, the former Ottoman colonies in the Middle East, such as Iraq and Syria, were re-cast as 'League Mandates', states in a condition of embryonic independence which were under the temporary protection of the imperial powers. (Iraq, in fact, was given independence in 1932, although it was the only League mandate to reach that stage.) Empire still continued as a global and seemingly slow-changing phenomenon, but it appeared to have stopped growing larger, at least as far as the European powers were concerned. The independent nation-state was now the standard model of what countries should become.

In this context, the Washington Treaties were crucial. A series of agreements signed between nine powers in 1921–2, they set the tone for much of the liberal atmosphere of international politics in the 1920s. The US, Britain, and Japan agreed to maintain navies at an agreed ratio of relative strength of 5:5:3. Among the most important declarations was that the powers should encourage China, still in a state of political flux, to strengthen itself. A crucial part of this strengthening was to restore the country's tariff autonomy, which had been removed in various treaties of the late nineteenth century under the Qing dynasty. Although a dispute with France meant that tariff autonomy was not fully restored, the overall intentions were to signal to China that it was being welcomed into international society. As a further gesture, the former German colonies in Shandong, which had been handed to Japan at the Paris Peace Conference, were now restored to China. And China, of course, became a member of the new League of Nations. Since colonies were not eligible to join, this made China one of the few non-European states allowed to do so.[29]

This rosy view of China's slow but steady absorption into the international community seemed plausible in Washington, London, and, to some extent, Tokyo. For patriotic Chinese themselves, though, the Washington measures seemed half-hearted and patronizing. Nonetheless, the Chinese governments of the 1920s, like the Nationalist government of Chiang Kaishek which would follow in 1928, were staffed by many sophisticated, often foreign-educated diplomats who knew that the world where the Chinese empire could unilaterally lay down its own prescriptions for dealing with the foreigners had died at the time of the Opium Wars some eight decades before. If the League of Nations and compromise with the imperial powers were necessary, then the Chinese would play that game to the best of their abilities. Participation, though, did not mean acquiescence.

A source of satisfaction for many Americans at the time was the extent to which Republican China seemed to be turning to the US as a model for progress. Certainly some Chinese authors wrote approvingly of role models such as George Washington and Abraham Lincoln, and reflections of a changing Chinese society were sent back to American readers through the pens of the writers of Henry Luce's *Time* magazine and novelists such as Pearl S. Buck. The US prided itself that, unlike the arrogant old imperial powers, it was seen as a force for freedom and liberation in China.[30]

This was not how things appeared to all Chinese. On the one hand, the sterling efforts of many American missionaries and educationalists were appreciated by many of the Chinese who had encountered them. On the other, the US blotted its record significantly by passing the Oriental Exclusion Acts in 1924, which stopped immigration from

East Asia in any significant numbers, and would continue to do so until the 1960s. In general, the belief of many Americans that what the Chinese really wanted and needed was for China to become more like America created misunderstandings that would lead, in part, to the tragic events of the Cold War. With their more overt resort to racism in the running of their Chinese empire (both territorial and economic), the British did not, for the most part, deceive themselves that the Chinese aspired to be like them and eventually came to understand, even if disapprovingly, the forces behind the rise of Chinese nationalism in the 1920s. For many Americans, this realization never came, and tokens of proof such as Chiang Kaishek's controversial conversion to Christianity helped to obscure the reality. Other countries, including those of western Europe, also provided cultural and political inspiration for many Chinese, and as will be seen, the emergence of the Soviet Union provided a new source of thought for more radical Chinese of the age.

Looking East in Europe

Many Chinese admired aspects of the west. But they did not, for the most part, aspire to *be* western, even at the height of May Fourth opposition to Chinese tradition. Even the term 'west' is misleading when assessing what it was that many Chinese admired about the European world. Most notably, when they turned to foreign examples, it was frequently not the powerful nations, the US, Britain, and France, that they cited. Instead, within Europe, it was often east, rather than west, where they looked. For many of the May Fourth generation, the newly freed nation-states that had emerged at Versailles were a far more relevant example for them than the great empires. First, these states had done what China sought to do. Oppressed by imperial powers, in their case the Austro-Hungarian or Ottoman rulers, they had created a sense of nationhood which was driven by will and determination. In 1931, the writer Cui Weizhou described the emergence of Czechoslovakia after World War I.

The Czech nation proposed revolution ... and everyone just laughed at their craziness, pitying their weakness and saying that they might sacrifice themselves but they would never be successful ... Their people struggled without concern for themselves and gave their strength to help them. Finally, after the Paris Conference of 1919, the Austro-Hungarian empire fell apart and they set up a state for the whole Czech people.[31]

Eastern Europe was also relevant to the Chinese because western Europeans had always considered the east of their own continent, like China, to be the 'Other', a dark, mysterious place not governed by the rules of reason. The 'Philosophic Geography' of the Enlightenment era defined eastern Europe as practically Asiatic, a place of irrationality and barbarism quite separate from the scientific and rational west. The British radical politician William Cobbett, speaking in 1801 on the subject of diplomacy with eastern Europe, made a specific comparison with China when arguing that one had to use go-betweens: 'What political relations can we have with countries situated between the Niemen and the Boristhenes [Dnieper]? We maintain communications with these countries by Riga, much in the same manner that we maintain a communication with China by Canton.'[32] Many of the western philosophers, including Voltaire and Rousseau, who wrote about eastern Europe had never actually visited the region. Nor, indeed, had many Chinese in the early twentieth century; but that did not stop the idea of this place looming large in their minds. Just as western Europe regarded eastern Europe and China alike as barbarous lands striving for modernity, so many thoughtful Chinese saw solidarity with the emerging European nations which were countering this image and seeking a strong role for themselves in the modern world.

Because few Chinese had visited the region, the Chinese view of eastern Europe was often one that bore little resemblance to reality. Poland had been dismembered and disappeared from the map of Europe in 1795, and this terrible fate gave it a mythical position in the minds of the late Qing Chinese: a new verb, 'to Poland', appeared in Chinese, meaning 'to be destroyed and vanish'. Yet this was just one of a plethora of references to the region.[33] The late Qing reformer Liang Qichao had also cited the Hungarian liberator Lajos Kossuth as an inspirational figure for the development of Chinese nationhood. The thinkers of the Qing, of course, were still having to deal with an eastern Europe whose national aspirations were embryonic. In the Republican period, in contrast, these same states now stood as a glorious example of what could be successfully achieved.

The fact that these Chinese writers were not drawing on direct experience of life in eastern Europe is indicative in its own right. Their willingness to learn from international examples and link their own lives and China's fate to currents that were seemingly far removed from their own concerns shows the cosmopolitan and eclectic way in which the May Fourth generation sought a new path for China. These people were not constrained by inward-looking or xenophobic ideas of what it meant to be Chinese. To create a strong, stable China, they would look anywhere, however unlikely-seeming, for inspiration.

Not Just West and East: Thinking Beyond Europe

Yet the European world, west and east, was not the limit of the May Fourth imagination. Zou Taofen, for instance, drew on a wide and refreshing range of influences to force himself and his readers to think about what China's crisis really meant. At that time, the number of non-European reformers who had modernized free states was limited, so perhaps it was inevitable that Zou Taofen used his platform at *Life* to explore the life of the most famous of them, although his subject would have balked at being described as non-European. That was one of the most prominent reformers of the era, Mustapha Kemal (known from 1934 as Atatürk), to whom Zou dedicated a three-part series in 1928, five years after the establishment of the Turkish Republic. 'Turkey in the Near East and China in the Far East have a lot of points in common', observed Zou. 'When we see how Turkey has pulled itself out of such a dangerous crisis, we must be even more sure to win out in China's future.'[34] In many ways, the Turkish experience was indeed most directly similar to what Chinese May Fourth nationalists wanted for China (and even the earlier 1908 Turkish revolution had been a source of interest to the late Qing nationalists).[35] Kemal had taken a decaying empire which had been defeated in war, overthrown it, and declared a political and cultural revolution from 1920 onwards. Zou explained the major reforms which had taken place in the new Turkish republic:

On 29 October 1923, the national assembly formally declared that Turkey had become a democratic republic [*minzhuguo*], and that Kemal was elected as the first president. From this moment, an extraordinary period [of revolution] came to an end, and a period of reconstruction began. On 21 April 1924, [Kemal] formally promulgated the Turkish constitution. In terms of reconstruction, he reformed national education, improved the law, encouraged agriculture, industry, and commerce, improved the position of women, and so forth. Everything was positively carried forward, and every day, it flourished more and more.[36]

This technocratic, progressive vision clearly appealed to Zou. In addition to the reforms he listed above, in Kemal's Turkey, the state was secularized, the script was reformed from Arabic to Roman letters, and Turkish nationalism was made a compulsory ideological element in all aspects of social and political life. This was different in many ways from the Meiji reforms in Japan, the other most obvious example of conversion from premodernity to modern nation-statehood in a short period: Japan had made religious ritual an integral part of its nationalism, women were not declared equal under the Meiji constitution (unlike Turkish women, who could vote and be elected in the 1930s, Japanese women had to wait until the American Occupation in 1945 to get the vote), and a remodelled version of the Japanese imperial past was embraced, not rejected, by the state. In other ways, too, the vision of Chinese nationalists such as Sun Yatsen was more like that of Kemal than Japan. In particular, Turkish 'democracy' meant a one-party state in practice; something, as we will see later, that Sun Yatsen believed was necessary as well. Japan, meanwhile, had developed multi-party democracy with wide male suffrage. Kemal, then, was an obvious choice for Zou to appeal to, as a successful secular, nationalist unifier of a nation-state.

Perhaps more surprising was another figure to whom Zou returned far more often than to Kemal: Gandhi. Gandhi was, of course, a powerful nationalist figure, although it was not clear at the time Zou wrote about him that he would in fact achieve his goals. Yet a great deal of what motivated him, in particular faith and spirituality, were very alien to the parts of the May Fourth Movement that rejected the past, or to the ideas of saving China through entrepreneurialism. Nonetheless, Gandhi got his own three-part series in 1929, celebrating his 60th birthday. 'India's caste system, religion and language are complex, this is famous around the world,' Zou wrote, 'but all are united in respect for Gandhi, and even his political enemies cannot help but be moved by his sacrificial spirit and character.' Although British military power was strong, 'in reality, the whole of India is controlled by this ordinary man with a weak body, short stature, and wearing torn clothes'.[37] In fact, Zou hardly touched on the religious nature of Gandhi's identity, and instead dwelled on the achievements which he felt would have most resonance for his readers. One of these was Gandhi's boycott of foreign textiles in favour of native homespun cloth, an agenda also encouraged by the National Products Movement.[38] However, Zou was hopeful in his summation of Gandhi's nationalist programme of non-violence and non-cooperation. 'This has a lot of value for consultation in China', he noted.[39]

In the end, Gandhian non-violence was a path not taken by Chinese political thinkers and actors in the twentieth century. The nature of the Chinese crisis turned it towards what the historian Hans van de Ven has termed 'cultures of violence', the result of attempts to mobilize a society which was highly internally divided, leading political actors to conclude that they had little choice but to use force to achieve their ends. Even though many of the May Fourth generation deplored this, they were forced to deal with violence or else be left behind by reality.[40] Nor was the May Fourth Movement itself free of taint in this regard. After all, the events of 4 May 1919, although they had started with dignified and peaceful protest, had ended up with a man left for dead covered with bruises 'that looked like fish-scales', and a house smashed and burned. The protestors who decried militarism were capable of mob action when it suited them. Significantly, the visit of Rabindranath Tagore, the Nobel

Prize-winning Indian poet, to China in 1924 met with scorn from the most radical of the May Fourth generation. Tagore gave lectures on the need for Asia to develop its spiritual and non-materialist qualities, only to be attacked by Chen Duxiu, by then the secretary-general of the CCP, and the novelist Mao Dun, who said that the best reply to imperialism and militarism was 'Reply to our enemies' machine guns with Chinese machine guns; answer their cannons with our cannons.'[41]

Organization was another reason why the Gandhian solution did not find much appeal in China. Among the reasons for Gandhi's success at home were his own great moral authority, but also crucial was the establishment of his political vehicle, the Congress Party, as the main exponent of non-sectarian Indian nationalism through a mass-membership party, united against one clear imperialist opponent. Although the Congress Party did not organize successfully across the whole of India, the party and leaders including Gandhi and Nehru had a geographical reach and political prestige that the Chinese political parties could not match in the 1920s. There was no Gandhi-like figure in China, nor did any of the parties, as we will see, achieve that kind of mass following, though they spoke often of trying to gain it. Marxism instead became the primary option for expressing political progressivism, and even Zou had turned to Marxism by 1930. Radical nationalism and Communism both also rejected significant parts of China's past, as expressed in folk religion, which they termed 'superstition'. Yet such religion was highly popular with the ordinary people; the experience of imperialism may have discredited China's past for some of the elites, but not for the population at large. Again, aggressive secularization could have perhaps worked to establish a nation-state if there had been an Atatürk-type figure with the control that he had had over the armed forces. As it was, there was not, much though Chiang Kaishek might have liked to fill a similar role.

Of course, Atatürk and Gandhi did not in the end provide political salvation for China. But it is worth remembering that Zou's essays, and their wide readership, offered a wide variety of political options to his readers. The decision that China's path might lie with the

Nationalist or Communist Party came quite late: in the 1920s, there was a ferment of options for people disillusioned by the tawdriness and hollowness of the political options available so early in the life of a Chinese Republic which had started, like Weimar Germany, with high hopes just a few years before.

Japan's Promise, Japan's Menace

The final non-European nation which influenced this generation, and the most controversial one, was Japan. Oppressor, imperialist, friend, mentor: Japan and the Japanese were all these and more during the May Fourth era. An old saying had it that the relationship between Japan and China was 'as close as that between lips and teeth', but that closeness was hardly a source of stability.

Japan and China had been in similar positions in the late nineteenth century. Both countries had been opened up at gunpoint by the western powers, primarily Britain for the Chinese and the US for the Japanese. Yet Japan had taken a radically different path from its larger neighbour. Where China had tried to limit the amount of impact that its clash with imperialism would have on the state, after a few years of attempted compromise, the centuries-old shogunate (regency) system which had closed Japan to the outside world was ended by a short civil war, and a new generation of oligarchs took over. The name they gave to their coup, the Meiji Restoration, became shorthand for the series of stunning political and social changes they made to Japan within a few decades. Learning from western techniques, the Meiji rulers decreed, was the only way to defeat them. Rather than take the ambivalent attitude towards reform of the Qing court, the Meiji rulers introduced constitutionalism, compulsory military service, and massive technological and industrial change. At the same time, they used a western political ideology, nationalism, to revise and revive premodern strands of Japanese thought, such as Shinto and Buddhism. There was rarely any question that the nature of Japanese reform had strong indigenous roots even while adhering to the demands of modernity.[42]

This synthesis did not happen in China. Over and over again, Qing authors lament the unwillingness of the Chinese court and wider society to learn from Japan.[43] Yet emulating Japan became more problematic as one particular aspect of their imitation of the west became more obvious: the drive for empire. To sit at the top table, the Japanese government decided, it must seek an empire in Asia, and with increased influence in Korea from the 1880s, it was clear that the formerly reclusive island state now intended to recast itself as a regional power. China, of course, had never been against empire in principle: in the eighteenth century, it had become one of the world's great land empires as it conquered much of central Asia. But this time, the victim was likely to be China itself. Struggles over influence in Korea led to the Sino-Japanese War of 1894–5, in which the Japanese victory forced the Chinese to cede the island of Taiwan. More humiliatingly, in 1904–5, two rival imperial powers, Japan and Russia, fought with each other for influence on Chinese territory in Manchuria, which the Qing could do nothing about; again, Japan won, leading to its foothold in southern Manchuria, which would eventually lead to the great crisis of 1931. Therefore, the real admiration that many Chinese had for Japan as an Asian power that had stood up to western imperialism was tempered heavily by the realization that Japan's own imperial ambitions were likely to target more and more of China, and that Japan often acted on Chinese territory every bit as arrogantly as western imperialists. Du Zhongyuan, in describing the path that had made him an entrepreneur, had said: 'I considered that we should certainly feel hatred for the Japanese invasion of China, but we should absolutely take their creative and hardworking spirit as a model.'[44] This ambivalence summed up the complex position that Japan held in the minds of the New Culture generation looking abroad for solutions to China's crisis.

Party Politics

We have taken quite a long time to get to the two groups most commonly associated with the politics of the Republican period: the Chinese Communist Party and the Nationalist Party. This has been deliberate. Elite party politics has so often been the most obvious, and most appropriate, framework in which to situate the narrative of modern China. Who could deny the importance of these two great parties who fought for power over a quarter of humanity? However, I have waited this long in large part to make clear the context of politics in China at this time. First, these two parties emerged from a welter of different possible paths that Chinese nationalism and modernity could have taken. As it turned out, China's two major political parties would both subscribe to a variety of secular Enlightenment modernity. Additionally, politics was not primarily a matter of party affiliation for most people, and political engagement for many, even in the May Fourth generation, was better achieved through committed journalism or literature. Certainly the party-based narrative that is appropriate to explain much about the US, Britain, France, or even Japan at this time fails to capture a great deal of what was important contemporaneously in China. The CCP would later claim that the May Fourth Movement's logical outcome was the foundation of the Party itself. Yet, as is clear, the movement was really a huge bundle of contradictory possibilities of which the Party's foundation was only one, and not even initially the most important.

Nonetheless, one cannot deal with the May Fourth era and ignore these immensely important bodies which emerged from the ensuing creative chaos and occupied most of the space that had been made available for free-thinking.

The Communists

The Chinese Communist Party did not start as a carefully disciplined organization, but changed drastically between 1921 and 1927.[45] At the start of that period, the future leaders of the party, such as Chen Duxiu, Cai Hesen, and of course Mao Zedong, were intellectuals and students associated with the heady atmosphere of possibility in China's cities, holding discussions in 'study societies' where exciting new ideas, often from the west, were analysed in an informal group of like-minded, politically engaged people. By the end of the decade, under the influence of the Soviet Comintern and after the bruising experience of war and strategy against the militarists who ruled

135

China, the party was a much more disciplined, ordered organization, with clear hierarchies and policies. How did the May Fourth period give birth to this machine which would eventually rule China?

To start with, the first writings that we have by the men (and they were practically all men) who founded the CCP were not about Communism at all, and in fact Marxism comes into their writings only late in the proceedings. Social Darwinism and the links between the body politic and the literal bodies of the Chinese population were much more on their minds, and many of the earliest writings of Mao are on the importance of physical exercise. Socialism, as opposed to Marxism, had been of great interest in China in the late Qing and early Republic. Anarchism in particular had inspired many, and Mao regarded the Russian anarchist Kropotkin as more of an influence on him than Marx in his early days.[46]

The 1917 Revolution in Russia changed views suddenly and radically. Marxism did not, as the Soviets later liked to imply, come fully formed into China after 1917, brought to innocent Chinese by wise Russian revolutionaries. The socialist background in China meant that by the time that the Bolsheviks took power in Russia, there was already a strong Chinese intellectual understanding of the different leftist positions. However, the Russian Revolution was crucial in letting at least some thinkers believe that Marxism, and Bolshevism in particular, might be a feasible way to bring about change in China.[47]

The close-knit intellectual atmosphere in Beijing made it a perfect spot for the big questions about Communism in China to be investigated. As it became clear that the change in government in Russia meant not just the fall of a regime, but a whole new system of government, interest grew. Here was another long-established empire which had collapsed; what lessons did its fall have for China? Li Dazhao, now the head librarian at Peking University, was the first to write extensively on the revolution. In 1918, he wrote a piece entitled 'The Victory of Bolshevism', published in *New Youth*. It was written in the aftermath of the Allied victory in Europe, but even before the Versailles Treaty which would trigger the 1919 May Fourth demonstrations, Li expressed doubts that the war's results would be good for China, and scorned his fellow-countrymen who believed that they

11. Mao Zedong, around 1935.
Mao Zedong was one of the founders of the Chinese Communist Party.
Outraged by the social injustice and desperate poverty he saw as a young man,
he came to the conclusion that only a radical political solution could save
China. In the mid-1930s, he began his rise to become the undisputed leader of
the Party.

would: 'politicians hold celebratory meetings, and generals who
never led a single soldier in the year or so that China participated in
the war, review parades of troops and are awe-inspiringly martial.'
Yet Li argues that it was in fact the victory of 'German socialism over
German militarism', not the Allies, which was the 'real cause for

victory', and that more widely, it was 'the victory of Bolshevism, the red flag, the working class of the world, and the victory of the new tide of the twentieth century'. The Bolsheviks, Li argued, aimed 'to break down the national boundaries which today are the obstacle blocking socialism,' and 'their war is class war ... Although the word Bolshevism was coined by Russians, its spirit is a spirit of enlightenment that every member of mankind can share'.[48]

A few months later, Li set up a discussion group, later more formally constituted as the 'Marxist Research Society', at his office in the university, where a few colleagues and students would discuss the implications of Marxist thought. Chen Duxiu, then dean of the university and editor of *New Youth*, decided to sponsor a special edition of the journal on the topic of Marxism. As the discussions on Marxism progressed over the next couple of years, the members of the group found themselves ready to commit to the formation of the first Chinese Communist Party, which held its first official Congress in Shanghai in 1921. Yet with just a few hundred members, it was a long way from any prospect of power.

The Nationalists

The Nationalists, or Kuomintang, have often been caricatured as the dark opposite to the Communists: tools of the imperialists, traitors to China, lackeys of a few privileged classes. Such a characterization does scant justice to a group who were very much part of the project of modernity which the May Fourth Movement embodied. Indeed, it was the similarity of the Nationalists to the Communists in so many areas that made their mutual hatred so much more intense.

For most of the period until the 1940s, the Nationalists, not the Communists, were the face of public party politics in China. Zhu Su'e recalled many years later that she had joined the Nationalists in college in 1928. This was the year after the event that would later be regarded as the great betrayal, the 1927 massacre of their former Communist allies in Shanghai. But that did not bother Zhu at the time: 'Guomindang [the Nationalist party] was led by Sun Zhongshan

[Sun Yatsen] and had overthrown the Qing dynasty. There was nothing wrong about that, and it was in power.'[49]

The Party itself had been born under pressure. The Revolutionary League of the late Qing activist Sun Yatsen, finding itself outpaced by the unexpected revolution in 1911, reconstituted itself in 1912 as the Nationalist Party. It ran in the 1912 elections on a platform that stressed the importance of reducing the power of the new president, Yuan Shikai, who had forced the provisional president, Sun himself, out of power after just a few weeks. The Party did extremely well in the elections, finding itself the largest single group in parliament, but its attempts to negotiate with Yuan were cut short by the assassination of the prime minister-designate, Song Jiaoren, on Shanghai railway station. The following year, Yuan declared the Nationalist Party illegal, and Sun had to flee to Tokyo, where he re-established his group as the Revolutionary Party (Gemingdang). Although he was able to return to China in 1916 after Yuan's death, Sun was buffeted by challenges to his leadership and an inability, or perhaps unwillingness, to deal firmly with the unstable and swiftly changing militarist politics which dominated China for the next decade. Having to move location and finding himself unable to settle a programme, he finally moved to Shanghai in 1920 and announced the re-formation of the Nationalist Party. In doing so, he found himself in the city shortly after the May Fourth Movement had extended its shockwaves beyond Beijing, leading to mass boycotts of goods produced by the imperial powers.[50]

What did the Nationalist Party believe? In one sense, it was founded in swift response to the welcome but disconcerting change in Sun's political circumstances in 1911. For the previous few decades, like so many other revolutionary thinkers, Sun had become convinced that the formation of a nation-state, drawn in large part from the model introduced from the west, was the way in which China should seek to strengthen itself. For Sun, as for late Qing anti-Manchu political activists such as Zou Rong and Zhang Binglin, the idea of the nation-state had become heavily tied to ideas of race by the turn of the century. Encouraged by western race theory and Social Darwinism, it became plausible for the revolutionaries to argue that China's problem lay not just in the symptom of oppression

12. Sun Yatsen, 1923.
Sun Yatsen was a prominent revolutionary activist against the Qing dynasty.
However, his attempt to gain power in the new Republic after 1911 failed in the
face of opposition from stronger militarist leaders. His memory is now
honoured in China, where he is revered as the 'father of the country'.

by western and Japanese imperialism, but the deeper cause of a decadent Manchu race, exemplified in the Qing dynasty, ruling over the
oppressed Han (ethnic Chinese) people which now had to be
recalled to its national 'destiny'. In this, they partly echoed the
Taiping rebels who had convulsed China half a century before, and
whose eccentric interpretation of Christianity (their leader, Hong
Xiuquan, believed himself to be Jesus's younger brother) incorporated virulent hatred for the Manchus.

Yet the downfall of the Manchu dynasty in 1912 quickly removed
the impetus from the racial element of the revolutionary message. In
the Republican era, a new era of citizenship, in which ordinary
Chinese accustomed themselves to modern symbols and ceremonies,
emerged. Urban and rural culture changed dramatically, from

the cutting off of men's queues (the long braid of hair which Han Chinese men had had to wear under the Manchus) to the wearing of new, modern suits of clothes (what we think of as a 'Mao suit' was originally a 'Sun Yatsen suit') to the use of new western-style calendars and the establishment of a calendar, still used in Taiwan today, that counted years 'since the Republic'.[51] Racial division within China, while not absent, was no longer a defining characteristic of the political scene, although outrage at the racial hierarchies perpetrated by the imperial powers remained strong. Therefore, the newly formed Nationalist Party sought to make itself suitable for a China which was growing into civic republicanism. It advocated democracy, though the precise definition of the term, itself relatively newly introduced to China, was elusive. The period in exile, though, gave Sun space to think in the longer term rather than having to deal with fast-changing events such as the revolution, the election, and their aftermath. In 1920, Sun gave speeches that put forward the political philosophy which would from then on be associated with his name: the Three People's Principles (*San minzhuyi*).

These principles have often been neglected or mocked as incoherent by later interpreters. It is certainly true that they were never as carefully worked through as Mao's variations on Marxism, nor did they have the international influence that Mao's did. Yet Sun was a powerful enough figure that Mao himself, in his 1940 speech 'On New Democracy', felt it necessary to pay homage to them and declare that the CCP was putting forward a new Three People's Principles as he sought to widen the Party's appeal. For Zou Taofen, Sun's thought continued to be a primary inspiration in the 1920s and remained important even when Zou moved towards Marxism in the 1930s. Furthermore, they reflected many of the concerns for freedom and modernity that so animated the May Fourth era, even though they are not generally considered part of that generation's legacy.[52]

The principles were *minzu, minquan,* and *minsheng,* most conveniently, if not entirely accurately, translated as 'nationalism, democracy, and socialism'. In fact, none of the terms could be translated quite that neatly, nor had they the fixed and relatively uncomplicated meanings that these later translations implied. Take *minzu* first. The

term itself, a neologism imported from Japan by writers such as Liang Qichao, meant literally something along the lines of 'people's descent group' or 'people's clan'. There was an implication of racial kinship that the western term 'nation' might imply, but would not necessarily demand. The difficulty in using this term was tacitly acknowledged by Sun and the early founders of the Republic, who referred to it as a state of five *minzu* (Chinese, Mongols, Manchus, Tibetans, and Muslims), but the ill-defined coincidence between the racial nation and the nation-state which dogged the Republic from the beginning was not resolved by this uneasy formulation.[53] Next, there was 'democracy'. China is not the only modernizing society where the term has been used in varying and competing ways. But in fact, the term that became the most common for 'democracy', *minzhu*, meaning 'people's rule', is not the one Sun uses here. *Minquan* has more of an implication of 'people's rights', but the implications of this are somewhat different from a system where the people themselves actually *embody* political power. The term harks back to the 'popular rights' (*minken*) movement in Meiji-era Japan, but democracy had only flowed slowly in Japan even after the flowering of that popular movement. Finally, *minsheng* translates best as 'people's livelihood', an alternative version which is less concise but also found fairly frequently. It was perhaps the most vaguely defined of Sun's aspirations, though, and 'socialism' perhaps gives too concrete an air to the well-intentioned programme of social reform which he failed to define. Yet these writings reflect the atmosphere of the new China too, as it emerged into an international atmosphere of 'rights' and political participation that marked the citizenry of a nation rather than the subjects of an empire. Furthermore, the ambiguity of the terms themselves reflects the fluid nature of the politics of the era as people scrambled to comprehend and interpret the new political vocabulary that had been thrust upon them.

Nationalists and Communists, United and Divided

The last phase of Sun Yatsen's life coincided with the first phase of the fledgling Communist Party. As the 1920s dawned, it was clear that

汉 蒙古
满 西藏
回

the outburst of anger which had been seen at all levels of Chinese society during the May Fourth demonstrations and their aftermath had not yet transformed itself into a coherent political movement. Sun had attempted to gain support from various sources for his dream of returning to power: militarist leaders, the western powers, and even the Japanese. But his courtship was in vain.

In any case, his disillusionment with the great powers, particularly after the slaughter of World War I and the betrayal of Chinese interests at the Paris Peace Conference, was becoming ever greater. Yet the changed international situation now came to his aid. The newly born Soviet Russia (as it was then generally known), still fighting for its own life in a vicious civil war, was also looking to export its revolutionary diplomacy abroad. In 1923, Sun met a representative of the Comintern, the organization of the new Soviet Russian state dedicated to fomenting international revolution, and sealed a pact that saw the next important stage in the parties' development: the United Front between the Nationalists and Communists, sponsored by the Soviets. All three participants benefited. For the Soviets, this was a chance to foment revolution. Marxist-Leninist theory held that China was too backward for a Communist revolution to take place immediately. Instead, a 'national bourgeois' revolution had to come first, and the Nationalists were the appropriate party to carry that revolution out: therefore, they needed to be supported at this stage. The Nationalists at last had the kind of powerful sponsor they had sought throughout their years in the wilderness. First, the Soviets gave them the kind of Leninist organizational discipline that had served the Russian party well. At least as importantly, they also helped organize a military training school, the Whampoa Academy, on an island south of Guangzhou (Canton). And for the Communists, who were still a small party without the wider popularity and reputation of the Nationalists, this was a chance to ride to power on the back of two powerful revolutionary forces, the Comintern and the Nationalists. For much of the period of the United Front (1923–7), it was often quite hard to distinguish between the Communists and the more left-wing, revolutionary members of the Nationalist Party.

A turning point, though it was only clearly perceived as such later on, was the death of Sun in 1925. Suffering from liver cancer, the iconic figure of the Chinese revolution, who had nonetheless enjoyed little real power throughout his life, left an uncertain legacy. It was unclear who was to be his true heir. Among the contenders were Wang Jingwei, who was more socially progressive, and Hu Hanmin, who was more conservative. Eventually to win out, though, was the head of the military section at the Whampoa Military Academy, Chiang Kaishek. Chiang did not have the ideological prestige of contenders such as Wang Jingwei, but his prominent role within the party's military organization, as well as his ties to local elites, meant that he was able to command sufficient clout to gain the leadership for himself. The alliance with the CCP and Soviets continued as it had before Sun's death, and an opportunity to strike against the forces of warlordism and imperialism, promoted as China's two principal enemies, emerged later the same year. Many accounts of the rise of nationalism in China have suggested that a direct line can be drawn between the events of 4 May 1919 in Beijing and those of 30 May 1925 in Shanghai.

Like the May Fourth Movement, the May Thirtieth Movement was a wide social phenomenon which took its name from a particular incident. Chinese workers organized a demonstration protesting against the violent ending of a strike and lockout over working conditions in a Japanese-owned factory in the International Settlement of Shanghai, as well as the arrest of several Chinese students. The settlement police, whose squad was made up of Indian and Chinese, became panicked by the crowd and fired into it, killing 11 people. Rage spread across the cities, resulting in demonstrations against imperialism and boycotts of foreign goods.

The Communists and Nationalists were able to take advantage of the heightened political atmosphere to launch their National Revolutionary Army on the Northern Expedition. Between 1926 and 1928, the Expedition, actually a powerful military campaign, moved up China's eastern seaboard, conquering or persuading the militarist leaders to join the Nationalist movement. Meanwhile, Chiang began to show an increasing reluctance to cooperate with his CCP allies, and negotiated forcefully with the Comintern adviser, Borodin, to restrict their role within the Nationalist Party structure. However, the revolutionary strategy of the Nationalists appeared to be paying off on the global scale, with the increasing willingness of the imperial powers to consider recognizing their government instead of the militarist-controlled one based in Beijing.

The endgame came with the Northern Expedition's capture of the most prestigious prize, Shanghai, in spring 1927. Although the United Front did not antagonize the imperial powers by attempting to seize the International Settlement or the French Concession, they fomented strikes and mass demonstrations which eventually led to the fall of the Chinese-controlled part of the city to Nationalist and Communist forces. However, Chiang had by now decided that the CCP were to have no further part in his vision of Nationalist China. He used his contacts among local elites and the underworld, in particular the notorious Green Gang crime cartel, to round up and massacre large numbers of the known CCP members and sympathizers in the city. The United Front was over, as far as Chiang was concerned. The summer of 1927 saw desperate attempts by the CCP and Comintern to form an alliance with the left wing of the Nationalists, based in Wuhan under the leadership of Wang Jingwei, who did not recognize Chiang's arrogation to himself of the leadership of the Nationalist revolution. But by the end of the year, the more radical Nationalists had made their peace with Chiang, recognizing the superior military and financial power that he had at his disposal, and the CCP, after another failed uprising in Guangzhou in December, found itself isolated and on the run.[54]

Did Sun Yatsen's political thought, which was supposed to underpin the Nationalist revolution and government, get significant popular exposure? Certainly, for Zou Taofen, he was the one contemporary Chinese figure worth writing about in *Life*.[55] For many people in Shanghai, marginally involved with or interested in political life, Zou's pieces may well have been one of the few ways in which the thought of Sun actually filtered into the real experience of ordinary people. As we noted earlier, political theory and political parties were hardly at the centre of the New Culture changes for grassroots Chinese and even for many more educated and elite urban-dwellers during that period: free love or new employment possibilities had a far greater direct effect on their lives. *Life* magazine was part of that new way of life too: something inspiring, interesting, and not too taxing to read at the end of a tiring day dealing with one's sexually harassing boss, demanding teacher, or tiring struggle with the petty cash accounts. If, in the midst of all this, there was an accessible essay by a trusted columnist, Zou Taofen, on Sun Yatsen and his thought, then it might well be read. Zou remained supportive of the Nationalist government into the 1930s; he did not desert Sun Yatsen's party until the Manchurian crisis led him to lose faith in their ability to keep the nation stable and whole.[56] However, Zou's concentration on Sun's thought is in part an indication of how threadbare the repertoire of indigenous, modern Chinese thought was at this time. The bald fact was that there had been only a few decades in which the various threads of western thought, including Enlightenment modernity and Christianity, had been available to Chinese thinkers to adapt, reject, or embrace. Still remaining was the long-standing treasury of pre-modern Chinese thought, epitomized by Confucianism. It was not surprising that people like Zou felt that Chinese thought should be allowed to engage with modernity, and that simply rejecting all that it had to offer was too hasty.

The Question of Woman

The urgent issues of gender relations were often marginalized or absent in the political discourses discussed in this chapter: Sun Yatsenism, revised Confucianism, Gandhianism, and even, to a large extent, Communism and nationalism. But in fact, there was a significant feminist movement in the era, although it was later suppressed both by the Nationalists and the CCP. From girls and young women working in the factories, to the new professionals such as Zhu Su'e, to the girls in the park fearing what foreigners would say about their harassers, women, and men, were in a new world where Confucian norms could no longer operate.

Discussions about how the Confucian family structure needed to be reformed were largely shaped by 'the search of young urban males for a new identity in a modernizing, industrializing society'.[57] In addition, the majority of the writing on the 'woman question' in journals such as *New Youth* was by men, and there were real difficulties in women gaining, or wishing to gain, 'independent personhood' (*duli renge*) in the context of May Fourth humanist liberalism which did not necessarily choose to emphasize the *differences*, as opposed to similarities, in the liberation of the sexes.[58]

Nonetheless, there was a powerful autonomous feminist voice during this period. The historian Christina Gilmartin declared that 'The Chinese revolution of the mid-1920s encompassed the most comprehensive effort to alter gender relations and end women's subordination of all of China's twentieth-century revolutions' – in other words, more even than the Communist revolution of 1949. During this time, women who joined the Communist Party in particular did so in significant part to articulate their own struggle against patriarchy. The most prominent female CCP leader of the era was Xiang Jingyu, though she found her path in the party was largely dependent on her relationships with prominent male leaders within the CCP, and that the concerns of female emancipation were repeatedly sidelined to accommodate the need to ingratiate the party with the prejudices of poor rural males whom the party wished to mobilize. Xiang Jingyu was executed in 1927 during a campaign of terror by the Nationalist government, which regarded the feminist movement as part of a wider social turmoil that would lead, unchecked, to anarchy.[59]

Yet there were hopeful signs too. Nominally at least, women were given suffrage and civil rights by the new Nationalist government after 1927 (as in Turkey but unlike Japan), although the reality of endlessly delayed democracy and flagrant civil rights abuses applied to men and women alike. Also, there were new working opportunities for women, although this is sometimes forgotten: as Wang Zheng observes in her introduction to her analysis of women's oral histories: 'As a woman born after 1949, I had absolutely no idea before I met these women that such a large number of independent career women existed before liberation.' Among the women interviewed by Wang was Zhu Su'e, who became one of the first women lawyers in China, qualifying in 1930.[60] Although most of Zou Taofen's stories of role models in *Life* were about men, he did identify inspirational women too, such as Marie Curie. 'Many countries have women poets, women writers, women educators and all types of leaders,' he observed, 'but which country has a woman scientist like Mme Curie?'[61]

Nonetheless, looking at the way in which the history of twentieth-century China has developed, it is clear that feminism has repeatedly been sacrificed for other goals: class warfare, conflict against Japan, and in the post-1978 reform era, the need to build up a strong, internationally competitive China. As with other aspects of free-thinking, the May Fourth era was more open and accommodating to feminism than the eras that have followed it. However, even at this time, feminism did not become a necessary, dominant theme. As we have seen, writers as different in tone and purpose as Lu Xun, Zou Taofen, and Ding Ling all came to grips both with gender relations and with what was then known as the 'woman question' (never, of course, the 'man question'). Yet for all of them, the goal of gender equality seemed to slip away. In Lu Xun's case, it fell victim to the wider lack of confidence that he felt for Chinese society as a whole; in Zou's case, it was subsumed by his over-willingness to assume that the patriarchy could not be tackled too quickly, and his later turn to Marxism which subsumed women's issues beneath the wider issues of (male) unemployment and war with Japan; and Ding Ling, who stuck to the feminist cause in her writings even after throwing in her lot with the CCP, found herself receiving public criticism from the Maoist party in the Yan'an base area in the 1940s for concerning herself with such bourgeois, urban matters. Zou and Du Zhongyuan, we must also remember, were commercial publishers and writers as well as activists: perhaps during the downturn of the 1930s, they felt that too strident a stress on feminist issues would alienate their core readership of men. Certainly the female characters in their journals from the mid-1930s are shriller and rather more one-dimensional than the complex voices that had appeared in the 'Readers' Mailbox' of the 1920s. Times of crisis seemed to throw male writers and politicians towards what were perceived as masculine values of martial prowess.

Conclusion: Goodbye May Fourth?

In many interpretations, 1927 is the year when Chiang Kaishek betrayed his CCP colleagues and sold out China's chance of revolutionary social change. Certainly Lu Xun and Ding Ling, both of whom were involved with CCP politics by that stage, felt deeply betrayed by the way that the Northern Expedition had turned out. They were not alone, and there was a turn towards the CCP on the part of many thoughtful Chinese worried about China's future and the political crises that continued to tear it apart.

Theirs was one very reasonable interpretation of events. However, it did not appear that way at the time to many others. The dominant understanding among those who were interested in politics was rather different. After years of feuding, China had a new government. Chiang Kaishek had declared the establishment of his Nationalist administration in Nanjing in 1928, and it was given international diplomatic recognition fairly fast. In retrospect, this has been seen as the recognition of a 'safe' government sympathetic to bourgeois and capitalist interests. Yet at the time, the Nationalist government was an unknown, and in some ways quite frightening, prospect for both of those groups. It was just a few months since British diplomats had referred to Chiang, then in alliance with the CCP, as 'the little red general'. Although it became clear, to the approval of these same groups, that the Nationalist government would be virulently anti-Communist, its other policies were hardly designed to offer comfort to the foreign powers. First and foremost, the Nationalists saw themselves as a revolutionary party, emphatically not a party of the status quo, and Sun Yatsen's declaration that 'the revolution is not yet complete' was stamped on official documents of the new government. Although the Nationalists certainly saw themselves as taking up the legacy of the 1911 revolution, they did not consider themselves yet to have completed their task. For that, they would need to work through the programme of Sun Yatsen: nationalism, democracy, and socialism.

The most notable aspect of the nationalism that the Nationalists espoused was anti-imperialism. Although they were prepared to take a relatively gradual approach with the foreign powers, there was never any question that Chiang's aim was to recover sovereignty over the Chinese territory ruled by the imperial powers, end extraterritoriality, and create a strong, stable Chinese nation-state. This was not a client regime of the imperialist powers, however much it might appease them on a tactical basis. With a government that was established but still unstable and buffeted from all sides, it would have been surprising if Chiang had been able to take a harder line than he did on imperialism.

On democracy, Chiang took refuge in the same formulation that Sun himself had done, claiming that while democracy was desirable, the Nationalist Party would have to offer a long period of 'tutelage' to the people to educate them into understanding what democracy meant. However, it is worth noting that the Nationalists always stuck to the language of democracy even when at their most corrupt and brutal. The dominant language of New Culture 'enlightenment' was not rejected even when they railed at many of its manifestations. Similarly, the USSR's determination to stick to a language derived from the Enlightenment does, in some fundamental sense, differentiate it from fascism and Nazism, which based their world-view on a conscious rejection of Enlightenment values, even if the results of 'Enlightenment' in the USSR were irrational and horrifying. Good intentions are not enough. But they are not irrelevant either. The model of modernity that the Nationalists put forward was still an Enlightenment one. The great failure of the Nationalist dictatorship was that, like other Chinese governments that came before and after, it failed to institutionalize difference, the ability to recognize that an alternative viewpoint was not necessarily treacherous. (This was, in contrast, the great insight of Chiang's son Chiang Ching-kuo when he finally allowed the democratization of Taiwan in the 1980s.) This unbending view is at least in part to do with the black-and-white view of moral behaviour bequeathed by Confucianism.[62] But it is also attributable to the Bolshevik influence, equally unbending, on the Nationalists and the Communists when they were under Soviet tutelage in the mid-1920s. In other words, there was no dominant and unchangeable 'Chinese culture' which forced the parties into viewing politics as a zero-sum game. Instead, historical circumstance and the luck of the draw as to which foreign advisers they took on led to that particular path.

What about Chiang's adoption of Sun's third great principle, 'socialism', or 'people's livelihood'? This, rightly, has been regarded as one of the great failures of the Nationalist government. This was not because of a lack of intention. CCP writing of the time argued that the 'feudal' values of the Nationalists and their lackeys meant that they had no concern for the misery and deprivation in the rural areas of China in particular. A fairer assessment, though, is perhaps that the Nationalist government recognized the scale of its task but never found adequate ways to deal with it. The government never managed to create a strong revenue base from which to pay for reforms. A vicious circle was created in the countryside, in which state-building was hampered by corruption caused in part by self-defeating methods of tax collection.[63] The Nationalists had also, throughout the 1920s, alienated many people by taking over local temples and shrines and forcibly secularizing them, turning them into party offices or schools, so as to press on the people the need for anti-religious, progressive reform. Unlike the Japanese state, which made state religion, Shinto, an integral part of the nationalism it had created, the modernizing Chinese vision, whether the Nationalist or Communist one, did not. The Nationalists had proposals for reform in the countryside, but they were never sufficient for the massive task they faced, and they started by alienating many who might have supported them through their own high-handed attitude as much as the details of their policy.

Things were different, though, in the cities, where the new regime did have more impact. The 'developmental state' created new government buildings in Nanjing, metalled roads, power stations, and so forth.[64] The regime also took advantage of populist nationalist movements where it could, supporting the National Products Movement, through which Chinese manufacturers since the early twentieth century had been encouraging consumers to favour Chinese-made goods in preference to foreign ones, even if the latter were cheaper or of higher quality.[65] For the first few years of the regime, in the cities at least, it was perfectly possible to find people who were prepared to give Chiang's regime the benefit of the doubt. If it was unstable and inclined to corruption, it was also nationalistic and progressive in language and intent. It was not, in the late 1920s, clear that the New Culture Movement had been brought to a halt because of the installation of the regime in Nanjing. Published discussion certainly continued to talk about China's future in the context of internationalism and anti-imperialism. The revolution, it was clear, was not yet finished. The increasingly menacing power on the other side of the Sea of Japan, though, would be largely responsible for deciding whether it would ever be finished – or, at least, whether it would be finished under the Nationalists.

PART II

Aftershock

5

A LAND OF DEATH

Darkness over China

In Datong, I met a group of three or five wounded soldiers . . . They were really in a pitiable state . . . [They said] 'Our side had no aircraft nor anti-aircraft guns, so when enemy aircraft came on raids, all you could do was wait to die, just enduring it.' I don't know how many times this sacrifice was made . . . But what was saddest was that when our side withdrew, a lot of our seriously wounded brothers had nobody to look after them. Some were crawling by the roadside, others shot themselves.[1]

Du Zhongyuan reported this scene in late 1937, during the greatest crisis that China had seen in the century, the War of Resistance against Japan (1937–45). As the country fell into a turmoil of bloody battle, refugee flight, and social breakdown, the political experimentation of the May Fourth era seemed a very long way off. Yet this eclipse of May Fourth was not limited to the years of the war against Japan.

For nearly 40 years, from the Japanese invasion of Manchuria in 1931 to the visit of President Richard Nixon to Beijing in 1972, China turned inwards. It is hard to compress the history of China during this period into just one story. The period contains World War, civil war, the Communist conquest of the mainland, massive social change and devastating, manmade famine. Yet those three and a half decades of turmoil have one common thread: many of the most important values and challenges to the status quo which were associated with the New Culture era were sidelined or attacked. During this time, political orthodoxy rather than free thinking came to the fore. The battle between the Communists and the Nationalists obscured the fact that neither wished to promote pluralist politics in China. Without intending to, the May Fourth era and the political climate of the early Republic had managed to institutionalize difference, a space for people to disagree openly and freely with each other. The problem was that they did so in an unstable way, and without explicitly acknowledging that pluralism was a positive good – many, in fact, used that freedom to argue that if they came to power, they would end that pluralist culture. This was the same problem that the Weimar Republic had had in Germany, where democratic freedom combined with an unstable state allowed parties to come to power on the promise that they would abolish the system which had allowed them to gain control in the first place.

There is another theme that gives this period unity: these decades are inexorably marked by constant, endless, numbing death. One reason that this reality has not been at the forefront of the historical record is, perhaps paradoxically, that the numbers involved are so large. The War of Resistance to Japan, China's theatre within the wider World War, saw around 20 million military and civilian Chinese deaths between 1937 and 1945. The Great Leap Forward, Mao Zedong's disastrous experiment in collectivized agriculture, killed some 30 million Chinese, perhaps more, between 1958 and 1962. These are merely the two most devastating single phenomena. One could take a couple of other disasters at random: disease (bubonic plague in Manchuria in 1947 killed 30,000 people), or floods (the Yangtze floods of 1931 drowned around 420,000 people).[2] This does not exhaust the list by any means: the civil war of 1946–9, other floods, famines, and droughts, and less well known but still hugely destructive civil wars between militarist leaders all added to the tally over these decades. Many of these phenomena existed before the 1930s, of course, and one of the primary targets of the May Fourth era was 'warlordism', which was already a problem by the 1910s. But after 1931, the more total experience of constant disaster and destruction inevitably reduced people's willingness to deal with matters that were not of the most immediate urgency.

The problems that China faced in this period were real, and many were no fault of its own. Had the Japanese not invaded China, then there are intriguing counterfactuals as to how the Republican and Nationalist state might have developed. Yet whether from outside or within, the type of crises that this new period brought about did not nurture the sort of pluralism of which May Fourth seemed briefly capable. The sense of crisis in the 1910s and 1920s had been real, but also ill-defined: there were so many targets, but few of them could be combated through one simply expressed policy. Ideas during the period 1931–66 narrowed, in contrast. They were often much simpler (Resist Japan! Destroy class enemies! Exterminate the Communists!), often for reasons of urgency, but the short cut they took was ultimately one which found acknowledgement of alternatives unwelcome and, at times, inadmissible.[3] Another characteristic of the ideas of these years was that they turned inwards. Chinese nationalism and Communism largely sought salvation from within a fixed set of boundaries, abandoning for the most part the trawl that had taken in Eastern Europe, Thomas Edison, Gandhi, or the other figures who had seemed to provide such an exciting array of possibilities a few years previously. The decades from the 1930s all the way until the late 1970s were not, with a few exceptions, ones in which China looked outwards, except, for a decade or so in the 1950s, to the USSR, and even then in a limited way.[4] As we have seen, May Fourth China did not look purely to the west – the colonial and non-European world was perhaps more exciting for them than for their equivalents in the 1980s who were more genuinely fixated on the west, and on the US in particular. But as the May Fourth era drew to a close, the dominance of conflict, both internal and external, seemed to force politics into a zero-sum mould, exacerbating Social Darwinist tendencies that had emerged in the late Qing, and encouraging the view that politics involved conquering or being conquered.

China Changes Shape, 1931–7

On 18 September 1931, a bomb exploded near a Japanese-owned train travelling on the outskirts of the city of Shenyang (then known in the west as Mukden) in Manchuria. The train was unharmed, but the Japanese Kwantung Army, which had been garrisoned in the region since 1905 under the settlement at the end of the Russo-Japanese War, declared that this was one provocation too far by Chinese 'bandits' who were being sponsored by the Chinese government in the region, led by the militarist leader Zhang Xueliang ('The Young Marshal'). A western adviser to the Nationalist government, Robert E. Lewis, recounted what happened next:

On Friday night September eighteenth the Japanese Army sent from Korea into Manchuria through Antung seven army railway trains fully loaded with soldiers . . . Japanese soldiers occupied every public office in Antung excepting the customs house which has Europeans in it, also placed guard over Chinese customs superintendent to prevent his free action . . . [Chinese] troops and military cadets were disarmed when captured and the arms and munitions of the Chinese arsenal were removed by Japanese including modern rifles field guns heavy guns military motor trucks.[5]

The bombing of the railway had been staged by two middle-ranking Japanese officers in the Kwantung Army, giving them an excuse for their rapid occupation of the whole of Manchuria. Chinese authority in the south of the region was expelled within days, and even resistance in the north ended within a few months. The Nationalist government calculated that it could not defeat the superior Japanese armaments, and protested to the League of Nations, but neither Chinese protests nor the League's condemnation of the Japanese action could budge the occupiers. The Japanese maintained that the Manchurians themselves had revolted spontaneously against oppressive warlord rule, and used local Chinese collaborators to help them establish a client state, supposedly independent, named 'Manchukuo' ('Land of the Manchus'). This new 'state' was recognized by few countries other than Japan, and the Japanese army exercised ultimate control in it. For the next 14 years, the northeastern provinces of China would be lost to the Nationalist government.

Yet in the immediate years after the Manchurian crisis of 1931, everyday life did not suddenly change in Beijing or Shanghai. Unemployment began to bite, and natural disasters affected many, but the Japanese menace affected few directly unless they lived in the occupied provinces. An exception to this was a brief but savage war between Chinese forces and the Japanese navy that broke out in Shanghai in February 1932.[6]

The massacre of the Communists within the First United Front by the Nationalists in Shanghai in spring 1927 made it seem that the CCP had been wiped out: their remnants either carried on a clandestine existence underground in Shanghai and other cities where they remained in danger from the Nationalist secret police, or else limped to rural areas where they could start afresh. It was in the most important of these rural base areas for the CCP in the wilds of Jiangxi province that Mao Zedong began seriously to develop his theory of rural, rather than city-based revolution, which would shape the eventual rise of his party to power. Between 1931 and 1935, the CCP reorganized before increasing pressure from Chiang Kaishek's 'extermination campaigns' forced them on the famous Long March northwest to Shaanxi province. There they made their new capital in the mountain city of Yan'an, in the base area which would come to be known as ShaanGanNing, after the shortened names of the three provinces which it covered. This period also saw the ascendancy of Mao Zedong to the paramount leadership of the CCP, aided by his concentration on mobilizing the peasants for revolution rather than on the cities, which had proved unreliable sources of Party power.

It is worth noting, though, that Chinese territory during those years maintained a rather bizarre variation on its May Fourth predecessor. Previously, political weakness had meant a plurality of views and lifestyles in any one city in China. From 1931, there was a variety of different approaches to politics – Nationalist, Communist, and Japanese-dominated – in existence at the same time within China. In addition, significant parts of the southeast and southwest were not controlled directly by the Nationalists (though their rulers were nominally allied to the Nanjing government), and there were semi-autonomous regimes, for instance, under the militarist leaders Yan Xishan in Shanxi province and Sheng Shicai in Xinjiang. The possibility existed, dangerous and difficult though it was, of moving to a part of China whose politics appealed more than those of one's current area of residence. Both Ding Ling and Du Zhongyuan, for instance, exercised this option. Manchukuo, the CCP base area, the autonomous militarist regimes and the official Nanjing government offered a choice that amounted to political pluralism: hardly an easy choice, but the choice was there.

This ended in 1937 with the war. The War of Resistance against Japan, as the China theatre of World War II is known in China itself, was the longest single conflict within the wider global war. It was also the moment when the juggling of political choices which, very precariously, the Republic had supported, stopped. Choices hardened.

Yet it had not been immediately obvious at the start of the decade that China would be plunged into total war. The 1930s were years of great turmoil in China on all fronts. The world depression began to bite, leading to the destruction of agriculture and many industries, and throwing millions out of work in the cities and the countryside. In the 1920s, Zou Taofen's *Life* journal had advised its readers how to cope with the new world of work (Chapter 3); now Du Zhongyuan, who edited the successor journal *New Life* in 1934–5, ran features on how to cope with the lack of work. A piece on youth unemployment noted that 'we must quickly recognize that the rapaciousness of imperialism ... the domestic economic system, and ... warlordism are the direct causes of our being thrust into unemployment and hunger'.[7] In contrast to this more abstract explanation, vivid accounts come from submissions to a newspaper project organized by Mao Dun, which asked people to send in accounts of life in China on one day, 21 May 1936. These gave a bleak picture of the human cost of the depression. In one piece, Ah Yuan, a young woman worker, is told that her night shift in the cotton factory has been cut to save costs:

Ah Yuan returned home and told her mother, 'The night shift has ended. We have to wait five days before there will be work.' Her mother listened, stunned. Last year in late June there were work cutbacks in the factory and there was no recovery until October. By pawning all their clothing and going into debt everywhere possible, they had managed to support themselves for three months of hungry living. This year, it was only May twenty-first and work cutbacks had already begun. ... The rice in the storage pot was used up too. How to get by in this life?[8]

As in the US, where the economic depression combined with environmental disaster in the 'dustbowl' states, China was also struck by natural disasters, or disasters combining human and natural agency. The year 1931 saw disastrous flooding on the Yangtze. The mid-1930s saw drought and famine through much of China.

Meanwhile, the Nationalist government of Chiang Kaishek, having proclaimed itself the only unitary, recognized administration for all China, found its authority repeatedly challenged. The Communists were the most notable dissidents from Chiang's rule, and Chiang made use of his central authority to target the CCP as the most deadly threat to the stability of the Chinese nation and state. Nationalist usage rarely referred to the *gongchandang* – the Communist Party – but only to *gongfei* – Communist bandits. For their part, the CCP condemned the Nationalists as reactionaries and traitors. This was no longer the world of the study societies at Peking University or the discussions about world cultures and philosophy in the news magazines of Shanghai. Eventually, the Nationalist 'extermination campaigns' against the CCP's Jiangxi base began to have their effect. In 1934, the party launched the famous Long March; 80,000 men (and around 2,000 women) began the retreat to Shaanxi province in the northwest, enduring Nationalist fire and intensely dangerous physical conditions. Only around 8,000 made it to the other end; among them was Mao Zedong, who now became the paramount leader of the Party. However, the CCP were not alone in challenging Chiang. Numerous substantial rebellions against his rule marked the period from 1927 to 1937, including a war against a group of northern militarists in 1930, a war with a group from Fujian in 1934, and opposition from within his own Nationalist Party from Cantonese rival Hu Hanmin. It was at this time that Chiang launched his 'New Life' Movement (see Chapter 4), which was primarily aimed at undermining the CCP, but also rejected much of the May Fourth agenda, instead promoting a revival of Confucian language as part of its nation-building effort.

Yet one crisis, the blame for which could hardly be laid at the feet of Chiang, continued to loom: the increasing imperialist aggression of Japan. From the late nineteenth century onwards, Japan had set itself on a path of imperialist expansion. While its plans were not driven by a long-term masterplan, as Chinese nationalists and others would later claim, the overall intention to expand in East Asia was clearly underpinned by a desire for prestige, fear of invasion, and paranoid sense of vulnerability, fuelled by Social Darwinist assumptions. It was, of course, Japanese imperialism that had triggered the May Fourth demonstrations in 1919, in the shape of the cessions of former German colonies to Japan by the Allies. By that time, Japan also held formal colonies in Taiwan and the Liaodong peninsula, as well as the substantial economic and political rights in Manchuria that came with their development of the South Manchurian Railway. Ironically, the 1920s now stand out as a respite in the advance of Japanese imperialism. Although the invasion of Manchuria had not initially been authorized at the highest levels of the Japanese government, Tokyo did not repudiate it. The 1930s were marked by attempts by Chiang Kaishek to sign agreements with Japan effectively acknowledging their conquests thus far, and banning anti-Japanese demonstrations and censoring sentiments hostile to Japan, on the understanding that Tokyo would then rest content with what it had conquered. But it was Japan, not China, that broke the compact. After a couple of years of uneasy peace between 1933 and 1935, the Japanese army moved into North China, creating a zone effectively under their control.[9]

The world had become a more hostile place in the 1930s. The world depression had triggered a series of protectionist measures around the world, as the United States and the British Empire retreated into closed trade blocs. The Japanese, whose economy had been hit particularly hard, started to develop their zone of economic influence into a 'yen bloc' which would eventually turn into a vast wartime empire. Meanwhile, democracy and liberalism seemed to be in eclipse as the most glamorous and seemingly successful forms in global politics appeared to be dictatorships, in particular the fascist states of Germany and Italy, which spoke of the need for expansion and conquest in Europe and elsewhere on the globe. In Japan, too, talk of that nation's 'destiny' developed from what had originally been more spiritual ideas of pan-Asianism in the early years of the century. Now military ultranationalists, inspired by philosophers who glorified the idea of Japan's unique race and culture, encouraged the country towards expansion on the mainland that was its buffer against western aggression – into China. Japan's rhetoric about the liberation of Asia from western influence sounded suspiciously like a plan for invasion to many Chinese. Du Zhongyuan, in a pointed editorial, stated: 'Pan-Asianism is Japanese imperialism: nothing more, and nothing less.'[10]

Chiang Kaishek, now increasingly worried, made even more active preparations for war from 1935. As early as 1934, in an anonymous article entitled 'Friend or enemy?', he warned that China could not accept endless territorial advances by the Japanese. Chiang's hand was forced in December 1936, when he was kidnapped by a militarist leader, Zhang Xueliang, the former ruler of Manchuria, whom he was about to demote from command; Zhang justified his capture of Chiang by explaining that he felt it necessary to force Chiang to unite with the CCP against the Japanese, rather than launching yet another campaign to eliminate the 'bandits'. Even when freed from captivity, Chiang eventually came to an accord with the CCP, and the two sides agreed to hold back from conflict with each other, while waiting for any further moves from Japan.[11]

The Choices of the May Fourth Generation

The darkness gathering over China also affected the men and women, now growing older and more worried, who had been at the heart of the New Culture era. The paths of Zou Taofen and Du Zhongyuan show the way in which choices and freedoms from the May Fourth era hardened during the drift to war and the war itself. Both remained heavily involved with journalism and the Shenghuo publishing company, which became more and more openly sympathetic to the CCP cause. This caused them both great problems during the years from 1931 to 1937 when the Nationalist government clamped down not only on Communism, but also on open opposition to Japanese imperialism. The government was justifiably afraid that the Japanese would use such opposition to foment disputes with China, but for the many nationalists who were outraged by increasing

Japanese aggression, it was hard to keep silent. The case of one book-seller in Shanghai in July 1935 who was arrested for selling books with titles such as 'Northeastern Volunteers' and '19th Route Army' was not an isolated incident: there was a market for writing of this sort which told stirring tales of the Chinese armies and guerrillas who had struck a blow for the national honour by fighting back against the Japanese.[12]

Du Zhongyuan, of course, had particular reason for outrage. The Japanese occupation of Manchuria in 1931 robbed him of his status and livelihood. His position in Shenyang as a porcelain entrepreneur, senior figure in the provincial chamber of commerce, and adviser to the Manchurian leader Zhang Xueliang were snatched away literally overnight on 18 September 1931, the day of the occupation. Now a refugee, Du escaped to Beiping, where he became part of a group which founded the Northeastern National Salvation Society.[13] This was one of the most powerful groups involved in spreading propaganda to counter Chiang Kaishek's policy of non-resistance to the occupation of Manchuria. Du's position as an editor on *Life* now came in very useful, as it gave him access to a wide section of the Chinese reading public. Du wrote blistering editorials that attacked Chiang Kaishek's refusal to send troops to recapture Manchuria from the Japanese and advocated resistance to Japan as the most important issue facing China. Eventually, censorship and the fear of arrest forced *Life* to close down and Zou to flee abroad in 1933.

A few months later, Du started up a new journal, waggishly entitled *New Life* [*Xinsheng*], to take on *Life*'s role of advocating resistance to Japan. It lasted until Du's arrest in 1935 for publishing an article (by another author) which caused a diplomatic incident by insulting the Emperor of Japan. The Japanese authorities demanded that the Nationalist government prosecute this blatant breach of the agreement not to allow publication of anti-Japanese material. According to a contemporary court report, angry patriotic students attended the trial to throw pamphlets and yell slogans such as 'Down with the fascist Kuomintang', 'Down with Traitor Chiang', and 'Down with the Imperialists' Running Dogs'. Du apparently opted for a more discreet defence, claiming that he had been away in another province when the offending article had been published. His lawyer claimed that 'the article was repugnant to Mr. Tu's [Du's] policy in the conduct of his magazine and that Mr. Tu was ready to express his sincere regret for the indiscretion'. One assumes that the lawyer had practised maintaining a straight face while preparing this argument, since the main distinguishing characteristic and primary purpose of *New Life* was its weekly columns attacking the evils of Japanese imperialism, resorting only to the figleaf of printing 'X X' instead of 'Japan' every time an author wished to refer to that country. The argument made no difference; Du was sentenced to 14 months in prison, and his appeal against sentence was denied.[14]

Zou Taofen, meanwhile, had also become angry and politically radicalized. By the mid-1930s, he was strongly sympathetic to the Communists, although he did not join the Party. He had been disillusioned by what he saw as the failure of the Nationalists to oppose Japanese aggression in Manchuria, and became more dismayed at the ravages that unemployment was causing for his core readership as the depression hit China. *Life* became a more strident voice: in its denunciations of the government, it reflected Zou's increasing sympathy with the platform of the CCP. Although *Life* was re-started under several different names after its closure in 1933 (including Du Zhongyuan's *New Life*), Zou himself had to go abroad for a year to avoid the attention of the Nationalist secret police. During this period, he visited both Hitler's Germany and the USSR; the former appalled him, but he found the latter inspirational. When he returned to China, he did not lie low, but instead became prominent in the National Salvation Association, an organization which agitated for action against Japanese aggression, and helped to foment public anger about the issue. Zou, along with several other prominent activists, was arrested in November 1936. 'When the six of us got to the police station in Shanghai', he later wrote, he and his fellows-detainees adopted the phrase 'We six people are one': in other words, they refused to be separated. In fact, public pressure led to their release the next year as war moved from probability to reality.[15]

The year 1936 also saw the death of Lu Xun, who had remained engaged but at a distance from Chinese politics all his life. He had only contempt for the Nationalist government, which he saw as corrupt, and which had executed many of his more politically minded friends. Yet he remained permanently suspicious of the all-embracing aims of the Communists, and never joined the Party himself. When he died, he seemed to have seen little that belied his lifelong pessimism. Knowing that he had terminal tuberculosis, he wrote a mordant piece in September 1936 simply entitled 'Death'. It mixed practicalities ('Get the whole thing over quickly. Have me buried and be done with it') with wry advice ('Don't take other people's promises seriously', 'Never mix with people who injure others but who oppose revenge and advocate tolerance'). It then went on to attack enemies ('Let them go on hating me. I shall not forgive a single one of them, either'), and signed off with the dry humour that had marked Lu Xun's career: 'If this is dying, it isn't really painful. It may not be quite like this at the end, of course; but still, since this happens only once in a lifetime, I can take it.'[16]

Lu Xun's life and writing had been one of scepticism and doubt, and he reserved much of his scorn for those who unthinkingly clung to political fashion or orthodoxy. Yet in future years, his memory would be revived by the CCP, an organization hardly tolerant of scepticism, as the purest expression of the meaning of the May Fourth era. In particular, that witty and downbeat farewell essay, 'Death', would be highlighted three decades later during the period in Chinese history most at odds with Lu Xun's values: the violent anarchy of the Cultural Revolution.

The year 1936 also saw Ding Ling make a momentous change in her life. The 1930s were a highly troubled decade for the writer. Following the execution of her lover Hu Yepin in 1931, she had been held under house arrest for several years. In 1936, she used a brief period of release to meet CCP contacts, who helped her plot an escape later that year, first to the Communist base area at Baoan, and then to the larger base area in the northwest with its capital at Yan'an.[17] By this stage, Mao Zedong had set up the political structures which would put Yan'an at the heart of the CCP's area of control during the whole of the period of the war against Japan. Ding Ling admired the selflessness of the many political activists who had come from huge distances to escape the Nationalists and oppose the Japanese. Yet her writing increasingly conflicted with the monolithic political line being set down by Mao Zedong. Feminism and individual autonomy, it seemed, had to give way to the demands of class struggle and resistance to Japan.

In late 1936, the Chinese public were on edge. The world was a colder place, and China was suffering as a result. The internationalist hopes of the 1920s seemed to have disappeared. Yet although there seemed to be menace on all sides, there was little that one could put one's finger on. Everything seemed to be balanced precariously, but people carried on with their lives.

Then the war came, and everything changed.

China Falls Apart, 1937–45

No-one can seriously believe that the Chinese government desires to engage in hostilities with Japan ... Responsible opinion in Tokyo is just as averse from embarking on further military activities on Chinese soil, whatever may be the fire-breathing ambitions of a limited section of Japanese officers.[18]

This editorial appeared in the *North China Daily News* on 13 July 1937, following reports of an outbreak of fighting between Chinese and Japanese soldiers at a small walled town named Wanping, a short distance outside Beiping (as Beijing had been renamed by the Nationalists in 1928). 'With the suddenness and unexpectedness of a lightning flash,' the same paper's Beiping correspondent had reported on 10 July, 'came the news of an outbreak of armed hostilities between Chinese and Japanese forces in North China.' The editorial, with its tone of slightly patronizing optimism, expressed the shared views of most of the western community in China. China and Japan had clashed verbally over Manchuria, and had gone to battle in Shanghai in 1932. Yet those disputes had calmed down: surely this one would also?

It quickly became clear that this time the situation was much graver. Already, visitors to the city were fleeing:

With the sound of guns and the roar of battle quite audible in Peiping [i.e. Beiping] a large number of foreign travellers decided that it was high time to depart. Hoping to leave Peiping last Friday morning, the tourists suddenly learned that all the gates to the city but one had been bolted shut and that there was no longer any rail service out of the city. [A train finally appeared at 6 p.m.] A veritable stampede including both Westerners and Orientals developed as people rushed through steady rain to the station. There they packed into the coaches like sardines sitting and standing among suitcases and bags of all descriptions while the rain leaked through the roof.[19]

It was unclear who had started the skirmish between the two sides, but the Japanese chose to regard the fighting as a provocation, demanding yet further territorial concessions from the Chinese in the Beiping area. This time, though, Chiang did not comply, knowing that if he let Beiping, which was a major railhead, fall to Japan, then his hope of controlling North China would be severely damaged. Instead, he fought back, undertaking a diversionary strategy by sending troops to Shanghai to draw the Japanese away from their area of greatest strength. Once again, the *North China Daily News* hoped that its words might wish away the reality of war. As fighting reached Shanghai, thousands of refugees fled from the Chinese-controlled areas of the city to the International Settlement, which was not controlled by the Chinese government and therefore neutral territory. 'The responsible authorities,' fussed the paper in early August 1937, 'will, it is hoped, take measures to stem the apparently quite unnecessary and highly dangerous exodus which has been proceeding from Chapei [Zhabei, a Chinese-controlled area of Shanghai].' It added forlornly, 'The admirable co-operation of the local Chinese and Japanese authorities has so far succeeded in preserving calmness and an absence of panic in Shanghai.'[20] The illusion was quickly shattered. On 14 August, Chinese air force bombers miscalculated and dropped bombs on Nanjing Road, the great boulevard at the heart of the International Settlement, killing around a thousand people. Yet it was the Japanese who brought the most death to Shanghai, reducing large parts of the city to rubble. After the Nantao railway station was bombed in late August, the *North China Daily News*, which had

13. **Civilian volunteers help survivors of an air raid in Canton, 1938.**
The War of Resistance against Japan (World War II) devastated China. Around 20 million Chinese were killed and 80 million became refugees in eight years of war, and the Nationalist government's state-building efforts were crippled. With pictures such as this one, the famous war photographer Robert Capa captured the desperation and heroism of the time.

admired the 'calmness' just a few weeks before, now pinned the blame firmly on Japan's Imperial Army:

It would seem as if the Japanese forces were being commanded to fill to overflowing the cup of bitterness with which their exploits will be associated in the eyes of the world. Here in Shanghai as the streams of refugees . . . are perceived in the streets . . . among them hosts of mothers desperately protecting their offspring and gallantly endeavouring to conceal their fears, the thought irresistibly rises that the Japanese mother . . . would be horrified if she could see what was being done to Chinese mothers and their children in the name of her people. Nantao stands for all, except Japan, to see.[21]

The Japanese paid no heed. Chinese and Japanese troops fought for Shanghai from August to October, and Chiang's troops were forced into submission, leaving behind 'a panorama of almost indescribable destruction'.[22] Over the terrifying months of summer and autumn 1937, Chiang's government was forced to withdraw to the central city of Wuhan, and in early 1938, to retreat once again to the far southwestern city of Chongqing. The Japanese made their determination to conquer China clear in the notorious Rape of Nanking in winter 1937–8, when the Imperial Japanese Army troops carried out a six-week orgy of murder, torture, and rape.[23] With the CCP still in control of their northwestern base area, China remained, broadly speaking, divided into three throughout the war years: Nationalist, Communist, and collaborationist. None of these divisions was stable or simple, but they dominated the shape of Chinese politics during the war years.

When Manchuria had been invaded by the Japanese in 1931, prominent nationalists had had little choice but to escape, if they could, to China below the Wall, and try and whip up support for their anti-Japanese cause from an often distracted public. Du Zhongyuan and Zou Taofen's reporting and propaganda had been crucial to that effort. Now millions more faced the same decisions in 1937. In a sense, many of the poorest had the easiest choice: none at all. Even though some 80 million Chinese became refugees during the war years, many millions more found themselves unable or unwilling to abandon their lives and leave. The parts of China taken over by the

14. Chinese try to enter the European concession area in Wuhan, but are prevented by barbed wire, 1938.

Foreign concession areas were neutral until 1941, and Chinese who managed to enter them were safe from Japanese air raids. Food supplies to many cities were cut off because of the invasion, and thousands of people had to beg for rice, as in this picture.

Japanese included the great cities of its cultural heartland – Beiping, Shanghai, Guangzhou, Nanjing – and the remoteness of Chongqing and the southwest was simply too much for many to contemplate. Better, perhaps, to see whether sitting tight or actively collaborating in the face of the enemy might lead to a quiet life not so different from what went before. In this respect, things were quite similar to much of Europe under Nazi occupation.

As in Europe, though, many people did flee, most of whom were among the better-educated and more elite parts of society, the groups most identifiable to the Japanese as the advocates of anti-imperialist Chinese nationalism. The writer Xiao Hong powerfully recreated the now-common scene of refugees gathering all their possessions in a desperate attempt to take the last train before the Japanese arrived:

At 5:20 He Nansheng's entire household was all together at the train station: There was his wife, the children – one boy and one girl – a willow suitcase, a pigskin suitcase, a net-covered basket and three rolls of bedding . . . Next to these three bundles, the net-covered basket had the greatest wealth of objects: steel cooking pots, black earthenware jars, empty cracker tins, curved wooden coat hangers, some clothesline, a chipped spittoon made in Shaanxi, a small piece of oilcloth that they put on the two-year old girl's bed at night in case she wet her pants, plus two broken wash basins, one for washing faces and one for washing feet.[24]

One of the most prominent choices made at this time was the decision of many of the faculty and students of China's great universities – Peking, Qinghua, Nankai (in Tianjin) – to go into exile as well. Thinkers and writers from outside the university world had to make the same decisions too.

Some went southwest. Those who went to the Nationalist zone decided not to relocate at the wartime capital of Chongqing, where Chiang Kaishek's security thugs and censors, given further justification by wartime, prevented much free discussion taking place. Instead, a new wartime campus, Lianda (short for the National Southwest Associated University) was established at Kunming, in Yunnan province, which was not under the direct control of Chiang, but one of his wary allies, Long Yun. The atmosphere there was freer and vibrant, although the constant pressure of air raids and scarcity of food made life more difficult as the war went on. 'For impoverished students, a simple meal of spicy chicken and noodles was considered a banquet', John Israel writes in his history of Lianda. Sometimes the fare was even more grim, with grains of sand and rat droppings turning up in the already poor-quality rice.[25] Yet in fields as diverse as languages, engineering, and social science, students and faculty created a sense of collective identity on campus which was combined with dedication to an individualistic search for truth. Lianda was a small outpost of the most liberal part of the May Fourth legacy at a time when that movement was devalued and under attack.

Meanwhile, the Nationalist regime concentrated on summoning up national unity from Chongqing. Since 1934, the government had been promoting the New Life Movement, which sought to promote Confucian values as part of their project of secular modernization. Even at that point, when the war had not yet begun, and Chiang was being condemned by the May Fourth radicals for the seemingly backward-looking nature of his Confucian project, others had remained more thoughtful about the possibilities of Confucianism. In his *New Life* journal, Du Zhongyuan, who was hardly a great supporter of Chiang Kaishek in general, mused in an article from 1934 on how and why Confucius should be commemorated:

In fact, [if you want] to respect Confucius's position in our culture, don't go and blindly worship Confucius, but instead regard Confucius as a brilliant personality of the history of the Chinese nation. Unlike Japanese imperialism in the Northeast [a reference to the Manchukuo client state], don't distort Confucius's thought on the Kingly Way [i.e. how to behave like a righteous king] . . . so as to intoxicate the people; only then will you really understand Confucius. Any type of sophisticated thought system is easy for people sometimes to misuse. The way of Confucius and Mencius can be reckoned as very valuable in terms of historical value. But used with evil intentions, it can be used as a tool for . . . intoxicating the masses. We should clearly recognize this point . . . and only then will we recall the righteous way of Confucius.[26]

15. **Young women are trained as soldiers for the Nationalist forces in Wuhan, March 1938.**
As the Japanese advanced, the Chinese government was forced to move to Wuhan, and then to
Chongqing. It mobilized as much of the population as it could as part of its strategy of total
resistance to the enemy.

This was hardly the voice of a May Fourth iconoclast at its most extreme. But a few years later, during the war, Chiang Kaishek now turned his attention squarely on May Fourth as a target. In his ghostwritten wartime work, *China's Destiny*, he declared:

After the May 4th [1919] Movement, the ideas of Liberalism [Democracy] and Communism spread throughout the country. But those that advocated these ideas had no real knowledge of the enduring qualities of Chinese culture; they were simply looking for something new. Moreover, they merely endeavored to copy the superficial aspects of Western civilization without attempting to adopt its basic principles for the benefit of the Chinese economy and the people's livelihood. As a result, the educated classes and scholars generally lost their self-respect and self-confidence. Wherever the influence of these ideas prevailed, the people regarded everything foreign as right and everything Chinese as wrong.[27]

The Nationalist government, however much it tied its rhetoric to ideas of nation, freedom, and self-determination, had now firmly decided that May Fourth had been destructive rather than progressive. The time for romantic, self-indulgent free-thinking, they implied, was over.

Some fled the Japanese by going northwest. Now that there was a united front again, the Communist zone was officially no longer bandit country, but instead the area controlled by the junior partner in the wartime coalition. The CCP also declared itself keen to welcome intellectuals disillusioned by the Nationalists and horrified by the ravages that the Japanese were inflicting on China. In clear contrast to the Nationalists, Mao declared devotion to the ideals of May Fourth:

Before the May 4th Movement of 1919 ... the petty bourgeoisie and the bourgeoisie (through their intellectuals) were the political leaders of the bourgeois-democratic revolution ... After the May 4th Movement, the political leader of China's bourgeois-democratic revolution was no longer the bourgeoisie but the proletariat, although the national bourgeoisie continued to take part in the revolution. The Chinese proletariat rapidly became an awakened and independent political force as a result of its maturing and of the influence of the Russian Revolution.[28]

The tone of Mao's speech 'On New Democracy', from which this extract is taken, aimed to encourage a united front across classes in the face of the Japanese invasion. Yet it also clearly claimed May Fourth primarily as a Marxist revolutionary movement:

... Since the May 4th Movement things have been different. A brand-new cultural force came into being in China, that is, the communist culture and ideology guided by the Chinese Communists, or the communist world outlook and theory of social revolution. The May 4th Movement occurred in 1919, and in 1921 came the founding of the Chinese Communist Party and the real beginning of China's labour movement ... Prior to the May 4th Movement, China's new culture was ... part of the capitalist cultural revolution of the world bourgeoisie. Since the May 4th Movement, it has become new-democratic and part of the socialist cultural revolution of the world proletariat.[29]

In the space of the decade or so spanned by these three quotations, Du Zhongyuan, Chiang Kaishek, and Mao Zedong were really all putting forward different models of what Chinese modernity meant. There is no doubt that all three of them wanted to see a 'modern' China. Yet although they agreed about the need for progress and economic expansion if China was not to be conquered, and shared Enlightenment assumptions about 'science' and development, they disagreed on the role of indigenous thought and the value of a Marxist framework. Social Darwinism also continued to underpin the assumptions of the different types of modernity which the Chinese debated, encouraged by the situation of total war.

Many of the intellectuals who had made their way to Yan'an were to find that the CCP used the forced isolation of their northwestern base area as an opportunity to remove dissent against the Party, and, as the Nationalists had done, end the May Fourth mindset of free-thinking, iconoclasm, and individualism. Although the CCP claimed to embrace May Fourth while the Nationalists repudiated it, both parties in practice clamped down on the type of critical thinking which it had encouraged. After 1941, the united front largely broke down as the Communists and Nationalists found themselves at log-gerheads. This was the cue for the 'Rectification' movements, when

Mao and his followers clamped down heavily on interpretations of the Communist revolution which differed from their own. Ding Ling was one of the writers who fell victim to the movement. She had exercised the opportunity to make the difficult journey northwest, but after arriving in Yan'an, she had begun to query the way in which women's issues had been sidelined as part of the CCP's drive for unity during the war. An example of this is her short story 'When I was in Xia village' [*Wo zai Xiacun de shihou*], which described the ambivalent way in which villagers welcomed back a young woman who had acted as an undercover agent behind Japanese lines by offering herself as a prostitute and consequently contracting a sexually transmitted disease.

Mao, however, brought a halt to the questioning nature of the May Fourth mindset, even though, unlike Chiang, he embraced the movement in name. In 1942, he gave talks (published the following year) at Yan'an in which he put forward the 'correct' policies on literature and art for writers and artists who had aligned themselves with the CCP. In these Yan'an Talks on Literature and Art, Mao stressed that artistic production must be 'for the masses', and intellectuals should abandon the attitude that they were in some way superior to the labouring classes. The concrete result of this was that literature in the CCP-controlled areas of China was no longer to concentrate on 'bourgeois' matters such as individual love, nor to criticize the Party itself. Negative and cynical writing was no longer necessary: 'What is wrong,' Mao asked, 'with praising the proletariat, the Communist Party, new democracy, and socialism?'[30] The idea of May Fourth as a symbol not of breaking boundaries, but instead following the CCP line, started to gain significance.

This period, in retrospect, marks yet another step in the creation of Mao's cult of personality. As he rose to power, Mao had a close, if often resentful, relationship with Stalin. Among the Soviet leader's tools of control that were relevant to Mao was the way in which the image of Stalin himself as national leader had far outstripped the status of his contemporaries or even the Party itself. The Rectification movements, with their intense and often coercive atmosphere, placed Mao himself, rather than the CCP, as the primary centre of devotion. Policy during the Yan'an period also accelerated the Party's orientation towards rural revolution. Land reform and adjustment of taxation, which had been tried out during the years that the CCP had been in Jiangxi, were now developed further in the wartime base areas.[31]

Some of the May Fourth generation, of course, did not go anywhere during the war. One notable example of this was Zhou Zuoren (Lu Xun's brother), who remained on the faculty of Peking University while the city was under occupation. He did so not out of ideological attachment to the invaders' regime, but at least in part because he was married to a Japanese woman, and also felt he had a duty to the students who could not flee to the southwest. Other intellectuals remained in occupied Shanghai, but most of their writing from that era bemoaned the fact that they had been born in such difficult times. There were, after all, no easy choices.[32] The Japanese attempted to court prominent Chinese politicians to collaborate with them. Although they had mixed success, their greatest coup was to entice Wang Jingwei, Chiang Kaishek's rival for the Nationalist leadership after Sun Yatsen's death, and sponsor his establishment of a 'reorganized' Nationalist government in Nanjing in 1940, which controlled much of south and central China until 1945. Wang justified his decision to collaborate by arguing that if he had not done so, China would have been subjected to even more years of destructive warfare, which would have been harmful in itself, and would also have allowed the Communists more opportunities to gain power. Although his decision was condemned after the Allied victory in 1945, Wang's choice did not seem wholly illogical at the time, although it quickly became clear that Japanese promises to him of autonomy were cruel deceptions.[33]

War and Confrontation

The outbreak of war liberated Du Zhongyuan. He had served his sentence and been freed from prison in 1936, and in 1937 he set off on yet another path in his picaresque journey through modern China. Now, freed from the political constraints that prevented him attacking the Japanese, he became a war correspondent, joining distinguished contemporaries such as Lu Yi and Fan Changjiang. Du's war reporting was part of a wider trend towards frontline reporting in China, and it made a special feature of detailed and empathetic reporting of the reality of total war for the Chinese population.[34] Du specialized in writing that shifted from the details of everyday experience to the wider political significance of the war itself; his language moved between strident, inspiring, folksy, and even vulgar as he judged the mood of his readership. At one point, he could talk about the problem that 'the knowledge of people in China's interior [about the war] is very backward', and that 'we . . . should set up a central agency [to shape] political opinion'; at another, he could give a shocking account such as the one at the start of this chapter, or describe hiding from an air-raid in a handy bath-house: when he and his companions finally got inside, 'everyone ate a couple of eggs and lay down for a deep sleep'.[35]

Although he wrote to gain empathy with his readers, Du also followed a nationalist line that demanded a centralized, unified government, a conclusion that was somewhat ironic considering his own attachment to his Manchurian regional identity, and his sufferings at the hands of the Nationalist government in Nanjing. War, for most political writers on either side of the divide, forced people into strait-jackets of limited choice.

However, there was still enough leeway in those choices to get Du Zhongyuan into what would turn out to be fatal trouble. By mid-1938, China had settled into the three uneasy zones of control that would last for most of the war. Frontline reporting of the terror of battle and refugee flight was less easy now, though journalists both Chinese and foreign continued to describe such scenes as the relentless air-raids on Chongqing, or life in the Yan'an base area run by the Communists. But Du, who had entered journalism as a way of promoting his political agenda, decided to turn his talents elsewhere. Since the mid-1930s, his concern with the ravages that unemployment was causing in China had turned him, along with Zou Taofen, into a sympathizer with the CCP, and he had reported favourably on the Party during his travels to the frontline. This did not make him an out-and-out critic of Chiang Kaishek. Particularly in the early years of the war, the CCP stuck to the line that Chiang was the acknowledged national leader against the Japanese, and Du followed this path in his reporting, savagely attacking fainthearts who doubted Chiang's ability to fight a war of resistance. Yet the CCP connection also meant that in 1939, Du accepted a new role. Having being an entrepreneur, journalist, and prisoner, he now became an educator. Sheng Shicai, the governor of the northwestern province of Xinjiang, the population of which was largely ethnic Uighur rather than Chinese, invited Du to take up the chancellorship of the Xinjiang Academy, the higher education institution for the province located in the city of Dihua (now known as Urumqi). For some years, Du had been in contact with Sheng, and had written extensively about the 'new Xinjiang' which Sheng was creating.

At the time, Sheng was sympathetic to the Soviet Union and the CCP, both of whose territories bordered his own, and which he regarded as a useful counterweight to Chiang Kaishek. Du was now openly sympathetic to the CCP, and therefore felt comfortable working in Sheng's Xinjiang. Du expanded the academy, making it something of a smaller, northwestern equivalent to the great university in exile at Kunming, with many faculty and students either allied to or at least sympathetic with the CCP. The novelist and CCP activist Mao Dun served as the academy's dean. However, in 1941, Sheng changed his mind. That year marked the effective breakdown of the united front between the Nationalists and the Communists, after the New Fourth Army Incident, when both parties blamed each other for refusing to back down over an ordered retreat, leading the Nationalist armies to attack those of the Communists. In the Communists' base areas, the new frostiness led to a heightening of class struggle against landlords, and a series of 'Rectification' campaigns which purged the CCP of figures who offered even the most constructive and mild criticism of the paramount rule of Mao Zedong. In addition, the USSR was invaded by Germany, making Sheng feel that a pro-Soviet orientation was less useful to him, and that it was time to become closer to Chiang Kaishek. The consequence in Xinjiang was the sudden rounding-up and arrest of hundreds of CCP sympathizers, including Du Zhongyuan. Du found himself imprisoned once again, and tried to summon help through his CCP contacts. It was in vain. After three years, in 1944, he was executed in prison, although Sheng claimed that Du had killed himself.[36]

Zou Taofen, meanwhile, had parted company with his old ally some time previously, and continued to run the Shenghuo publishing business in Chongqing. Yet his politics had also become highly sympathetic to the CCP, and after 1938, the enterprise came more and more under the Party's influence, being used to spread literature and propaganda on social reform via branches throughout Nationalist China and even into some Japanese-occupied areas. By the end of the war, though, Zou himself was becoming ill with cancer, and he died in Shanghai in 1944, having reportedly asked on his deathbed to be admitted to the CCP. The request was granted.[37]

Zou and Du did not live to see the victory over Japan, nor the victory of the Communists over the Nationalists. Yet their stories, particularly that of Zou Taofen, were to reappear decades later in China as symbols of what the May Fourth Movement had meant.

The New World

Even as Du and Zou died, the world in which the war took place was changing rapidly. The War of Resistance against Japan which had broken out in 1937 had become part of the World War that had engulfed Europe in 1939 and the United States in 1941. The entry of the US into the war after Pearl Harbor meant the slow but inevitable defeat of Japan, but China would suffer a great deal before the war finally ended. The inclusion of China into the World War did, however, lead to one goal which the Nationalists, Communists, and all Chinese patriots had sought for a century: the ending of the hated 'unequal treaties' with the west, and the system of extraterritoriality. After Japan declared war on the Allies, it declared that western privileges, including the maintenance of concession areas in cities such as Shanghai, were abolished. Not to be outdone, the Allies negotiated a similar agreement with Chiang Kaishek, and in 1943, a century and a year after the signing of the Treaty of Nanjing in 1842, it was declared that Chinese sovereignty alone would apply in Chinese territory (although the British insisted on the retention of Hong Kong). At the time, this was not a practical commitment, since Shanghai and the major treaty port cities were mostly under Japanese occupation, but the symbolic gesture had been made: China was no longer to be treated as a second-class nation in global politics.

In 1944, the Japanese military, aware that it now had the best part of a million troops bogged down in the quagmire of what they had called the 'China Incident', launched Operation Ichigo, a last attempt to drive through Nationalist lines to the west and break down Chinese resistance. It succeeded in conquering a large part of central China, but Allied victories in the Pacific meant that Japan's advantage was shortlived. By late 1944, Japan's home islands were coming under relentless bombardment, and it was clear that, however slow and painful the attack might be for the Allies, Japan could not now win. In the event, Allied estimates that the war in Asia might last into 1946 were proved wrong by the unleashing of the most devastating weapon of the entire war, the atomic bombs which destroyed Hiroshima and Nagasaki, and led to Japan's immediate unconditional surrender.

China was allowed no space to breathe, though, as it moved from World War to Cold War. Buffeted by global currents since the mid-nineteenth century, the destruction of two empires (Japan's and Britain's) and the rise of two newer ones (those of the US and USSR) in the region forced yet more stark choices on the Chinese.[38] Japan's surrender was followed by an immediate race between the Nationalists and Communists for territory and influence. Uneasy truce, leading to failed negotiations organized by General George C. Marshall, was rapidly followed by all-out civil war. The war raged from 1946 to 1949, and ended with Chiang Kaishek and his Nationalist government fleeing to Taiwan to set up a government in exile, while Mao Zedong stood at Tian'anmen in Beijing and declared the establishment of the People's Republic of China (PRC), announcing that 'the Chinese people have stood up'.

This was a momentous change in world politics. Just four years earlier, Japan had been the west's great Asian enemy, and China had been one of the 'four policemen' designated by President Roosevelt to guard the postwar world against a re-emergence of fascism. Now the two countries' fates were reversed. Japan had been occupied by the US and was now a staunch ally in the emerging Cold War. But the rise to power of the CCP in China was a severe blow to American hopes of containing Communism in Asia. 'Who lost China?' became the cry of right-wing American politicians sure that internal treachery within the US must have allowed the Communists victory.

In fact, though, China had never been the Americans' to lose. Chiang Kaishek had needed US support and tolerated their presence in China, but had never been culturally or personally sympathetic to the US. And while the CCP had done an excellent job of liaising with US military advisers during the war, the ideological commitment of Mao Zedong to revolution would have made him very unlikely to form any lasting alliance with the Americans. Yet foreign influence is only one factor in explaining the CCP's success. Both the Nationalists and the Communists tried to influence the new imperial powers – the US and the USSR – to back them in their civil war, and for a while, it looked as if the USSR would opt for the quiet life in China and give its support to the Nationalists while concentrating on taking territory in Europe instead. Domestic factors, however, played a key role. The War of Resistance against Japan had devastated China. Chiang Kaishek's military had been heavily battered by eight years of struggle, whereas the CCP had not undertaken major campaigns in the last years of the war and had fresher and better-trained troops. Chiang Kaishek's government had lost large parts of its legitimacy. The areas under its control showed massive price inflation, food supply remained insufficient, and as the government returned to the parts of China which had been occupied during the war, it often acted like a new colonial occupier, treating the locals who had had to stay put during the war with arrogance and brutality. Yet the economic and social crisis which the Nationalists had to cope with was not, as reporters sometimes claimed, caused purely by wilful corruption on the part of Chiang's government. The Japanese invasion had destroyed so much of China's industrial and agricultural productivity that any government would have found it difficult to restore order even in conditions of peace. And China was not at peace for long.

The CCP was determined to seize its chance for power, just as Chiang was determined finally to eliminate it. It had also learned the lessons of its periods in Jiangxi in the early 1930s, and then in Yan'an during the war years, when the idea of mobilizing the peasants in rural revolution, rather than concentrating on the cities, was crystallized. The May Fourth era had turned the cities into the richest source of thinking on reform and revolution. It was the CCP under Mao that achieved revolution based on the farmers, who made up the majority of China's population. Therefore, in the areas it controlled, the CCP often achieved local goodwill by instituting reform policies that distributed land to poor peasants, and enabled them to accuse and humble local elites who had oppressed and humiliated them in the past. Ding Ling's novel *The Sun Shines over the Sanggan River* (1948) brings the joy, as well as the violence, of this period powerfully to life. 'Schemer Qian', a local landlord and notorious bully, is hauled to a mass meeting to face his former victims:

At this point a man suddenly leapt out from the crowd ... Rushing up to Schemer Qian, he cursed him: 'You murderer! You trampled our village under your feet! You killed people from behind the scenes for money. Today we're going to settle all old scores, and do a thorough job of it. Do you hear that? Do you still want to frighten people? It's no use! There's no place for you to stand on this stage! Kneel down! Kneel to all the villagers!' He pushed Qian hard, while the crowd echoed: 'Kneel down! Kneel down!' The militiamen forced him to kneel down properly.[39]

The CCP did not rely on land reform alone. It also made sure that its troops were well armed (the Soviets handed over captured Japanese arms to the Communists) and trained. In contrast to the flailing of the demoralized Nationalist government, the Communists gave off an air of purpose and morale. Without arms, these psychological weapons would not have been enough. But put together, all these factors eventually spelled the end of Nationalist rule and the triumph of the CCP.

For a long time, this was where 'history' ended in China. For

16. **Refugees flee the advancing Communist armies during the Civil War, Nanjing, April 1949.** Even after Japan's defeat, China was not at peace. For three years, civil war raged between the Nationalist government and the Communist forces, ending in Communist victory in 1949. Chiang Kaishek's regime fled into exile in Taiwan.

western and Chinese accounts alike, 'liberation', the Communist victory in 1949, marked the end of China's 'feudal' past and 'old' society. The watershed year marked the time when everything changed, and a 'new China' emerged from the past. For analysts, everything post-1949 was the province of contemporary political science, and the tactics and successes of the Communist Party were the stuff of live and relevant debate in understanding world politics.

The view looks different more than half a century later. As in Eastern Europe, ideological communism as a system of governance seems to have had its day in China, although unlike in Europe, the Communist Party itself survives in reformed guise. Later chapters will deal with the links between global and internal change in China, and the way in which the ever-changing memory of the May Fourth legacy helped to shape those changes in China. But before that, it is worth observing how our picture of Maoist China has changed in recent years. Many things did indeed change in and around 1949. Yet there were also many continuities between the 'old' and 'new' societies. Decreeing 'liberation' did not automatically mean that people accepted that life must change.

What, then, were the major changes under the rule of the CCP and of Mao? First, and perhaps most notable, was the far more explicit and widely penetrating influence of politics, both in rhetoric and in action. Mass campaigns in endless succession marked the most public face of Mao's China. These could be practical in orientation, such as the land reform campaigns of the earliest years of the PRC, or the anti-opium and anti-prostitution campaigns of the early 1950s. They might be primarily ideological, such as the 'Aid Korea, Resist America' campaign of 1950–1, launched to support China's intervention in the Korean War, or the Anti-Rightist campaign of the 1950s, or the Socialist Education Campaign of 1962. The CCP used its political control and ideological fervour to achieve the mass awareness of politics that had eluded leaders such as Sun Yatsen or Chiang Kaishek.

Yet awareness did not necessarily guarantee acceptance. The CCP aspired to the ideal of colonizing all spheres of life, governmental, public, and private. They did not necessarily succeed. For instance, in rural villages, widows of martyrs to the Communist revolution were not always in practice given the respect the state demanded that they be shown, and some were driven to suicide because of the continuing patriarchal domination of their lives. Schoolteachers in Shanghai were often surprised to find that local connections meant that people with 'bad' political records from the pre-1949 era were nonetheless given higher salaries than certain teachers who had been in excellent party standing.[40]

Nonetheless, the Maoist state was very different indeed in its public politics from the fractured yet precariously pluralist model that had held sway during the Republic, at least until 1937. Ironically, the May Fourth Movement now became a staple image that was used over and over again by the CCP's image-makers. Inspired by selfless patriotism, their account went, the students had protested against warlords and imperialists who threatened to destroy China. From the turmoil of protest emerged the force that would finally lead China to liberation and self-sufficiency: the Chinese Communist Party itself. It was true, of course, that the CCP had emerged at the height of the movement, in 1921. Yet by the time the People's Republic was established, much of the enthusiasm to embrace the world, and the nationalism that looked outward as well as inward to Gandhi, Atatürk, and Edison as well as Sun Yatsen, was now turned instead on China itself, with some genuflection to the USSR which remained its only ally. The petulance of the United States, which refused to recognize the new regime in Beijing (unlike France and the UK), added weight to the CCP's feeling that the west was no longer any sort of ally, and drove them further into the bloc divisions that marked the onset of the Cold War. Many figures from the May Fourth era survived into post-1949 China. Lu Xun, Du Zhongyuan, and Zou Taofen were all dead, but Ding Ling and Mao Dun became prominent ministers in the new government.

Political uncertainty in the May Fourth era had led to an intellectual life that teetered on the balance, an often exhilarating leap between certainty and the unknown. In contrast, the rhetoric of Maoist China was built on political certainty: the certainty of the Party. The mass campaigns did not allow for ambiguity or individualism, now seen as self-indulgence. Beijing, the intellectual origin of the May Fourth Movement, was physically transformed to reflect the new world. While many of its narrow alleyways, known as hutongs, remained in the backstreets, the centre of the city was remodelled to reflect Soviet-influenced ideas of architecture as power: grandiose neoclassical buildings with pillars and pediments, such as the Great Hall of the People, the Martyrs' Revolutionary Monument, and, most notably, a massive, kilometre-wide new square in front of the Tian'anmen, the Gate of Heavenly Peace, where the Emperor had traditionally entered the Forbidden City, and in front of which the nationalistic students had gathered in 1919.[41] Shanghai underwent fewer immediately obvious architectural changes. The Bund, the famous waterfront symbol of imperialism's presence at the centre of China, remained (and remains) as it was in the 1920s, although the International Settlement of which it was part was abolished in 1943. The occupants of the imposing buildings, however, changed swiftly after 1949. Most notably, the building which had previously housed the Hongkong and Shanghai Bank now held the People's Municipal Government instead.[42] Yet Shanghai came under particular scrutiny from the country's new masters in Beijing. While the city's role in China's revolutionary history was not in doubt, its reputation for decadence, cosmopolitanism, and pluralism, as well as its decades of rivalry with Beijing, made it a prime target for 're-education'. For decades, Shanghai's formerly lively intellectual and cultural life was firmly discouraged by central diktat. Yet the city's instincts for contrarianism would manifest themselves elsewhere, when it became the crucible of the Cultural Revolution in 1966–7.

Mao himself appeared everywhere in the new China, particularly after his Politburo colleague Lin Biao orchestrated the cult of Mao's personality during the 1950s and 1960s. If he did not appear in person, waving from a podium on top of the Tian'anmen gate, then his image turned up in posters or photographs, or his words in the *People's Daily* [*Renmin ribao*] newspaper. Although these campaigns were carefully controlled, one should not underestimate the genuine prestige and respect which Mao, along with the rest of the CCP, enjoyed in the early days of the PRC. The country was united, and the twin horrors that had fuelled May Fourth patriotism, warlordism, and imperialism, had been vanquished. (Awkward questions about the economic and territorial concessions in the northeast and northwest won by the USSR as a price of helping the new state, which looked suspiciously like imperialist conquests, were not asked in public.) There was a clear sense of purpose and drive about many of the campaigns and public works which the new regime initiated. The most popular with the wider population was probably land reform, where poorer peasants were encouraged to 'speak bitterness' in public criticisms against those who were seen as oppressive landlords. Although the Party was at first cautious about mass redistribution of land, not wishing to disrupt the harvests that fed the country, as the regime became firmer, it also authorized harsher treatment of landlords and more wide-ranging land reform. The endless campaigns also encouraged the Chinese to think of the policies which affected their own lives as part of a wider project to create a wholly new society.

The obsession with renewal and the growing isolation of China from its one significant outside influence, the USSR, led Mao and the Party in yet another direction. Although Mao's relationship with Stalin had always been somewhat dysfunctional, it was marked by wary respect on both sides. The same could not be said of Mao's dealings with Stalin's ultimate successor, Khrushchev, which became ever frostier as the 1950s moved on. However, Khrushchev's first major post-Stalin policy shift, the swiftly leaked 'secret speeches' of 1956 that condemned Stalin's terror, caused a significant change in Chinese policy. Mao was unhappy about what he perceived as a betrayal, but the Hungarian uprising later the same year persuaded him that perhaps the time had come to test the waters of political liberalization. In 1956–7, after a hesitant trial run, Mao declared open season for constructive criticism of the CCP's record so far. 'Let a hundred flowers bloom in culture', he declared, and 'Let a hundred schools contend in thought'. Mao was confident enough, just seven years into the new regime, that society had changed so completely that there would be only moderate criticism of the details, rather than the fundamentals, of life in the new China. In particular, he pinned his hopes on comments from the 'intellectuals', a term used to

describe the more educated elements in society, although not necessarily the high-flown type that the term implies in western usage.
The May Fourth era, of course, had drawn on the longstanding tradition of scholars criticizing unjust government to bring about reform.
Was the Hundred Flowers going to be a new May Fourth?

It was not. First, the reaction was not at all what Mao had expected
when pushing the policy through the Politburo, at which time many
of his colleagues had been unenthusiastic. Rather than gentle criticism, there was a torrent of abuse, ranging from the specialized, such
as academics who could no longer read foreign journals to keep up
with their fields, to the widespread, such as the violent opposition of
many peasants to the mass collective farms which Mao had advocated
from 1955, in a reversal of the redistribution of smaller, individual
plots that had proved so popular in the early 1950s. Fearful that hard-
liners in the Politburo would interpret these outbursts as loss of
control on his part, Mao changed his mind just a few weeks after the
official start of the Hundred Flowers Movement on 1 May 1957, and
now declared the movement to be 'rightist' – in other words, a subversive attempt by enemies of the revolution to undermine it and
him. In an abrupt crackdown, some 300,000 intellectuals were condemned to re-education or internal exile. Among them were an
abruptly demoted and disgraced Ding Ling, along with the young
journalist Liu Binyan and the scientist Fang Lizhi. Liu and Fang
would become prominent again in the aftermath of the Cultural
Revolution and then the 1989 Tian'anmen Square events.[43]

The Cold War

Yet even had the voices briefly freed by the Hundred Flowers been
allowed to speak a little longer and more boldly, the campaign was
still a long way from the promise of May Fourth. Of course, the
earlier era had hardly been a liberal paradise. Various terrors had
waited for those who spoke their minds and offended the men in
power, whether warlords, imperialists, or Chiang Kaishek. Yet the
fragmentation and lack of penetration of political power had meant
that radicals could flee to or from the International Settlement, the

Communists could escape to Jiangxi, and the wartime radicals could gather in Kunming rather than Chongqing. In Mao's China, there was nowhere to run, which made the words of those who spoke out even braver. Nor was there the *de facto* pluralism of the Republican era which made up in part for the fact that no powerholders had ever felt able to agree to disagree with their opponents. Now, disagreement meant exile or death. Nor was there the consuming interest in the outside world that had marked the New Culture era.

This was, in significant part, a cultural shift that emanated from the Cold War. The Cold War was the first time in modern global politics when choices were in large part reduced to the starkness of bipolarity. The interwar world had portrayed itself as shaped by clear choices: fascism versus democracy, imperialism versus anti-colonialism, communism versus capitalism, and so forth. Yet, as was discussed in Chapter 4, there were at least three dominant versions of modernity competing with each other for global dominance in the interval between the World Wars. Two of them, liberal democracy and communism, despite their seeming mutual detestation, arose from the same Enlightenment-derived language of rationality and secularism. The third, fascism, drew a picture of modernity which consciously rejected the Enlightenment and embraced anti-rationality, primordial ideas, and drew more explicitly on quasi-religious and spiritual themes. These messages could not, of course, be neatly divided up and distinguished from each other in practice. Liberal democracy betrayed its founding principles by permitting imperial domination of subject peoples, although the contradictions in that position led to the post-Versailles guilt that resulted in such uneasy compromises as League of Nations mandates, which were supposedly not real colonies. Soviet Communism took on many of the quasi-religious aspects of fascism as Stalin's cult of personality dominated the supposedly rational, if also murderous, bureaucracy of the Leninist state. Anti-colonial movements, even ones like Gandhi's which were expressed in terms of non-European thought, were heavily shaped by ideas such as democracy, nation-state, class, and race. Underpinning the system were a variety of powers: the rising embodiments of the two differing Enlightenment models of anti-imperialism, the US and USSR; a rising imperial power, Japan; and two significant status-quo advocates of empire, Britain and France.

World War II changed this scene violently. Not only did the three openly imperial powers find themselves destroyed or bankrupt, but the idea of imperialism itself was, on a global stage, discredited, even though it would be a couple of decades before the European empires would finally fade away. This was not a direct consequence of one of the three pre-war models of thought, the fascist one, being thrown out of contention – after all, Britain and France had fought fascism – but the new dominance of the anti-imperial powers made it impossible to argue for ideas that had previously been acceptable, if not universally shared, such as liberal imperialism, 'education' of colonial peoples towards a slow independence, and so forth. Empire, despite occasional provocative attempts to rehabilitate it as a concept, has not been a viable political tool since 1945 in a world of 'United Nations'. The US and USSR both ran huge empires after 1945, of course, but were careful never to use the term in self-reference, only in accusation of the other.

Nobody of consequence mourned for fascism. However, the reduction in the number of modes of thought during the Cold War had significant consequences for societies around the globe. In addition, the fact that the two dominant modes of thought, capitalism and communism, shared many assumptions and rejected many of the same ideas meant that they were frequently in competition for interpretation of the same political vocabulary: democracy, freedom, progress. Quarrels between neighbours are often much more bitter than those against enemies who are more distant, as the quarrel between the Nationalists and Communists in China had shown for the previous two decades. In the case of the global Cold War, much of the animus and paranoia came from the fear of subversion from enemies who looked 'just like us'. In the US, this gave birth to McCarthyism; in the USSR, to the purges of the very late Stalin era, which had a particularly anti-Semitic overtone. The tone spread to the superpowers' client states: in Japan, thousands of war criminals were rehabilitated under the 'reverse course' policy, their most important quality now being defined as anti-Communism, whereas in Hungary and Poland, persecution and purges marked the early years of the new Soviet satellite regimes.

Mao's China, though, could not be termed anybody's client state after 1949, any more than Chiang's had been before that date. Mao and his Party never ceased to take pride in the fact that their revolution had, effectively, been an internal one. The policies which had turned the Party from a bedraggled mob on the run from Chiang Kaishek's Nationalists to the controllers of the world's most populous nation, and in particular the policy of agrarian revolution, had often been carried out in the teeth of opposition from Stalin and the Soviet Communist Party. China's turn to the USSR after 1949 was ideological in nature, a combination of political inclination and lack of choice. For the starkness of the Cold War choices crucially affected China's orientation towards the outside world. It was the United States that insisted on continuing to recognize Chiang Kaishek's exiled regime on Taiwan as the true rulers of China. This was a fundamentally different policy from the American policy towards the USSR, which it had recognized in 1933, and with which it always maintained diplomatic relations even during times of crisis. Refusal even to acknowledge the reality of the new People's Republic was justifiably taken by Beijing as a signal that it had no choice but to turn towards Moscow for support both financial and ideological. Not that Mao became any sort of Soviet stooge, regardless of attempts by McCarthy-era Washington to portray him as such, and to silence those foreign service officers who knew better. His reaction to Khrushchev, in particular, was furious, regarding him as a traitor and, worse, a Trotskyite. Yet Mao's internal political choices became more and more driven by the boxes within which the Cold War had enclosed him. The US was closed off, and the USSR was rapidly cooling into enmity. Attempts in the 1950s to pose as a leader of the newly emergent Third World evoked interest from the rulers of many of the newly independent states of Africa and Asia: yet this was a role to which China, which had never had the global ambition that had defined the European powers, took somewhat half-heartedly, and China was in turn not fully trusted by Third World leaders such as

Nehru who were suspicious of its aims. There were some spectacular examples of Mao's willingness to spread revolution outside China's borders. China's intervention in the Korean War less than a year after the establishment of the PRC showed Mao's commitment to reversing what he saw as injustice in the global order. Yet despite his support for 'wars of national liberation', Mao's heart was not fully on the global stage: although he had been bathed in May Fourth internationalism, he had, after all, only left China twice in his life, both times on visits to Stalin in Moscow in the early years of the PRC. Instead, as the 1950s drew on, China was increasingly left to look inward.[44] If nobody would help China, China would help itself. The notion of self-sufficiency and the desire to provide some alternative to the now alienated dyad of Cold War superpowers led to one of the single most extraordinary and traumatic policy decisions of the Mao era: the Great Leap Forward.

The Great Leap Forward

Agriculture was the engine on which China ran. With such a huge population to feed, everything that the CCP wanted – industry, military strength, construction and development – flowed from the availability of food. The late nineteenth and early twentieth centuries had been marked by regular famines all over China, caused by a combination of unresponsive political leadership and particular environmental factors which are not yet fully understood. The lack of food in Nationalist China had undermined Chiang Kaishek's government fatally during the war.[45] Mao's fixation with the rural revolution and agricultural production was entirely understandable.

Agriculture had been efficient after 1949, in part because of the regime's pragmatic application of the land reform policy. As early as 1955, however, Mao had claimed to detect a 'high tide' of socialism in the countryside, and used this as the basis for reorganizing much of the countryside into collective farms. The policy was not universally popular, as criticisms made during the Hundred Flowers showed, but Mao, whose concern for ideological purity was always as strong as his concern for the pragmatic success of the revolution, was not

17. An exhibition in Beijing to show bridges and railways constructed under the Communist government, 1958.
Although Mao had promoted a rural revolution, his government was fixated with technological modernity, a legacy of the May Fourth Movement's determination that 'science' should be the counterpart of 'democracy'. The great photographer Henri Cartier-Bresson recorded many of the happier scenes from the Great Leap Forward period.

disheartened. Following the debacle of the Hundred Flowers, he came back to the Politburo convinced that China was doing well, but could do better. Now that successful collective farming was embedded, why not use the power of the planned economy to show what China was really capable of? Mao's enthusiasm, it should be noted, now found strong support among his Politburo colleagues. Cooperative farms were organized into 'people's communes', which were much larger units. Social changes followed this radical reorganization of work. One of the most notable results was the enforced breakdown of the patriarchal relations that had persisted among China's farmers even after 1949.[46] Because both men and women needed to be deployed to work the massive farms, often at great distance from their home villages, duties which had generally fallen to women, such as childcare and cooking, were now centralized within the communes. Initially, the CCP's promises of hugely increased food production led to slogans such as the one promoted in Jiangsu province: 'Eat as much as you can and exert your utmost in production.' People ate huge amounts of rice and meat, which they normally would have saved for the hard seasons of the year, or as a safeguard against natural disaster.[47] Mao also encouraged the people of China to combine industrial modernization with domestic self-reliance. This led to phenomena such as the 'backyard smelter' scheme, where farming communities were supposed to produce industrial-grade steel in home-made furnaces. Unsurprisingly, such steel as was made turned out to be useless, and often consisted of old pots or railings that had been melted down, but people were ordered to fulfil their quotas regardless of the usability of the end product. Yet there was, in the initial year of the Leap, a real sense of purpose and drive to Chinese society. New building works and construction projects were started, and peasants were encouraged to write poetry and enjoy art forms that had in the past been an elite preserve. The renowned photographer Henri Cartier-Bresson produced a portfolio of pictures showing the inspirational and confident mood that the Great Leap Forward had stimulated in many parts of Chinese society.

The visions of a bright new dawn, however, turned out to be fatally deceptive. The motivation for the Great Leap went beyond the idea that the command economy was superior to *laissez-faire*, which underpinned the Soviet challenge to the west, expressed in Khrushchev's famous promise 'We will bury you'. Rather, Mao and his supporters believed that ideological fervour and sheer will could propel China's masses to exceed the laws of economics altogether and reach agricultural and industrial targets massively in excess of anything either superpower claimed was possible. In an attempt to satisfy CCP cadres, false statistics were sent up from the countryside giving the impression that the inflated production targets were being met. As a result, 'surplus' grain was exported to the USSR, when the hidden reality was that poor harvests and inappropriate techniques had led to a severe, deadly lack of food.

Jasper Becker has documented the famine that hit China in 1958–61

18. A giant parade to mark ten years of Communist rule in China, 1959.
The early Communist period was marked by mass mobilization of the
population, and early policies such as land reform helped to make the new
government popular. However, overconfidence led to the Great Leap Forward
policy promoted by Mao from 1958. This policy caused a famine which killed
some 30 million people.

as a direct result of the Great Leap Forward policies. Unlike any
previous famines in China, this one covered the entire country, and
killed perhaps 30 million people – 1 in 20 of the rural population,
where most of the deaths occurred.[48] One woman from Anhui province who survived the famine remembered:

My legs and hands were swollen and I felt that at any moment I would die.
Instead of walking to the fields to look for wild grass [to eat], I crawled and
rolled to save energy . . . All the trees in the village had been cut down. Any
nearby were all stripped of bark. I peeled off the bark of a locust tree and
cooked it as if it were rice soup . . .

More than half the villagers died, mostly between New Year [1960] and
April or May . . . The production team chief's daughter-in-law and his
grandson starved to death. He then boiled and ate the corpse of the child
but he also died. When the village teacher was on the verge of death, he said
to his wife, 'Why should we keep our child? If we eat him then I can survive

and later we can produce another child.' His wife refused to do this and her husband died.[49]

The Great Leap Forward was not officially repudiated until 1981. But the policy was in effect reversed from 1962, as the Politburo marked the changes by moving towards a more pragmatic policy in the countryside, breaking up the massive cooperative farms and allowing people to move back to smaller agricultural units. In 1959, Mao had agreed, somewhat under pressure, to give up one of his positions, as head of state, although he remained the head of the CCP. By the mid-1960s, food production had returned to normal levels. Yet Mao's ideological ardour was by no means exhausted. Even while China recovered economically, Mao was gripped by two emotions, anxiety and resentment. He was anxious that 'economism', the concern both of his senior colleagues and the Chinese masses for personal prosperity, was blunting their collective revolutionary edge. At the same time, he was angered by his comrades' attempts to lever him out of power, and despite his occasional wistful suggestions that he might retire to the 'second line', he seemed to have little inclination to withdraw from political life.

The stage was set for the next great trauma in China, and one that would be a poisoned, strange legacy of the May Fourth ethos which Mao had inherited: the Cultural Revolution.

Conclusion: May Fourth in Abeyance

In just three and half decades, from the early 1930s to the mid-1960s, many societies across the globe changed. Few, however, changed as much as China. Yet the long period of time in this chapter has continuities in it. The period was marked by endless death, caused by war, disasters both natural and manmade, and the consequent disorientation and disruption of everyday life. Ordinary life had to be lived in a state of immediate crisis.

As a consequence, this was a time when May Fourth values largely disappeared from view in China. They did not vanish completely. Even while Chiang Kaishek was blaming the New Culture for

China's inability to define its own identity, writers such as Lu Xun and Ding Ling tried to come to terms with China's fate through literature, and Zou Taofen and Du Zhongyuan did so through journalism. Post-1949, May Fourth was transformed through sterile hagiography into nothing more than the birthplace of China's vehicle of destiny, the CCP. The Great Leap Forward showed an obsession with ideas of science and destiny, which certainly had precedents in the May Fourth era. But overall, individualism, free-thinking, and iconoclasm, as well as an embrace of the foreign as *part* of what it meant to be Chinese, all typical of the New Culture thinkers, were not at a premium at a time of mass unemployment, war, famine, and revolution. Nor did the mass campaigns that shaped the early Mao era encourage these values, and those who tried to challenge them soon found themselves in trouble.

The Cultural Revolution would be different, though. On the one hand, it certainly did not encourage free-thinking, individualism, or a love of the foreign. On the other, it did something that had not been a feature of other events or campaigns since the 1930s: it provided a very different interpretation of some of the implications of the original May Fourth Movement. In effect, the Cultural Revolution became a *reductio ad absurdum* of what May Fourth could have been if China had not, in the 1920s, been weak, divided, and unsure of its own path. It was not an *inevitable* consequence of May Fourth, any more than Nazi Germany was the inevitable consequence of the weakness of the Weimar Republic. However, in that earlier era, paradoxically, China's weakness had been its safety net; few ideas were strong enough to dominate. By the 1960s, China's reunification under a government that, paradoxically, was actually solid but *thought* itself vulnerable, gave it the strength that allowed the next wrenching story to take place.

6

TOMORROW THE WHOLE
WORLD WILL BE RED

The Cultural Revolution and the
Distortions of May Fourth

On the night on 30 August 1966, Nien Cheng, who worked for the Anglo-Dutch Shell Oil Company in Shanghai, was forced to open the door to her house and let in a gang of Red Guards, teenage enthusiasts for the policies of the Great Proletarian Cultural Revolution. In this campaign, set in motion earlier in the year, Mao Zedong declared that the Communist Party still held large vestiges of the 'old thinking' and 'feudal customs', which had slowed down the pace of the Chinese revolution, and had led to major leaders such as state president Liu Shaoqi taking 'the capitalist road'. Mao demanded that China's youth, untainted by the past, should 'bombard the head-quarters', bringing down authority figures all across the country, from top Party leaders to schoolteachers, doctors, and anyone else who, he claimed, thought themselves superior because of their education or knowledge of the world outside China. Being 'red' in one's ideological devotion to the words of Chairman Mao was far more valuable than being 'expert' in the bourgeois worlds of technical knowledge or expertise.

Nien Cheng, in a memoir written after she had moved to the United States in 1980, recalled a dialogue with a young Red Guard who had started smashing her priceless Kangxi era (seventeenth-century) porcelain wine cups:

I picked up one of the remaining winecups and cradled it in my palm.

200

Holding my hand out, I said, 'This winecup is nearly three hundred years old. You seem to value [my] cameras, watches and binoculars, but . . . no one in this world can make another winecup like this one again. This is a part of our cultural heritage. Every Chinese should be proud of it.'

The young man whose revolutionary work of destruction I had interrupted said angrily, 'You shut up! These things belong to the old culture. They are the useless toys of the feudal Emperors and the modern capitalist class and have no significance to us, the proletarian class. They cannot be compared to cameras and binoculars which are useful for our struggle in time of war. Our Great Leader Chairman Mao taught us, "If we do not destroy, we cannot establish." The old culture must be destroyed to make way for the new socialist culture.'[1]

China seemed, to the outside world, to have been turned upside down by the Cultural Revolution. China-watchers who had carefully traced the various ups and downs in the Politburo suddenly found that prominent politicians had disappeared from the line-up with new, little-known ones taking their place (in particular the politicians who would later be condemned as the 'Gang of Four', which included Mao's wife Jiang Qing). Almost all China's diplomats were brought home, and government offices often stood idle as the bureaucrats found themselves being pulled out for public 'struggle sessions' where they were forced to confess 'counter-revolutionary' crimes and admit being 'demons' and 'ghosts'. The educated were often forced into labouring jobs, either elsewhere in the city or by being 'sent down' to the countryside. Meanwhile, young men and women took advantage of free train travel to go around the country taking part in revolutionary demonstrations, crowding into Beijing to attend mass rallies addressed by the Cultural Revolution's guiding light, Mao himself.

Yet, for those who cared to look, there were clear connections with the past, although those connections were disturbing and seemed to make little sense. An example of this could be seen on 31 October 1966, when some 70,000 people gathered in Beijing to commemorate Lu Xun, who had died 30 years before. The rally was attended by Zhou Enlai, among other top leaders, and addressed by Yao Wenyuan, one of the 'Gang of Four', Xu Guangping (Lu Xun's widow, or more strictly speaking his partner), the former May Fourth era romantic poet and now cultural official Guo Moruo, and propaganda chief Chen Boda. Lu Xun, caustic, dry, and ironic, seemed like the last figure who would be praised during the Cultural Revolution. With a keen sense of the absurd and a dislike of dogma and authority, his ironic pessimism was in stark contrast to the bombast and fanatical certainties of the Red Guards. Yet Lu Xun was praised as a 'fearless and thoroughgoing revolutionary spirit' and, in Mao's words, 'the chief commander of China's cultural revolution'.[2]

Lu Xun is generally acknowledged as China's greatest twentieth-century author, and his status was burnished because he was taken up by the CCP and praised by them as the most important May Fourth intellectual. Why Lu Xun? His aesthetic excellence is widely acknowledged, though that was hardly a major issue for the CCP. He was certainly a Marxist by the end of his life, and a fellow-traveller of the Communist left, although maddeningly for the CCP, he never joined the Party. He also embodied the anti-traditional and nationalist strand of thought in the May Fourth Movement, in other words, the strand with which the CCP identified itself and wished to portray as the most important. He had also been an enemy of the writer Zhou Yang, who had gone on to be a high-level cultural official in Mao's China, and had now come under fierce attack in the Cultural Revolution; praising Lu Xun was a way of denigrating Zhou Yang. But perhaps most importantly, Lu Xun had the great good fortune to be dead.

Between Lu Xun's death in 1936 and 1966, when the Cultural Revolution began, China had gone through the most intense changes: the war with Japan, the civil war and the Communist takeover, the Great Leap Forward, and then the Cultural Revolution itself. Emotionally, the end of the May Fourth era and the start of the Cultural Revolution seemed centuries apart. In reality, though, many people who had been young and active as the New Culture took hold, born around the turn of the century, would still be alive and indeed not particularly old in the 1960s. That held perfectly true for the May Fourth generation of writers and thinkers. Some, such as Zou Taofen and Du Zhongyuan, had died during the war. But many others were alive. However, the length of time they had survived also made them politically problematic. Ding Ling, after being publicly humiliated during the Rectification movement of 1942, had been condemned in the Anti-Rightist campaign of 1957, and was in exile and prison in Heilongjiang province in the frozen far northeast for 20 years. Mao Dun had been dismissed as minister of culture in 1964, and had anyway not written any significant fiction since the period of the war against Japan. Lu Xun, though, had not lived to see the CCP take power, and therefore had said nothing about the regime which could get him into political trouble. However, it is hardly speculation to say that Lu Xun would have hated Mao's China. Unlike, say, Guo Moruo or Ding Ling, whose Marxism was fuelled in large part by their penchant for romanticism, Lu Xun had aligned himself with the radical left more in despair with the hollowness of the Nationalists than in joyous embrace of the certainties of leftist ideology. (Unlike Guo or Ding Ling, he had never been a romanticist, although his work was always marked by a weary, humanist compassion.) Nor, as we have seen, was he particularly keen on being told what to do, which was his main quarrel with the League of Left-Wing Writers, the CCP-oriented organization of the 1930s. Had he lived, it seems unlikely that he would have taken kindly to Mao's 1942 Yan'an Talks on Literature and Art, when Mao had declared that art's primary purpose was to serve the revolution (see Chapter 5).

No matter; the Party needed a literary icon, and enough of Lu Xun fitted the bill to get him the role. As early as 1940, at the time of his speech 'On New Democracy', Mao had singled out Lu Xun for praise as the only 'correct' May Fourth thinker; in the same speech, he had also developed the term 'cultural revolution' to describe the May Fourth Movement.[3] In 1966, Lu Xun's apotheosis went further and he was even transformed into a sort of revolutionary martyr: 'Lu Hsun [Lu Xun] died for the people', declared Huang Bingwen, a student at the Peking Institute of Geology, although the writer had actually died of tuberculosis.[4] The commemorative meeting of October 1966 was itself a travesty of Lu Xun's wishes. In his essay 'Death', he had specifically given his wishes for his funeral: 'Get the whole thing over quickly, have me buried and be done with it . . . Do nothing in the way of commemoration.'[5] This essay was one of the ones chosen for reprinting in the special edition of *Chinese Literature*

203

attached to the rally, so it seems that one of Lu Xun's most notable traits, irony, had not been transmitted to his literary successors. What qualities did they find, then, in Lu Xun, and why did they suit the iconoclasm of the Cultural Revolution?

First, Lu Xun was praised for his intolerance of the past: an editorial in the Party journal *Red Flag*, referring to his emblematic story 'Diary of a Madman', declared that he 'had an implacable hatred for all man-eating systems and cultures'.[6] 'A new world can only be discovered in the course of repudiating the old world', the editorial went on; 'This was precisely the course followed by Lu Hsun [i.e. Lu Xun]'. The editorial then went on to claim that this repudiation was expressed in the struggle against the Trotskyites which turned Lu Xun 'from a radical democrat into a great communist fighter' who 'stood with Chairman Mao' (again unlikely, since the latter only began to achieve paramount power in 1935, the year before Lu Xun's death).

Even though Lu Xun had never joined the CCP, the Party was not manipulating the truth in respect of his strong hostility to traditional culture, which other figures of the era such as Zou Taofen and Du Zhongyuan had dealt with more flexibly. Nonetheless, their representation was highly selective. Guo Moruo, one of Lu Xun's literary contemporaries, gave a speech at the meeting entitled 'Commemorating Lu Hsun's Rebellious Spirit'. 'The life of Lu Hsun,' wrote Guo, 'was one of fighting and rebellion'. This was Lu Xun reinterpreted as revolutionary romanticist, in other words someone like Mao or like Guo himself. The rest of Guo's piece goes to extraordinary lengths to show that Lu Xun's very late writings, particularly those in favour of an anti-Japanese front, 'can be regarded as an application for Party membership shortly before his death ... Chairman Mao later confirmed Lu Hsun to be a Communist, and that can also be regarded as approval of Lu Hsun's application by the Party.' With these links made, Yao Wenyuan, another of the 'Gang of Four', could make the leap and declare that the 'heroic Red Guards' who were 'vigorously destroying the "four olds" (old ideas, culture, customs, and habits) and fostering the "four news" ' were the true inheritors of Lu Xun's legacy.[7] One of the Red Guards, Liu Lu of the Long March Middle

School in Beijing, declared: 'In commemorating Lu Hsun, we Red Guards must learn from his revolutionary spirit, to rebel against imperialism, against the bourgeoisie, against revisionism; learn to be like him.'[8]

The pieces in the forum pay Lu Xun the dubious compliment of treating his works like those of Mao in the famous 'Little Red Book': isolated chunks of quotation taken out of context and imbued with meaning. The couplet from his poem,

> Fierce-browed, I coolly defy a thousand pointing fingers
> Head-bowed, like a willing ox I serve the children

was meant, according to Huang Bingwen, to show 'a concentrated reflection of his proletarian outlook', and his essay on 'beating a dog in the water' was meant to show that 'we must put destruction first and daring in the lead'. Chen Boda, the CCP's propaganda chief, was particularly impressed by the passage from the essay 'Death', in which Lu Xun declared of his enemies: 'Let them go on hating me. I shall not forgive a single one of them.'[9]

Yet the reduction of Lu Xun in this interpretation can be seen in a comment from the later part of Guo's speech, where he derided a contemporaneous tribute to Lu Xun in a Soviet magazine, which 'deliberately distorted and negated Lu Hsun's revolutionary fighting spirit, describing him as a writer "with deep humanity and love for people" '.[10] Lu Xun himself would probably have regarded such a tribute as a high compliment: for Guo, in the context of the Cultural Revolution, it was now the deepest insult. In this short, almost throwaway comment, the way in which the May Fourth legacy was perverted is summed up neatly. Throughout the essays in tribute to him, Lu Xun is given praise for his refusal to compromise and in particular for his lack of tolerance and moderation. Certainly his opposition to moderation, as we have seen, was an integral part of his rebellion against the 'man-eating' Confucian culture. Yet what makes this a bizarre reading of his legacy is that what Lu Xun was intolerant of was rigidity, authoritarianism, bombast, and hypocrisy. While, as the 1966 forum pointed out *ad nauseam*, he was permanently enraged at the Trotskyists, reactionaries, and Nationalists, he expressed his rage not because of a Damascene conversion to CCP ideological purity, but precisely because, in the words of that despised Soviet journal, he was a figure 'with deep humanity and love for people'. Xu Guangping, Lu Xun's pupil and lover, was wheeled out as an authority to rebut this foul claim, but had to deal with statements she had made a decade earlier to a Soviet journalist, when she had supposedly called Lu Xun a 'humanitarian' with a 'pacifist tendency'.[11] Xu now denounced this report as 'shameless slander of the worst kind'.

However, the pieces from which the quotations are taken, when read in full, do not have the certainty and confidence that Chen Boda and the others attributed to them. The piece ' "Fair Play" should be put off for the time being' observes 'Do not Chinese and foreign-style gentlemen often say that China's special features make foreign ideas of liberty and equality unsuitable for us? I take this to include fair play.'[12] Once again, this surely showed Lu Xun at his most mordantly ironic, something that escaped or was ignored by the literal-minded interpreters of the Cultural Revolution. Perhaps the comment most pertinent to the Cultural Revolution, though, was in the essay 'Thoughts on the League of Left-Wing Writers', from a talk given in 1930, when Lu Xun observed: 'Revolution is a bitter thing . . . not as romantic as the poets think. Of course there is destruction in a revolution, but construction is even more necessary to it; and while destruction is straightforward, construction is troublesome.'[13] In this last sentence, spoken more than three and half decades before, Lu Xun had put his finger on the essential problem at the heart of what would become the Cultural Revolution.

Lu Xun's memory did well during the first phase of the Cultural Revolution, in contrast to that of Zou Taofen. Zou had been praised during the 1950s for his move towards Marxism, portrayed as the model of a 'progressive' intellectual. Now, instead, he was condemned as yet another of the bourgeois humanists without whom China would have been better off. The Shenghuo bookshop which he had pioneered was condemned, after 'investigation' by Cultural Revolution inquisitors, as a 'black' (that is, counter-revolutionary) 'shop of the 1930s'. Considering what happened to the living intellectuals who fell foul of the Red Guards, perhaps Zou was also fortunate to have died two decades previously. His associates were condemned as 'renegades, secret police agents, and capitalists'. He and they would not have their reputations rehabilitated until the late 1970s, when the official verdict on the Cultural Revolution was reversed.[14]

Considering the Cultural Revolution

One way to deal with trauma is to erase it from memory, or at least separate it out from 'normal life'. It is not always a good idea to transfer the psychology of individual human beings to the 'psyches' of nations as a whole, but it is noticeable that nations do tend to deal with the most horrific parts of their histories by treating them as anomalous, in the way that a person claims that he did some dreadful deed while he was 'not himself'. Nazi Germany, Rwanda during the Hutu genocide of the Tutsis, or Cambodia under the Khmer Rouge are just some of the prominent examples of this phenomenon which our writing of history neatly sections off with the final-sounding dates of 1933–45, 1994, or 1975–8. Something similar has often occurred with the Cultural Revolution, 1966–76.

The first problem is that, in fact, that neatly defined decade, which has become known openly in China as the 'Ten Years' Disaster', has come under serious questioning: can the manic phase of 1966–9 be equated with the political doldrums of the following years, when relative political inactivity at home was punctuated only by the arrival of President Nixon from abroad? More widely, though, this sectioning off of the Cultural Revolution allows people to say that it was a terrible period when unspeakable wrongs were done, but it was a product of a particular time, and largely due to the actions of one man, Mao Zedong. There will likely never again be a would-be totalitarian state with a cult of personality in China, so the circumstances in which the Cultural Revolution took place would not recur.

It is indeed most unlikely that a new Cultural Revolution could happen in China. But the circumstances, and in particular the ideas that fuelled it, can only be fully understood in the wider context of

Chinese modernity. Nazism was a dead-end perversion of German modernity, but the years 1933–45 were shaped by trains of thought that had developed decades, even centuries, before the period itself; similarly for the Rwandan and Cambodian genocides, the latter being heavily influenced by both the Great Leap Forward and the Cultural Revolution.

The Cultural Revolution in China was largely caused by the obsessions of one man concerned both with the purity of his revolution and his own personal position. However, the patterns of thought that defined the path he took were largely ones that had shaped him in May Fourth. Mao's Cultural Revolution is an explicable end-point of the darkest side of May Fourth – obsession with youth, destruction of the past, arrogance about the superiority of one's own chosen system of thought – without the enlightenment that tempered the original – cosmopolitanism, critical enquiry, and universalism. The historian Prasenjit Duara has observed that 'The May 4th movement demanded, as did the Cultural Revolution in a different context, the break with the past in order to achieve Enlightenment self-consciousness.'[15]

The Cultural Revolution was a particularly strange time in Chinese history: different from the rest of post-1949 China as well as from the earlier part of the century. It is sometimes hard to see that, because China has had no shortage of extreme events: the War of Resistance to Japan saw perhaps 20 million deaths, and the Great Leap Forward killed over 30 million. But in those events, one can relate the reality to something ultimately explicable, events that can be traced more or less rationally, even if the results were irrational: the clash of nationalism and imperialism, or a tragic over-enthusiasm for a potent mixture of scientism and ideology. The Cultural Revolution killed far fewer people than either of the other disasters. But as one wanders in reports and documents, trying to reconstruct the period, one is continually struck by how hard it is to find one's bearings. A large part of this is to do with the way in which the Cultural Revolution used language as a tool. Violence in language can be a means of promoting physical violence. In addition, though, there is a further connection between linguistic disorientation and disorientation in understanding. The Cultural Revolution is per-haps the time in the twentieth century when language was most separated from meaning. Terms such as 'class', 'bourgeois', 'demon', or 'capitalist-roader' could take on whatever meaning a group or person in control chose to assign to them. 'Humanist' and 'com-passion' could become hideous insults; 'destruction' could become a term of immense praise.

This is not a trivial point. It mattered during the immediate events of the Cultural Revolution, because to be given the 'wrong' label could lead to persecution, suicide, or murder. But more widely, a society in which language divorced itself so thoroughly from mean-ing, particularly in relation to terms that contained value judgements, was one that also ended up abandoning responsibility. What people say generally matters because they are expected to be held to the meaning of their words. If that meaning is infinitely flexible and reversible, then its only determinant is whether the person using it is powerful or not. If you do not mean what you say, because what you say has no meaning beyond the immediate present, then it is impos-sible to imbue language with any system of values. 'Investigations' of past 'wrongdoing' during the Cultural Revolution were often seem-ingly based on meticulous examination of documents written by or relating to the accused (an echo of the *kaozheng* literary critical trad-ition in imperial China). But the interpretations of those documents were not subject to any constraints of context or meaning.

This led to the overall moral nullity of the Cultural Revolution during its most manic phase. The Red Guard period (1966–9) was defined almost entirely according to power relationships. It could hardly be governed by moral norms or understandings when there was no fixed meaning for linguistic terms which governed those norms. Those norms had been distorted hugely by the CCP before 1966, of course, and by the Nationalists and militarist government before them: 'peace', 'democracy', and 'progress' had always been loaded terms. The Great Leap Forward had created a world where norms of scientific and rational understanding were bent and stretched almost beyond imagining. But the early Cultural Revolu-tion cut those norms adrift from any anchored meaning.

The Cold War isolation of China during this period helped the process along. One of the advantages for China during the May Fourth era (and again during the 1980s) was that the forced exposure to ideas from abroad meant that its thinkers had to engage with the question of meaning. With so many new ideas and terms entering China and needing translation and interpretation, and with interaction between China and the outside world so constant, any interpretation could be (and was) questioned and criticized. The combination of a dominant governing party, a leader with a particular political agenda, and a culture hermetically sealed from the outside world meant that there was no tempering mechanism when that leader's project turned out to involve the assignation of violent meaning to words as part of a political project with devastating psychological and physical consequences.

Other societies have done something similar, of course. Victor Klemperer located the power of the Nazis in part in 'L. T. I.' (*Lingua tertii imperii*, or 'Language of the Third Reich'), a bureaucratized and sanitized linguistic cover for mass murder: phrases such as 'Special treatment', 'Final Solution', and 'Work will make you free'.[16] Nor was Stalin's regime reluctant to use bureaucratic language to make the Terror seem less like the state criminality that it was. Yet both these regimes had to stabilize even their perverted use of language over the years, a price to pay for relative fixity of their regimes. The Cultural Revolution did not truly stabilize in the 1966–9 period, and meaning remained inconstant on an almost daily basis during much of it. Force, rather than natural stabilization, was what ended this period.

What Was the Cultural Revolution?

The storm began brewing in 1965, when an attack on Beijing Vice-mayor Wu Han's play 'Hai Rui Dismissed From Office' by the critic Yao Wenyuan was published in Shanghai. The play was interpreted as critical of Mao, and came in for harsh comment. This paved the way for the announcement, in early 1966, of the policies that were to define the 'Great Proletarian Cultural Revolution'. Mao announced that too many of the Party's bureaucrats, from the highest levels down, had taken the 'capitalist road' and had let the revolution lose momentum. Top leaders such as State President Liu Shaoqi and Politburo members such as Deng Xiaoping and Peng Zhen were purged and subjected to humiliating and violent treatment during 'struggle sessions'. The most public face of the movement, though, was Mao's appeal to China's youth to take up the challenge of renewing the revolution which their elders had let slip. Mao enjoined China's youth in particular to 'smash the four olds', by which he meant 'old thinking, old customs, old habits and old culture'. Forming groups of 'Red Guards', young Chinese in cities all around the country vied to prove themselves the most loyal followers of Mao. While the demonstrations seemed spontaneous, there was in fact a significant amount of direction from the radicals in the Party leadership to destabilize their opponents.

To some outside observers, this was an inspiring way to breathe new life into the revolution. The British economist Joan Robinson wrote in 1968 of the importance of children and teenagers being encouraged to become Red Guards:

For some years, there had been talk of the problem of the third generation, the lucky children who take New China [the People's Republic] for granted and begin to think of what they can get out of it for themselves more than of what their fathers gave to build it . . . Now another generation of teenagers and students have been plunged into the revolution and become committed to it. Running their organizations without the aid of grown-ups, and later on Long Marches, they learned more about politics and about their own country in a few months than they ever could have learned out of books.[17]

She did note a darker tone to the movement: 'Violence was not in the rule book, but it broke out from time to time.'[18] Others, however, could not put such a rosy interpretation on the events. First, it was clear that violence, far from being 'not in the rule book', was in fact one of the most defining characteristics of the movement, and that a tremendous psychological oppression and loss of life was taking place. Then, smashing the old culture was being taken very literally

211

in many cases, as Nien Cheng's account showed. Red Guards went to many of China's finest monuments and landmarks, and systematically defaced them. For an item to give aesthetic pleasure without greater social utility was a crime in itself, and the guilty objects – statues, porcelain, books – were destroyed for their temerity. The Thousand Buddhas at Qixia Temple in Nanjing, the sculptures of which largely dated from the height of Chinese Buddhist culture in the Tang and Song dynasties, had many of their stone faces smashed. In Tibet, many of the most impressive monasteries were destroyed. Religious imagery in general was targeted as a particularly noxious relic of feudal society. Some of the most important places, such as the Forbidden City and Lama Temple in Beijing, were saved, apparently through the intervention of Prime Minister Zhou Enlai, but all across China the country's cultural heritage was smashed, in many cases beyond repair.

This type of wholesale destruction had not happened when the Communists took power in 1949, although the regime had not been slow, particularly in Beijing, to build new architecture that flaunted its power. Why did it happen in 1966? Before considering the way in which ghosts of May Fourth, although they were distorted and perverted, can be seen in the Cultural Revolution, we must briefly look at how and why the events of 1966–9 happened as they did.

The period between 1949 and 1966 had seen Mao take great political risks, not always with success. In the initial period after the victory over the Nationalists, the CCP had instituted wide-ranging land reform and redistribution policies, thereby shoring up their support among the rural population, as well as redistributing urban jobs away from the privileged classes who had previously held them, instead assigning them to people of now acceptable class background. However, Mao's enthusiasm in the nation-building project began to outrun reality, leading to the Great Leap Forward (see Chapter 5). Although the Great Leap policies were never openly repudiated, they did lead to Mao's position within the leadership being somewhat downgraded: although he remained chairman of the Party, the pragmatic Liu Shaoqi became the head of state. However, Mao was not content to fade into retirement. Although he turned 70 in 1963, he still harboured a number of concerns and obsessions which led to the Cultural Revolution.

First, his own personal power was clearly a consideration. Mao had resented the way in which Liu Shaoqi, Deng Xiaoping, and Chen Yun, the pragmatists in the leadership, had forced an end to the Great Leap, and he was determined to reduce their influence and raise his own.[19]

Second, Mao was genuinely distressed by what he saw as a slackening in revolutionary fervour by the 1960s. His version of the revolution had always been romantic. He was tied to the idea that an individual could lead a people to greatness through the force of his own will (shades of Lu Xun's Mara poets); he was also simultaneously attracted to an idealized picture of 'the masses' as a revolutionary force. By the mid-1960s, Mao was increasingly at odds with his colleagues' willingness to use themselves as a mediating point between the masses and the Party. Instead, Mao wanted the masses to be brought back directly into political action.

Third, and related, was Mao's obsession with youth. Though now in his eighth decade, Mao had never lost the fascination he had gained early in the century with the overturning of Confucian respect for age and hierarchy, and the exaltation of youth. The idea of turning once more to youth for his final battle was immensely appealing. More cynically, he also calculated that students in particular were the least immediately economically productive group in society, and therefore could be mobilized at less cost to the economy than workers.[20]

The most violent confrontations were in the cities, from which Mao felt the greatest corruption of his ideals had come. However, the countryside received large numbers of youths 'sent down' to the rural areas to learn from the farmers. The farmers were not always overjoyed to be cast in the role of teachers to their uninvited visitors. The total of deaths was far smaller than in the Great Leap Forward, but the social effects of the Cultural Revolution would in some senses be far longer-lasting. Schools and universities closed down for several years, and even when they re-opened, 'revolutionary' qualifications were often preferred to scholastic achievement when entry

213

19. A Cultural Revolution poster urging 'Resolutely Support the Anti-Imperialist Struggle of the Peoples of Asia, Africa, and Latin America'.
The rhetoric of anti-imperialism stressed China's role as a Third World mentor, and substantial foreign aid was given to newly independent African countries. However, the Cultural Revolution was highly xenophobic at home.

criteria were decided. Furthermore, the curriculum tended to be sterile and based largely on the study of Maoism. Many in that generation of youth later saw the period as one not of liberation, but the theft of their possibilities for education, something made even more bitter during the science- and technology-oriented 'open door' period after Mao's death.

The Cold War and the Cultural Revolution

The original May Fourth era was shaped in large part by the international atmosphere. It was the time of liberal internationalism, not just among statesmen, but also intellectuals, travellers, and readers. The era of World War II was, it goes almost without saying, shaped by the globality of that conflict: values became, at least in rhetoric, collective and focused much more on state and society and less on the individual for both the Allied and Axis powers. Mao's China was also inevitably shaped by the global framework of its own time, the Cold War, and in particular the First Cold War, from the late 1940s to the late 1960s, up to the period of détente. (The Second Cold War, from the late 1970s to the late 1980s, would also shape Deng Xiaoping's China, but in rather different ways.)

The Cold War in many ways provided a framework much more fitting to Mao's project than the original New Culture era because of its binary nature, the tendency to divide the world neatly into two (see Chapter 5). But for China, détente in the late 1960s became a Cold War crisis in its own right. The early Cold War, with its stark divisions, suited the tendency in Chinese politics for both the Communists and the Nationalists to define the country's issues in good/bad terms – Nationalist patriots versus Communist bandits, or bourgeois lackeys versus noble peasants. There were at least two major influences on this binarism. One was the continuing influence of the Confucian division of the world into moral and immoral. However, many of the ethical elements of the old Confucian system had been rejected by the CCP during the May Fourth years, and they had not yet managed to define what the new morality might be. The other major influence was Soviet Bolshevism. While this system of thought had been driven by ideas of political reform and techno-logical progress, it also contained the seeds of a Manichaean world-view which divided the world, again, into good and evil. In the USSR, the Stalinist purges and terror had been the ultimate expression of this tendency.[21] Both of these influences, Confucian and Bolshevik, had been apparent in the New Culture era, but the other political choices available then meant that the political system was not her-metically sealed, and other, more pluralist or sceptical ways of thought diluted the influence of these uncompromising political models. Maoist China, in contrast, did not allow pluralism, and became a world of good and bad choices, people, and classes, that bore less and less relation to actual behaviour, past or present, and had more to do with political decree and background.

20. **A demonstration in support of the Vietnamese Communist movement, Beijing, 1966.**
Support for anti-imperialist Third World movements was an important part of Chinese Communist foreign policy. Part of the reason for the split between the USSR and China in 1960 was Mao's contempt for what he saw as Soviet accommodation with the US.

The détente between the US and USSR in the 1960s threw this black-and-white binarism into a crisis. Khrushchev's condemnation of Stalin in 1956 was, for Mao, a betrayal not only of a great revolutionary leader, but also of the understanding that one did not betray one's own side in the two-way struggle. This threw the state into a crisis of identity which was somewhat different from the one it had suffered in the New Culture era. Then, foreign imperialism was a source of China's troubles, but also a resource on which the country could draw to strengthen itself. In the Cold War, China had shut off most external political options early on. There were attempts to break out of its binary affiliation, such as Zhou Enlai's attendance at the Bandung Conference for newly decolonized nations in 1955, where he attempted to put China forward as a leader of the emergent Third World group. However, Zhou's proposals did not fully reassure many of the newly independent Third World nations about China's good intentions. Instead, the increasing frostiness of the Sino-Soviet split led China, at least initially, to decide that its only option was to turn inward and trust to its own resources. Those resources included not just material goods, but ideological and intellectual resources. The Cultural Revolution happened as it did because China entered a somewhat artificial 'either/or' internal discussion about the options open to it, partly because the nature of the binary Cold War forced it to, and partly because the nature of the political system, Maoism, by which it maintained itself, made that sort of inward-looking binarism the most natural path to follow at that time.

Life and Death during the Red Guard Period

Back in the 1930s, Du Zhongyuan had pandered to his readers' prejudices by mocking the clothing of the ultra-modern young revolutionaries who wore 'swallowtail beards and leather shoes'. During the Cultural Revolution, wearing leather rather than cloth shoes might lead not just to mockery, but outright injury. 'From the outset,' noted the correspondent of the *Far Eastern Economic Review*, the Hong Kong-based news weekly,

Red Guard vs. fashion

The Red Guards had declared war on 'teddy' boys and 'flapper' girls, soon extending these words to include all with any pretension to fashion or those who wore any individual, unusual clothes. Boys with tapered trousers, girls with slacks, boys wearing 'rocket' (sharp-pointed) shoes – or even just leather shoes – and girls with stylish hairdos were the main targets ... Not a few girls and young ladies were escorted to the nearest barber shops to cut off their hairdos.[22]

It is as true for the Cultural Revolution as for the New Culture and wartime eras that the circumstances in which people lived shaped their understanding of events and their behaviour during them. For the leadership in Beijing, the decade from the late 1950s to the late 1960s marked the era of greatest isolation from the international community. For ordinary Chinese, the machinations of the Cold War were of little direct relevance. Yet the characteristics of China's position in the international community – isolated, paranoid, in fear of disruption and instability – were reflected in the country's domestic social organization. Ironically, the state and Party's fears about their own weaknesses were exacerbated by the reality of those two bodies' actual strength. In the New Culture era, the Chinese state was genuinely weak, and could not choose the option of being isolated because imperialism would not permit it: the by-products of cosmopolitanism and pluralism that emerged in China at that time were unintended, but were in a real sense a result of China's weakness. Now, in the 1960s, China was still vulnerable, as were all Cold War powers, and shared with those powers fear of invasion from without or subversion from within. But in this case, the strength of the state's power meant that turning inward was a realistic option. Turning inward did not have to mean doing so destructively. Tokugawa-era Japan (1600–1868) had kept itself mostly closed off from the outside world, and had developed a stable and culturally rich society. However, the combination of state strength with an ideology which was obsessed with the new, and praised dynamism, interpreted along class-based lines, proved both powerful and ruinous.

It is still much harder to document everyday life in Maoist China than in the Republican period before it or the reform era which

21. **Girls of the 'Little Red Guard' practise bayonet drill, Shanghai, 1973.**
The Cultural Revolution stressed the role of youth. Mao hoped to overcome what he saw as the stagnation of the revolution by encouraging the younger generation to rise up against their elders and renew the country's enthusiasm for eliminating 'feudal' and 'capitalist' practices.

followed. The lively intellectual and public culture of the Republic and the revived one of the decade following Mao's death were not paralleled at the height of Mao's control. Foreigners were a rarity in Mao's China; famously, huge curiosity was provoked by any tourist who appeared even in large cities in China after the reform policies opened the country up from the early 1980s. Foreign reporters, missionaries, business travellers, and novelists were all an integral part of the scene in the New Culture era, and some of them reappeared after 1978. So for the Tian'anmen demonstrations of 1919 and 1989 alike we have news reports and pictures from non-Chinese observers. In the last few years, archives have begun to open to enable researchers to consider the post-1949 period as history. However, the materials often peter out at the start of the Cultural Revolution; just as 1949 used to be the stopping-point for 'history', so 1966 now fulfils that function for many studies. Yet archival records do exist for that period, and slowly researchers from within China and even from outside are beginning to get access to them. In addition, materials from the Red Guard groups, government organizations, and of course the multiple memoirs of the era, many from participants still alive, have added to the resources that we can use to reconstruct the period.

What was life like, then, during the Cultural Revolution? The first three years, 1966–9, mark its most startling phase, when the mass movements, including the Red Guards, seemed to take over China and transfix the world. Some movements seized the opportunity to liberate themselves from the bureaucracy which seemed to many to have ossified the revolution. The most prominent example of this came from Shanghai, a city that kept its long-standing radical reputation even in the new politics of Mao's China. In January 1967, revolutionary workers announced that they had set up the 'Shanghai Commune', based on the Paris Commune of 1871, which for a few weeks attempted to collectivize property and social roles in a more egalitarian fashion than had ever been seen in China. This show of spontaneity worried the central Party leadership and they rapidly infiltrated and changed the leadership of the Commune to bring it more under control.[23] Yet the renamed organization, the Shanghai Revolutionary Committee, still had to acknowledge in its

declarations that the movement had started with 'the Shanghai proletarian revolutionary clique who had ... raised high the red flag of
Mao Zedong thought ... and bravely battled against the counter-
revolutionary black wind of economism ... and brought about a new
phase in the Great Proletarian Cultural Revolution in Shanghai.'[24]

Probably the most powerful feeling of liberation was that enjoyed
by China's youth, and one cannot underestimate the genuine elation
which they experienced. Dai Hsiao-ai, who later escaped China,
recalled his time as a Red Guard in Guangzhou, when he persecuted
'class enemies':

In truth, this part of the movement was, in some ways, the most fun of all.
We were free to do as we pleased, nobody checked on us, and we controlled
ourselves. ... I thought that what we were doing was important; therefore I
enjoyed myself fully. It was a great deal of fun![25]

Dai also enjoyed another privilege of the time: free train travel
around the country. This was ostensibly for the purpose of *chuanlian*,
revolutionary 'interaction' and exchanges of experience, but for
many young Chinese, it was the first chance they had had to widen
their horizons and see more of their own country:

The train was so packed that four of us were assigned to every three seats;
we struggled to find a place to sit amid quarrels and shouting. The fracas
tapered off after the train pulled out of the station, and our spirits were soon
restored. There was much singing of revolutionary songs. One fellow said
exultantly, 'Even when dreaming I never imagined being able to go to
Peking without spending a cent!' ... Others expressed their determination
to see the famous Yi Ho Garden ... whose beautiful scenery they had often
read about. A few even had great expectations of sampling Peking's famous
cuisine.[26]

Yet the ultimate joy was to catch a glimpse of the man who had made
it all possible. 'Comrades: let me tell you the great news, news greater
than heaven,' wrote a schoolteacher, Bei Guancheng, to his colleagues in Shanghai after he had taken the opportunity of joining the
crowds flocking to Beijing. 'At five minutes past seven in the evening
of the 15th September 1966, I saw our most dearly beloved leader

Chairman Mao! ... Today I am so happy my heart is about to burst ... After seeing the Red Sun in Our Hearts, I just ran around like crazy all over Beijing.' Bei concluded the letter, 'I have decided to make today my birthday. Today I started a new life!!!'[27]

 The streets of cities were marked by the verbal violence of the 'big-character poster' (*dazibao*) which was a principal means for factions to express their anger with their victims or with each other. One such poster, written by a Red Guard at the Beijing Aeronautical Institute, gloated over the demotion of Zhou Tianxing, a former high CCP official within the Institute, and his wife Lu Wen:

I was delighted to see that ox-monster and snake-demon couple Zhou and Lu shorn of their old prestige, laboring under our surveillance ... They are a pair of vampires, neatly dressed and smelling of perfume all over, but with souls putrid and rotten to the core. If you threw them in the latrine, you'd end up soiling the latrine! ... A joyous event like this one could only have taken place in today's Great Proletarian Cultural Revolution.[28]

People's experiences could be turned against them in an instant. The top leaders whom Mao perceived as his enemies came in for particular criticism. One of the most famous writers of 'big-character posters', Nie Yuanzi, was politically active at Peking University. With official blessing, she attacked two of the Politburo's biggest names in unequivocal terms. 'We recognize,' she said in November 1966, 'that in the clique in our party which wants to take the capitalist road, is [state president] Liu Shaoqi, and his number two is [Politburo member] Deng Xiaoping.' In its structure, Nie's denunciation was typical of many such accusations during this period. It contained many specifics, usually twisted to fit the political needs of the moment. For instance, it claimed that in 1962, when the economy was in 'temporary difficulties' (that is, the end of the Great Leap Forward disaster), Deng Xiaoping had unleashed a 'capitalist windstorm'. What was the nature of the storm? The answer: he had 'openly called for peasants to be given back their individual plots of land, and said that "It doesn't matter if a cat is black or white; if it can catch mice, it's a good cat."' This phrase would later become the slogan associated most strongly with Deng Xiaoping's reforms when he became paramount leader in the 1970s and 1980s: perhaps it is no surprise that he was so keen to rehabilitate it, since in 1966, it had been part of the 'proof' that he had been trying to destroy China through capitalist subversion. Further 'crimes' that had taken place in 1964 and 1965 were listed throughout the document to make the case. But the nub of the matter came at the end, where the seemingly forensic analysis of Deng's actions ended with the verdict that abandoned pretences of balanced judgement:

Clean out [Deng's] influence.
Whoever opposes Chairman Mao is our enemy and we must beat him down, and never let him be free.
Defend Mao Zedong to the death!
Uphold Mao Zedong thought to the death!
Ten thousand years of life to Mao Zedong! Ten thousand times ten thousand years of life to Mao Zedong![29]

The barrage was maintained over the weeks and months. Another one of Nie's attacks, in December 1966, increased the hysteria:

Everybody take a look at what a serious pass Liu Shaoqi and Deng Xiaoping's reactionary capitalist path has already led to – they are just like the reactionary clique of the Nationalists, they have openly oppressed the revolutionary masses, have carried out a 'white terror' [the term used for the 1927 massacre of Communists by Nationalists at the start of Chiang Kaishek's period of rule] and created counter-revolutionary methods which led to bloody incidents![30]

Liu Shaoqi and Deng Xiaoping were swiftly purged, and Liu would die from lack of medical attention while held under house arrest in the city of Kaifeng.

Ironically, Nie Yuanzi was herself later arrested and persecuted. But this did not end the attacks on other prominent victims. One of these was Wang Guangmei, wife of Liu Shaoqi, who was interrogated by young Red Guards, screaming at her for her 'bourgeois' tendencies because she had worn an attractive dress on state visits to Indonesia and Pakistan. The party veteran Bo Yibo was persecuted for having some 30 years previously renounced his membership of the CCP so as to be released from a Nationalist prison. He had done so on Party orders, yet now found himself the victim of a struggle session, where he appeared in a stadium in Beijing with a plaque around his neck denouncing his 'crimes'.[31]

Bo Yibo faced accusations because of association with the Nationalists at a time of great national crisis: the war against Japan. Something similar seems to have happened to a man whose name is not even known. The Sichuanese writer Fan Jianchuan, a collector of memorabilia from the War of Resistance and the Cultural Revolution, wrote many years later about a cracked earthenware cup he picked up at a sale. The cup was of no aesthetic merit, but it had scrawled across it in marginally literate characters the agonized message: 'I only remember the eight years of the War of Resistance. I fought the Japanese, and I took a bullet in my leg. I determinedly fought to the end and never left the line of fire! 15 September 1966.'[32] As Sichuan was the Nationalist stronghold during the war, it seems likely that this man was a veteran of Chiang Kaishek's armies, and had suffered persecution as a result. Fan observed:

Looking at this string of characters, I felt saddened and angry. In the eight years of the War of Resistance, he had dodged death and had for many years been considered to have had an honourable experience, and suddenly, overnight, it was considered shameful?! He ... had no place to appeal, in the political high temperature of that era, the majority of people didn't believe him ... so all he could think of was to write on this cup, and write down some words from his heart; he was surely sad and angry.[33]

Violence in language was intimately related to physical violence. It is hard to put a precise figure on how extensively either form was used and how one categorizes its results: for instance, how does one classify the many people who were not killed, but were pressured into suicide? But there were certainly many cases of people being physically attacked and even murdered. Nien Cheng's daughter, Meiping, was murdered by Red Guards. And Bei Guancheng, the young teacher who had written to his colleagues with such joy about his far-off glimpse of Mao in Beijing, fell foul of colleagues in his Shanghai school. There were several witnesses to his fate. A staff worker recalled, 'I saw some twenty students surrounding Bei Guancheng on the terrace of Building No. 5. Three or four students were beating him up ... A student by the name of XXX was most vicious and threw Bei to the concrete floor maybe five or six times.' A Red Guard and a teacher also remembered, 'From afar you could hear the noise and the "slam, bam, slam, bam" sound of him being beaten', and a Red Guard who participated in hitting Bei, but who later claimed to regret it, told the investigators, 'We got some bamboo sticks and other weapons to thrash him with and got all fired up'.[34] Bei's tormentors later admitted that they had gone too far; but it was too late for the young teacher himself, as on 2 October 1966, following the attack, he committed suicide.

Violence could reach extremes beyond even these levels. One of the most notorious, and still controversial, stories to come out from the Cultural Revolution is the incidence of cannibalism. This is one story for which the CCP has not permitted publication, even during the period of 1978–81 when people were encouraged to speak out against the abuses they had suffered. The most famous account of this phenomenon was Zheng Yi's book *Scarlet Memorial* [*Hongse jinianbei*], published in Taiwan in 1993, and banned on the mainland. Zheng took advantage of the more open atmosphere of the 1980s to investigate persistent rumours that in Guangxi province, in the southwest, local officials had encouraged not only the violent persecution of people whom they disliked, but also took the flesh from their corpses and cooked and served it for the local population. Wu Hongtai, a school principal from the town of Wuxuan, told Zheng Yi about the beating to death of Wu Shufang, a geography teacher at the school. This was a sadly common occurrence all over China. What happened next was not. Wu Hongtai recalled that his colleague Qin Chineng was forced to cut chunks of flesh from the corpse:

After he had cut out the heart and the liver, along with the flesh from the victim's thigh, the crowd took off. They carried some hunks of the flesh away in plastic bags ... Wu Shufang's flesh was cooked in three places: One was the school kitchen ... When the flesh was cooked, seven or eight students consumed it together.[35]

Cannibalism, of course, was very rare, and the reports of its occurrence have been disputed in later years. What is not in doubt is its immensely powerful symbolism. For centuries, Chinese culture had used the image of cannibalism as a symbol of society's values being turned thoroughly upside down, and so it made sense to use it to portray the most extreme part of an extreme period. Lu Xun, of course, had written during the May Fourth era in his short story 'Diary of a Madman' that Confucian culture had made China into a society in which people ate each other. Zheng Yi followed his account of the schoolteacher's gruesome fate by writing wryly, 'In its time, Lu Xun's short story . . . was merely a symbolic literary work, but unfortunately it had been realized under the great and glorious banner of socialism . . . When [children] are taught to consume their own species, surely that nation has lost all hope and its future.'[36] Zheng Yi's book came out when the bloody quelling of the Tian'anmen uprising was still a fresh and bitter memory. So 1989 as well as 1968 may well have been on his mind when contemplating the meaning of cannibalism.

Changing the Guard

The Cultural Revolution marked a generational midpoint between the May Fourth era and the new liberalization that would come after 1976. The key figures of the latter period were coming of age while those of the older generation began to leave the stage. For many of these elders, their departure was enforced, as writers and political leaders became victims of the purges.

Meanwhile, a generation that had known nothing but Mao's China came of age in the adrenaline-filled atmosphere. Among them was Su Xiaokang, who would go on to write much of the controversial television documentary *Heshang*, which would symbolize the last flowering of the optimism of the 1980s before Tian'anmen. Su was born in 1949 in Hangzhou, and in 1966 became a 'rebel' (that is, extreme Maoist) Red Guard in Henan, from where he made the journey to see Mao in Tian'anmen Square. 'The Cultural Revolution,' wrote the critic Richard Bodman, 'appears to have been crucial in forming his character, both as a rebel against the establishment, and as a self-critical thinker.'[37] When his father fell from grace during the political struggle, and he himself was dismissed from his post as a newspaper reporter, Su began a train of thought that would force him to bring a discussion of the Cultural Revolution into public discourse.[38] Also formed by their experiences were Chen Ziming and Wang Juntao, Red Guards from relatively elite families who would go on, like Su, to become involved with the political discussions on democracy in the 1980s via thinktanks and newspapers.[39]

Why, though, was Mao's call to 'bombard the headquarters' taken up so enthusiastically in so many quarters, and particularly among

MAO ZHU XI SHI WO MEN XIN ZHONG DE HONG TAI YANG

22. Poster of worker holding 'Quotations from Chairman Mao', proclaiming that Mao is the 'red sun in our hearts'.
Mao's cult of personality, built up since the late 1950s, was central to the Cultural Revolution. The 'Quotations', small excerpts from his writing collected in the 'Little Red Book', became immensely powerful verbal weapons in the battles between competing factions.

youth? Mao's prestige was beyond question, despite the debacle of the Great Leap Forward, and the Socialist Education Campaign and 'Learn from the PLA' Campaign of the early 1960s fuelled the cult of Mao's personality and thought in crucial institutions such as the Army. (This was promoted in a campaign coordinated by Defence Minister Lin Biao and Party propaganda chief Chen Boda.) Yet the call to overthrow the whole structure of the new society which had been created less than two decades before was a step beyond even the mass mobilization campaigns that had characterized the PRC since its foundation. One cannot overestimate the importance of Mao's persona in the development of the Cultural Revolution: it seems reasonable to say that if Mao had dropped dead in 1964, then there would have been no Cultural Revolution at all, at least in the form in which it happened. Mao's image and his thought, turned into an almost theological set of precepts, was essential to the movement. Lin and Chen's enthusiasm can be attributed to their concern for their own personal positions. But why did people in the wider society respond to the Cultural Revolution?

In large part, it was because society remained deeply riven. The purpose of the constant class warfare since 1949 was to remove those elements of the 'feudal', 'old' society which were held to blame for the shortcomings of pre-1949 China. And just as the New Culture Movement had attempted, at least in part, to redefine terms such as 'morality' and 'virtue' in the face of a new society, so the PRC had attempted to do so as well. Just as large parts of the New Culture redefinition had had to do with terms such as 'liberty', so the early years of the PRC saw morality linked inexorably with class background, as defined by the state. To be a large landholder or former Nationalist Party official, however low-level, was not simply a factual description, but a statement about how a person was to be perceived in a new hierarchy of morality as well as of status. The Cultural Revolution went back to this reconfiguring of society and declared that it, like earlier pre-1949 attempts, had failed. In doing so, it found some unusual allies.

The problem with Chinese society by the mid-1960s, at least in Mao's analysis, was that it was over-bureaucratized, complacent, corrupt, and inclined to think of 'economistic' goals such as growth or productivity without considering the importance of revolutionary ideology. Whether they shared that analysis or not, however, large parts of that society had a vested interest in the kind of complete overturning that Mao advocated. For a start, the establishment of the PRC had seen a baby boom in China, as had also occurred in the United States. Now that the country was at peace and that, at least initially, economic growth seemed to be a real possibility, people began to have families. As the population grew larger, though, it seemed less likely that there would be higher education, good jobs, or party positions for all the new citizens. The Cultural Revolution marked the coming of age of the baby boom generation; they would be teenagers who remembered nothing before the establishment of the PRC and now feared that society would not be able to live up to its promises to them. In combination with Mao using his prestige to blame this situation on his colleagues in the governing Party itself, this was clearly a potent complaint. This goes some way to explaining the pragmatic, as well as the emotional appeal of the Cultural Revolution to urban youth in China. However, the political scientist Lynn White has also observed something of a paradox that made the composition of the Red Guards even more interesting. In 1949 and after, as one would expect, it was the children of people from good 'red' backgrounds (peasants, workers, CCP cadres, and so on) who were given professional and educational opportunities. Children of 'black' class backgrounds (landlords, capitalists, Nationalist Party officials, and so on) were usually given much lower priority.[40] Class became a hereditary attribute: one's parents' class status privileged or disadvantaged one. But by 1966, many of the 'red' workers and their families were now comfortably esconced in the jobs and schools which the Communist revolution had made available to them. To them, the prospect of society being turned upside down once again was most unwelcome. In contrast, the children of the 'black' classes could see a chance to shrug off their seemingly indelible negative class label by backing Mao's campaign to the hilt. This led to the bizarre spectacle of ultra-radical Red Guard groups being made up of people whose class background was regarded as reactionary or bourgeois, while those of worker and peasant background formed relatively defensive or conservative Red Guard groups who wanted to try to preserve as much of the status quo as possible.

May Fourth or Not?

The May Fourth era was associated most with nationalism, 'science and democracy', enlightenment, and openness to the outside world. Surely it is hard to claim that the Cultural Revolution, notable for its xenophobia, intolerance, and scorn for technical knowledge, is the child of that earlier period of possibility?

Mao's use of the term 'Cultural Revolution', echoing his usage of the term in his 1940 speech 'On New Democracy', made the events of the 1960s his self-declared follow-up to the original May Fourth. In this, it is different from, say, the Tian'anmen Square uprising of 1989, which as we will see very consciously took on the mantle of the earlier movement at a grassroots level. However, the Cultural Revolution was not an uncomplicated inheritor of May Fourth's legacy. Its xenophobia, if nothing else, means that it was a distorted interpretation of the values of the New Culture Movement. Nonetheless, the mindset that inspired Mao, who had been in the thick of May Fourth and shaped by it in many ways, bears many indelible marks of the earlier era.

How useful is it, though, to argue that the Cultural Revolution was in some sense shaped by May Fourth? Let us again make a comparison with the European experience. It is absurd to argue that Italian fascism or Nazism were the *only* logical conclusion of European modernity. On the other hand, it is clear that they were heavily shaped by modernity, even while reacting against it in many ways, much though political expediency after 1945 has wished to argue that they were wholly anomalous experiences with no connections either to the past or the present.[41]

What, then, are the areas where the Cultural Revolution shows a debt to ideas that originated wholly or in large part during the May Fourth Movement, and which do not conform with the cultural traditions of premodern China?

First, the stress on youth. One of the most notable features of the most radical strain of May Fourth was its overturning of the Confucian veneration of age, wisdom, and experience. The journal *New Youth* was one of the most obvious aspects of this, but more widely, the messianic nature of the new thought systems, particularly of the radical left and right, that came into China from Europe, helped to fix the idea more strongly in the minds of urban youth that they, not the older generation, were destined to 'save the country'. The ideological machines of the Nationalist, collaborationist, and Communist regimes had harnessed the appeal to youth in the next few decades. The war against Japan in particular had forced a nationalist agenda (and even Wang Jingwei's regime, which had collaborated with the Japanese, portrayed itself as nationalist) on all sections of society, which meant that the opportunity for young people to express their own agendas was now heavily restricted. After the foundation of the People's Republic, top-down impositions of ideology were even more dominant, and the role of 'youth' was shaped heavily by the requirements of the state. So the Cultural Revolution was the first movement since May Fourth genuinely to place seemingly autonomous, free youth in the forefront of the political agenda. Since the May Fourth generation had also been deeply critical of the patriarchal nature of the traditional Chinese family, the calls to attack one's parents and elders took this part of the May Fourth agenda to an extreme conclusion.

Closely linked to the prominence of youth was the stress on iconoclasm, and related to that, violence. The defining characteristic of that most radical strain of May Fourth had been rejection of the Chinese tradition and the embrace of western thought. In the May Fourth era, the more porous nature of the political atmosphere meant that the strongest iconoclasts were tempered by the moderates (such as Zou Taofen) and the traditionalists who wanted to adapt or reject the May Fourth agenda. However, the writings and actions of Lu Xun, Chen Duxiu, and other influential thinkers did explicitly make the link between acceptance of western modernity and the utter rejection of the Chinese past. Mao's early writings show the strong influence that these ideas had had on him as a young man in

Hunan. Nor was violence absent in the May Fourth era. One of the Nationalist Party's strongest threads during that era had been 'anti-superstition' campaigns. Nationalist activists smashed or took over long-standing town and village temples on the grounds that they were representative of 'feudal' culture, ignoring the tremendous hurt that this caused to local communities for whom the temples had been a central part of their way of life.[42] The smashing of temples and other aspects of the 'old culture' in the Cultural Revolution was in some sense a direct inheritance by Mao from the most radical Nationalists in the May Fourth era. It was also influenced by the 'culture of violence' which shaped the Nationalist and Communist political culture during the Northern Expedition that brought Chiang Kaishek to power, and had also affected the wider society in which the two parties operated.[43] A statement in January 1967 by a group of Red Guards at Beijing Normal University condemned a 'discussion society on Confucius' in terms of which Chen Duxiu might have approved:

The cow-demons and snake-spirits who have taken part in this 'discussion society on Confucius' have called out for something or other called 'benevolent government' [*renzheng*] and 'virtuous rule' [*dezhi*]. They have attacked the socialist system and the dictatorship of the proletariat, and have openly advocated a comeback for counter-revolutionaries.[44]

Finally, one unacknowledged but clear cultural debt that Mao owed to May Fourth is clear not just from the Cultural Revolution, but also his other policies such as the Great Leap Forward. The Cultural Revolution was supposedly rooted in the idea that all external influences in Chinese culture should be rooted out, as well as all pre-Communist indigenous influences. Yet the mindset Mao revealed in setting the policy forward is heavily rooted in European romanticism, one of the most powerful cultural threads of May Fourth, exemplified by writers who had become prominent in the 1920s such as Yu Dafu and Guo Moruo. Romanticism encouraged the belief in a transcendent hero, in a figure who could drag an entire people into the future through the force of sheer will. The personal element in romanticism also helps us to understand why the often-made comparison of Mao with the emperors is not entirely helpful. This was very much a cult of the individual, not rooted in a tradition of ritual as the cult of the emperor had been in premodern China. To create the cult of Mao, both a modern sense of the self and the techniques of the modern mass media had been necessary.

In his celebration of youth, of violence, and of iconoclasm, Mao slotted neatly into one facet of May Fourth thinking. His language tended to be ideological and abstruse, but as he started to rise to power in the 1930s, his prose becomes far less distinctive, and it is harder, though not impossible, to see the romanticist threads in it – until the Cultural Revolution. Mao's romanticism also had several sources. From early youth, he had read and re-read classic Chinese novels of outlaw fiction, such as *The Water Margin*, whose knight-errant (*wuxia*) heroes had become literary archetypes. His contemporaries had also embraced European romanticism. Guo Moruo, one of the most prominent romanticists, became a Marxist in 1924, and found membership of the CCP a logical conclusion to his literary and political instincts. In 1958, in the midst of the Great Leap Forward, Guo declared that Mao was 'the greatest romanticist', though this did not save Guo from being persecuted during the Cultural Revolution, and having to confess that all his written works were of 'no value at all'.[45]

The Cold War and the Romance of Technology

Lu Xun once explained why he had become disillusioned with his membership in the Communist-sponsored, Soviet-influenced League of Left-Wing Writers in the 1930s. The Soviet idea of a perfect poem, he observed caustically, ran: 'O steam whistle! O Lenin!'[46]

Lu Xun was prescient as ever. The mixture of technological fetishism and ideological hero-worship in that 'poem' describes exactly one of the most notable threads in the Cultural Revolution, and one that can be traced directly from the debates on modernism of the Republican era. There is a strong romanticist tinge in the tendency to glorify industrial technology not for its scientific qualities, but for the virility and power which it seemed to offer the nation. Ironically, this obsession with technology was a first step towards the policy of the Four Modernizations which began in the late Cultural Revolution, and which, shorn of its associations with that period, have underpinned the whole era of Chinese reform from 1978 onwards. The early phase of the Cultural Revolution was less fixated on technology, although there are exceptions (such as the obsession in 1967–8 about the building of the bridge across the Yangtze at Nanjing). But the concern of the leadership for the state in which the manic phase of the Cultural Revolution might leave the economy meant that the emphasis on technology increased from 1970 onwards. The journal *Chinese Literature* introduced two sets of essays which were said to have been written by workers on the two major prestige engineering projects of the 1960s, the bridge over the Yangtze at Nanjing and the 'Shanghai 125,000 kw. steam turbo-generating set with inner watercooled stator and rotor' under the headline 'Heroic Songs of the Working Class'. In the same journal, another poet, Li Shouyi (who, a footnote states, is 'a PLA man'), also gives his verdict on the launch of the first Chinese manmade satellite, declaring 'Looking Happily into Space I Declaim my Determination'.

Spring thunder shakes/ Heaven and earth,/ The East is Red resounds/ Throughout the universe;/ The whole country rejoices/ Over the successful launching/ Of our first/ Manmade earth satellite . . .
A red propagandist – Our satellite,/ Revolution – /Its signal. /Doubled is the Revolutionary strength/ Of people the world over /When the signal reaches their ears . . . What the foreigners have/ We will have, /What they have not/ We will create. /Behold! /The red satellite is circling the universe; / Scared to death are U.S. imperialism/ And Soviet revisionism . . .
. . . Tomorrow/ The whole world/ will be red.[47]

Space technology has a particularly potent role in the political discourse of this era, not only in China but internationally. First, along with atomic weapons, space exploration was, at least in the popular imagination, at the cutting edge of scientific modernity. (A few decades later, it would perhaps be genetics that took that place in the west, although the launch of the Chinese Shenzhou spacecraft in 2003 showed that space still had high prestige in the

Chinese official mind some three decades later.) Second, the space race (again, like atomic weapons) was emblematic of the Cold War. Space exploration was both a literal and metaphorical arena for competition between the capitalist and communist blocs. For the most part, this was a battle between the US and the USSR; few other states had the resources to compete, even if they had the will, and even American politics was thrown into panic when the Soviets drew first blood with their successful launch of Sputnik in 1957. However, the Sino-Soviet split of 1960 meant that the Chinese, never entirely happy with being subsumed rhetorically within the Soviet embrace, now had to create a new language in which neither the Soviets nor the US had any influence on them, and in which they instead followed 'self-reliance' (*zili gengsheng*).

This rhetoric reflected both the existing concerns of the Cold War and the cultural preoccupations of the pre-1949 era. This led to one of the internal contradictions which ultimately showed the hollowness of the Cultural Revolution. On the one hand, as in the May Fourth era, it was obsessive about catching up with foreigners ('What the foreigners have/ We will have'), yet also with opposing them ('Scared to death are/ U.S. imperialism/ And Soviet revisionism'). This was a different combination to the anti-imperialism of May Fourth, which acknowledged (perhaps too much) the potency of foreign ideas while condemning their application in the form of imperialist aggression. The Cultural Revolution, like the Qing, wished the end results of technological modernity, but to fit them into a frame in which they were constructed as purely Chinese products. Yet the xenophobia (expressed as anti-imperialism, but in fact violent anti-foreignism) meant that this was always a well that would run dry eventually: the techniques that had been learned from the west before 1949 and then the Soviets until 1960 could be adapted to Chinese circumstances to a certain point, but the desire simultaneously to create a Chinese knowledge base drawing on western modernity without any foreign input, and furthermore condemning any association with foreign knowledge (Soviet or western), led to a dead end of spectacular proportions. The Cultural Revolution wanted the technology, but not the means of creating the knowledge base that went with it.

However, the earlier nostrums of the Cultural Revolution had not been rejected in 1970, as they would be in 1976–8 in a decisive and declared break with the past. Instead, the new emphasis on technology had to be made compatible with the declaration that it was better to be 'red' than 'expert', and that foreign influence must be avoided at all costs. This led to a series of uncomfortable confluences, as in the tales of the workers on the Nanjing bridge. This bridge was symbolic of the split between China and the USSR in the early 1960s, when the increasing fractiousness between Mao and Khrushchev had led to all Soviet engineers being withdrawn suddenly in 1960. A railway bridge across the Yangtze at Nanjing was one of the engineering projects that had been left half-built. The bridge was intended to be the first to span the river, and would for the first time make it possible for trains to run directly from north to south China without having to be ferried across the river on a transporter ship. The Soviets presumably thought that the Chinese would be unable to complete the project without outside help. It became the mission of Mao's regime to prove them wrong.

One short story dealt with the building of the Yangtze bridge in fictional form.[48] The hero, Wang Chao-chu, is an engineer who has worked his way up the Party ranks and has just been elected to the Central Committee of the Party at the Ninth Congress. The moment he has finished listening to Mao's talk, he rushes back to Nanjing to continue work on the bridge there, as an ordinary worker. However, the project seems in danger when the assistant chief director wails that 'the Party committee has informed us they're not inviting a single foreign adviser'. His colleague 'pompously' cuts in to say that when he worked for the Nationalists before 'liberation', 'an American bridge expert' had said that 'jumping up into heaven would be easier than building a bridge at Nanking [i.e. Nanjing]'. Wang Chao-chu would have none of this. 'Be self-reliant, work hard', as demanded by Mao Zedong Thought, was the only formula necessary to get the bridge built. Wang is inspired by remembering an improvised pile-driver he had managed to rig together when he had helped blow up a bridge during the Korean War; he then uses the same technique to piledrive the foundations for the Nanjing bridge. The workers on these projects were 'Heroes of the working class' who had carried out often near-superhuman feats, such as Hu Pao-ling, who dived beneath the surface of the Yangtze and 'explode[d] the myth that whoever goes deeper than 45 metres to survey underwater foundations for the bridge will be crushed'.[49]

It is not just to western eyes that this story, with its bulging muscles and heroic dialogue, has a touch of camp about it. Lu Xun would no doubt have been sceptical of it, although it might have appealed to Zou Taofen and Du Zhongyuan in their more hopeful and optimistic days. And indeed, the bridge was finished in 1968, and was used by the regime to show triumphantly that they did not need imperialists of either Cold War bloc to help them build up their own country. The trouble was that in reality, the overall expertise to finish the bridge existed because of the training provided by Soviet engineers between 1949 and 1960, and western ones before that. Continued development of technological progress, as the May Fourth generation had acknowledged, meant choices. China could continue to attack those who refused to believe in superhuman feats and the power of will, and could instead insist on valuing ideological purity ('being red') over technical expertise ('being expert'). However, to do that in practice meant that they would have to keep relying on Soviet aid and technical capacity. Or else China could develop its own indigenous technical capability, but to do so, it had to give technical expertise higher status. The bridge at Nanjing could be finished, in practice, because of the institutional memory of Soviet engineering advice; but anything new would be difficult, if not impossible, to develop. The opening up to the US came in part as an unacknowledged realization of this dilemma.

Zhou Enlai and his protégé Deng Xiaoping had little choice but to make learning from the west a key part of their Four Modernizations for the post-Cultural Revolution order, even before the Cultural Revolution itself had officially ended. High technology, peasant agrarianism, utter rejection of the outside world, and ideological hero-worship were not sustainable as a combination. They coexisted very potently for a few years, but this was high-octane fuel that would quickly leave the engine of state running dry. The late Qing had also seen an unsustainable combination of a desire for political introversion with foreign-influenced technological modernity. That had led, in reaction, to the May Fourth Movement and its all-out embrace of westernization. Perhaps it is therefore not surprising that the aridity of the Cultural Revolution led directly to the similarly uncritical pro-westernism of the 'new era' of the 1980s.

Divisions: Red, Black, Men, Women

The Cultural Revolution perpetrated stereotyped roles for women and men without admitting that it did so. While emancipation of women was one of the stated aims of the revolution, the showdown between Mao and Ding Ling in 1942 showed that in practice, the struggle of women was often subordinated to class struggle, as the endless campaigns of the post-1949 era ground on. The reality of women's advances in the PRC should not be denied, as they continued to be given significant roles in the labour market and to increase their numbers at the lower, if not the top, levels of the CCP. In practice, some liberation from patriarchal roles also occurred in events whose ostensible rhetoric was directed elsewhere, such as the Great Leap Forward. The Cultural Revolution, however, made class the defining lens through which everything else in society was refracted. Yet 'class' in the Cultural Revolution was more a political label of convenience than an attempt to define social status or position: terms such as 'bourgeois' or 'capitalist' became insults rather than descriptions, although they became so embedded in official writing that fiction written during the period is marked by casual descriptions of people as, for instance, 'a lower-middle peasant of short stature'. In this context, the default definition of these various roles was always masculine. This was not only because male exemplars tended to be given most prominence, although the dominance of men among these images is striking: Lei Feng the model worker, the workers at the model commune of Dazhai, the builders of the bridge over the Yangtze at Nanjing. The workers who built the 125 kW generator are described as willing to 'break with the convention that their job cannot be done when it is snowing. They vow: "We'll sink piles even though it snows iron."[50] 'Such are the heroes of our era, men who have created wonders', the article concludes. Virile and capable of working beyond what nature allows: these are not merely men – they are supermen. Their writings are also praised as differing from 'literary works of the bourgeoisie in their powerfulness and loftiness in sentiment. There are no mawkish passages, no personal wavering and sickly sentimentality.' Although this differentiation is made in class terms, there is an element of condemnation of perceived effeminacy behind it too; the condemnation of writers such as Yu Dafu, Ding Ling, and others in the past had often been in terms that castigated them as weak and lacking in bravery and masculine values. The Social Darwinist thread of the New Culture is at play here as well; once again, as had happened during the May Fourth era, China is painted as being under threat if it does not become stronger and more masculine.

These values seemed to leak into the reality of the Cultural Revolution as well. The May Fourth generation's multifaceted concerns, which had in fact allowed some feminist space, ended up being subsumed to a centralized, masculine nationalism in the 1930s as the sense of national crisis grew stronger. One of the results of the permanent sense of crisis that enveloped Maoist China during the Cold War and Cultural Revolution was that revolutionary women's lives, needs, and habits were portrayed as being identical to those of men, and often in terms of the same bulging muscles and calls for violence that decorated male icons: posters of the period make this clear. And in practice, female Red Guards and authority figures at that time are frequently recorded as being just as ready to use violence as their male counterparts.[51] Yet this was also a highly prurient and sexually repressed time: the May Fourth ideals of free love and escape from arranged marriage seemed a long way off. Marriages were now arranged by the head of one's work unit, with little way out of an unsuitable match except suicide. In 1919, a young woman named Miss Zhao had killed herself in Changsha because the patriarchal head of her family had insisted on her marrying a man she detested: Mao had written sympathetically about the case at the time.[52] Little seemed to have changed in the mid-1960s, except that one's work-unit leader,

239

23. Women's artillery squad (picture by Ding Zhuang and Yao Zhongyu, 1974).
During the Cultural Revolution, society and culture became highly militarized, and both men and women were portrayed in ways that stressed confrontation, violence, and virility. Images of women often used poses that had traditionally been confined to men.

rather than one's parents, had ultimate power. Sexual histories could also be used, particularly against women, to persecute them and accuse them of promiscuity. As a result, frank discussions of love and sexuality ceased. The Cultural Revolution was a profoundly reactionary phase in the history of personal relationships in China.[53]

Conclusion: A Strange May Fourth

This chapter has stressed that the Cultural Revolution was a distortion of May Fourth values, though its genealogy was clear, and that it was not the sole logical conclusion of those values. It is important to remember the major areas where the Cultural Revolution rejected important values that were central to the New Culture agenda.

Perhaps most notable was the Cultural Revolution's xenophobia. This was the diametrical opposite of the May Fourth era, which often unthinkingly embraced western ideas. By the mid-1960s, of course, the PRC was isolated from both major Cold War blocs, and therefore people associated with the Soviets might be as much in trouble as those who had had connections with the west before 1949. Yet it is worth remembering that the xenophobia of the Cultural Revolution was not the reverse side of a new devotion to indigenous values: in that sense, it was not the counterpart of the new cultural nationalism of the 1990s (see Chapter 8), nor of the cultural chauvinism of societies such as interwar Japan. Rather, xenophobia was the complement to the rejection of Chinese culture, meaning in this case not just Confucian culture, but all aspects of modernity, including much of the culture of the PRC, except for a very narrow selection of newly created works such as the model 'revolutionary operas' which were performed all over China.

The problems of China in the twentieth century have sometimes been attributed to an inherent 'cultural' problem with pluralism and inability to deal with the outside world. Yet this is surely not the case. There have been plenty of other political options offered to China, in which many politically aware Chinese have showed interest. There is no inherent reason within Chinese political culture that differentiates it from other societies in which foreign ideas have been able to hybridize and indigenize when they are given the right circumstances: after all, in China, the strength and optimism of the Tang dynasty saw a rise in Buddhist and Central Asian culture that was confidently incorporated into what it meant to be 'Chinese', and, as the makers of the documentary *Heshang* noted, the Tang is now regarded as China's cultural high point. The failure of modern political pluralist models to take root has been in large part because the options that have been chosen are ones which inherently do not permit difference. This is partly choice, but also global circumstances, including World War and Cold War, have pushed China into a situation where pluralist choices seemed frivolous or self-indulgent

241

at a time of greater crisis, whether that crisis was real or perceived. Confucian hierarchy and a morality that refused to recognize legitimate disagreement is blamed for much of the political inflexibility that has led to a harsh environment for pluralism in China since the late nineteenth century. But this is, once again, to take the most radical anti-traditional May Fourth activists at their own word, and to accept their definition of Confucianism as definitive. Chen Duxiu and Mao Zedong may have stressed the very real and devastating damage that Confucian hierarchy had done to women, the poor, and the oppressed in society. But neither would give any extensive consideration to whether the other side of Confucianism, the inherent obsession with ethics and mutual obligation, might be relevant to righting the wrongs in society. This possibility was brushed aside by these thinkers, whose train of thought became ultimately dominant, even though Confucian ethics continued to have relevance for the likes of Zou Taofen or Du Zhongyuan. But the Communists and Nationalists alike would make much greater allowances for cruelties caused by their own preferred system of thought, arguing that in this case the ultimate goal of a great, if undefined future outweighed the individual suffering of a few (or few million) living now.

The food metaphor of broken eggs being needed to make omelettes brings one naturally to Mao's most famous aphorism on the topic of revolutionary morality. 'A revolution is not a dinner party', he said. 'It cannot be so kind, so refined.'[54]

This is a sentiment that is utterly removed from what a Confucian could openly say, and in part marks Mao's lifelong and continued exhilaration with his liberation from the norms of the old society. This was, after all, the man whose first published article had stressed the need to 'shake the mountains by one's cries'. And it is true, unarguably so, that life in much of late Qing and Republican China was wretched and marked by an abandonment of all that the old Confucian social contract had claimed to offer. But it is hard to restrain one's thought that Mao, by the time that he made this particular remark, was already *inherently* opposed to the idea of being kind or refined. Confucian moderation could mean compromise with injustice, which was what had turned the May Fourth generation

242

against it; yet it could also mean mercy and generosity. Lu Xun had also condemned moderation and reconciliation in his final testament which had been so fêted at the mass meeting in 1966, yet one cannot help but see that statement tempered by his own humanism. For Mao, the romantic revolutionary, similar words take on quite a different tone, one of joy in refusing to acknowledge human bonds, 'old' morality, restraint, moderation, and the supposed 'virtues' of the Confucian world. Those values, in the 1960s as in the 1920s, belonged to those who refused to acknowledge the brave new world of the May Fourth radicals. In a China which seemed to have changed beyond recognition between the 1960s and the 1920s, the rejection of those values led to the Cultural Revolution.

China's reckoning with the Cultural Revolution is not yet over. Many who lived through it are alive today, yet discussion of the period has only just begun in earnest in China itself. It will not go away.

7

UGLY CHINAMEN AND DEAD RIVERS

Reform and the 'New May Fourth'

Tian'anmen Square was tense on the evening of 2 June 1989. A student from Qinghua University later recalled:

When we were close to Tian'anmen Square, we saw some military trucks being stopped. Many workers were trying to break tires and smash the trucks. They also cast bricks at soldiers and pulled them out to beat them... At that time the soldiers did not fight back.[1]

These were the last days of the protest, although the demonstrators could not know it at the time. For much of the last month, huge numbers of students, workers, and farmers had gathered in the Square, a million or so of them at the movement's peak, to protest against a wide variety of ills: the lack of democracy, high prices, social instability, and the seeming inability of the CCP to deal with the crises that seemed to be assailing China. Over and over again, the student leaders proclaimed the need for a 'new May Fourth movement'. The British reporter John Simpson recalled the atmosphere at a more relaxed time, a few weeks earlier, when the whole Square had the air of gentle carnival:

Ideas flourished. Several of the students I came to know told me they had learned more from their time in the Square than in the rest of their university education. It wasn't just hyperbole; everywhere you went, from the tents on the side to the encampment in the middle, people were talking about politics. They argued passionately, haranguing each other, issuing documents, writing reports ... And they believed what they told themselves: that the government wasn't capable of doing anything about them.[2]

The students were wrong. On the night of 3 June, the Chinese government sent tanks and heavily armed troops into Tian'anmen Square and the neighbouring boulevard, Chang'an Avenue. The number of people killed and injured that night has never been disclosed. But on the morning of 4 June, the square had been emptied. An era of openness and reform in Chinese history appeared to have ended. How, only a decade or so after the CCP had repudiated the excesses of the Cultural Revolution, could the confrontation between the government and its people have ended in such violence? What did it mean for the fate of post-Mao China?

In the 1980s, the world got used to 'China after Mao'. Deng Xiaoping's China, with western fashions in the streets and invitations to foreign companies to invest, was a very different proposition from the sullen giant of the Cultural Revolution. Visitors' expectations of collective farms and workers all wearing identical blue denim uniforms faded as people saw China turning to the outside world in a way that had not happened since 1949. To a large extent, that division of Communist China into Mao and post-Mao eras still operates today in the thinking of many in the west. The uprising at Tian'anmen Square bloodily punctuated the post-Mao period, but China's reforms and opening to the west seem to have gone on regardless since 1989.

The time that has elapsed since the Tian'anmen confrontation is now longer than the time between Mao's death and Tianan'men. We can now look at the aftermath of the 1989 tragedy in more perspective than the writers who had to assess its impact in the months and years immediately afterward. That reassessment has been visible in China itself, where the term 'new era' (*xin shiqi*) has been used to describe the decade between 1978 and 1989, a shimmering time of political and cultural promise whose attraction lay in its instability; the critic Xudong Zhang has compared it to Weimar Germany or the French Second Empire.[3] The May Fourth period and the 'new era' share similarities in that they mark a period that is past; not just in the literal sense, of course, but in the sense of being cultural moments that are fundamentally different from what followed them. It was a time of reassessment, of openness, and, like the May Fourth era, it has gone.

The Late Cold War

Since 1989, it has become commonplace to say that China is in a new era of nationalism. This formulation ignores the reality that a nationalist agenda has underpinned all of China's modern regimes. But it does seem that after 1989, the nature of that nationalism became more defensive and more self-glorifying.

One reason for this is that 1989, as well as being the year of the Tian'anmen uprising, was also the year when the Berlin Wall fell. The Chinese regime retained its power on a national level after the first event, but its place in the international system looked much more shaky after the second. In retrospect, of course, the 1980s were the last decade of the Cold War. But it is sometimes forgotten that the early 1980s were one of the coldest periods of that war: the election of Ronald Reagan in the US; the succession to Brezhnev by two geriatric and distrustful leaders, Yuri Andropov and Konstantin Chernenko; and the crisis caused by the Korean airliner shooting in 1983 all raised the global temperature in what has been termed the 'Second Cold War', after the fading of détente. Then, it was unclear until the very end of that decade that the old Cold War divisions were ending. In that light, China's 'new era' has to be interpreted not just as a domestic cultural phenomenon, reflecting some kind of return to May Fourth and the Republican era, but also part of the cultural orientations of the late Cold War, when the world thought that the international system needed to be adjusted, not that it was about to fall apart. Having been part of the Soviet cultural sphere in the early Cold War, China drew heavily on western cultural norms in the later part of that conflict.

The 'new era', after all, was the high point of China's leaning toward the west, and the US in particular. Having spent the 1960s isolated from both superpowers, the opening to China by Richard

Nixon in 1971–2 marked the beginning of China's re-entry into the international system. While it would be an exaggeration to characterize China as an ally of the US during this period, Deng Xiaoping kept a balance in his pronouncements by characterizing himself in 1984 as being worried about Soviet 'hegemonism', even while cautioning against American support for Taiwan.[4] Deng moved to an 'independent' foreign policy which would tie China to neither superpower. By the mid-1980s, after the rise of Gorbachev, there was a decided thaw in Chinese relations with the USSR, which would culminate in the Sino-Russian agreements of the 1990s. But this time, unlike in the 1920s, it was American culture, not Soviet, which dominated the arguments about China's way forward during the 'new era'. The 'culture fever' of the 1980s was shaped by the dynamics of the Cold War as the last of the twentieth century's 'grand narratives', and that makes the phenomena of this chapter, such as the apocalyptic television show *Heshang* and the obsession among Chinese readers with futurology, much more understandable as phenomena of their time. The Republic, after all, was a product of the Wilsonian interwar order culturally as well as politically. Similarly, the 'new era' was part of the international late Cold War order culturally as well as politically. In the early Cold War, the strongest cultural influence had been Soviet; in the middle part, China had rejected all foreign influence; and in the last part of the conflict, it turned to the other dominant cultural stream, the market-oriented culture epitomized by the US.

Because the CCP survived its 1989 crisis, unlike the regimes of Eastern Europe, it is too easy to assume that the government that remained in power was essentially the same as it had been prior to 1989. But even without the Tian'anmen confrontation, the nature of the government would have changed because of the new post-Cold War world of the 1990s. Unlike May Fourth, there is a clear, sharp end to the 'new era' of the 1980s because of that violent domestic confrontation that forced radical changes at home. But as in the 1930s, the changes in the 1990s would have led to domestic changes in atmosphere in China too, and the 'new era' would have disappeared, even if not as spectacularly as it did in 1989.

What was the nature of this 'new era' that lasted from 1978 to 1989?

Life and Liberty in the 'New Era'

Most of the people who work for the bus company go out with the people they work with. For example, a ticket seller might date a driver, or two ticket sellers might get together; it makes life a lot easier . . .

What do I like to do after work? Well, I read magazines and novels. I go out and buy them myself . . . What do I like to read? I read everything I can get my hands on. My favorite magazine is *The Younger Generation*. There's a lot of interesting things in it . . . The two of us are taking classes at a tailoring school. The tuition is six yuan a month.[5]

Bao Mujie, a 20-year-old bus conductor, gave this account of her life while clipping tickets on the number 44 route around Beijing in 1984. Her story is just one of a remarkable set of interviews conducted by the journalists Zhang Xinxin and Sang Ye in 1984 and published under the title *Chinese Profiles*. Their subjects were young, old, wealthy, poor: what they had in common was that they were part of the generation trying to make sense of life after the Cultural Revolution, mostly in Beijing. Bao Mujie's life story would have sounded very familiar to Zou Taofen: young, doing an unskilled job but taking night classes to move up in the world, loves reading (but nothing too complicated), keen to go on dates, but keeps her love life within the workplace to make things easier. A perfect target reader for *Life*, he might have thought, if his ghost were doing market research from beyond the grave. Yet although Bao's lifestyle might have seemed familiar to anyone who knew urban China in the 1920s, it would have been dangerous and near-impossible just fifteen years or so earlier at the height of the Cultural Revolution. Reading for pleasure, dating rather than having relationships decided for one, and trying to increase income by gaining education were all taboos until a few years before that interview. The political changes of the late 1970s and 1980s were, as in previous episodes of China's twentieth-century history, reflected in changes in everyday life.

Below, we will see how the intellectual, political, and cultural legacy of May Fourth reappeared in the 'new era'. But as in the first New Culture Movement of the 1920s, and in all the periods when Chinese thought went through revolutions, it was in everyday life that the context for new thought emerged. The original May Fourth Movement is inseparable from the teahouses, the narrow streets, and the Peking University campus where people met, argued, and ate and drank together while developing a genuine 'cultural revolution'. So first we need to know, how did life change in the Chinese cities of the 'new era', and what triggered those changes?

The period 1969–76 was an uncertain one in Chinese life. The chaos of the initial Cultural Revolution period had been shut down in 1969 by the People's Liberation Army (PLA) at Mao's command, and in the following years, few people dared to make any kind of individual gestures on a large or small scale: they had seen what happened to people who stood out. The major events of the period were the mysterious death of Mao's supposed chosen successor, Lin Biao, who was accused of having plotted against his ageing leader, and the visit of the US President, Richard Nixon, to China, opening up relations between the two powers which had been frozen since the Communist takeover in 1949. But there was little popular discussion of either. The 'Gang of Four' still had access to the highest levers of power.

That access ended with Mao's death in September 1976. In what was effectively a palace coup, the faction around Mao's eventual successor, Hua Guofeng, arranged for the sudden arrest of the Gang of Four, who were in the early 1980s placed on trial and given long prison sentences. Hua Guofeng represented what was known as a 'whateverist' faction, accused by his enemies of agreeing that 'whatever' Mao had said must be right; yet he also steered away quickly from the excesses of the Cultural Revolution, and permitted new liberalization in the economy, as well as opening up avenues for freedom of speech. However, the windows were only opened a little way. The aim was to allow the public to express their grief at the tragedies of the Cultural Revolution, and to lay the blame for that period squarely at the feet of the Gang of Four. It was not to sow any doubts about the CCP's legitimacy to rule in principle. Two new important types of writing emerged in 1978 as a result. One was called 'Scar literature' [*shanghen wenxue*], sometimes translated as 'literature of the wounded'. This was fiction about the experiences of the

Cultural Revolution, named after its archetypal piece, 'The Scar' by Lu Xinhua, which detailed the way in which a family had been split up during the Cultural Revolution. The story was first published on 11 August 1978 in the newspaper *Wenhui bao*. Its protagonist, Xiaohua, has seen her mother condemned as a counter-revolutionary in Shanghai in 1969. The only way that her daughter can redeem herself in front of her Red Guard friends is to disown her mother:

Young and hurt, she boarded a train and left her home in Shanghai, aged only sixteen . . . When her mother returned home she would find a note:
'June 6th, 1969
I've decided to break off all ties with you. Don't try to find me.
Xiaohua'
Her mother would weep and be desolate. Xiaohua thought of the love her mother had for her. But why had she become a renegade? There was no room for sympathy.[6]

Nine years later, Xiaohua is racked with remorse and arranges to meet her mother, who has been rehabilitated by Hua Guofeng. But in a melodramatic finale, her mother dies of a stroke just a few minutes before Xiaohua can reach her. The story is not written in a very elegant style. But in its ability to capture the effects of the Cultural Revolution on the social cohesion of an entire generation and their families, it caught the public mood very effectively.

At this time, a genre termed 'reportage literature' also re-emerged; while this was not fiction, but rather accounts of current and recent events, it was written in a self-consciously literary style.[7] One of the best-known examples is 'People or Monsters?' by the investigative journalist Liu Binyan, which detailed abuses of power by a party cadre in Heilongjiang province, again during the Cultural Revolution. Liu had originally been exiled to Heilongjiang in the crackdown after the 1957 Hundred Flowers Movement. Unlike the emotional simplicity of 'The Scar', 'People or Monsters?' was a savage, ironic piece worthy of Lu Xun:

Nineteen seventy-two certainly was an historic year in modern Chinese history. In Bin County, cadres' banqueting and drinking – and pilfering, grabbing, embezzling, and appropriating – all reached a new high that year . . .

[Corrupt official Liu Zhen] got a nickname: 'The Old Lady Official.' And another: 'Liu Ha-ha.' He would always nod his head and say, 'Ha-ha, fine, fine, fine.' . . . Was he born with this kind of character? Probably not. If one attributes such things to nature, one has to account for a remarkable coincidence. Why is nature so concentrated? Why, out of three members in the County Party Secretariat, were all three notoriously 'slippery' and 'treacherous'?[8]

This genre of writing followed in the footsteps of 'reportage' on social crises which had developed in the New Culture era. In the 1970s, it reflected a new openness, which increased as a power struggle developed between the newly installed Chairman Hua, and the long-standing Politburo pragmatist, Deng Xiaoping. Deng had been committed to revolution from an early age, studying in France during the May Fourth period, and taking part in the seminal events of the Communist march to power, such as the Long March. Yet he had usually been associated with the more moderate wing of the Party, leading to his being named 'number two capitalist roader' during the Cultural Revolution, and being purged twice (in 1966 and shortly before Mao's death in 1976) before rising to power.

Deng used his alliances within the Party to leverage Hua out of his positions of power between 1976 and 1978. Although Hua kept many of the grand titles he had acquired on Mao's death, the decision-making power seemed to flow more and more to Deng, until the latter was effectively made paramount leader of China from the Party Central Committee meeting of December 1978. Deng managed to remove Hua formally from most of his positions by 1980. A curious consequence of the new leader's campaign was that he authorized yet further protest against the past by the public (in a move to promote his agenda, which was aimed at reversing the policies of the Cultural Revolution). Most famously, he allowed 'Democracy Wall', an area in central Beijing where, for a brief period in late 1978, people were encouraged to put up posters praising Deng and condemning the excesses of Mao's period in power. Yet there were clear limits. The activist and former Red Guard Wei Jingsheng put up a poster demanding full democracy in China; he was arrested and sentenced to 15 years in prison, while Democracy Wall itself was quickly shut down. Deng was now firmly in control and no longer needed the 'spontaneous' expressions of support from the street which had helped him get there.

Wei Jingsheng's arrest was not the beginning of a period of immense repression, although the following decade saw periodic campaigns against 'spiritual pollution' and 'bourgeois liberalism' (notably in 1983 and 1987). In practice, a much wider arena for discussion of China's direction opened up. This was an inevitable part of the economic reforms for which the Deng era has become best known. The policy formulation that has shaped the post-1976 era is the 'Four Modernizations'. This was originally the invention of Zhou Enlai, developed in the last years of the Cultural Revolution, but the idea that China needed to modernize its agriculture, industry, science and technology, and national defence has been shared by all leaders since Mao's death. The policy disputes have come over how far and how fast China should follow that route, not whether it should be doing so in the first place. The reforms allowed Chinese farmers to set aside a proportion of their crops to sell on the private market, for entrepreneurs to set up their own businesses, and for universities and research institutes to devote themselves to developing specialist knowledge rather than obsessing about ideological purity. Typical of the era was a speech by Deng at the opening ceremony of a National Conference on Science held on 18 March 1978, when he said:

When views diverge on scholarly questions, we must follow the policy of 'letting a hundred schools of thought contend' and encourage free discussion. In scientific and technical work, we must listen closely to the opinions of the experts and leave them free to use all their skills and talents so as to achieve better results and reduce our errors to the minimum.[9]

Deng's words were carefully chosen. By mentioning 'a hundred schools', he was paying homage to Mao's legacy, but deliberately bringing to mind the brief open period of the Hundred Flowers Movement in 1957 rather than the Cultural Revolution. Explicit in

24. **Giant portrait of Deng Xiaoping, Shenzhen, 1978.**
Deng Xiaoping became paramount leader of the Chinese Communist Party within two years of Mao's death. This poster celebrates his famous speech which advocated that China should once again open to the outside world to promote the 'Four Modernizations' (agriculture, science and technology, defence, and industry).

this was a need to reverse one of the Cultural Revolution's most notable obsessions, xenophobia, and to learn from foreign countries. Chinese students began stream out of the country to study abroad, and 'foreign experts' in all sorts of areas came in to dispense their advice, often for handsome consultancy fees.

Chinese everyday life changed everywhere, as collective farms were dismantled, and new freedoms came to the cities. During Mao's period in power, the wide boulevards and squares which had been created during this period were generally bare, apart from banners with revolutionary slogans emblazoned on them. The 1980s, though, saw the return of private enterprise, and with it, advertising. The variety of clothes and make-up available was also widened, enabling people to express their own personal style much more strongly. The western press, at first slow to realize the sea-change happening in China's values, noted such innovations as China's first fashion show, or the opening of a branch of Pierre Cardin's restaurant *Maxim de Paris* in Beijing, with a brasserie attachment named *Minim*. These were not, in themselves, the changes that ordinary Beijingers or Shanghainese found most important. Another interviewee in *Chinese Profiles* noted: 'I've been to all the Western food restaurants in Beijing except Maxim's and Minim's. It's not worth going to them ... The biggest is for foreigners, the smallest is for Chinese, so I don't want to go!'[10] However welcome foreign investment was, the return of hierarchies from the era of western imperialism was not. Yet some of the most interesting changes were taking place in areas less immediately related to the foreign presence, though undoubtedly stimulated by it.

In some areas, it seemed as if the story of the early twentieth century was being replayed. The willingness of the authorities to show some cautious opening up was shown by the experience of the radio journalist Xinran, who was given permission in 1983 to run a 'women's mailbox' advice section on her Nanjing-based radio show 'Words on the night breeze'. Women wrote in on all manner of subjects, among which sexuality was a particular concern. 'One woman wanted to know why her heart beat faster when she accidentally bumped into a man on the bus. Another asked why she broke out into a sweat when a man touched her hand.' The Cultural Revolution's atmosphere of paranoia and prurience, which belied its iconoclastic rhetoric, had made such matters taboo, so 'all discussion of sexual matters had been forbidden ... As a result, two generations of Chinese had grown up with their instincts in confusion.'[11] The role played by Zou Taofen's 'Readers' Mailbox' was clearly not redundant half a century after *Life* magazine had ceased to publish. Sexuality, in the 1980s as in the 1920s, was yet another source either of joy or terrible danger in a new and untested world.

The roles of women and men, and the relations between them at work and in love changed again in the 'new era', in both positive and negative ways. The restrictions of the Maoist era were relaxed: women could wear stylish clothes and make-up again without fear of the Red Guards sending them down to the countryside by way of the barber. But the agenda of equality that the Maoist era had promoted also began to fall away. Of course, that agenda had always been heavily compromised. There were few top-level women cadres in China even at the height of Mao's prestige, and 'equality', in the Cultural Revolution, had often meant an equal opportunity to behave in ways considered to be the preserve of men, glorifying in machismo and violence. Periods such as the Great Leap Forward, when gender roles were broken down most successfully, were packaged in a project of such overall irresponsibility that it made the advances in gender relations almost beside the point. Yet in the mid-1980s, newly liberated employers now tried to squeeze women out of the workforce, encouraging them to take early retirement or cutting childcare facilities which the state would previously have paid for.[12] In addition, the reforms gave local Party leaders more autonomy to revive patriarchal behaviour that had never fully disappeared, and to let the state impose a 'one-child' policy that may have been demographically necessary but also put the onus of obedience squarely on women in their role as mothers.

Xiahai: 'Jumping into the Sea' of the New Society

The May Fourth era was notable as a period when intellectuals and students were genuinely influential in shaping modern China's ideas about itself. The 'new era' of the 1980s was also such a period. The opening-up of China impressed many of the urban educated elites: after the stultifying years of the Cultural Revolution, it was now permitted, even encouraged, for the Chinese to take on board ideas from the west. Universities could study foreign topics, the study of English and other languages was also permitted, and travel abroad was possible, although at a high cost. The long-standing thirst for education, which had been pushed out of the way by the Cultural Revolution, was clearly back. Li Xiaohang, born in 1949, had been a Red Guard as a teenager, and had used the opportunity to learn to swear and to abandon the frock she wore for trousers. But by 1984, as with so many of her generation, she realized that the liberation from school that the Cultural Revolution had provided was of little use in the reform era. 'I need a university qualification if I'm going to get security in the job I have been doing for four years,' she said. 'The management is going to start to grade our posts and without qualifications we'll be nowhere.' Others cashed in on the new boom in education. The manager of a new magazine declared:

I've started things off with a magazine correspondence course. I wanted to target in on young people who are interested in getting a higher degree by doing a correspondence course, so we've been using the magazine ... My magazine also provides its readers with information on how to pass exams as well as publishing self-improvement teaching materials. There's a knack to passing exams, especially the way the examination system is set up.[13]

China was slowly opening again, in the way that had been the norm until the long hiatus caused by the war against Japan in the 1930s and the coming of the Cold War in the 1940s.

However, the economic reforms brought serious problems. At Maoism's height, when China had practically no private markets, the fixed state salaries and the assignment of the whole population to 'work units' (*danwei*) meant that prices were strongly controlled from above. The opening of private markets meant that fixed prices no longer applied for large numbers of essential goods such as food. This was good for farmers and entrepreneurs, who made a profit from the higher prices, but problematic, often disastrous, for employees on state salaries that were not pegged to inflation and rapidly shrank in value, preventing these people from buying even basic necessities. Discontent about prices ran alongside resentment over the changes in China's employment structure. Having received a college-level education, many young people felt they deserved prestigious and well-paid jobs, but found that the only work that was made available to them was in unfancied provincial towns, and sometimes not even that. This resentment was no doubt fuelled by the long-standing tendency of the educated classes in China to regard themselves as more worthy of opportunity than the less literate groups in society. Gender disparities, which had always existed in China, but had in some areas been reduced during the Maoist period, now began to re-emerge and grow. In addition, student protests, taking advantage of the more open atmosphere, became louder. In 1985, for instance, the astrophysicist Fang Lizhi, also back from long exile in the provinces, toured university campuses around the country, including Peking University, encouraging students to stand up for more democracy in China.[14] These social problems fuelled a wider sense of political crisis, which shapes much of the writing and broadcasting of the 1980s.

Nonetheless, the opportunities that opened up were real. Another echo of the New Culture era was the revival of entrepreneurial culture as a way of creating a modern China, something which, of course, the Maoist era had frowned on heavily. Now, association with the 'capitalist road', provided that the term itself was not used, was much easier. Thirty-four-year-old Feng Yichun, who had developed a local building and repair team into a large construction company, said:

Now I'm the manager, my wage is 115 yuan a month, the same as a grade fourteen state cadre. On top of that, I get a responsibility supplement and other things that bring it up to 290. The joke is that I get more than the mayor. Of course some people object to me making this much. 'We've been making revolution all these years, and this is all we get, you so-and-so.' What I'd like to ask is, how many of them do as much work as I do? ... People can say what they like ... The situation's changed.[15]

Du Zhongyuan, with his brickworks and porcelain factory, would have found Feng a kindred spirit, and Zou Taofen might well have sniffed out the subject for a profile for *Life*. But they would have had to adjust their reporting style in at least one crucial way. Unlike the 1920s, when Du Zhongyuan could restrict his discussion of national salvation through business to men, women could also get involved in the new possibility of *xiahai* – 'jumping into the sea [of private business]'. Rural women could and did take part in the new agricultural private market. Urban women had an even wider range of possibilities open to them. The journalist Xinran recalled an interview with a university student, a young woman from a well-off background who dismissed the worth of reading 'dusty old tomes' and recommended titles such as *Modern Commercial Management*, *The Study of Personal Relations*, or *The Life of an Entrepreneur* for a real insight into 'human needs and desires'.[16] Fiction also reflected these changes, including the emerging phenomenon of 'neon-light literature', whose themes include the glamorous new women entrepreneurs in China's cities. 'Zhang Xin's business women wear Karl Lagerfeld and Valentino', observed the critic Daria Berg in her study of one of the best known of these writers, Zhang Xin, '. . . Coffee shops, revolving restaurants in five-star hotels, clubs and beauty parlours, places perceived to be the most modern and glamorous sites of the city, feature as the main places of action.'[17]

In many ways, then, there were echoes of the plurality of choices from the 1920s in the 'new era' of the 1980s. Also echoed, though, was that earlier era's sense of crisis.

What Sort of Crisis?

Many of the new voices who criticized aspects of the new China put themselves very consciously in the tradition of the May Fourth protesters. The uncertainty about the path China should take to achieve modernity was at the heart of the discussions of the 1920s and the 1980s. As with the consideration of the importance of May Fourth in the Cultural Revolution, though, the May Fourth legacy did not come down to later generations untouched: it had significant differences as well as similarities.

Let us look at the differences first. 'Saving the nation' was one of the most important ideas of the May Fourth era, and this was prompted by the politically divided and vulnerable state in which China found itself. In the 1980s, China was not divided between warring factions as it had been in the 1910s and 1920s, nor could its government meaningfully be termed weak, as the militarist-backed governments or even the Nationalist government of Chiang Kaishek had been. Furthermore, the other great enemy of the earlier period, foreign imperialism, was no longer a significant factor. There was still the question of Hong Kong, but even that was solved relatively easily in the 1980s, as the power relationship between China and Britain had been reversed in the preceding decades.

On the other hand, the similarities with May Fourth are striking. First, although traditional territorial imperialism no longer threatened China, there were certainly fears that the 'neo-imperialism' of the globalized (meaning westernized) economy and society could invade and subvert China. Then, the touchstones of 'science' and 'democracy' which had motivated the May Fourth intellectuals were once again brought into play. Both the state and its critics agreed on the importance of 'science', although its implications were strongly debated. The Cultural Revolution had done terrible damage to China's knowledge base, and its technology could not be improved without a crash-course in western-derived science. 'Democracy' remained much more contested. Again, the word itself was praised on all sides: the CCP reiterated, as it always had done, that it aimed to take China towards an ever more democratic future.[18] Yet the right to question the path of the CCP beyond what the Party itself would allow was one of the most important themes of the 'new era'. During May Fourth, finding political space had also been a problem. Although there was rather more variance of views in May Fourth China, which had been an ironic benefit of the very political disunity which the nationalist reformers of the age had condemned, during both the 1920s and 1980s the protesters had to work out the boundaries of what they could talk about, and what they could not. Finally, both eras show a remarkable willingness to take on board ideas from abroad. During May Fourth, Europe and Japan were the main sources of new thought, whereas America played a much more prominent role in the later period. But both periods contrasted with the more inward-looking nationalism that followed them in the 1930s and 1990s – in the first case, as a product of the war against Japan, and in the second, the more insecure world created by the end of the Cold War. The 'new era', just like the 'New Culture', ultimately seemed 'new' because both periods were imbued with a strong sense that things had to start again, and that what had come before did not provide a useful guide to how things could be in future.

The Culture Fever Debates

The early Mao era, at least until the Cultural Revolution, had seen Chinese political culture shaped by terminology taken not just from Marxist theory, but from Soviet experience. The 'new era' was notable for its openness, for the first time in China since the Republican era, to western and in particular American strains of thought. As in May Fourth, there was a significant school which introduced this type of thinking in uncritical terms: as the critic Xudong Zhang puts it, 'Throughout the 1980s, Western literary, aesthetic, and theoretical discourses were introduced to China, not as ideology, but as knowledge as such, that is, as science'.[19] The phrase 'culture fever' (*wenhua re*) was frequently used to describe this enthusiasm that was attached to the new knowledge.

Notable among the writers who found favour among China's more intellectual reading public were the American 'futurologists' who extrapolated huge, often apocalyptic, visions of the future from present trends. 'Nowadays,' said one interviewee in *Chinese Profiles*, 'Alvin Toffler's *The Third Wave* has itself become a wave,' though he added that 'John Naisbitt's book *Megatrends: Ten New Directions Transforming Our Lives* has turned out to be more useful and inspiring to us.'[20] This type of 'big picture' book was snapped up, still potent in a world where the last big story to date, the Cold War, was still very much operative, and the choice between a market and a command economy was still a valid one. Some of these writers, such as Toffler, were actually invited to China to give lectures and seminars, in the same way that Dewey, Shaw, and Russell had been invited in the May Fourth era. Chinese advocates of this school were very much working consciously in the tradition of the most westernizing strain of May Fourth thought. The historian Jin Guantao produced a well-known series of books entitled 'Toward the Future', which characterized China as an unchanging culture forced to deal with the impact of the west; Jin would later advise the makers of the documentary *Heshang.* In this way, the most radically pro-western strain of New Culture thought from the 1910s and 1920s was echoed once again.[21] In the meantime, the last members of the original May Fourth generation were finally disappearing. Ding Ling, rehabilitated and respected again after the end of the Cultural Revolution, died in 1986.

Typical of the enthusiasm among the intellectual classes for globalizing their discussions was the magazine *Reading* [*Dushu*]. Edited by Wang Hui, it was in some senses a spiritual successor to *Life*, since it was (and is) published by the Shenghuo-Dushu-Zhishi company, started in its original form by Zou Taofen. However, *Reading* was more highbrow in its writing and concerns. Starting in 1979, the journal's range of topics summed up the eclectic and enthusiastic consideration of the outside world which was finally permitted after three decades of Maoism. The editions for the 1987–8 year give some flavour of the variety on offer. Among the authors considered are the Welsh poet R. S. Thomas, the American anthropologist Margaret Mead, the South African novelist Nadine Gordimer, and the Soviet Nobel laureate Boris Pasternak. Engagement with then-contemporary politics is also evident: for instance, an analysis of Gorbachev's policy of *glasnost* (openness), examining the precedents for the term in Leninist thinking. In the mid-1980s, after all, the Soviet experiment in opening-up was running parallel with the Chinese one, and the results of neither was yet clear. A 'correspondent at Harvard' also provided regular despatches on topics such as management theory, which also turned up repeatedly as an intellectual point of reference in the now enterprise-oriented culture. Nor was Chinese thought neglected. The contradictions between Confucian culture and modernization were considered, as were articles by and about prominent thinkers of the post-Mao era such as

Wang Huning and Li Zehou.[22] The editors, writers, and readers of *Reading* were clearly making up for lost time.

The Ugly Chinaman and *Heshang*

Two of the best-known and most symbolic examples of the culture fever were a book and a television series.

The book, ironically, was written in Taiwan. Entitled *The Ugly Chinaman* [*Chouluo de Zhongguoren*], this was a tract by Bo Yang, the pseudonym of the gadfly Guo Yidong. Guo was born in the mainland in 1920, and had left for Taiwan in 1949. His politics were strongly anti-Communist, but he was also intolerant of dictatorship in any form, which soon got him into trouble with the Nationalist authorities on Taiwan. In the 1960s, he began to write satirical essays rather like those in the later work of Lu Xun, which dealt with the eternal dilemma of Chinese modernization. At this time, most political discussion on Taiwan ran in grooves shaped by debates from the mainland, as Chiang Kaishek's regime maintained the increasingly unconvincing stance that it was temporarily in exile and preparing to retake the mainland. Therefore, the May Fourth debates still had relevance for the Chinese population of the island, although they were more directly of concern to the incoming exiles such as Guo Yidong himself rather than the Taiwanese Chinese who had only formally become part of the Republic of China in 1945, and had never experienced the May Fourth Movement as part of their own cultural history. Though a mainlander, Guo Yidong was in favour of democratic modernization, if not wholesale westernization. However, his satirical essays drew the attention of the authorities, and in 1968 he was sentenced to 18 years in prison on trumped-up charges of association with the Communists. He was released early in 1977, after Chiang Kaishek's death had led to a loosening of the political climate under Chiang's successor as leader, his son Chiang Ching-kuo. By the early 1980s, Bo Yang was able to publish more openly, and in 1985 his signature essay *The Ugly Chinaman* went on sale to a storm of controversy.[23]

The 1980s was in some ways a similar time in Taiwan and in the mainland; neither state was a democracy, but they had retreated from the strong authoritarianism of their previous rulers (Mao and Chiang) and were exploring the possibilities of creating new spaces for discussion. Bo Yang's tract had therefore within a couple of years appeared in unofficial form in the mainland too, and was the subject of heated discussion on both sides of the strait. What did this controversial tract say?

The 'ugliness' of the Chinese, said Bo Yang, was not physical, but spiritual. His book was a denunciation of the Chinese national character; after decades of revolution and reform, the Chinese were still selfish, egocentric, unable to work together. He wrote:

Why are Chinese people's voices so loud? Because we do not feel secure. Therefore Chinese people shout especially loud, because the louder our voices are, the more right we must be. If we shout loud . . . the right side of the argument must flow towards us, otherwise why would we be making such an effort? I think that this has caused damage to Chinese people's characters, and has made our mental balance insecure. Noise, filth and chaos can also naturally influence our mental balance. Living in cleanliness or in filth is like living in two different worlds.[24]

The debt to Lu Xun, or to even earlier Qing reform writers such as Yan Fu, was clear, and the tone had hardly changed at all in five decades, or even ten. The tone also echoed the Nationalist New Life Movement of the 1930s, which also condemned the seemingly anarchic personal habits of the Chinese as a menace to the wider society. Bo Yang's most powerful metaphor was the soy vat. In China, vats full of soya beans are left to ferment, unexposed to the outside air, to create soy sauce. Chinese culture, according to Bo Yang, had also got itself into this kind of rancid stew, focused in on itself and unable to take positive influences from outside:

Owing to the pernicious influence of a very long period of a social system that was dictatorial and feudal, the Chinese people have been fermenting away for too long in the soy paste vat. Our thinking, judgement, and outlook have all been marked by the soy paste vat. Being within the confines of an inescapable soy paste vat for years on end has made us lose our ability to tell right from wrong, and we lack the courage of moral principles.[25]

Bo Yang's writing on 'The Ugly Chinaman' could never possibly have been published if it were not by a Chinese. (There is a long tradition, after all, that criticism from within a community is acceptable in a way that criticism from outside it is not.) Its political bravery is not in doubt. One should bear in mind that this was the period when political opponents of the Nationalists had been frequently tortured or killed, not just imprisoned.

However, Bo Yang echoed thinkers of the late Qing through the May Fourth era who argued that some essentialized 'nature' of the Chinese people was what caused their continuing crisis. 'I do not believe there is an [inherent] problem with the Chinese character', Bo Yang was careful to say. But he did believe that 'we Chinese should neither blame our parents, we should not blame our ancestors, but if we want to blame something, we should blame rather the sort of culture that our ancestors have handed down to us'.[26] These cultural characteristics apparently included 'noisiness, filth, and chaos'.

The television series *Heshang* was, in many ways, very different from Bo Yang's piece. If there is one phenomenon that sums up the 'new era', it is probably this programme. The title is not easy to translate succinctly, and has been rendered variously as *River Elegy, The River Dies Young,* or *Deathsong of the River;* we will use *Heshang* here. It may be the single most-watched documentary in the history of television, although it was only ever shown in China twice, in June and then again in August 1988. The show created a national debate, even a scandal, with top-level Politburo politicians reportedly fighting with each other about whether to praise it or ban it. What was the show, and why did it matter?

It is hard even to give a generic term for what *Heshang* was. It was a six-part series shown weekly which gave an account of Chinese culture and history accompanied by voiceover narration and carefully collated visual images. It is difficult to get hold of a copy these days, as it is banned in China, although copies circulate in Hong Kong and the west. Yet it is well worth the effort. Even now, the programme gives off a powerful energy. Each episode starts with a title sequence which takes in shots of large assemblies of Buddhists and Muslims prostrating themselves on the ground, followed by aerial shots of a huge bend in the Yellow River, giving way to close-ups of boats on the river. The theme music starts with ominous drumbeats, then segues into a haunting song: 'How many bends does the Yellow River make in the empire? On the bends, how many boats are there? On the boats, how many poles are there? And on the bends, how many boat-men steer the boats?'[27] Throughout the episodes, historical footage of railways, battles, and mass campaigns is mixed with reconstructions, interviews, and powerful abstract images. The first episode, 'Search-ing for the dream' [*Xunmeng*], ends with a shot of the planet Saturn; the final one, 'Deep Blue' [*Weilanse*] is punctuated by repeated images of crashing waves breaking on the shore. Throughout, stirring music is used as a backdrop.

Heshang was not a 'straight' documentary, though much of the footage was borrowed from another series which was. Instead, it was a polemic, arguing that nearly 70 years after May Fourth, Chinese culture was still in thrall to an outdated culture which was suffocat-ing China's development as a modern nation-state. The series used various symbols of Chinese identity, such as the dragon, the 'yellow earth' loess soil of the north, the Great Wall, and, most notably, the Yellow River, and suggested that far from being the symbols of a proud and sound civilization, they were emblems of a culture that had remained inward-looking and violent. Instead, *Heshang* argued, China should abandon its 'yellow' culture (yellow soil, yellow river) and instead embrace the 'deep blue' of the ocean; in other words, the outward-looking influence of the west.

Heshang was not a text by dissidents, in the sense of underground rebels. It could hardly have been shown on Chinese national televi-sion if it had been. Instead, it was a product of the uneasy compact between intellectuals and the state in Communist China.[28] A whole generation of thinkers emerged in post-1949 China who were often supportive of the CCP, but saw their role as offering advice to it, rather than obeying its orders without question. At times of repres-sion, this led these intellectuals into trouble. At more open moments, such as the brief Hundred Flowers and the longer 'new era', this could lead to a genuine and highly creative debate about China's future.

Heshang condemned what it saw as China's tendency to look inward, most markedly during the Cultural Revolution. It acknowledged that China's civilization had not always been dead and unwilling to open up to outside influence. The series praised the Tang dynasty (618–906) in particular, characterizing it as a time when the influence of Indian and Central Asian culture, particularly Buddhism, had made Chinese culture particularly glorious. The Vairocana Buddha at the Longmen Caves in Henan was the epitome of the way in which Indian culture influenced Chinese art to reach some of its finest achievements: even when using foreign artistic techniques 'they did not feel that the great Middle Kingdom [China] had lost face'.[29]

While alarmist, *Heshang* is less pessimistic in tone than Bo Yang's vision of the 'ugly Chinaman'. It was also a political manifesto, explicitly tying itself to a western-style modernization. The touchstone phrases of the May Fourth era were visible throughout the programme. China needed to 'receive the new light of science and democracy', and the Great Wall was condemned for holding in this 'peaceful, thoroughly ripened, agricultural civilization'.[30] The first episode ended with a challenge: 'It is industrial civilization! It is calling us!'[31] The combination of modernization and the condemnation of a supposedly somnolent and peaceful Chinese culture (largely a western construction) as contrasted to a Dionysian, creatively destructive modernity were staples of the earlier May Fourth discourse as well.

Heshang was the brainchild of Su Xiaokang, the former Red Guard, with various co-writers including Wang Luxiang and Yuan Zhiming. Su had emerged, like many of his generation, determined that the Cultural Revolution should never recur in China, and his reaction to that movement's xenophobia is reflected in the television series' fervent embrace of western modernity. It created a huge storm in the summer of 1988, when it was broadcast on CCTV-1, the central television station in China based in Beijing. The programme immediately received thousands of letters of support from viewers, as well as severe criticism. After Tian'anmen Square, in which *Heshang*'s writers and producers had become involved, the series was officially condemned in specially convened academic roundtables.[32] Among the accusations thrown at the authors were that they were slavish followers of westernization, that their history was inaccurate and tendentious, and that they called upon western theories such as geographical determinism and authorities such as the historian Arnold Toynbee that had long since fallen from favour in their culture of origin. Clearly, these arguments were more about the circumstances of 1989 than they were about the substantial content of *Heshang*.

However, it is possible to criticize what *Heshang* has to say, and by doing so, show why the positive as well as the negative in the May Fourth agenda continued to live on in China's intellectual and political culture some 70 years on. The destruction of the Cultural Revolution and Mao's cult of personality come under fierce attack in *Heshang*. Yet it can be argued that it was in part the willingness of some May Fourth figures such as Mao to follow up the destructive and near-nihilistic possibilities opened up by Lu Xun and others that allowed the ideology of the Cultural Revolution to form. And the desire to smash 'old culture, old thinking' in *Heshang* is clearly there; perhaps this is unsurprising in a generation made up of ex-Red Guards, even ones who utterly rejected the Cultural Revolution. The attack on Chinese culture as too somnolent and peaceful is also perhaps surprising from a generation who ostensibly rejected the Cultural Revolution. Clearly, the xenophobia of the Cultural Revolution was not shared by either *Heshang* or indeed the original May Fourth thinkers. However, there is a dangerously primordial tone to the series' desire to see fundamental changes in the Chinese 'national character', or *suzhi*.

Heshang was also the child of the late-flowering May Fourth Movement for other reasons. Its authors were overwhelmingly motivated by the desire to 'save China', but like their 1920s predecessors, they regarded change, destruction, and upheaval as positive phenomena. We saw earlier how the May Fourth ideals of free love, of youthful exuberance, and embrace of foreignness led many ordinary Chinese to retreat back into their familiar world. Even when they welcomed aspects of the new world, there were always others that left them terrified, as Xinran had found: how to fall in love, how to find a job, how to avoid being thrown out onto the streets.

The social changes which came with the reform period were almost certainly inevitable: the Maoist command economy, at least as it had been run in practice, was no longer a practical alternative. And yet for many Chinese, the old system meant guaranteed work, food, and status. Being encouraged to *xiahai*, jump into the sea of private business and enterprise, was a terrifying rather than liberating experience for many. Little of this emerges in *Heshang*. Instead, those who clung to the old system, in this case Maoist rather than Confucian, were treated as backward-looking. In Part Four, 'A New Era', there is an interview with Yuan Zhiming, then a doctoral candidate at Renmin University, later to go into exile after 1989, who declares that if China wants to change its psychology and character, 'then we will have to endure a great deal of pain'. In an earlier episode, the voiceover describes reform as 'a hugely painful period in which a civilization is transformed'.[33] The sense of crisis of the May Fourth era, and the equation of virtue and suffering, had come back to haunt China in its 'new era'.

The May Fourth thread that is least clearly acknowledged in the programme itself is *Heshang*'s stress on commercial culture. *Heshang* turned the tables on traditional Communist and Confucian hostility to private enterprise by praising it as the only way forward for a prosperous China; this was also a sensible manoeuvre to keep the economically radical, if politically moderate CCP secretary-general Zhao Ziyang in support of the programme. Zhao is mentioned by name in the episode that states 'only . . . a healthy market' can ensure 'opportunity, equality, and competition'.[34] This was not the 'classic' CCP model, which had been largely shaped by the choice made in the early Cold War to take the Soviet command economy as a guide. Instead, *Heshang*'s makers turned to the alternative choice in the Cold War binary.

Heshang self-consciously embraced a big, overarching narrative about modernity, stressing the need for 'national reconstruction'. With its stress on science, technology, market economics, and intellectual scepticism, it reflected the most Enlightenment-oriented models of modernity which had emerged during the original New

Culture period. Yet while embracing the grand narrative of May Fourth, the series also questioned it. In the last instalment, 'Deep Blue', the commentary stated:

The May Fourth movement of 1919, for the first time and with a thoroughly uncompromising spirit, unfurled the banners of 'science' and 'democracy.' Western cultural thought, including Marxism, was spread widely in China. But this progressive cultural tide did not completely wash away the accumulated sediment of feudalism in politics, economics, and in individuals. Over the past few decades, from time to time it has resurfaced, and at other times, it has frozen things solid.
It is as if many things in China ought to start afresh from May Fourth.[35]

The other driving concern of May Fourth, reflected again in *Heshang*, is the concern of the educated elites (the 'intellectuals') that China's success or failure is ultimately about them. This does not mean that they are given unstinting praise; episode six of *Heshang* declares that 'for thousands of years they have been vassal-like dependents'. Yet the commentary goes on to say that 'It is they alone who can direct the deep blue spring-water of science and democracy onto the yellow earth'.[36] Yet the conviction that the educated classes were the only ones who could save China, an idea which had so infuriated Mao, had clearly not been driven out by the Cultural Revolution, and once again echoed a mindset that went back even before May Fourth to the era when Confucianism had dominated.

Echoes of May Fourth: The Different Crises

Two of the biggest cultural phenomena of the 'new era', then, were considerations of China's crisis. They both consciously echoed the era of May Fourth, *Heshang* even more so than *The Ugly Chinaman*. Yet despite their shared sense of uncertainty at China's fate, the two works offer rather different, though related, takes on the May Fourth tradition. Bo Yang was very much in the tradition of Lu Xun. In contrast, *Heshang* brings to mind not so much Lu Xun as the sweeping social canvas of Mao Dun, or the exuberance of Guo Moruo. *Heshang* reflected the romanticist strain of the New Culture Movement, just as Bo Yang reflected a more restrained, small-canvas tradition. The attitude of the two writers towards China's perceived crisis was also reflected in their successors. Famously, Lu Xun regarded his mission as being to try and wake up a few of the sleepers in an 'iron house' in which they were burning to death, and from which there was still no guarantee of escape. The message mixed bleakness and hope, with perhaps more emphasis on the bleakness. In contrast, the impatience of the romanticists was for a better world which they felt they could almost touch; they just had to motivate the nation and the people to reach it. A similar division can be seen in the treatment of modern China in these more contemporary works. Bo Yang's account of the Chinese people is dark and suggests that a long, painful process will be necessary before China will be saved. *Heshang*, in contrast, argued that there was a swift, if not easy, solution to China's problems – 'It is industrial civilization! It is calling to us!' Perhaps this is unsurprising, as *Heshang*'s authors were, of course, critics within the system, whereas Bo Yang (like Lu Xun) made his criticisms while declining to join a political party. Again, like Lu Xun, Bo Yang was of an older generation when his essay was finally published (65 years old), whereas Su Xiaokang and Wang Luxiang, while not striplings, were only in their late 30s.

The romantic urge, seen also in the May Fourth and Cultural Revolution, meant that even while China was declared to be in crisis, that crisis was made to seem somehow glamorous and grandiose; the sheer size and depth of China's problem gave it a certain importance at the same time as making the scale of the crisis more daunting. In contrast, Bo Yang's Chinese crisis seemed more sordid and inward-looking. *Heshang*'s crisis was of a people who had followed Mao, a false 'peasant emperor', and had been led astray by the mighty river when they should have looked to the wide, blue ocean. Bo Yang's crisis was about a people who spat on the street, shouted too loud, and were too selfish and inconsiderate to think of others. *Heshang* gave the impression of a noble people waiting for salvation; Bo Yang, of a childish crew who needed a good slapping.

The two pieces, though, shared certain characteristics. First, they were both predicated on a centralized notion of what China should be. Although Bo Yang discussed events in Taipei as grist to his mill of 'proving' that the Chinese were uncouth and uncivilized, he did not try to differentiate between mainlanders and Taiwanese, nor Han Chinese and aboriginal peoples on that island. Nor did *Heshang*, despite its discussion of the significance of the 'yellowness' of the North China loess plains, seek to define any clear regional or ethnic differences within China. They reproduced the May Fourth agenda of 'saving the nation', defining the nation in a rather uncomplicated, centralized way in which local culture was of less importance, and women and men had the same needs and political agendas.

The other shared assumption was that China was in crisis in the first place. It seemed obvious to many that China was in trouble, but even though the May Fourth nostrums were being transmitted some seven decades later, the world had changed profoundly. The nature of the crisis of the 1910s and 1920s lay in several areas; first, imperialism; second, mass poverty; and third, a disillusionment with Chinese tradition. These problems did not exist in the same forms by the 1980s. Territorial imperialism was no longer an issue, although economic imperialism was an alternative source of concern (though not, it seems, to *Heshang*'s authors or Bo Yang); although China's per capita GNP was still very low, the terrible famines of the 1930s had recurred only when Mao was at his most fanatical; and Confucianism, as such, hardly had the grip on minds that it did in the early twentieth century (although folk religion continued to grow). Therefore, the crisis, such as it was, was at least in part self-created. China was in trouble in significant part because people *said* it was. The crisis did not relate so much to specific goals, for instance poverty reduction according to statistical targets, as to the continuing, only half-defined sense that China was something special, and there ought to be more to life than just being a large, populous developing nation. The implied, and sometimes stated, message of both pieces was that they were only so harsh in their judgements on the Chinese people and character because they thought it mattered. An offended commentator on post-imperial Britain in the 1960s once sniffed that the country was going to 'sink, giggling, into the sea'. The question that was not asked, in the case of China, was what did it matter if the nation succumbed to giggling and frivolity? The feeling seemed to be common at all levels of society that China *ought* to matter, and the rest of the world *ought* to take it seriously.

Both pieces, in retrospect, were very much products of their time. From the vantage point of the early twenty-first century, they seem to be period pieces, if not as distant as those of the original May Fourth era, then certainly not speaking to current concerns at the turn of the millennium. They are part of the 1980s now, as much as Reagan's talk of the Soviet Union as an 'evil empire', Gorbachev's policies of *perestroika* and *glasnost* (reconstruction and openness), and DeLorean cars. *Heshang* in particular was a product of the 'new era'. Its sensibilities and its ideas are rooted in 1988; the same programme could not have been made in 1998. This is not just because the programme itself was banned. The cultural climate of the 1990s and beyond was one in which the May Fourth agenda, the openness to outside ideas, was much less attractive as it implied wholesale westernization, where westernization now meant slavish adherence to the values of the one superpower left, the United States.

In the case of Taiwan, Bo Yang's argument had been superseded for perhaps happier reasons. For in the decade or so that followed the publication of *The Ugly Chinaman*, Taiwanese politics changed fundamentally from right-wing Leninism to liberal democracy. In 1989, Chinese politics on the mainland took a different path.

Tian'anmen and the End of an Era

More than one class, and more than one generation, were involved with the Tian'anmen demonstrations of 1989. Participants such as Su Xiaokang and Fang Lizhi were not students, and were shaped by the experience of Mao's China. But the prominent students in the Square, such as Wang Dan, Wu'er Kaixi, and Chai Ling, were much younger, in their early 20s. They had been born during the Cultural Revolution, but were too young to have been shaped directly by it. Yet, as we will see, even for this new generation, the ideas of May Fourth continued to have potency.

Why did the Beijing spring of 1989 end in bloodshed? The Cultural

Revolution had seized those aspects of May Fourth which it found most appealing: among them, the uncompromising anti-traditionalism and anger of Lu Xun. The 'new era' saw some of the Red Guards turn to other aspects of May Fourth: the need to open up to the outside world to help China develop, and the mystical, melancholic longing informed by a sense of crisis that saw a 'deathsong'. The spring of 1989 saw a new generation, many of whom had been babies during the Cultural Revolution, take up the challenge of May Fourth, and, moreover, saw a clash between two rival May Fourths.[37] One such version was the now 'official' one of the Communist Party, whose senior leaders such as Deng Xiaoping remembered the original events of 1919 and now strove to imprint their interpretation on them 70 years later. The other one belonged to the students, who sought to take up the mantle of their predecessors in protest when they had in turn been young and angry.

The generational change is important. Much of the story we have seen throughout the book has been the handover of the talismans of

25. Front entrance of Peking University, Haidian district, Beijing.
The old Peking University campus had been at the centre of the political ferment of the May Fourth era. In the 1980s, the new campus was also a hotbed of student activism for political reform. Professors and students also participated in the influential *Heshang* television series.

May Fourth from one generation to the next, with different people and different eras taking certain elements and ignoring others. May Fourth itself was the implicit absorption of the changes that had been brewing since the 1890s and before. The Cultural Revolution saw at least some figures from the triumphant strain of May Fourth put forward their own version of that legacy: Mao, most obviously, but also Guo Moruo, for instance. Yet at the same time, then unnoticed, the Red Guard generation that would, ten or twenty years later, produce Wei Jingsheng, Su Xiaokang, and Wang Luxiang was coming into being. And so in 1989, the talismans were handed on again, as the middle-aged Red Guard generation, which had tried to negotiate a space with the CCP in the 1980s, found itself caught up in a movement whose motivating force was a younger generation which preferred confrontation to compromise.

As in 1919, Peking University was the dynamo behind the Democracy Movement. This was not accidental: the students who led the movement were very aware of the legacy that their predecessors had left them, and spoke at length of the need for a new May Fourth Movement as the way to rescue China from the political and economic stagnation which it appeared to have reached. Wang Dan, a student at the university, had founded a journal named *New May Fourth* in late 1988, and had organized 'democracy salons' to discuss both issues of wider politics and conditions in the university and the city.[38] The study societies and small cliques of the university and its surrounds had also given rise to radical movements in 1919, among them the CCP. Other universities also became involved in the gradually growing movement for change.[39]

On 3 April, Wang Dan was instrumental in putting up an open letter to the authorities at Peking University, again noting that it was nearly 70 years since May Fourth, and recalling the legacy of Cai Yuanpei, the university's president at that time. The university, said Wang's letter, 'should serve as a special zone for promoting the democratization of politics'.[40] This was a sharp dig at Deng's economic reforms, which set up 'Special Zones', mainly on the coast, where tax breaks and other incentives were provided to attract foreign investment. The idea that the university could allow foreign 'investment' in ideas of democracy echoed Wei Jingsheng's call for 'the fifth modernization' in the face of the eminently economistic first four. Yet at the time, this petition was not much noticed. The real spark for the movement was the sudden death from a heart attack of former Party general secretary Hu Yaobang on 15 April 1989. Hu had been purged from the leadership (though not physically harmed, as Liu Shaoqi had been during the Cultural Revolution) in 1987 after student demonstrations in various cities had been blamed on him by his Politburo colleagues. While he was among the more liberal of the CCP leaders in the 1980s, his death now enabled the student radicals to portray him as an out-and-out democrat, an incorruptible who had been purged because he dared to speak truth to power (even though he had been in power). However, Hu himself was not the point, any more than Lu Xun the man had been the point of the 1966 commemoration at the start of the Cultural Revolution. The memory of Hu was the starting point for a much more radical programme, one that would have surprised even the dead former leader.

Wu'er Kaixi, the ethnic Uighur student leader who became one of the best-known faces of the movement, issued the 'New May Fourth Manifesto' on 4 May 1989 in Tian'anmen Square. He started by recalling the original event, 70 years earlier, and declared that it was the demonstrators' mission to 'carry forward the May Fourth spirit of science and democracy'. The Communist Party, he stated, 'has emphasized the role of science' but 'has not valued the spirit of science – democracy'. Bureaucracy, corruption, inflation, and the undervaluing of intellectuals had all prevented the reforms from genuinely advancing democratic reform. 'If the spirit of science and democracy, and their actual processes, do not exist, numerous and varied feudal elements ... which are antagonistic to large-scale socialist production, will reemerge in society ...' Wu'er Kaixi also emphasized patriotism: 'Prosperity for our nation is the ultimate objective of our patriotic student movement.'[41]

The most wounding May Fourth reference, perhaps, was to the existing regime as having 'feudal' tendencies; the idea that the CCP had ended up no better than the late imperial culture against which the original New Culture Movement had battled had also been a theme of *Heshang*. The 'feudalism' jibe was made even more explicit in an unsigned big-character poster of 3 May, which declared 'We must do away with the Confucianism that has made dogs of us! We must seize back the people's rights and power!'[42] This reference to 'Confucianism', though, as in the original May Fourth, is a constructed idea: not a flexible and potentially ethical Confucianism, but the kind of people-eating monster that Lu Xun had railed against.

The democracy movement, however, was not simply a movement to install free-market multiparty democracy in China, as some foreign media outlets portrayed it later; nor was it a failed version of the 'velvet revolutions' of 1989 in central and eastern Europe. Rather, it was an amalgam of various different agendas, often shaped by class, generation, and geographical background. For a start, the 1989 demonstrations were not limited to Beijing. Other cities, most notably Shanghai and Guangzhou, had large and noisy demonstrations, but they were dispelled much more peacefully than the symbolically most powerful ones in Beijing. (Jiang Zemin's rise to the top came in part because of his successful dispersal of the demonstrators when he was mayor of Shanghai.) Then, the student demonstrators dominated the movement both at the time and in much retrospective analysis, partly because they were more articulate and literate. By tying the demonstrations so specifically to the May Fourth agenda, the focus was always going to be on the students, who had their own concerns. Among the issues Wu'er Kaixi put forward were 'to respect intellectual work', an issue of specific interest to the students, permission for private newspapers, valuing education, and, more generally, reduction of corruption and establishing a 'democratic' government. Some of the documents produced by the students purported to put forward the views of workers and peasants, but these were reported as being entirely uncritical. One transcript of a conversation with a peasant ran: 'These students are terrific … They don't have any intention other than to speak for the people, and to try to improve the country's situation.'[43] Nonetheless, the peasant's account is linked with a reasonable and convincing-sounding analysis of how the economic situation had deteriorated for workers in the late 1980s. The tendency of Chinese elites to speak on behalf of the ordinary people had not diminished in 70 years since May Fourth, but the protests that they were making were linked to real concerns and problems.

The Communist Party's concern about 'bourgeois liberalism', by which it meant western-oriented liberal individualism, was expressed in its own definitions of 'democracy', based on Deng Xiaoping's 1979 declaration of the 'Four Cardinal Principles' in response to the Democracy Wall movement. The principles were adherence to socialism, maintenance of the leadership of the CCP, support for Marx-Lenin-Mao thought, and the people's democratic dictatorship. However, the status of the Principles as, as one critic put it, 'fundamental laws of nature, not subject to doubt or questioning', gave rise to serious questioning from participants in the movement. As the Confucian orthodoxies of the past had come under the fire of the May Fourth protesters, so did the Communist orthodoxy find itself criticized for having led China to a new period of stagnation in which 'China is facing the danger of being expelled from the world community'.[44]

There were attempts at compromise throughout May 1989, with top CCP leaders talking to student hunger strikers on television, and negotiators among the protesters trying to get the students to back down. The students attracted the most attention among the demonstrators, particularly from the international media, although the movement in fact contained a variety of different social classes. Just as their predecessors in 1919 had printed up banners in English to deliver at the foreign embassies during their demonstration, so university students in 1989 wrote English-language posters calling for freedom and democracy that would catch the eye of CNN and the BBC. (This did not make them any less sincere; just savvy.) Yet there were also prominent workers within the movement's leadership, who drew attention to the difficulties that the reform had caused for the ordinary labouring classes in China's cities, and even rural-dwellers came and participated at the movement's height. The movement's leaders were later criticized for not exercising enough control over their followers and ordering them to go home. But this gives a misleading impression of the nature of the movement: it grew under its own dynamics, not because its instigators had orchestrated it. To that extent, it was even less planned in advance than the 1919 demonstrations, which had been quite carefully arranged. It also differed from 4 May 1919 in another powerful respect: violence was not a significant part of the 1989 movement. There were cases where the police and soldiers were assaulted, particularly when the demonstrators felt threatened, but in as much as they were able, the movement's leaders prevented and sternly discouraged these actions. In contrast, the original May Fourth generation seemed to show little regret at the damage to people and property that their own demonstration had brought about in just one day, rather than the month or more that the 1989 movement lasted. Fang Lizhi's wife, Li Shuxian, lamented a decade later of the students: 'They thought they could imitate Gandhi.'[45] As it turned out, they were misguided in the face of a regime that was prepared to use violence against them. But in 1919, the students could also have imitated Gandhi: he and his tactics were famous enough by then, and Rabindranath Tagore's messages of spirituality and non-violence were also well known at the time, although they were rejected by most of the May Fourth generation when he visited China in 1924. Xu Deheng and other participants in the demonstrations of 4 May 1919, which had ended with assault and arson, could have condemned the violence of their fellow-participants. For the most part, they did not do so. In 1989, the message of non-violence was far more prominent.

Arguments still rage about whether the demonstrators or the government could or should have done more to bring the demonstrations to an end. The Party leaders did try to compromise. On 18 May, CCP secretary-general Zhao Ziyang was in a group of senior figures who visited hospitals in Beijing where hunger-striking students had been taken. He told them:

Your enthusiasm for democracy and the rule of law, for the struggle against corruption, and for furthering reform is very valuable ... The aims of the Party and government are the same as your aims ... So please don't continue fasting. You're young, and you've got a long time ahead of you for making contributions to the nation and the people, so you should take care of your health first.[46]

26. Exuberant demonstrator in Tian'anmen Square, Beijing, spring 1989.
The social pressures stimulated by the reform programme culminated in the
mass occupation of Tian'anmen Square in April 1989. There were attempts to
mediate between government and the demonstrating students and workers, but
the movement ended in bloodshed on the night of 3–4 June.

Other student leaders were given a meeting with Li Peng and other
prominent politicians on the same day. However, despite this clear
sign that a compromise was possible, the students and the politicians
were unable to agree. Ultimately, an agreement would have been
dependent on both sides trusting each other, and it was clear that this
was unlikely to happen. Soon afterwards, the CCP's senior leaders
decided to declare martial law. Over the next couple of weeks, military forces were discreetly brought into Beijing, ready for the final
showdown. By late May, the number of students in the square had
sharply reduced from the peak of mid-May, with tens rather than
hundreds of thousands staying overnight.[47] Yet this was still a situation out of control, as far as the government was concerned. At
6.30 p.m. on 3 June, loudspeakers in the square began to repeat an
ominous message: 'Beginning immediately, Beijing citizens must be
on high alert. Please stay off the streets and away from Tian'anmen

Square. All workers should remain at their posts and all citizens should stay at home to safeguard their lives.'[48]

As darkness fell, there were last-minute evacuations by demonstrators who sensed what was to come. Hou Dejian, a well-known rock singer who had been prominent in the square, spoke over a loud-speaker to those still present:

We know you're not afraid to die. Even if you now peacefully withdraw, you have already shown you're not afraid of death. We are like you; we are not afraid of death, either. So we hope everybody will leave the Square now. We must stick with our principles of non-violence as we leave, so clubs, bottles and anything else that might be used as a weapon all should be turned in at the monument.[49]

At around 4 a.m., troops and tanks moved in. On the way, they destroyed the 'Goddess of Democracy', a polystyrene replica of the Statue of Liberty that had become one of the best-known symbols of the movement. Although it seems that few, if any, people were killed in the square itself, there were reports of pitched battles and massacres along Chang'an Avenue, the wide boulevard that cuts through central Beijing and runs along the north of the square. Hospitals and mortuaries were filled that night, and although the full death toll has never been given, it seems likely that the dead ran into thousands rather than hundreds.

The Beijing spring was over.

The Nature of the New Era: Towards Chinese Democracy?

The 'new era' reflected many influences. It was a reaction to China's immediate history during the Cultural Revolution; it was a product of the binary choice between command and free-market economies that the global culture and framework of the Cold War had encouraged; and it reflected the longer patterns of thought that had run through the preceding century in China, in particular the May Fourth discourse on 'science and democracy'.

One of the repeated claims made about the student demands in Tian'anmen Square was that their calls for democracy were ill-defined and vague. This may be true, but as the whole of the twentieth century has seen Chinese thinkers trying to grapple with the question of what democracy means, it seems a little harsh to condemn a group of 20-something students for not having come up with the answer in a few months. Throughout the century, Chinese politicians and thinkers turned 'science', the rhetorical partner of 'democracy', into an object that needed no further analysis. The notion that science was disputed and that the scientific mentality was as dependent on doubt and scepticism as on certainty, was anathema to those who saw it as a type of panacea for all China's premodern troubles; science became a solution to the crisis of modernity, rather than a cause of it. At its most extreme, this overconfidence in the notion of 'science' could lead to the Great Leap Forward.

The same simplifying tendency has affected the debate on democracy. Democracy often became a sort of panacea: it is no surprise that the character *de* which was used to transliterate 'democracy' in the May Fourth era was also the character which literally meant 'virtue' or 'morality'. By seeking a new political vehicle in democracy, thinkers of the May Fourth generation were at least in part seeking a restitution of an old, lost sense of indisputable morality which had disappeared in a shameless age. The same criticism, then, was levelled at the Communist Party in 1989, which was repeatedly labelled 'amoral'.[50]

The uncomplicated notion of democracy, however, had the disadvantage that all essentialized concepts have. Being used as a means to power rather than an end in itself, 'democracy' in rather different senses was used throughout the century by political actors. For the Nationalists, it was the vaguely defined period after the period of 'tutelage' (that is, dictatorship). For the Communists, it was the victory of one class over another. Only for a few relatively isolated and powerless actors did it mean liberal, multiparty democracy. In the later part of the century, when the calls for 'democracy' as an answer to Communist authoritarianism became louder, there were people who did wish to interpret democracy on western lines. But it is important to understand the nature of much of the democratic debate of the 1980s. Contrary to the arguments of some that the Chinese do not understand the concept of democracy, there are many very sincere advocates of the concept. However, the essential-ized nature of the concept of 'democracy' in Chinese discourse has not put it in the best position to show two features that the American/West European tradition have come to consider important (and which have become important in democratic Taiwan; see Chapter 8): diversity and liberalism.

The notion of 'collective democracy' sounds a little forced to western ears, like one of the confections such as 'democratic dictator-ship' which Leninist regimes regularly threw up. Yet a constant theme in the democracy movement of the 1980s, just as in the 1920s, was that 'democracy' would be a means to create a strong, united China; the same has also been true of 'science'. The rights of the individual were stressed – the student leader Wu'er Kaixi observed that 'a democratic spirit is ... the protection of each individual's interests' – but generally, again, as a means to nation-building.[51] As such, the ideas of 'the people' and 'the nation' were often turned into a collective whole so that the individual was hard to discern, just as happened during the political rethinking of the 1890s and 1900s. This has meant that democratic issues that involve not binding, but rather breaking down, the ideas of the 'nation' and the 'people' have gener-ally been either ignored or rejected. As in previous moments of crisis, gender issues, for instance, were hardly ever brought up in 1989, even though one of the most notable things about the Chinese Communist leadership since 1949 was that it consisted almost entirely of men (Jiang Qing being the kind of exception few feminists would wish to embrace). More acutely, perhaps, 1989 marked a period of ethnic uprising in Tibet and Xinjiang, yet the idea that greater Chinese democracy must mean a platform for autonomous regional voices was rarely voiced. One could suggest that the demonstrators in 1989 could not deal with abstractions such as gender and ethnicity when there was a real crisis to be dealt with on their doorsteps. But the idea, implicit in this formulation, that such issues were an optional bolt-on to be dealt with when serious urban, male Han ethnic

Chinese concerns had been dealt with, is an integral part of the reason why the Chinese democratic movement has been less substantial than it might have become (or might become in future). This idea echoes that put forward by the Communists themselves that class struggle was the only true issue, and that other concerns, feminist, ethnic, and so on, would be resolved automatically in the wake of the breakdown of class structures. It also echoes the Nationalist reformers of the earlier part of the century, including the May Fourth era, who argued that imperialism and warlordism were so urgent that other concerns needed to be sidelined. Crisis was always a reason to abandon pluralism.

Another, seemingly unrelated event, also in 1989, shows why one could not necessarily expect democracy in China to be liberal. In April that year, male African students were surrounded in their university dormitories in Nanjing by screaming mobs of Chinese students yelling 'Kill the black devils!'. The African students became the victims of racist resentment because they were thought to be getting too friendly with Chinese girls. It is hard to know how many of the rioters subsequently took part in the student demonstrations of that spring.[52] But the race riots and the democracy movement are not necessarily entirely removed from one another as phenomena. Race, as in the May Fourth era, remains a much more essentialized concept in Chinese thinking even in the contemporary era, with a much stronger conception that it is a biological reality, rather than a social construction.[53] In a rather different sort of way, this can be seen in *Heshang*'s repeated agonizing over the *suzhi*, or essential nature, of the Chinese people. While in the case of *Heshang* the intention was noble, the idea that there was something fundamental to all Chinese that needed changing once again showed the concentration even of Chinese reformers on the collective over the individual. For this reason, the advent of democracy need not in itself mean the rise of liberal ideas. A China informed by ideas of racial essence could easily be democratic in voting terms within its own borders, yet monolithic and hostile to diversity politically.

Most of the democracy protesters – old-timers such as Liu Binyan and Fang Lizhi, middle-aged ones such as Su Xiaokang, and the young and rash such as Wang Dan and Chai Ling – went into hiding, and many into exile in the United States or elsewhere. The May Fourth era had allowed a precarious pluralism that let people who had gone too far politically slip away before being arrested or shot. The 'new era' may have given the appearance of a new May Fourth, but when the crisis came, the state showed that it had the power to crush the appearance of pluralism and reveal its true strength.

The students and workers in 1989 did not have clear political beliefs, and would have had little concrete idea of what to do if the CCP had, as they demanded, stepped down from office. They were arrogant towards senior leaders who were probably genuine in their desire for compromise (if only to relieve themselves from an embarrassing situation under the eyes of the world media). They misjudged their own authority. But they were also mostly in their early 20s, or in some cases just teenagers. Although they were verbally rude, they showed more physical restraint than their predecessors in 1919, who had nearly beaten a man to death and burned a house down but were nonetheless released after indulgent elders interceded for them. The most persistent and prominent demonstrators in 1989 were guilty of showing that their government could not cope and was inclined to panic. They were also guilty of being young, over-confident, and disrespectful.

These are not generally crimes that carry the death penalty.

8

LEARNING TO LET GO

The May Fourth Legacy in the New Millennium

It was thunder in springtime, calling forth the people's great consciousness of patriotism; it was a seed, bringing forth the great spirit of progress, democracy and science; it was a monument crystallizing the Chinese nation's limitless strength to flourish and develop; it was a bugle call announcing the song of a noble and undying epoch.

Looking out at the red building of Peking University, and casting one's eyes on the 'democracy square,' we praise the immortal 'May Fourth' spirit; we look back at history, look forward to the future, and move forward toward the glory of tomorrow.

Inscription on the reverse of the memorial to the May Fourth Movement, Wusi dajie (May Fourth Avenue), Beijing

In June 1989, when the protests in Tian'anmen Square ended in bloodshed, and China's 'new era' was equally abruptly frozen, the wider world still maintained the Cold War framework that had held it in place for over 40 years. The accession to power of the Soviet leader Mikhail Gorbachev in 1985 had changed the world utterly, and the Washington summit conference of 1987 had, in practice, ended the superpower confrontation. Yet the USSR still existed as a one-party state, and its eastern European satellites varied in condition from moderately lively to comatose. At that time, Poland, for so long an object of interest for Chinese thinkers, was the country most likely to break out of the Warsaw Pact mould, with its world-famous Solidarity opposition group, led by the former shipyard worker Lech Walesa, compelling the moribund government of General Jaruzelski to offer it places in government. But at the other extreme, on the

27. Monument to the May Fourth Movement, central Beijing.
A prominent memorial to the spirit of May Fourth. At the start of the
twenty-first century, the Chinese government showed its interest in claiming
the legacy of the movement by opening the 'old red building' of Peking
University as a museum in 2002.

surface, it did not appear as if the hardline government of Erich
Honecker in East Germany or the pseudo-monarchical regime of
Nicolae Ceaușescu in Romania were planning to give up their grip
on power any time soon. The failure of the 1989 Beijing Spring gave
no hint of what was to happen in Europe just three months later.

In the end, it was Hungary, another country Mao had looked at
with great concern in 1956, which set off the chain reaction, opening
its border with Austria in September 1989 and starting a series of
popular movements which forced Communist governments in central and eastern Europe, one by one, to cede power, whether in the
'velvet' revolution in Czechoslovakia, achieved almost without violence, or the bloody coup that saw the Ceaușescus fall over Christmas.
The next two years saw the USSR itself collapse internally. By summer of 1991, Gorbachev's country was running on empty: inflation
meant that foreign visitors could drink champagne for the price of a

soft drink in the west, housing estates peeled, dripped, and cracked for want of infrastructural repair, and popular feelings ran high against the reformist president. In August 1991, Gorbachev was briefly ousted by a small clique of conservative Politburo and KGB old-schoolers. The poverty of their alternative programme, which they appear to have thought through hardly at all, combined with anger among the population at large, expressed most vividly in the defiant resistance of Russian (as opposed to Soviet) President Boris Yeltsin, saw the coup collapse after just a few days. But it precipitated an event which neither the plotters nor Gorbachev himself had wanted: the downfall of the Communist Party, which Yeltsin declared illegal within Russia. Shortly afterwards, it became clear that the USSR, which had lasted for nearly three-quarters of a century, and had shaped world history for a large part of that period, was breaking up into its constituent republics. On 25 December 1991, the country of which Gorbachev was president disappeared. A great reformer who proved unequal to the hugeness of the task which he had set himself – a task too great for any one person, perhaps – disappeared from the world stage. He joined instead the twilight community of former statesmen and -women who appear in the public gaze only through occasional sententious editorials in newspapers, and, in the case of Gorbachev, an advertising campaign for a pizza chain, which quit its Russian business shortly afterwards.

Deng Xiaoping had no intention, even if the option had become available, to retire and become a jobbing editorialist and pizza salesman. The CCP leadership had to cope with the aftermath of Tian'anmen at home as well as the collapse of Communism as an alternative ideology to capitalism. 'Zhao Ziyang is China's Gorbachev', protesters in Tian'anmen Square had declaimed. Zhao, the prime minister who had been praised by the makers of *Heshang*, was hastily sent into house arrest during the crackdown, as his comrades thought fearfully about the fate of the Soviet Union befalling China. For the rest of 1989, rumours of civil war and rebellion circulated within China, being reflected in the foreign press even while official publications declared the uprising a 'counter-revolutionary rebellion' and showed pictures of concerned citizens offering slices of watermelon to thirsty soldiers cleaning up calmly after the tur-moil. A new national campaign of Socialist Education was promul-gated, as the leadership changed to reflect the new hard line: Li Peng, the Prime Minister, was a Soviet-trained engineer whose stolid con-servatism was a long way from the theatrics of Hu Yaobang or Zhao Ziyang. Nobody would be touting *him* as the face of a new open China if a second *Heshang* were ever to be made.

And what is obvious, now that the events of 1989–91 have faded into contemporary history, was that it worked, at least in the short term. China did not break up into civil war. The regime may have lost legitimacy in many important sectors of society, though the difficul-ties of asking such questions on the ground in China make this hard to quantify, but it certainly did not lose power. Even its international position, which seemed potentially shaky after sanctions were imposed in the wake of the uprising, was aided by the Bush adminis-tration's signals that business as usual with China would continue, and the willingness of China not to veto the 1991 Gulf War in the United Nations Security Council placed it firmly back in the good books of the now western-dominated international community.

Yet the wider changes following the end of the Cold War affected Chinese political culture deeply, even if there was no sharp break with the past in terms of a change in the governing party. Clearly the after-effects of Tian'anmen shaped developments in a significant way. But even if Tian'anmen Square had not happened, or if the demonstrations had been peacefully broken up, as in 1985 or 1987, or as in other cities in China in 1989, the ending of the Cold War binary would have altered China's self-presentation and self-confidence very strongly. In addition, the often naïve optimism of the 'new era' would likely have given way to more cautious assessments of the impact of foreign culture, just as happened in the aftermath of the initial, often uncritical pro-westernism of the original May Fourth era.

Yet the new political leadership did not entirely live up to the hardline reputation that it earned in the years immediately after Tian'anmen. There were figures who felt that the economic reforms had been responsible for the showdown and wished to slow or reverse them, but Deng Xiaoping, in his last spurt of reforming energy, made it clear that he continued to place his personal prestige behind their continuation. He also promoted a new generation of leadership. The former mayor of Shanghai, Jiang Zemin, was promoted to the top positions of State President, Secretary-General of the CCP, and Chairman of the Central Military Commission (the powerful body controlling China's armed forces), and during his decade in control, China's economic reforms accelerated, probably irreversibly. Deng died in February 1997, but his legacy now seemed safe. In 2002, under the arrangements encouraged by Deng to prevent the arbitrary changes in leadership that had happened in Mao's China, there was a seemingly smooth and publicly announced change at the top, as Hu Jintao was promoted to replace Jiang as Secretary-General of the Party, and then as State President. It was expected that the third prize, control of the military, would also transfer to Hu shortly afterwards, although the Beijing rumour mill buzzed with stories that Jiang had moved on only reluctantly, and was clinging by his fingertips to the last of his positions for as long as possible. Nonetheless, none of these changes caused the wider turmoil in society that the Cultural Revolution or the arrest of the Gang of Four had done a generation earlier.

The Two Cities Revisited

The aftermath of 1989 profoundly affected the two cities which had run through the story of China's twentieth century, Beijing and Shanghai. The 1989–92 period, when it seemed briefly that reform might be stymied by the conservative counter-reaction to the 'turmoil' in 1989, in retrospect seems more like a last gasp of the old order. What was to come instead was a complex mixture: relative economic liberalism, but a turn away from uncritical internationalism to an ambivalent nationalism which craved acceptance by the world order while also seeking not to be dominated by it. These tendencies were reflected in the development of Beijing and Shanghai.

Beijing, of course, had to come to terms with the violence that had ended the 'new era'. Tian'anmen Square remained heavily policed on the anniversaries of 4 June, particularly in 1999, when the entire square was shut down for 'renovation'. Yet the global changes of the post-Cold War era gave the CCP a new opportunity to legitimate itself. For in the 1990s, the Chinese government projected an image very similar to the one that the 1930s equivalent, the Nationalist government, had done, and used similar logic to condemn the excess freedoms of the 'new era' just as the Nationalists had attacked the wilder shores of the New Culture period. And just as in the earlier period, although the sense of crisis was in part created by the government itself, it found a wider resonance among the population as a whole. In the 1930s, China projected itself as a developing nation-state attempting to enter Woodrow Wilson's world of international order, but being thwarted by the forces of imperialism, and after 1931 Japanese aggression in particular. In such a climate, frivolous free-thinking was a luxury that had to be discarded. In the 1990s, China reinvented itself as a developing state, no longer revolutionary but instead keen to participate in the wider world order, while staying on guard against outside threats. These threats were far less easy to define clearly than the Japanese invasion of the 1930s, but many of them originated in the new American-dominated international order. Among the fears were economic imperialism, protectionist barriers that would bar Chinese goods to the US market, and attempts by outside powers to prevent unification between the mainland and Taiwan. Common to them was a growing perception in China that the new order ought to allow China to emerge as the major regional power in East Asia, or even as a world power, and that US hegemony was preventing this from happening. This conviction united people at all levels of society – political leaders, intellectuals, and citizens whose opinions were sought in polls.

This feeling manifested itself in one of the most important campaigns in Beijing, run once unsuccessfully, and once triumphantly. This was the battle to win the Olympic Games. In 1990, the Asian Games were held in Beijing, something of a success for the regime considering that rumours that the country would dissolve into civil war had been circulating only a year before. The Chinese leadership then nominated Beijing as a candidate city for the 2000 Olympics. Yet painstaking efforts, involving plastering the city with Olympic posters and placards, came to nothing when, in 1993, the winner was announced as Sydney. The rejection of Beijing, though, fuelled the sense of nationalist resentment, with conspiracy theories about how dark forces, probably linked to the US, had manoeuvred to prevent the Chinese capital from winning. To be sure, there was probably a significant level of concern in the Olympic Committee about the Chinese bid, though it would have had more to do with an unease that it was just four years after Tian'anmen rather than a desire to crush China's hopes of being seen as a global player. Yet the realization that another Olympic snub might turn China away from international society probably helped China's second bid along, and in 2001 it was announced that Beijing would hold the Olympic Games of 2008. In addition, Tian'anmen was now more than a decade in the past, and China had successfully held the UN International Conference on Women in 1995, as well as lobbied for entry into the World Trade Organization in the same year as their Olympic bid. China was firmly back in the world community.

The Olympics are used by all cities as an excuse to upgrade their infrastructures, but Beijing used the years before and after its bid to rebuild on a monumental scale. A massive metro railway network and the clearing of miles after miles of the old alleyways (*hutongs*) of small houses were among the more notable changes in the city. Many mourned the destruction of a long-standing way of life in Beijing backstreets. Fewer people regretted the anti-pollution measures that the Beijing authorities imposed on the city, giving it blue rather than smoke-grey skies for the first time in decades, although rumour had it that the factories, which of course gave thousands of people their livelihoods, were closed down at sometimes brutally short notice. In addition, the transformation of much of Beijing into an internationalized modern Asian city like Tokyo or Seoul continued at great speed. In 1990, China's first McDonald's opened in Shenzhen, across the border from Hong Kong. A decade later, there were hundreds all over the country, with two on Wangfujing Dajie, the most prestigious shopping street in Beijing, alone. Japanese and western brand names – Kodak (Zou Taofen might have been pleased to see the return of

28. The Bund, Shanghai, 1995.
The architecture of this waterfront street has changed little since the 1920s, although Shanghai has gone through numerous changes since 1949. The city was highly radical during the Cultural Revolution, but from the 1990s the government encouraged Shanghai to become an international commercial centre, as it had been half a century earlier.

his old hero George Eastman), Coca-Cola, Shiseido, Toyota, Volkswagen, 555 cigarettes – all gave Beijing, like other cities, the advertising-rich patina of internationalism that had marked Shanghai and the treaty ports in the 1920s and 1930s.

Yet in some ways, the major landmarks of Beijing – the Forbidden City, Tian'anmen Square, the Beijing Hotel – did not change much between 1989 and the turn of the millennium. Not so Shanghai. Shanghai's most visible spot, the waterfront Bund, had survived 1949 much better than Beijing's centre, and it remained (and remains) a central point of reference for the city. But the view in 1990 from the top of the art-deco Peace (formerly Cathay) Hotel over the Huangpu River which separates the Bund from Pudong, the eastern bank of the city, bore no resemblance to what one saw just ten years later. For in the 1990s, central government policy towards Shanghai changed. For the 40 years that the CCP had controlled China, the old Shanghai had been the epitome of everything of which the Party disapproved: obsessed by commerce, shaped by imperialism and internationalism, full, at least in popular perception, of millionaires and prostitutes, bandits and opium addicts. Furthermore, Shanghai's reputation as a centre for radical dissent, of which the CCP itself was an excellent example, was not something that the new regime appreciated once it had obtained power and turned its face away from the cities towards the countryside. So one of Asia's most international cities, already battered by a decade of war and the chaos of the return of the Nationalists in 1945, was deliberately reformed and restrained by the puritans of the new order. Even during the era of Mao, as we saw in Chapter 6, the repression of Shanghai was not entirely successful, as it briefly reinvented itself in 1966–7 as the crucible of the most radically egalitarian manifestation of the Cultural Revolution, the 'Shanghai Commune'. But for the most part, Shanghai spent the post-1949 era as a ghost of its former self. The memories of the clubs, banks, neon-light advertising, and dance-halls that had shaped this most vibrant and brutal of places was gone, seemingly forever. The public city was in bed by 9 p.m.

Until the 1990s. As part of the strategy of encouraging China's growth and also making it a place that mattered in the global hierarchy, Shanghai was given permission to grow. The most visible manifestation of this change was the new cityscape in the Pudong district. In the early part of the twentieth century, this had been a muddy area full of godowns (warehouses) and cotton mills, populated by impoverished manual labourers, many controlled by mafia-linked syndicates such as the famous Green Gang. The area had been a flat wasteland in the years after 1949, with little of architectural distinction to complement the imperial pomp of the Bund which faced it. But after 1990, developers were given full rein. The old godowns went down, and in their place came a twenty-first-century megalopolis, with tens of gleaming skyscrapers in silver and gold appearing and dominating the skyline. Suddenly, the once-imposing Bund looked dwarfed in comparison. While not generally sharing the architectural excellence of Hong Kong's cityscape, the new buildings

29. The Oriental Pearl Tower dominates Shanghai's skyline, 1995.
In contrast to the Bund, the Pudong bank of the Huangpu River has been
transformed beyond recognition since 1990. Space-age skyscrapers have sprung
up in the former warehouse area.

had an undeniably brash self-confidence. Most notable was the
Oriental Pearl television tower, an eye-scorching tower some
450 metres high, with bright mauve stripes across a silver shaft, with
two bulbous onion-like projections along it. As a symbol of virile,
modernizing intent, the tower could hold its own with the Cultural
Revolution's great symbol, the bridge over the Yangtze at Nanjing,

any day, although at the turn of the millennium, many in the city already felt that it was looking dated. More generally, Shanghai is once again full of the things that made it so distinctive in the 1920s: French cafés, American banks, German cars, Japanese advertising. The great goal for the first decade of the new century, just as Beijing aimed at the Olympics of 2008, was the Shanghai World Expo of 2010. Given its head, Shanghai no longer aims to outclass Beijing or even Hong Kong. It wants to return to the days, more than half a century ago, when it was spoken of in the same breath as New York, London, or Paris, as one of the few cities of the international elite.

Coping with the Past

It seemed that the attempt to reclaim the May Fourth legacy by the demonstrators in 1989 had been crushed. Yet the 1990s did not see the wholesale destruction of free expression that some had expected after Tian'anmen. Instead, China's past, both ancient and recent, crowded into the present in often unexpected ways.

First, the government made copious use of history to bolster its legitimacy. A striking use of the past was the official support for the memory of Confucius. During the Mao period, Confucius was criticized heavily, in line with the radical May Fourth influence on the CCP regime, culminating in the 'Criticize Confucius, Criticize Lin Biao' campaign of 1973–4, when the sage was associated with Lin Biao, the former favourite of Mao who was alleged to have plotted against him and died in an air crash while fleeing Beijing. (The campaign's immediate political target was the pragmatic Prime Minister, Zhou Enlai.) But in the 1980s, in line with the new emphasis on education, Confucius was now portrayed as a great teacher who thought about moral issues, and was a suitable exemplar for the young. In the 1990s, as China's reforms made the enterprise culture into a political fixture, Confucius was turned, through an extraordinary sleight of hand, into an advocate of profit and economic growth. Symbolically, in 1994, Kuang Yaming, a senior member of the CCP and former president of Nanjing University, came to open an officially sanctioned statue of Confucius in his birthplace, the small northern town of Qufu.[1] If the May Fourth generation had been alive to see these changes, one imagines that Chen Duxiu would have been appalled that the CCP had reversed itself into welcoming the philosopher whom he felt was at the heart of China's cultural crisis, whereas Zou Taofen would have perhaps been gratified that his attempts in the 1920s to integrate capitalist modernity and Confucianism had borne fruit, even if a detour of four decades had been necessary to get there.

At least Confucius had been safely dead for more than two millennia. What about a more recent corpse, Mao Zedong? One of the oddest popular phenomena in the year following the Tian'anmen uprising was the emergence of the 'Mao craze', a sudden enthusiasm, particularly notable among many of the young, for wearing Mao badges and listening to songs (such as 'The East is Red' and 'I Love Beijing's Tian'anmen Square') from the Cultural Revolution era, although in a piece of enterprising cultural hybridity, a popular recording of the songs was reissued with a driving disco beat in the background. Although the 'Mao craze' of 1990 subsided somewhat, the whole decade saw a widespread cultural reassessment of the pre-1976 era.[2] Karaoke parlours made singalong versions of revolutionary songs available. Cultural Revolution nostalgia restaurants, with simple 'peasant-style' meals became briefly popular in the mid-1990s among the big cities' new rich (although the prices were not similarly peasant-like, nor was there any sign of parallel 'Great Leap Forward' themed restaurants featuring empty plates). This phenomenon echoed the kitsch treatment of dictatorship in other societies in the 1990s, including former East Germany, where restaurants and clubs had their staff dress up as Stasi (secret police) agents, and Russia, where Stalin was re-cast in the 1990s as a great strongman and, in his native Georgia, a favourite son. In China, as in the other countries, the reliving of a traumatic past as black comedy seemed to serve at least two purposes. First, it soothed recent painful memories by taming the past, and ridiculing its most frightening features so that they no longer had the power to hurt. Yet the phenomenon was also a dig at the new rulers. In post-Communist Europe, the praise for Stalin or the nostalgia for East Germany was for many a way to complain about the breakdown in order that post-Soviet Russia suffered, or the materialist and selfish culture that West Germany was accused of bringing to its poorer eastern neighbour. In China, although the governing party had not changed in name, the Deng Xiaoping era was clearly different from Mao's. By wearing a Mao badge or reviving the songs of the 1960s, a pointed comment about the materialism of the Deng era could be made. In this rose-tinted view of the recent past, Mao's era was the one when the Chinese people had 'stood up' against the foreigners, been economically self-sufficient, and when people had been much more equal in both status and income. Although this was all empirically dubious, the idea of a golden Maoist age seemed powerful to some who disliked the materialism and obeisance to foreign culture that they seemed to detect under Deng. And clearly, 'protesting' in this way forced the CCP into a sly complicity with the protester: for how could the Party openly object to glorification of the founder of the People's Republic, and the man still immortalized with his portrait hanging in Tian'anmen Square?

Elsewhere, though, the Party and the people both sought other sources of legitimacy. Mao could not be abolished, but he could no longer be at the centre of Chinese identity in the early 21st century. One historical event that the Party now sought to reclaim was the experience of the War of Resistance to Japan in the 1930s and 1940s. This had been a physically and emotionally devastating culmination to the Republican era, yet in contrast to the other countries which had gone through World War II, whether as victors or vanquished, China never fully explored the legacy of the War of Resistance. Unlike the Soviet Union, which used the memory of the 'Great Patriotic War' to encourage love for the motherland, or Britain, which could draw honour and prestige from its noble stand against dictatorship (assisted, of course, by millions of empire troops of all colours), China was unable to draw patriotic sustenance from its eight-year agony of war and occupation.[3] The political terrain was simply too complex. Chiang Kaishek's Nationalist government had borne the brunt of the resistance against Japan, yet he and the CCP were plunged almost immediately into civil war in 1946. Once the CCP had won control of the mainland, it was hardly in their interests to allow any positive assessments of Chiang's war record, as he was now cast as a reactionary puppet of the Americans, waiting off the mainland for a chance to retake China. (Nor were the CCP wrong about Chiang's intentions.) The 1980s brought a change in attitude, though. Mao and Chiang, the great enemies, were both dead within a year of each other, in 1976 and 1975 respectively. The new leadership was anxious to reunify Taiwan with the mainland peacefully. In 1984, it gained great national prestige through its negotiations on Hong Kong, which, it was agreed, would be returned to China by Britain in 1997. Now Taiwan should be encouraged to take similar steps. At the same time, the reversal of Maoist policies under Deng, and national disillusionment caused by the Cultural Revolution, forced the CCP leadership to search for something in the recent past that could unite the Chinese people around their rulers. The War of Resistance was a logical choice, therefore: the last great event when the Chinese, regardless of whether they were Nationalist or Communist, were united against a brutal, outside enemy. Huge museums of the war were opened in the late 1980s in Beijing, Nanjing (at the site of one of the massacres of 1937), and Shenyang (at the site of the railway bombing that sparked off the Manchurian crisis in 1931). Films, novels, television shows, and both academic and popular histories of the war emerged in profusion. Even Chiang Kaishek came in for reassessment: from being a reactionary tool of capitalism, he was now recast as a man who had made serious mistakes, but who had nonetheless played an important patriotic role in the war against Japan, and whose government had carried out some reforms that had helped to modernize China. The Taiwanese were wary of this olive branch from the mainland. However, on the mainland, there was strong popular enthusiasm for the new freedom to attack Japan's savage wartime record in China, reactions exacerbated by attempts by right-wing Japanese to deny events such as the Nanjing massacre; an opinion poll in 1996 suggested that 83.9 per cent of youth surveyed associated Japan with the massacre above all else.[4]

Suspicion at the post-Cold War order and its intentions for China were not directed solely at Japan. The US, as the dominant power in the new order, came in for much more explicit criticism, particularly as it was perceived as trying to hold China back from its rightful position of dominance in East Asia. Chinese explanations of their own position veered between declarations that they wished to be moderating players in the new world order, a statement backed up by regular Chinese restraint in forums such as the UN Security Council where the PRC used its veto rarely and tended to abstain on controversial matters,[5] and encouragement of popular nationalist sentiment at times of crisis, most notably in 1999, when NATO forces bombed the Chinese Embassy in Belgrade during the Kosovo war, and large anti-American crowds protested shortly afterwards in the streets of the Chinese capital, with government authorization. Eighty years after May Fourth and ten years after Tian'anmen, a springtime crowd was now gathering in the centre of Beijing to *support* the government's position, although many of the demonstrators did echo the voices of 1919 by protesting that the government had not responded even more robustly to the American insult to the Chinese national honour. The CCP even became worried at the enthusiasm with which the anti-American agenda was taken up by some activists. Two academics who started an Internet petition in February 2003 to oppose American plans for war in Iraq found themselves under official surveillance, despite their strongly nationalist position. 'Most countries, including ours, are afraid to criticise the US', claimed one of the scholars. 'This will only encourage the US to be even more aggressive in future.' Yet although the group was monitored, it was not banned. The government was clearly ambivalent about the emergence of this type of organization which was patriotic but not directly controlled by the Party.[6]

A strong Chinese nationalism, both official and popular, became a theme of the post-Cold War period. It could take political, historical, and cultural forms: the 1999 Kosovo demonstrations, remembrance of the war against Japan, and the new praise for Confucius were all part of it. In stark contrast to the Cultural Revolution and the most radical May Fourth agenda, this sentiment was not all confrontational, but now included a nuanced and critical appreciation and even enjoyment of China's past. A boom in interest in Republican China emerged in the 1980s and showed no signs of stopping at the turn of the millennium. Biographies were written on characters both good and bad, including Shanghai businessmen and bandits, and New Culture writers who had long been ignored in the PRC because they had not become members of the CCP. Restaurants opened in the old French Concession area of Shanghai, recreating the atmosphere of the roaring Twenties, again with high prices to match. The idea that China could look back to the 1920s to see where it might go in the new millennium became a strong one, particularly as the cities once again became prominent in China's vision of itself. One institution that epitomized this tendency was the powerhouse of the original May Fourth Movement, Peking University. Even though the PRC government made it known from the 1970s that it preferred its capital to be known as 'Beijing', a translation that corresponds much more accurately to its pronunciation in Chinese, the University had let it be known that it preferred to be known in English as 'Peking University', the name under which it had achieved international fame in the early twentieth century. The Chinese government made efforts in 1998 to associate the University's centenary celebrations with the rise of the CCP, and President Jiang Zemin's speech praised the University's 'glorious tradition of patriotism, progress, democracy and science' – the CCP's version of the May Fourth agenda again – as well as stressing the importance of commitment to the Party. Elsewhere, however, a professor published an essay in the journal *Reading* in which he instead praised Cai Yuanpei, the University President whose enthusiasm for 'absolute academic freedom' had enabled Peking University to place itself at the heart of the May Fourth Movement.[7] And it is notable that the May Fourth atmosphere of intellectual exploration, carefully balanced with wariness about an ever-fragile political situation, has carried on post-1989 in a way that would have seemed unlikely to most people looking at the wreckage in Tian'anmen Square on the morning of 4 June 1989.

The revival in interest in the Republican era was a relatively safe nostalgia as far as the state was concerned, and the opening of the old 'red building' of Peking University as a museum in 2002 was a sign that the dangerous alternative memories of May Fourth which had emerged in 1989 were no longer a source of fear for the government. Heroes of the era such as Zou Taofen were remembered as well: a newspaper article said that he 'used his pen to try to save his country from the Japanese invaders', and his old home, like Lu Xun's, is now kept as a shrine where his personal items are on display to visitors.[8] There were even overtones of a revival for the much-mocked 1930s New Life Movement of Chiang Kaishek: in the run-up to the Beijing Olympics, the city authorities announced that they were instituting a 'morality evaluation index' which would give high scores for 'displays of patriotism, large book collections, and balconies full of plotted plants', while downgrading residents who indulged in 'alcohol abuse, noise complaints, pollution or a violation of licences covering internet cafes and karaoke parlours'.[9] And concern for China's trading position, seen in the National Products Movement of the early twentieth century, came back too. One newspaper article had a very familiar ring:

Why is the world outdoing China at china? Chinese porcelain products used to sell like hot cakes in stores right around the world . . . But nowadays, people seldom seek out the products that carry the English name for the Middle Kingdom in overseas porcelain stores . . . Chinese-produced porcelain products are designed mostly for everyday use, making the quality very poor. If Chinese porcelain manufacturers want to make a fortune in the international arena, the driving forces will be the product's design and quality, and the recognition of the brand name around the globe.[10]

Du Zhongyuan might have been disappointed that nothing he wrote in 1931 (Chapter 3) seemed to have changed in seven decades.

New Thinking

At the heart of the New Culture of the 1920s and the 'new era' of the 1980s was the willingness of Chinese thinkers to draw on a wide range of resources to fashion solutions for the problems China faced. The post-Tian'anmen, post-Cold War era also produced a new generation of thinkers who gave an intellectual edge to the atmosphere of political change.

Many of the most prominent activists of the 1980s were no longer in a position to contribute to the debate, as their association with the 'counter-revolutionary' uprising had made it unsafe for them to remain in China. Liu Binyan had already left for exile in the US in 1988. In the wake of Tian'anmen, most of the prominent student leaders managed to escape China, although Wang Dan was arrested and imprisoned for several years. Their fates varied; as they had all been so young in 1989, they still had time to start new lives. Wang Dan, for instance, went to study at Harvard, while Wu'er Kaixi became a radio talk-show host in Taiwan. Fang Lizhi, although much older than the student leaders, was also a marked man, even though he had kept silent during the events of 1989. He and his wife managed to escape to the United States embassy in Beijing, and after a year of diplomatic stand-off was given permission to emigrate. The writers of *Heshang* also had to seek new lives: of the five main writers, four escaped to the United States, and, in an exchange of one transformative vision for another, two of them became evangelical Christians. Su Xiaokang, the main driving force behind the programme who had also made an appearance at Tian'anmen Square during the demonstrations, was not one of those who found religious faith. For him, the destruction of the promise of the 'new era' had led to a huge sense of personal loss. 'I tried hard,' he said in conversation with the writer Ian Buruma over a decade after Tian'anmen, 'but I can't believe in anything at all.'[11]

Many of the makers of the 'new era' of the 1980s were forcibly removed from the debate about China's future, and although the initial period after Tian'anmen Square gave them prestige and a certain amount of glamour, the world's fickle attention quickly moved on when it was clear that the Beijing regime was not about to collapse. It was generally the most pro-westernizing thinkers, the equivalent of the most radical May Fourth figures such as Chen Duxiu and Hu Shi, who left the scene in 1989. But even in the 1980s, there had been many more cautious voices, echoing the May Fourth era thinkers who had cautioned against a simplistic belief that solutions from abroad could deal easily with China's problems. These figures would now form the intellectual debates of the 1990s and the

new century. And that debate would be much freer and more productive than many would have predicted in spring 1989.

This was in large part because the global changes that made the
Chinese government more cautious about the west after the collapse
of the USSR in 1991 also changed the intellectual atmosphere in
China. Although the dominant tone of much of the politics of the
1980s was that political reform needed to be even more extensive than
the CCP was prepared to permit, from the 1990s the tone changed,
with a more wary nationalism shared by the government and by
prominent thinkers. If anything, the government was now often criticized not for being too politically repressive, but rather for being too
compliant in the face of outside (particularly American) pressure.
Even in exile, Su Xiaokang regretted his uncritical optimism about
western industrial culture in *Heshang*, admitting that because he had
known little about the west at that time, he had also been unable to
understand its shortcomings.[12] Many of those writing in China after
1991 were even harsher in their assessment of the new world order.

Wang Hui, editor of *Reading* (the journal which had provided such
an important source of 'liberal' thought in the 1980s), came to prominence as one of the most thoughtful commentators on the uncritical
May Fourth-type 'enlightenment' thought in the 1990s. Wang and
those who thought like him argued that the promise of western capitalist modernity had not in fact led to democracy and social justice,
but rather to a dangerous entwining of political and economic
power.[13] He and other intellectuals, such as Zhang Kuan, argued that
the western categories such as liberal democracy and individualism
forced Chinese reformers into a straitjacket of thinking that was not
necessarily appropriate for the situation China faced in a globalized
and sometimes hostile world. Zhang also criticized Chinese writers
who wrote for the western market, such as Nien Cheng (whose Cultural Revolution memoir appeared in Chapter 6), arguing that they
produced a distorted, 'fantastic and unreasonable' impression of
Chinese reality to appeal to foreign readers who understood little of
China. To be sure, there were also 'liberal' thinkers who defended the
May Fourth tradition strongly even into the 1990s.[14] Yet the dominant
tone has been highly critical of a simplistic acceptance of western

categories and models for reform in China. Nonetheless, it is notable that, whatever their political position, many of the most important Chinese intellectuals of the 1990s have shown a sophisticated and nuanced understanding of western theories such as postmodernism as well as of premodern Chinese thought. Although the state continues to maintain ultimate control over publication and distribution of political writing, there is a genuine and informed debate going on in China that is highly reminiscent of the intellectual foment of the May Fourth era itself. These debates, while not receiving a wide Chinese readership in themselves, are reflected at a more popular level, for instance in the bestselling polemic *China Can Say No* (1996), which attacked the United States for attempting to keep China from becoming a global power with a strong economy. The book became a publishing phenomenon.[15] In rather different circumstances, Zou Taofen and Du Zhongyuan had achieved bestseller status in the 1930s with their attacks on Japanese expansionism in China in the journals *Life* and *New Life*. At times of real or perceived crisis, there was clearly a market for popular writing that portrayed China with its back to the wall, needing its people to come to the rescue.

It was not always easy to speak out in the May Fourth era, yet it was not a period of complete repression. The same is often true in the contemporary literary and political scene. Some critics of the government are still silenced through arrest and imprisonment. But the situation of the writer Yu Jie is also a suggestive example of how the state has come to an unspoken compromise with some writers. Yu Jie has written a number of books, of which his 1998 collection of essays, *Fire and Ice* [*Huo yu bing*], was one of the most noted. He has offered severe criticisms of targets including Mao Zedong, the current regime, and the 1989 Tian'anmen crackdown. One of his models is Lu Xun. Yu Jie's books have been banned in the mainland, or prevented from going to press, or published only in Hong Kong. Along with other known critics, he has been placed on a semi-official blacklist, which makes it very hard for him to be published in any officially registered publication. On the other hand, Yu Jie has not been arrested, and has been permitted to travel to the US. Just as the May Fourth generation played unspoken, sometimes dangerous games with the censors, so Chinese writers at the turn of the millennium are pushing at the boundaries of what is permissible.[16]

Across the Straits

The story of Taiwan's development is not one that has appeared much in this narrative. That is because, throughout the twentieth century, Taiwan's main political and social developments have gone through a significantly different journey to those on the mainland. The Chinese government has repeatedly made it clear that reunification with Taiwan is the last piece of unfinished business from the era when imperialists and foreign powers tried to carve China up. Yet since 1895, Taiwan and China have been part of the same united political entity for only four years, during the last unstable period of the Nationalist government from 1945 to 1949. In 1895, the island was ceded to Japan after the Sino-Japanese War, and for the next 50 years was a colony run by Japanese administrators who promoted a new middle-class Taiwan elite to assist them in running the island smoothly. The defeat of Japan in 1945 meant that the island reverted to Chinese rule, but the Nationalists quickly squandered goodwill among the Taiwanese when they sent a brutal and corrupt governor to rule the island, and then put down an uprising by the Taiwanese in 1947 with mass killings and arrests. After 1949, the Nationalists ruled Taiwan under military law, bringing with them millions of mainlanders who wished to flee the Communist advance. The Nationalists maintained the position that they were on the island only temporarily until they could recapture the mainland, yet this argument became steadily less plausible as it became clear that the CCP were in China to stay. In 1975, Chiang Kaishek died, and his son, Chiang Ching-kuo, succeeded him. Under the elder Chiang, political dissent had been ruthlessly suppressed, as Bo Yang had found out when he was imprisoned for his subversive writing. But during the rule of the younger Chiang, slow but sure moves were made to liberalize Taiwan's political atmosphere. The illegal opposition groups were legalized and then formed into the first legitimate political parties permitted to oppose Nationalist rule. Among the most prominent was the Democratic People's Party (DPP), which advocated that Taiwan should become an independent state. Reforms quickened after Chiang Ching-kuo's death, as freedom of speech and publication became ever greater, and free multiparty elections were held for local government, parliament, and, finally, for the presidency. In 2000, for the first time, an opposition politician was elected president: Chen Shui-bian of the DPP, who just 20 years earlier had been a persecuted dissident. Taiwan had come from dictatorship to democracy in less than a generation.[17]

The experience of Taiwan is important for what it says about China's future path. The differences are often stressed: Taiwan is much smaller than China, and has a population of just 20 million or so. It is also much richer and has a far lower level of inequality; few people are desperately poor in Taiwan in the way that they are in the impoverished rural parts of China. It is also worth noting that the nature of the democracy movement in Taiwan was significantly different from the various experiments with democracy on the mainland. Even when May Fourth reformers spoke of 'science and democracy', whether in 1919 or 1989, there continued to be an assumption that these desirable entities would flow down from educated elites, who understood them, to the grassroots level. The inbuilt feeling of superiority among China's educated classes which so infuriated Mao Zedong continued (and continues) to be visible in much of the discussion of democratic reform in the mainland. Taiwan's dissident movement, however, started with different bases. The Taiwanese were ethnic Chinese, but after 1945, their resentment was not aimed at some foreign imperialist power, but rather against their own ethnic Chinese Nationalist government, which refused to accept demands for more localized Taiwan autonomy, and treated Taiwan as a temporary base in service of the supposedly much more important task of retaking the mainland. As the dissidence grew louder in the 1970s, other marginalized groups, such as Taiwan's aborigines, who numbered a few tens of thousands, also began to find their voices. The aborigines had been subjected to an assimilation programme under the Nationalists which would have been familiar to European colonial governors everywhere, discouraging them from using their own languages and cultures (which are not ethnic Chinese but Malay-Polynesian, dating from prehistoric times) and forcing them into becoming 'Chinese' whether they wished to or not. Therefore, while the aims of the democratic movement in Taiwan were ones common to many democracy movements, such as freedom of speech and varied political representation, the origins of the movement forced the recognition of issues such as ethnic plurality and identity politics which had never been so fully acknowledged in the mainland. The democracy movement in Taiwan was not really the product of the May Fourth discourse of 'science and democracy', as its principal proponents had been part of a different political structure, Japanese colonialism, at the time when the May Fourth Movement had appeared in China itself. So the Chinese world's most successful democratization did not stem from China's most famous movement for democracy.

Yet this irony does not by any means discount the validity of Taiwan's experience for China. For the enthusiasm of the government and political conservatives in the mainland for Confucianism in the post-Mao era has been largely fuelled by their conviction that China has underlying 'Confucian values' that ultimately make western liberal democracy unsuitable for China. (Rephrased as 'Asian values', the same argument was very popular in places such as Malaysia and Singapore during much of the 1990s.) Yet Taiwan has always maintained Confucian norms much more strongly than the mainland has, as it experienced neither May Fourth anti-Confucian radicalism, nor Communist rule and the Cultural Revolution. Everyday life in Taiwan recognizes Confucian norms in many ways, even while the island is now a raucously liberal and pluralist democracy. Clearly there is a political willingness among some conservatives in China to maintain the position, reminiscent in some ways of the May Fourth radicals, that Confucianism can only be defined in one specifically authoritarian way, and similarly to argue that liberalism and pluralist democracy are purely western ideas that can only be built on the specific basis of 300 years of post-Renaissance European experience. Taiwan stands as an embarrassing counter-argument to this tendency to make culture a restrictive prison rather than an enabling tool.

The writer Ralph Wiley once replied to the haughty question asked by a Nobel Prize-winning author, 'Who is the Tolstoy of the Zulus?' with the retort: '*Tolstoy* is the Tolstoy of the Zulus – unless you find a profit in fencing off universal properties of mankind into exclusive tribal ownership'.[18] Similarly, the answer to the question, 'What is Chinese democracy?' might well be '*Democracy* is Chinese democracy'. Even 'liberal democracy' does not exist in just one model, although its common elements are recognizable even in its variations in American, British, or German forms, and, more recently, its Taiwanese form: if the latter system is 'western', then it seems to have bedded down remarkably well in an unimpeachably 'Chinese' society. Of course every society has its own cultural characteristics that shape its politics. Nor can political ideas be transferred in an instant from one society to another. Simply translating Tolstoy into Zulu is not sufficient; yet nobody would surely argue that a Zulu-speaker could never read or understand Tolstoy. The experience of the late Qing and the May Fourth era shows that there was a whole repertoire of choices available to thinkers who wanted to reform China's politics: western ideas, of course, but also Chinese indigenous thought and ideas from outside Western Europe and North America. China's twentieth century has shown no difficulty with the *ability* to adapt ideas from other places or times (such as Social Darwinism or Marxism); the problem seems to lie with a frequently spread and shared perception that certain of these options are too risky to try at a time of political crisis. Even today, one hears from official Chinese sources that too much democracy may cause chaos in China; the idea that democracy may be what is needed to bring stability to China, by providing a pluralist environment that may lessen internal dissent, is less often heard.

Searching for a New Story

There is a new self-confidence in China in the early twenty-first century, yet the country still seems to be in search of a new narrative about what the country is, and what it should become. The May Fourth legacy is part of that search.

The symbolism of May Fourth has continued to be important for the Chinese government. As described in Chapter 2, in 2002, the old 'red building' of Peking University, behind the Forbidden City, reopened as a museum of the New Culture Movement, with a modernist memorial to the patriotic students of 1919 placed prominently nearby. The building known to Cai Yuanpei, Chen Duxiu, and Mao Zedong was open to visitors again. The spirit of 'science', if not necessarily 'democracy', continued to be powerful for the government also. In the late 1990s, a Buddhist group of mysterious origins known as Falun Gong ('the wheel of the law') emerged, recruiting large numbers of Chinese. Such millennial groups were well known to Chinese governments in the past, and had been responsible for destabilizing dynasties, so the CCP was keen to crack down on this latest manifestation of the phenomenon. While the techniques of mass arrest which they used were not so different from those used against democracy protesters in the 1980s, the rhetoric they deployed against Falun Gong had a very May Fourth air: they argued it was necessary to use science and technology to combat this sort of superstition which threatened to take China back to the dark ages. In 2001, a Foreign Ministry spokesperson replied to complaints from the European Union about suppression of the group: 'China's constitution guarantees religious freedom ... [but] "Falun Gong" is a thorough cult that goes against humanities, society and science.' After a long history of aggressive anti-religious activism, the CCP had now reached a position that, once again, closely resembled that of Chiang Kaishek's New Life Movement: organized, state-approved religion was fine, but religions that were not controlled by the state were evil cults leading people away from the path of secular modernity.[19]

Elsewhere, one of the most visible projects through which the government displayed its authority in the 1990s was the Three Gorges Dam on the Yangtze. When it started filling in 2003, this was the world's biggest dam project, which would create in effect a huge inland lake out of several hundred miles of the river's length. Environmental objections had been made early in the project's life: perhaps, it was suggested, building several smaller dams would be safer, and have the same effect. But several small dams would not

30. **The Three Gorges Dam on the Yangtze at Sandouping, creating a lake some 550 km (342 miles) long.**
One of the biggest and most environmentally controversial projects in the world, the Three Gorges Dam has been closely associated with the Chinese government's rebuilding of its own legitimacy and authority since 1989.

have the air of virile, scientific modernity that the politics of the project demanded. The often stark definition of 'science' that emerged in the early twentieth century had clearly not disappeared at the start of the new century. 'Science' was also politics, and the Enlightenment model of modernity, with its stress on the scientific and rational world-view as a necessary starting point for development and progress, continued to be dominant in Chinese political thinking. In 2003, China carried out its first successful launch of a manned spacecraft, Shenzhou, which orbited the Earth. At a time when spaceflight seemed to have fallen from favour in the west as a relic of a Cold War past, this project symbolized the Chinese desire to take over the prestige of this arena of scientific endeavour from the now reluctant Americans and Russians.

It is unsurprising that the Chinese government has continued to make use of the May Fourth ideas that serve its purposes: after all, that movement's history and legacy are still known to all educated Chinese. Yet it may be in a rather different aspect of May Fourth that China finally finds the solution to its quest for identity. For one of the most important realizations about the original New Culture was not to do with any one specific thread of thought, but rather, the ability of China to sustain competing ideas about how to 'save the nation'. Not Communism, Gandhianism, nationalism, or Confucianism on their own could come up with solutions to China's earlier crisis, but it was not inevitable that politics should turn to ideologies that were intolerant of any alternatives or dissent. The 1930s did not turn out to be a propitious time for social experiment, but this was a comment on the crisis caused by the aggression of Japanese imperialism, not on the viability of Chinese pluralism. China's thinkers, when given space and opportunity, however precarious, could come up with a variety of different solutions, all of them with something to contribute. Chinese Communism put forward solutions for the countryside, but said little about individual enterprise. The National Products Movement suffered from perhaps the reverse problem. The Nationalist government did not have enough faith in its own prescriptions for democratic governance. Gandhianism provided a potential answer to the quandary of Chinese political violence and the

311

31. **A family in the town of Wanxian in Sichuan are relocated from their bulldozed house.** The building of the dam has meant huge change all along the Yangtze. Many towns are disappearing as the water levels rise, and their inhabitants are being moved to new homes elsewhere. Some are pleased to move, but others are unhappy at leaving familiar places and memories behind.

seeming destruction of indigenous morality, but may have needed more time and space to develop as an idea.

Yet although the sense of crisis is back in contemporary China, and has been a constant throughout the century, the country is perhaps less at risk than it has been in well over a century. Both Du Zhongyuan in the 1930s and the authors of *China Can Say No* in 1996 wrote bestselling publications that warned of the imminent invasion of China, and the political atmosphere in China allows explicit comparisons between the drift to war with Japan before 1937 and China's international situation now. Yet the differences are more striking than the similarities. China really *was* about to be invaded in the 1930s, and by 1937 large parts of its territories were under occupation. Even Chinese military planners are unlikely to argue that a territorial invasion from any other power is imminent, and cultural and economic imperialism, while worrying, are not likely to cause the 20 million deaths for which the War of Resistance against Japan was responsible.

China has always given rise to apocalyptic sentiments from both inside and outside: the world's biggest market, an environmental disaster waiting to happen, a nascent superpower with uncertain intentions. The mixture of the premodern conviction of the country that it was the source of all civilization with the more recent embrace of romanticist ideas that make all crises into a life-or-death struggle, has contributed to the reality of China's struggle to free itself from imperialism and hegemony throughout the century. Even the top-down nature of much of the discussion of how China can develop towards democracy reflects the sense that at a time of crisis, China cannot afford to allow too many varying voices and agendas to battle for attention. In many ways, China at the start of the twenty-first century gives the appearance of being in the same situation as at the start of the twentieth, simultaneously trying to ward off internal social collapse and external pressure.

Nonetheless, a sense of crisis is at least in part self-created. Perception does not necessarily match reality. China may well find that the solution to its quest for modernity is to let the best part of May Fourth re-emerge: the ability to put forward a variety of experiments in happiness, and to choose between them. This is not to say that any one political solution, whether neo-Confucianism, western liberal democracy, or *laissez-faire* capitalism, will provide all or indeed any answers. But the circumstances of the new century could bode far better for a new May Fourth. All that is necessary is that China is willing to try it out. Despite the gloomy declarations of *Heshang* that China must go through terrible pain to reach salvation, letting go might hurt a lot less than some people think, even though it might be at the tolerable risk of China's twenty-first century being blessedly less exciting than its twentieth. Revolution, as Lu Xun observed, was a bitter thing in the twentieth century. China can make choices to make it less so in the twenty-first.

Guide to Further Reading

There is a huge literature surrounding aspects of the May Fourth Movement, and this book has been able to touch on only a small part of it. There are extensive discussions of literary, linguistic, historiographical, political, and philosophical debates during the movement; studies of its impact all over China; and studies of influences from all over the globe on the movement itself.

I have prepared this guide primarily for readers who do not know Chinese. This guide cannot provide a complete bibliography for the May Fourth Movement and still less so for the whole of modern Chinese history. Instead, I have indicated a few useful or stimulating works in various relevant areas. No slight is intended to works that do not appear here: they are just too numerous to list.

In addition to this guide, the Notes also give references to works that are relevant to specific topics taken up in the book.

Twentieth-century Chinese History

There are many excellent surveys of Chinese history, including Immanuel Hsu, *The Rise of Modern China* (Oxford, 2000); Richard Phillips, *China since 1911* (Basingstoke, 1996); and Jonathan D. Spence, *The Search for Modern China* (New York, 1999). For detailed essays on particular topics accessible to a non-specialist, turn to the volumes of the *Cambridge History of China* (general editors John K. Fairbank and Denis Twitchett): volumes 10 and 11 deal with the late Qing, volumes 12 and 13 with the Republic, and volumes 14 and 15 with the People's Republic.

The May Fourth and New Culture Movements

I have sketched out the approach of several of these books in Chapter 1: Chow Tse-tsung, *The May Fourth Movement: Intellectual Revolution in Modern China* (Cambridge, Mass., 1960); Benjamin I. Schwartz, *Reflections on the May Fourth Movement: A Symposium* (Cambridge, Mass., 1972); Lin Yu-sheng, *The Crisis of Chinese Consciousness* (Madison, WI, 1979); Vera Schwarcz, *The Chinese Enlightenment: Intellectuals and the Legacy of the May Fourth Movement* (Berkeley, 1986); and Milena Doleželová and Oldřich Král (eds.), *The Appropriation of Cultural Capital: China's May Fourth Project* (Cambridge, Mass., 2001). On the movement outside Beijing, Joseph T. Chen, *The May Fourth Movement in Shanghai: The Making of a Social Movement in Modern China* (Leiden, 1971); Wen-hsin Yeh, *Provincial Passages: Culture, Space, and the Origins of Chinese Communism* (Berkeley, 1996); and James R. Carter, *Creating a Chinese Harbin: Nationalism in an International City, 1916–1932* (Ithaca, NY, 2002).

On the diplomatic crisis that led to the May Fourth demonstrations, a recent revisionist work is Bruce Elleman, *Wilson and China: A Revised History of the Shandong Question* (Armonk, NY, 2002).

For those who read Chinese, a very useful listing of Chinese works on the movement is Sha Jiansun and Gong Shuduo, *Wusi yundong yu ershi shiji zhongguo de lishi daolu* [The May Fourth Movement and the Path of Twentieth-Century Chinese History] (Beijing, 2001), 186–197.

Biographies of Key Figures

The May Fourth generation: A study highly accessible to the non-specialist, tracing the lives of key figures in the May Fourth Movement, including Lu Xun, Ding Ling, Lao She, Xu Zhimo, and Qu Qiubai, is Jonathan Spence, *The Gate of Heavenly Peace: The Chinese and their Revolution, 1895–1980* (New York, 1981).

Lu Xun: There are many studies of this influential author; see, for instance, William A. Lyell, *Lu Hsün's Vision of Reality* (Berkeley, 1976), and Leo Ou-fan Lee, *Voices from the Iron House: A Study of Lu Xun* (Bloomington, IN, 1987).

Ding Ling: Studies include Yi-tsi Mei Feuerwerker, *Ding Ling's Fiction: Ideology and Narrative in Modern Chinese Literature* (Cambridge, Mass., 1982), and Charles

Alber, *Enduring the Revolution: Ding Ling and the Politics of Literature in Guomindang China* (Westport, CT, 2002).

Zou Taofen: There is no full biography of Zou Taofen in English. An important analysis of his life and work is Wen-hsin Yeh, 'Progressive Journalism and Shanghai's Petty Urbanites: Zou Taofen and the Shenghuo Weekly, 1926–1945', in Frederic Wakeman, Jr. and Wen-hsin Yeh (eds.), *Shanghai Sojourners* (Berkeley, 1992). Zou's development in the 1930s is detailed in Margo S. Gewurtz, *Between America and Russia: Chinese Student Radicalism and the Travel Books of Tsou T'ao-fen, 1933–1937* (Toronto, 1975). Full biographies in Chinese include Mu Xin, *Zou Taofen* (Hubei, 1978) and Chen Hui, *Zou Taofen* (Shanghai, 1999).

Du Zhongyuan: There is little work on Du Zhongyuan in English. A tentative analysis of his significance in the 1930s is Rana Mitter, 'Manchuria in mind: press, propaganda, and Northeast China in the age of empire, 1930–1937', in Mariko Asano Tamanoi (ed.), *Crossed Histories: New Approaches to Manchuria in the Age of Empire* (Honolulu, forthcoming). A good biography in Chinese is included in Du Yi and Du Ying (eds.), *Huan wo heshan: Du Zhongyuan wenji* [Going back to my rivers and mountains: Du Zhongyuan's collected works] (Shanghai, 1998).

There are useful short biographies of Zou Taofen and Du Zhongyuan in Howard Boorman (ed.), *Biographical Dictionary of Republican China* (New York, 1968).

Mao Zedong: This central figure in modern Chinese history has been the subject of many biographies; newer ones have taken full advantage of the availability of fresh Chinese materials. A full account of his life is Philip Short, *Mao: A Life* (London, 1999); shorter reflections on his life are the biographies by Shaun Breslin (*Mao*, London, 1998), Delia Davin (*Mao Zedong*, Stroud, 1997), and Jonathan Spence (*Mao*, London, 1999).

Chiang Kaishek: Another key figure in Chinese history, but one far less well served by biographers. Jonathan Fenby, *Generalissimo: Chiang Kai-shek and the China He Lost* (London, 2003), is a highly readable reassessment of his life.

Su Xiaokang: The chief writer and creator of *Heshang* has published an autobiography, *A Memoir of Misfortune* (New York, 2001). He and other exiles from the 1989 Tian'anmen uprising are profiled in Ian Buruma, *Bad Elements: Chinese Rebels from Beijing to Los Angeles* (London, 2003).

Primary Accounts and Sources

Many of the authors and texts dealt with in the book are available in English translation. This is a representative selection of their works. The translators are listed in the Notes where individual works are cited in the main text of the book.

May Fourth authors: Lu Xun, *Silent China: Selected Writings of Lu Xun* (ed. and tr. Gladys Yang) (Oxford, 1973); *Call to Arms* (Beijing, 1981); *Diary of a Madman and Other Stories* (tr. William Lyell) (Honolulu, 1990). Ding Ling, *Miss Sophie's Diary and Other Stories* (Beijing, 1985); *The Sun Shines over the Sanggan River* (Beijing, 1984). Xiao Hong, *Flight from Danger and Other Stories* (Beijing, 1982).

Zou Taofen and Du Zhongyuan's works are not available in English, but representative selections of their work in Chinese are Xu Xing and Jing Zhen (eds.), *Taofen sanwen* [Selected essays of Zou Taofen] (Beijing, 1997) and Du Yi and Du Ying (eds.), *Huan wo heshan: Du Zhongyuan wenji* [Going back to my rivers and mountains: Du Zhongyuan's collected works] (Shanghai, 1998).

Mao Zedong: Stuart Schram, *Mao's Road to Power: Revolutionary Writings 1912–1949* (Armonk, NY, 1992–), is a fully comprehensive translated edition of all Mao's works until his rise to power. *Selected Works of Mao Tse-tung* (5 vols., Beijing, 1975), covers certain post-1949 materials too.

Cultural Revolution: An essential selection of documents, with detailed commentary, is Michael Schoenhals (ed. and tr.), *China's Cultural Revolution, 1966–1969: Not a Dinner Party* (Armonk, NY, 1996). The most comprehensive single source of Cultural Revolution documentation in Chinese is Song Yianyi *et al.*, *Chinese Cultural Revolution Database* (Hong Kong, 2002). The memoirs used here are Nien Cheng, *Life and Death in Shanghai* (London, 1986) and Gordon A. Bennett and Ronald N. Montaperto, *Red Guard: The Political Biography of Dai-Hsiao-ai* (London, 1971).

Scar Literature: Liu Xinwu, Wang Meng, *et al.*, *Prize-winning Stories from China 1978–1979* (Beijing, 1981); Liu Binyan, *People or Monsters? and Other Stories and Reportage from China after Mao* (Bloomington, IN, 1983).

The 1980s 'new era': For interviews giving views on everyday life in mid-1980s Beijing, see Zhang Xinxin and Sang Ye, *Chinese Profiles* (Beijing, 1986); a powerful account of the impact of broadcasting on women's lives is Xinran, *The Good Women of China* (London, 2002). *Heshang* is translated with comprehensive notes and commentaries as Su Xiaokang and Wang Luxiang (ed. and tr. Richard Bodman and Pin P. Wan), *Deathsong of the River: A Reader's Guide to the Chinese TV Series* Heshang (Ithaca, NY, 1991). Bo Yang, *The Ugly Chinaman and the Crisis of Chinese Culture* is translated and edited by Don J. Cohn and Jing Qing (London, 1991).

The 1989 Tian'anmen crisis: Important documentation is in Michel Oksenberg, Lawrence R. Sullivan, and Marc Lambert (eds.), *Beijing Spring, 1989: Confrontation and Conflict: The Basic Documents* (Armonk, NY, 1990); Han Minzhu (pseud. ed.), *Cries for Democracy: Writings and Speeches from the 1989 Chinese Democracy Movement* (Princeton, 1990). Insider documents on the leadership's decision to crack down on the demonstrators are in Zhang Liang, Andrew J. Nathan, and Perry Link (eds.), *The Tiananmen Papers* (London, 2001).

Literary and Intellectual Debates during the May Fourth Era

An overview of these debates throughout the twentieth century is Merle Goldman and Leo Ou-fan Lee (eds.), *An Intellectual History of Modern China* (Cambridge, UK, 2002). On literary questions, see Shih Shu-mei, *The Lure of the Modern: Writing Modernism in Semicolonial China, 1917–1937* (Berkeley, 2001); Leo Ou-fan Lee, *Shanghai Modern: The Flowering of a New Urban Culture in China, 1930–1945* (Cambridge, Mass., 1999), and *The Romantic Generation of Modern Chinese Writers* (Cambridge, Mass., 1973); Susan Daruvala, *Zhou Zuoren and an Alternative Chinese Response to Modernity* (Cambridge, Mass., 2000); Michel Hockx, *Questions of Style: Literary Societies and Literary Journals in Modern China, 1911–1937* (Leiden, 2003). On historiographical debates, see Q. Edward Wang, *Inventing China Through History: The May Fourth Approach to Historiography* (Albany, NY, 2001).

Intellectual Change in China

Wm. Theodore De Bary and Irene Bloom, with the collaboration of Wing-tsit Chan, *Sources of Chinese Tradition* (New York, 1960, 1999) is an excellent set of readings on the foundations of Chinese premodern thought. On philosophical thought in premodern China, see Joel Kupperman, *Classic Asian Philosophy: A Guide to the Essential Texts* (Oxford, 2001). On the transition from Confucian to modern thought, see Hao Chang, *Chinese Intellectuals in Crisis: Search for Order and Meaning (1890–1911)* (Berkeley, 1987); and Philip Huang, *Liang Ch'i-ch'ao and Modern Chinese Liberalism* (Seattle, 1972). The significance of the late Qing reform movement is reassessed in Rebecca Karl and Peter Zarrow (eds.), *Rethinking the 1898 Reform Period: Political and Cultural Change in Late Qing China* (Cambridge, Mass., 2002). On the importance of the press in creating Chinese modernity, see Joan Judge, *Print and Politics: 'Shibao' and the Culture of Reform in Late Qing China* (Stanford, 1996).

Nationalism in China

The development of nationalism in the late Qing and early Republic is over-viewed in Jonathan Unger (ed.), *Chinese Nationalism* (Armonk, NY, 1996). Important studies include Prasenjit Duara, *Rescuing History from the Nation: Questioning Narratives of Modern China* (Chicago, 1995); Rebecca Karl, *Staging the World: Chinese Nationalism at the Turn of the Twentieth Century* (Durham, NC, 2002); and Arthur Waldron, *From War to Nationalism: China's Turning Point, 1924–1925* (Cambridge, UK, 1995). On the development of ideas of citizenship, see Henrietta Harrison, *The Making of the Republican Citizen: Political Ceremonies and Symbols in China 1911–29* (Oxford, 2000). On the importance of ideas of race, see Frank Dikötter, *The Discourse of Race in Modern China* (London, 1992). On student nationalism, see John Israel, *Student Nationalism in China, 1927–1937* (Stanford, 1996), and Jeffrey Wasserstrom, *Student Protests in Twentieth-Century China: The View from Shanghai* (Stanford, 1991). On proletarian nationalism, see S. A. Smith, *Like Cattle and Horses: Labor and Nationalism in Shanghai, 1895–1927* (Durham, NC, 2002).

Ordinary Life

Vivid portraits of street life in Beijing and Shanghai are in David Strand, *Rickshaw Beijing: City Politics and People in the 1920s* (Berkeley, 1989) and Lu Hanchao, *Beyond the Neon Lights: Everyday Shanghai in the Early Twentieth Century* (Berkeley, 1999). A detailed account of university life in China during the May Fourth era is Wen-hsin Yeh, *The Alienated Academy: Culture and Politics in Republican China, 1919–1937* (Cambridge, Mass., 1990). On the politics of everyday consumption of goods, see Karl Gerth, *China Made: Consumer Culture and the Creation of the Nation* (Cambridge, Mass., 2003). For the contemporary era, see Michael Dutton (ed.), *Streetlife China* (Cambridge, UK, 1998).

Political Parties and Chinese Democracy

On the rise of the Nationalists, see Joseph Fewsmith, *Party, State, and Local Elites in Republican China: Merchant Organizations and Politics in Shanghai, 1890–1930* (Honolulu, 1990); C. Martin Wilbur, *The Nationalist Revolution, 1923–1928* (Cambridge, UK, 1983); John Fitzgerald, *Awakening China: Politics, Culture, and Class in the Nationalist Revolution* (Stanford, 1998). On the rise of the Communists, for an overview, see James Harrison, *The Long March to Power: A History of the Chinese Communist Party, 1921–72* (London, 1973). On the origins of the Party, see Arif Dirlik, *The Origins of Chinese Communism* (Oxford, 1989); Hans J. Van de Ven, *From Friend to Comrade: The Founding of the Chinese Communist Party, 1920–1927* (Berkeley, 1991); S. A. Smith, *A Road is Made: Communism in Shanghai 1920–1927* (Honolulu, 2000). On smaller Chinese parties, see Roger Jeans (ed.), *Roads Not Taken: The Struggle of Opposition Parties in Twentieth-Century China* (Boulder, CO, 1992); and Edmund S. K. Fung, *In Search of Chinese Democracy: Civil Opposition in Nationalist China, 1929–1949* (Cambridge, UK, 2000). For a concise assessment of Nationalist foreign policy, see William C. Kirby, 'The Internationalization of China: Foreign Relations at Home and Abroad in the Republican Era', *The China Quarterly*, 150 (June 1997). On the development of democracy, see Suzanne Ogden, *Inklings of Democracy in China* (Cambridge, Mass., 2002) and Andrew Nathan, *Chinese Democracy* (New York, 1985).

Women's History and Gender History

On feminism in the early Communist movement, see Christina Gilmartin, *Engendering the Chinese Revolution: Radical Women, Communist Politics, and Mass Movements in the 1920s* (Berkeley, 1995). On women professionals in the Republican era, see Wang Zheng, *Women in the Chinese Enlightenment* (Berkeley, 1999). Two stimulating collections are Susan Brownell and Jeffrey N. Wasserstrom, *Chinese Femininities/Chinese Masculinities: A Reader* (Berkeley, 2002), and Christina Gilmartin *et al.* (eds.), *Engendering China: Women, Culture and the State* (Cambridge, Mass., 1994). In the post-1949 era, see Harriet Evans, *Women and Sexuality in China since 1949* (Cambridge, UK, 1997); Elisabeth Croll, *Changing*

Identities of Chinese Women: Rhetoric, Experience and Self-perception in Twentieth-century China (London, 1995); and Ping-Chun Hsiung, Maria Jaschok, and Cecilia Milwertz, with Red Chan, *Chinese Women Organizing: Cadres, Feminists, Muslims, Queers* (Oxford, 2001).

Imperialism

The British imperial presence in China is analysed in Robert Bickers, *Britain in China: Community, Culture and Colonialism 1900–1949* (Manchester, UK, 1999); British empire life in Shanghai is brought to life in Robert Bickers, *Empire Made Me: An Englishman Adrift in Shanghai* (London, 2003). The Japanese presence in China is detailed in Peter Duus, Ramon Myers, and Mark Peattie (eds.), *The Japanese Informal Empire in China, 1895–1937* (Princeton, 1989). The invasion of Manchuria in 1931 is analysed in Sadako Ogata, *Defiance in Manchuria: The Making of Japanese Foreign Policy, 1931–1932* (Berkeley, 1964); attempts to create a sense of 'authentic' sovereignty for Manchukuo are analysed in Prasenjit Duara, *Sovereignty and Authenticity: Manchukuo and the East Asian Modern* (Lanham, MD, 2003); and grassroots Chinese reactions to the invasion are in Rana Mitter, *The Manchurian Myth: Nationalism, Resistance and Collaboration in Modern China* (Berkeley, 2000).

The War against Japan (1937–45) and the Civil War (1946–9)

The response of Chinese politicians to Japanese aggression in the 1930s is analysed in Parks M. Coble, *Facing Japan: Chinese Politics and Japanese Imperialism, 1931–37* (Cambridge, Mass., 1991). There is no single standard history of the War of Resistance to Japan in English. In Chinese, an essential volume is Zhang Xianwen (ed.), *Zhongguo kang-Ri zhanzheng shi (1931–1945)* [History of the War of Resistance to Japan, 1931–1945] (Nanjing, 2001). Hans van de Ven, *War and Nationalism in China, 1925–45* (London, 2003), contains substantial chapters on the war against Japan and on military culture more widely. One of the most notorious incidents during the war is chronicled starkly in Iris Chang, *The Rape of Nanking: The Hidden Holocaust of World War II* (New York, 1997). The social impact of warfare is detailed in Diana Lary and Stephen MacKinnon, *Scars of War: The Impact of Warfare on Modern China* (Vancouver, 2001). On the Communist base areas, see Chalmers Johnson, *Peasant Nationalism and Communist Power: The Emergence of Revolutionary China, 1937–1945* (Stanford, 1964); Mark Selden,

The Yenan Way in Revolutionary China (Cambridge, Mass., 1971); Yung-fa Chen, *Making Revolution: The Communist Movement in Eastern and Central China, 1937–1945* (Berkeley, 1986); Gregor Benton, *New Fourth Army: Communist Resistance along the Yangtze and the Huai, 1938–1941* (Richmond, UK, 1999); and David Goodman, *Social and Political Change in Revolutionary China: The Taihang Base Area in the War of Resistance to Japan, 1937–1945* (Lanham, MD, 2000). On the areas where collaboration with the Japanese took place, see David P. Barrett and Larry N. Shyu, *Chinese Collaboration with Japan, 1932–1945: The Limits of Accommodation* (Stanford, CA, 2001). On intellectual choices, see Poshek Fu, *Passivity, Resistance, and Collaboration: Intellectual Choices in Occupied Shanghai, 1937–1945* (Stanford, 1993). On the Civil War, see Odd Arne Westad, *Decisive Encounters: The Chinese Civil War, 1946–1950* (Stanford, 2003).

The Great Leap Forward and the Cultural Revolution

The politics of this period are fully documented and analysed in Roderick MacFarquhar, *The Origins of the Cultural Revolution* (Oxford, 3 vols., 1974–96). On the effects of the famine, see Jasper Becker, *Hungry Ghosts: China's Secret Famine* (London, 1996) and Dali L. Yang, *Calamity and Reform in China: State, Rural Society, and Institutional Change since the Great Leap Famine* (Stanford, CA, 1996). There is a clear account of the causes of the Cultural Revolution in Lynn White, *Policies of Chaos: The Organizational Causes of Violence in China's Cultural Revolution* (Princeton, 1989). Among many important studies of this period are Elizabeth Perry and Li Xun, *Proletarian Power: Shanghai in the Cultural Revolution* (Boulder, CO, 1997), and Anita Chan, *Children of Mao: A Study of Politically Active Chinese Youths* (Seattle, 1985). A stimulating set of essays is William A. Joseph, Christine P. W. Wong, and David Zweig (eds.), *New Perspectives on the Cultural Revolution* (Cambridge, Mass., 1991). Harriet Evans and Stephanie Donald (eds.), *Picturing Power in the People's Republic of China: Posters of the Cultural Revolution* (Lanham, MD, 1999) examines the dramatic poster art of the era in detail. A concise history of the whole period will be Roderick MacFarquhar and Michael Schoenhals, *The Cultural Revolution in China* (Cambridge, Mass., forthcoming).

Politics and Society since the Death of Mao

The elite politics of the period are detailed in Richard Baum, *Burying Mao: Chinese Politics in the Era of Deng Xiaoping* (Princeton, NJ, 1994) and the changing relationship between state and society is analysed in Vivienne Shue, *The Reach of the State: Sketches of the Body Politic* (Stanford, 1988). For the relationship between intellectuals and the state, see Merle Goldman, *Sowing the Seeds of Democracy in China: Political Reform in the Deng Xiaoping Era* (Cambridge, Mass., 1994). On the 1989 Tian'anmen Square crisis, see Frank Pieke, *The Ordinary and the Extraordinary: An Anthropological Study of Chinese Reform and the 1989 People's Movement in Beijing* (London, 1996); and Dingxin Zhao, *The Power of Tiananmen: State-Society Relations and the 1989 Beijing Student Movement* (Chicago, 2001). A comprehensive account of politics and ideological change since 1989 is Joseph Fewsmith, *China After Tiananmen: The Politics of Transition* (Cambridge, UK, 2001).

Culture and Literature since the Death of Mao

On the 1980s 'Culture Fever', see the highly informed analyses in Jing Wang, *High Culture Fever: Politics, Aesthetics, and Ideology in Deng's China* (Berkeley, 1996); Xudong Zhang, *Chinese Modernism in the Age of Reforms* (Durham, NC, 1997), and Chen Fong-ching and Jin Guantao, *From Youthful Manuscripts to River Elegy: The Chinese Popular Cultural Movement and Political Transformation 1979–1989* (Hong Kong, 1997). Tang Xiaobing, *Chinese Modern: The Heroic and the Quotidian* (Durham, NC, 2000), explores literary connections between the early twentieth century and the reform era. For the post-1989 period, stimulating analyses include Geremie Barmé, *Shades of Mao: The Posthumous Cult of the Great Leader* (Armonk, NY, 1996) and by the same author *In the Red: On Contemporary Chinese Culture* (New York, 1999); and Shiping Hua (ed.), *Chinese Political Culture, 1989–2000* (Armonk, NY, 2001). Contemporary intellectual debates are explored in Xudong Zhang (ed.), *Whither China? Intellectual Politics in Contemporary China* (Durham, NC, 2001).

Notes

CHAPTER 1

1. *North-China Herald* (hereafter *NCH*), 10 May 1919, 348. The *North-China Herald* was the weekly digest of the most important articles in the *North China Daily News*, published in Shanghai.

2. Vera Schwarcz, *The Chinese Enlightenment: Intellectuals and the Legacy of the May Fourth Movement* (Berkeley, 1986), 15–17.

3. Luo Jialun, 'Beijing daxue yu wusi yundong' [Peking University and the May Fourth Movement] in *Wusi yundong qinli ji* [Personal experiences of the May Fourth Movement] (Beijing, 1999), 64.

4. *NCH*, 10 May 1919, 348.

5. *NCH*, 10 May 1919, 348.

6. Luo, 'Beijing daxue', 66.

7. *NCH*, 10 May 1919, 348; Luo, 'Beijing daxue', 66.

8. Luo, 'Beijing daxue', 66–7.

9. Luo, 'Beijing daxue', 67.

10. *NCH*, 10 May 1919, 343.

11. Xu Deheng, *Wusi yundong qinli ji*, 14.

12. Schwarcz, *Chinese Enlightenment*, 19.

13. Cui Wenhua (ed.), *Heshang lun* [*Discussions on* Heshang] (Beijing, 1988), 76.

14. Wm. Theodore De Bary and Irene Bloom, with the collaboration of Wing-tsit Chan, *Sources of Chinese Tradition* (New York, 1960, 1999), is an excellent set of readings on the foundations of Chinese premodern thought.

15. The definition of 'culture' and 'cultural history' are huge areas in their own right. Two key starting points remain Clifford Geertz, *The Interpretation of Cultures* (New York, 1973), and Robert Darnton, *The Great Cat Massacre and Other Episodes in French Cultural History* (London, 1984).

16. Rudolf Wagner, 'The Canonization of May Fourth', in Milena Doleželová

and Oldřich Král (eds.), *The Appropriation of Cultural Capital: China's May Fourth Project* (Cambridge, Mass., 2001), 69.

17. Chow Tse-tsung, *The May Fourth Movement: Intellectual Revolution in Modern China* (Cambridge, Mass., 1960), 358–9.

18. Lin Yu-sheng, *The Crisis of Chinese Consciousness* (Madison, WI, 1979).

19. Joseph T. Chen, *The May Fourth Movement in Shanghai: The Making of a Social Movement in Modern China* (Leiden, 1971); Wen-hsin Yeh, *Provincial Passages: Culture, Space, and the Origins of Chinese Communism* (Berkeley, 1996), James R. Carter, *Creating a Chinese Harbin: Nationalism in an International City, 1916–1932* (Ithaca, NY, 2002).

20. Schwarcz, *Chinese Enlightenment,* 24–5.

21. Doleželová and Král (eds.), *Appropriation of Cultural Capital.*

22. Jonathan D. Spence, *The Gate of Heavenly Peace: The Chinese and their Revolution, 1895–1981* (London, 1981).

23. A recent survey is Sha Jiansun and Gong Shuduo, *Wusi yundong yu ershi shiji zhongguo de lishi daolu* [The May Fourth Movement and the Path of Twentieth-Century Chinese History] (Beijing, 2001) which has an excellent bibliographical guide to Chinese work.

24. Wagner, 'The Canonization of May Fourth', 69.

25. Douglas R. Reynolds, *China, 1898–1912: The Xinzheng Revolution and Japan* (Cambridge, Mass., 1993); Roger R. Thompson, *China's Local Councils in the Age of Constitutional Reform, 1898–1911* (Cambridge, Mass., 1995).

26. Henrietta Harrison, *The Making of the Republican Citizen: Political Ceremonies and Symbols in China, 1911–1929* (Oxford, 2000), ch. 2.

27. Vera Schwarcz, 'Strangers no more: personal memory in the interstices of public commemoration', in Rubie S. Watson (ed.), *Memory, History, and Opposition under State Socialism* (Santa Fe, NM, 1994).

28. Fei Xiaotong, ed. and tr. Gary Hamilton and Wang Zheng, *From the Soil: The Foundations of Chinese Society: A Translation of Fei Xiaotong's* Xiangtu Zhongguo, *with an introduction and epilogue* (Berkeley, 1992).

29. Mark Elvin, 'The Inner World of 1830', in Tu Wei-ming (ed.), *The Living Tree: The Changing Meaning of Being Chinese Today* (Stanford, 1994), 44.

30. An excellent introduction to the sweep of early Chinese history is Valerie Hansen, *The Open Empire: A History of China to 1600* (New York, 2000). On Marco Polo, see Frances Wood, *Did Marco Polo Go To China?* (London, 1995).

31. On Manchu–Han relations, see Pamela Crossley, *A Translucent Mirror: History and Identity in Qing Imperial Ideology* (Berkeley, 1999); Mark Elliott, *The Manchu Way: The Eight Banners and Ethnic Identity in Late Imperial China* (Stanford, 2001).

32. On the High Qing period, a fine survey is Susan Naquin and Evelyn S. Rawski, *Chinese Society in the Eighteenth Century* (New Haven, 1987).

33. Susan Mann Jones and Philip A. Kuhn, 'Dynastic decline and the roots of rebellion', in John K. Fairbank (ed.), *Cambridge History of China*, vol. 10 (Cambridge, UK, 1978), 128.

34. There is a lively and developing literature on the culture of opium in China. See, for instance, Timothy Brook and Bob Tadashi Wakabayashi, *Opium Regimes: China, Britain, and Japan, 1839–1952* (Berkeley, 2000); Frank Dikötter, Lars Laaman, and Zhou Xun, 'Narcotic Culture: A Social History of Drug Consumption in China', *British Journal of Criminology*, 42 (2002).

35. Pei-kai Cheng and Michael Lestz with Jonathan D. Spence, *The Search for Modern China: A Documentary Collection* (New York, 1999), 119.

36. Marius Jansen, *The Making of Modern Japan* (Cambridge, Mass., 2000); Carol Gluck, *Japan's Modern Myths: Ideology in the Late Meiji Period* (Princeton, NJ, 1985).

37. Cheng and Lestz, *Search for Modern China*, 171.

38. Robert Bickers and Jeffrey N. Wasserstrom, 'Shanghai's "Dogs or Chinese Not Admitted" Sign: History, Legend, and Contemporary Symbol', *The China Quarterly*, 142 (1995).

39. Benjamin Schwartz, *In Search of Wealth and Power: Yen Fu and the West* (Cambridge, Mass., 1964), 19–20.

40. Joshua A. Fogel, *Politics and Sinology: The Case of Naito Konan (1866–1934)* (Cambridge, Mass., 1984), 10.

41. Rebecca Karl and Peter Zarrow (eds.), *Rethinking the 1898 Reform Period: Political and Cultural Change in Late Qing China* (Cambridge, Mass., 2002).

42. On Yuan Shikai and Confucianism, see Ernest P. Young, *The Presidency of Yuan Shih-k'ai: Liberalism and Dictatorship in Early Republican China* (Ann Arbor, MI, 1977), 202–5.

43. On the politics of this period, see Arthur Waldron, *From War to Nationalism: China's Turning Point, 1924–1925* (Cambridge, UK, 1995); Andrew Nathan, *Peking Politics, 1918–1923: Factionalism and the Failure of Constitutionalism* (Berkeley, 1976).

44. Weili Ye, *Seeking Modernity in China's Name: Chinese Students in the United States, 1900–1927* (Berkeley, 2001).

45. Cheng and Lestz, *Search for Modern China*, 241.

46. Akira Iriye, *Cultural Internationalism and World Order* (Baltimore, 1997), 47–8. On pan-Asianism, see Eri Hotta, 'The Fifteen Years' War: Pan-Asian Ideology and Japanese Expansionism, 1931–1945' (doctoral dissertation, Oxford University, 2003).

47. 'The meaning of the Republic of China', in Sun Yat-sen, ed. Julie Lee Wei, Ramon H. Myers, and Donald G. Gillin, *Prescriptions for Saving China: Selected Writings of Sun Yat-sen*, 129.

48. A fresh, post-Cold War assessment of Chiang's career until 1949 is Jonathan Fenby, *Generalissimo: Chiang Kai-shek and the China He Lost* (London, 2003).

CHAPTER 2

1. Chen Tu-hsiu (Chen Duxiu), 'Call to Youth' (1915), in Teng Ssu-yu and John K. Fairbank, *China's Response to the West: A Documentary Survey, 1839–1923* (Cambridge, Mass., 1979), 240.
2. Paul Fussell, *The Great War and Modern Memory* (Oxford, 1975); Jay Winter, *Sites of Memory, Sites of Mourning: The Great War in European Cultural History* (Cambridge, UK, 1995).
3. Robert Bickers, *Empire Made Me: An Englishman Adrift in Shanghai* (London, 2003), 39.
4. For an explanation of why I refer to the city as 'Beijing', but to 'Peking University', please see the note at the front of the book.
5. David Strand, *Rickshaw Beijing: City People and Politics in the 1920s* (Berkeley, 1989), 7.
6. Strand, *Rickshaw Beijing*, ch. 7.
7. Schwarcz, *Chinese Enlightenment*, 48.
8. Zhu Hǎitao (Zhu Wenchang), 'Beida yu Beidaren' [Peking University and Peking University People] in Wang Shiru and Wen Di, *Wo yu Beida: 'Lao Beida' hua Beida* [Peking University and Me: Former Students Talk about Peking University] (Beijing, 1998), 475, 480.
9. Zhu, 'Beida yu Beidaren', 476–7.
10. Zhu, 'Beida yu Beidaren', 477–8. For an account of Peking University under Cai Yuanpei's presidency, see Schwarcz, *Chinese Enlightenment*, 46–54.
11. *All about Shanghai: A Standard Guidebook* (orig. Shanghai, 1934–5), (Hong Kong, 1983). Robert Bickers, *Britain in China: Community, Culture, and Colonialism, 1900–1949* (Manchester, 1999), deals with the British settler community and their views of Shanghai. On Chinese conceptions of the city, see Leo Ou-fan Lee, *Shanghai Modern: The Flowering of a New Urban Culture, 1930–1945* (Cambridge, Mass., 1999), ch. 1.
12. 'Rushing', in Ding Ling, *Miss Sophie's Diary and Other Stories* (tr. W. J. F. Jenner) (Beijing, 1985), 191.
13. Cheng and Lestz, *Search for Modern China*, 258–9.
14. Bickers and Wasserstrom, 'Shanghai's "Dogs and Chinese Not Admitted" Sign', 460.
15. Bryna Goodman, *Native Place, City, and Nation: Regional Networks and Identities in Shanghai, 1853–1937* (Berkeley, 1995), 27–8.

16. Mao Tun [Mao Dun] (tr. Hsu Meng-hsiung and A.C. Barnes), *Midnight* (Beijing, 1957), 16–17.

17. Lee, *Shanghai Modern*, 21, 120–1, 122–30.

18. Wen-hsin Yeh, *The Alienated Academy: Culture and Politics in Republican China, 1919–1937* (Cambridge, Mass., 1990), 65, 135, 141, 283.

19. Lu Hanchao, *Beyond the Neon Lights: Everyday Life in Early Twentieth-Century Shanghai*, 118–19, ch. 5.

20. Margo S. Gewurtz, *Between America and Russia: Chinese Student Radicalism and the Travel Books of Tsou T'ao-fen, 1933–1937* (Toronto, 1975), 3.

21. 'Wode muqin' [My mother] in Xu Xing and Jing Zhen (eds.), *Taofen sanwen* [Selected essays of Zou Taofen] (Beijing, 1997), 377.

22. For Zou's life and development as a writer and publisher, see Wen-hsin Yeh, 'Progressive Journalism and Shanghai's Petty Urbanites: Zou Taofen and the Shenghuo Weekly, 1926–1945', in Frederic Wakeman, Jr. and Wen-hsin Yeh (eds.), *Shanghai Sojourners* (Berkeley, 1992). See also Mu Xin, *Zou Taofen* (Hubei, 1981) and Chen Hui, *Zou Taofen* (Shanghai, 1999).

23. Mu Xin, *Zou Taofen*, 49.

24. *Chinese Literature* 1967:1, 87.

25. 'Preface' in Lu Xun, *Call to Arms* (tr. Yang Xianyi and Gladys Yang) (Beijing, 1981), iii.

26. Spence, *Gate of Heavenly Peace*, 101–2.

27. 'A Certain Night', in Ding Ling, *Miss Sophie's Diary*, 186.

28. A powerful account of the National Products Movement is Karl Gerth, *China Made: Consumer Culture and the Creation of the Nation* (Cambridge, Mass., 2003).

29. Charlotte Furth, 'Intellectual Change: From the Reform Movement to the May Fourth Movement, 1895–1920', in Merle Goldman and Leo Ou-fan Lee (eds.), *An Intellectual History of Modern China* (Cambridge, UK, 2002), 88–92; Arif Dirlik, *The Origins of Chinese Communism* (Oxford, 1989), 11–15; Hans J. van de Ven, *From Friend to Comrade: The Origins of the Chinese Communist Party, 1920–1927* (Berkeley, 1991), 38–43.

30. Spence, *Gate of Heavenly Peace*, 115, 165, 170; Van de Ven, *From Friend to Comrade*, 22–6.

31. Jerome B. Grieder, *Hu Shih and the Chinese Renaissance: Liberalism in the Chinese Revolution, 1917–1937* (Cambridge, Mass., 1970), 124.

32. Leo Ou-fan Lee, 'Literary Trends: The Quest for Modernity, 1895–1927', in Goldman and Lee, *Intellectual History*, 163–7.

33. Dingxin Zhao, *The Power of Tiananmen: State-Society Relations and the 1989 Beijing Student Movement* (Chicago, 2001), ch. 8.

CHAPTER 3

1. 'Shenme shi pingdeng?' [What is equality?] (orig. in *Life* 2:36, 10 July 1927) in *Taofen sanwen*, 22.

2. S. A. Smith, *Like Cattle and Horses: Nationalism and Labor in Shanghai, 1895–1927* (Durham, NC, 2001), 17.

3. Smith, *Like Cattle and Horses*; Elizabeth Perry, *Shanghai on Strike: The Politics of Chinese Labor* (Stanford, 1993); Emily Honig, *Sisters and Strangers: Women in the Shanghai Cotton Mills, 1919–1949* (Stanford, 1986).

4. On professionals, see Xu Xiaoqun, *Chinese Professionals and the Republican State: The Rise of Professional Associations in Shanghai, 1912–1937* (Cambridge, UK, 2001); on petty urbanites, Wen-hsin Yeh, 'Progressive Journalism', 191–4 and Lu, *Beyond the Neon Lights*, 61–3; on the bourgeoisie, Marie-Claire Bergere, *The Golden Age of the Chinese Bourgeoisie, 1911–1937* (Cambridge, UK, 1989).

5. On footbinding, see Maria Jaschok, *Concubines and Bondservants: A Social History* (London, 1988), 24–5.

6. Wang Zheng, *Women in the Chinese Enlightenment: Oral and Textual Histories* (Berkeley, 1999), 188.

7. 'Nü kexuejia shuo de ji ju hua' [Some words about a woman scientist] (orig. in *Life* 5:6, 5 January 1930) in *Taofen sanwen*, 682.

8. Honig, *Sisters and Strangers*, 139, 161, 172.

9. On anti-religious radicalism in Nationalist politics, see Prasenjit Duara, *Rescuing History from the Nation: Questioning Narratives of Modern China* (Chicago, 1995), ch. 3.

10. Rudolf Wagner, 'The Role of the Foreign Community in the Chinese Public Sphere', *The China Quarterly* 142 (1995); Chang-tai Hung, *War and Popular Culture: Resistance in Modern China, 1937–1945* (Berkeley, 1994), 40.

11. Lee, *Shanghai Modern*, ch. 2.

12. Denise Gimpel, *Lost Voices of Modernity: A Chinese Popular Fiction Magazine in Context* (Honolulu, 2001); Perry Link, *Mandarin Ducks and Butterflies: Popular Fiction in Early Twentieth-Century Chinese Cities* (Berkeley, 1981), 117.

13. Wang Zheng, *Women in the Chinese Enlightenment*, 191.

14. See Leo Ou-fan Lee and Andrew J. Nathan, 'The Beginnings of Mass Culture: Journalism and Fiction in the Late Ch'ing and Beyond', in David Johnson, Andrew J. Nathan, and Evelyn S. Rawski (eds.), *Popular Culture in Late Imperial China* (Berkeley, 1985).

15. See Jiwei Ci, *Dialectic of the Chinese Revolution: From Utopianism to Hedonism* (Stanford, 1994), 68–9.

16. Leo Ou-fan Lee, *The Romantic Generation of Modern Chinese Writers* (Cambridge, Mass., 1973), 295.

17. 'Miss Sophie's Diary', in Ding Ling, *Miss Sophie's Diary* (tr. Jenner), 19, 40.

18. 'Miss Sophie's Diary', 52, 60, 64.

19. Spence, *Gate of Heavenly Peace*, 300.

20. Zhu, 'Beida yu Beidaren', 478.

21. Wen-hsin Yeh, 'Progressive Journalism', 205–16, has a detailed analysis of many of the issues which Zou's readers brought up in their letters.

22. Guan Dongsheng (ed.), *Taofen 'Duzhe xinxiang'* [Taofen's 'Readers' Mailbox'] (Beijing, 1998), 137.

23. *Taofen 'Duzhe xinxiang'*, 150.

24. *Taofen 'Duzhe xinxiang'*, 151.

25. *Taofen 'Duzhe xinxiang'*, 138–9.

26. *Taofen 'Duzhe xinxiang'*, 140.

27. Yeh, 'Progressive Journalism', 214.

28. *Taofen 'Duzhe xinxiang'*, 134.

29. *Taofen 'Duzhe xinxiang'*, 135.

30. Spence, *Gate of Heavenly Peace*, 267.

31. *Taofen 'Duzhe xinxiang'*, 135, 136.

32. *Taofen 'Duzhe xinxiang'*, 141.

33. The novel is analysed in detail in Link, *Mandarin Ducks and Butterflies*.

34. Du Zhongyuan, 'Jiuguo zhishi zai nali?' [Where are the national salvation patriots?] in Du Zhongyuan, *Yuzhong zagan* [Feelings while in prison] (Shanghai, 1936), 38.

35. Lu Xun, 'Preface', ii.

36. Elisabeth Köll, *From Cotton Mill to Business Empire: The Emergence of Regional Enterprise in Modern China, 1895–1949* (Cambridge, Mass., 2004). On biographies of entrepreneurial patients in the Republic, see Gerth, *China Made*.

37. 'Zui youyi yu quan shijie de lao touzi' [The most useful old man in the world] (orig. in *Life* 2:33–37, 5 to 19 June 1927), in *Taofen sanwen*, 644–6.

38. See Peter Kornicki, *The Reform of Fiction in Meiji Japan* (London, 1982).

39. Gerth, *China Made*.

40. Du Zhongyuan, 'Ba nian nuli zhongde yuanwang' [My hopes during my eight years of hard work] (orig. in *Life*, July 1931), in Du Yi and Du Ying (eds.), *Huan wo heshan: Du Zhongyuan wenji* [Going back to my rivers and mountains: Du Zhongyuan's collected works] (Shanghai, 1998), 2.

41. 'Ba nian', 4.

42. 'Ba nian', 2.

43. 'Ba nian', 3.

44. 'Ba nian', 3.

45. 'Ba nian', 4.

46. On warlord politics of the period in Manchuria, see Gavan McCormack, *Chang Tso-lin in Northeast China, 1911–1928: China, Japan, and the Manchurian Idea* (Stanford, 1977); Ronald Suleski, *Civil Government in Warlord China: Tradition, Modernization and Manchuria* (New York, 2002).

47. Rana Mitter, 'Manchuria in mind: press, propaganda, and Northeast China in the age of empire, 1930–1937', in Mariko Asano Tamanoi (ed.), *Crossed Histories: New Approaches to Manchuria in the Age of Empire* (Honolulu, 2004).

48. 'Ba nian', 7–8.

49. Lloyd Eastman, *Family, Fields, and Ancestors: Constancy and Change in China's Social and Economic History, 1550–1949* (Oxford, 1988), ch. 5.

50. Rana Mitter, *The Manchurian Myth: Nationalism, Resistance and Collaboration in Modern China* (Berkeley, 2000), 226.

CHAPTER 4

1. Xu Deheng, 'Huiyi wusi yundong' [Remembering the May Fourth Movement], in *Wusi yundong qinli ji*, 14.

2. On smaller parties in Republican China, see Roger Jeans (ed.), *Roads Not Taken: The Struggle of Opposition Parties in Twentieth-Century China* (Boulder, CO, 1992); Edmund S. K. Fung, *In Search of Chinese Democracy: Civil Opposition in Nationalist China, 1929–1949* (Cambridge, UK, 2000); Roger Jeans, *Democracy and Socialism in Republican China: The Politics of Zhang Junmai (Carsun Chang), 1906–1941* (Lanham, MD, 1997); for differing varieties of socialism in the late Qing and early Republic, see Dirlik, *Origins of Chinese Communism*.

3. On the US, see Maurice Isserman and Michael Kazin, *America Divided: The Civil War of the 1960s* (New York, 2000).

4. On Gandhi, see Judith M. Brown, *Gandhi: Prisoner of Hope* (New Haven, CT, 1989).

5. Gewurtz, *Between America and Russia*, 8.

6. Chen Tu-hsiu (Chen Duxiu), 'Call to Youth' (1915), in Teng and Fairbank, *China's Response to the West*, 240.

7. Leo Ou-fan Lee, 'Incomplete Modernity: Rethinking the May Fourth Intellectual Project', in Doleželová and Král, *Appropriation of Cultural Capital*, 31–2, 58.

8. See Pei-yi Wu, *The Confucian's Progress: Autobiographical Writings in*

Traditional China (Princeton, 1990), on premodern Chinese writings on the self.

9. Spence, *Gate of Heavenly Peace*, 167.

10. Mao Zedong, edited by Stuart Schram, *Mao's Road to Power: Revolutionary Writings 1912–1949*, vol. 1 (Armonk, NY, 1992), 124.

11. Lu Xun, 'Diary of a Madman', in *Call to Arms*, 3–4, 12.

12. Lee, *Romantic Generation*, 111.

13. 'Miss Sophie', 42.

14. See Daniel H. Bays (ed.), *Christianity in China: From the Eighteenth Century to the Present* (Stanford, 1996).

15. Van de Ven, *From Friend to Comrade*, 33.

16. 'Zui youyi yu quan shijie', 649.

17. Hans van de Ven, *War and Nationalism in China, 1925–1945* (London, 2003), 166.

18. 'Zenyang huifu womende minzu jingshen' [How to recover our national spirit] (orig. in *Life* 2:33, 19 June 1927), in *Taofen sanwen*, 17.

19. Schwarcz, *The Chinese Enlightenment*, 217.

20. See Harry Harootunian and Tetsuo Najita, 'Revolt against the West: Political and cultural criticism in the twentieth century', in Peter Duus (ed.), *Cambridge History of Japan*, vol. 6 (Cambridge, UK, 1988). For a stimulating revisionist view of Nishida, see Christopher Jones, *The Political Philosophy of Japan* (London, 2004).

21. Frank Dikötter, *The Discourse of Race in Modern China* (London, 1992), ch. 4; Rebecca Karl, *Staging the World: Chinese Nationalism at the Turn of the Twentieth Century* (Durham, NC, 2002), 139–44; Joan Judge, *Print and Politics: 'Shibao' and the Culture of Reform in Late Qing China* (Stanford, 1996), 83–119.

22. Duara, *Rescuing History from the Nation*, ch. 6; John Fitzgerald, *Awakening China: Politics, Culture, and Class in the Nationalist Revolution* (Stanford, 1996), 150–4.

23. Norman Davies, *Europe: A History* (Oxford, 1996), 597.

24. Davies, *Europe*, 783.

25. There is a huge literature on this subject, of which Benedict Anderson, *Imagined Communities: Reflections on the Origin and Spread of Nationalism* (London, 1983, 1991), is one of the most important examples.

26. Marilyn A. Levine, 'Zeng Qi and the Frozen Revolution', in Jeans, *Roads Not Taken*; Frederic Wakeman, Jr., 'A Revisionist View of the Nanjing Decade: Confucian Fascism', *The China Quarterly*, 150 (1997).

27. Shih Shu-mei, *The Lure of the Modern: Writing Modernism in Semicolonial*

China, 1917–1937 (Berkeley, 2001), 14–15. For a powerful model of an 'East Asian modern', see Prasenjit Duara, *Sovereignty and Authenticity: Manchukuo and the East Asian Modern* (Lanham, MD, 2003).

28. William C. Kirby, 'The Internationalization of China: Foreign Relations at Home and Abroad in the Republican Era', *The China Quarterly*, 150 (June 1997), 433.

29. Arthur Waldron, *From War to Nationalism: China's Turning Point, 1924–1925* (Cambridge, UK, 1995), 31–3.

30. Richard Madsen, *China and the American Dream: A Moral Enquiry* (Berkeley, 1995), ch. 2.

31. *Jiuguo xunkan* [National Salvation journal] 1 (29 February 1932), 2.

32. Larry Wolff, *Inventing Eastern Europe: The Map of Civilization in the Mind of the Enlightenment* (Stanford, 1994), 6–7, 282.

33. Karl, *Staging the World*, 33–8.

34. 'Zhengjiu Tuerqi yu weiwang zhong de Kaimoer' [Kemal, who saved Turkey when it was in danger of destruction] (orig. in *Life* 4:1–3, 18 Nov. to 2 Dec. 1928), in *Taofen sanwen*, 598.

35. Karl, *Staging the World*, 177–93.

36. 'Zhengjiu Tuerqi', 597–8.

37. 'Jingcheng gandong quan Yindu de Gandi' [Gandhi, whose sincerity has moved all India] (orig. in *Life* 25:4, 19 May 1929), in *Taofen sanwen*, 601.

38. Gerth, *China Made*, p. 116.

39. 'Gandi de jiuguo fang'an' [Gandhi's plan for saving the nation] (orig. in *Life* 27:4, 2 June 1929), in *Taofen sanwen*, 611.

40. Van de Ven, *War and Nationalism*, 128–30; Schwarcz, *Chinese Enlightenment*, ch. 4.

41. Spence, *Gate of Heavenly Peace*, 214.

42. Gluck, *Japan's Modern Myths*, ch. 5.

43. Teng and Fairbank, *China's Response to the West*, 179.

44. 'Ba nian', 3.

45. Van de Ven, *From Friend to Comrade*, 240–6.

46. Dirlik, *Origins of Chinese Communism*, ch. 5.

47. S. A. Smith, *A Road is Made: Communism in Shanghai 1920–1927* (Honolulu, 2000), 4.

48. Li Dazhao, 'The Victory of Bolshevism' (1918) in Cheng and Lestz, *Search for Modern China*, 239–41.

49. Wang Zheng, *Women in the Chinese Enlightenment*, 194.

50. Marie-Claire Bergère (tr. Janet Lloyd), *Sun Yat-sen* (Stanford, 1998).

51. Harrison, *Making of the Republican Citizen*, ch. 2.

52. Fitzgerald, *Awakening China*, is a highly sophisticated analysis of the

development of Nationalist ideology. On Sun thought, see Audrey Wells, *The Political Thought of Sun Yat-sen: Development and Impact* (Basingstoke, UK, 2001).

53. Dikötter, *Discourse of Race*, ch. 4.

54. C. Martin Wilbur, *The Nationalist Revolution in China, 1923–1928* (Cambridge, UK, 1983), 147–91; Van de Ven, *War and Nationalism*, chs. 2, 3.

55. Gewurtz, *Between America and Russia*, 8.

56. Yeh, 'Progressive Journalism', 217–18.

57. Susan Glosser, ' "The Truths I have Learned": Nationalism, Family Reform, and Male Identity in China's New Culture Movement, 1915–1923', in Susan Brownell and Jeffrey N. Wasserstrom, *Chinese Femininities/Chinese Masculinities: A Reader* (Berkeley, 2002), 121.

58. Christina Gilmartin, *Engendering the Chinese Revolution: Radical Women, Communist Politics, and Mass Movements in the 1920s* (Berkeley, 1995), 23; Wang Zheng, *Women in the Chinese Enlightenment*, 20.

59. Gilmartin, *Engendering the Chinese Revolution*, 201, 212.

60. Gilmartin, *Engendering the Chinese Revolution*, 214; Wang Zheng, *Women in the Chinese Enlightenment*, 26, 192.

61. 'Nü kexuejia shuo de ji ju hua', 682.

62. Lin Yusheng, *The Crisis of Chinese Consciousness*.

63. Prasenjit Duara, *Power, Culture and the State: Rural North China, 1900–1942* (Stanford, 1988), 256.

64. William C. Kirby, 'Engineering China: Birth of the Developmental State, 1928–1937', in Wen-hsin Yeh (ed.), *Becoming Chinese: Passages to Modernity and Beyond* (Berkeley, 2000).

65. Gerth, *China Made*, ch. 4.

CHAPTER 5

1. Du Zhongyuan, 'You Taiyuan dao Fengzhen' [From Taiyuan to Fengzhen] (orig. in *Dikang* [Resistance] 13, 29 September 1937), in *Huan wo heshan*, 264.

2. Steven I. Levine, *Anvil of Victory: The Communist Revolution in Manchuria, 1945–1948* (New York, 1987), 149; van de Ven, *War and Nationalism*, 131.

3. The link between annihilation of biological pests and the extermination of state enemies in modern China is suggestively argued in Ruth Rogaski, 'Nature, Annihilation, and Modernity: China's Korean Germ-Warfare Experience Reconsidered', *Journal of Asian Studies*, 61:2 (May 2002).

4. Kirby, 'The Internationalization of China', 458.

5. Guoshiguan (Academia Historica, Taiwan), 172–1:1068 (Lewis telegram to Nanjing).

6. Donald A. Jordan, *China's Trial by Fire: The Shanghai War of 1932* (Ann Arbor, MI, 2001).

7. *New Life* [*Xinsheng*] 1:1 (10 February 1934).

8. Sherman Cochran, Andrew C. K. Hsieh, with Janis Cochran (ed. and tr.), *One Day in China: May 21, 1936* (New Haven, CT, 1983), 39.

9. Parks M. Coble, *Facing Japan: Chinese Politics and Japanese Imperialism, 1931–1937* (Cambridge, Mass., 1991), ch. 7.

10. 'Dayaxiyazhuyi' [Pan-Asianism] in Du Zhongyuan, *Yuzhong zagan* [Various thoughts in prison] (Shanghai, 1936), 68.

11. Van de Ven, *War and Nationalism*, ch. 5.

12. Donald Jordan has shown that Chiang Kaishek did in fact give covert support to Chinese units who fought in Shanghai in 1932. See Jordan, *China's Trial by Fire*, 237–8.

13. Mitter, *Manchurian Myth*, ch. 5.

14. *NCH*, 17 July 1935, 89, 100. On Du Zhongyuan's encounter with the Nationalist censors, see Michel Hockx, 'In Defence of the Censor: Literary Autonomy and State Authority in Shanghai, 1930–1936', *Journal of Modern Literature in Chinese*, 2:1 (July 1998).

15. 'Liu ge ren shi yi ge ren' [Six people are one] (orig. in Zou Taofen, *Jingli* [Experiences] (Shanghai, 1937)), in *Taofen sanwen*, 277. On this incident, see Parks M. Coble, 'The National Salvation Association as a Political Party', in Jeans, *Roads Not Taken*, 140–2.

16. *Chinese Literature* 1967:1, 87.

17. Spence, *Gate of Heavenly Peace*, 301–2.

18. *NCH*, 14 July 1937, 49.

19. *NCH*, 14 July 1937, 60.

20. *NCH*, 11 August 1937, 219.

21. *NCH*, 1 September 1937, 327.

22. *NCH*, 3 November 1937, 181.

23. See Iris Chang, *The Rape of Nanking: The Hidden Holocaust of World War II* (New York, 1997).

24. Xiao Hong, 'Flight from Danger,' in *Selected Stories of Xiao Hong* (tr. Howard Goldblatt) (Beijing, 1982), 136–7.

25. John Israel, *Lianda: A University in War and Revolution* (Stanford, 1998), 313–14.

26. *New Life* [*Xinsheng*] 1:30, 1 September 1934.

27. Chiang Kaishek, *China's Destiny* (tr. Philip Jaffe) (London, 1948), 98.

28. Mao Zedong, 'On New Democracy', in Mao Tse-tung [Mao Zedong], *Selected Works*, vol. 2 (Beijing, 1975), 348.

29. Mao, 'On New Democracy', 371–2.

30. Bonnie S. McDougall, *Mao Zedong's 'Talks at the Yan'an Conference on Literature and Art': A Translation of the 1943 Text with Commentary* (Ann Arbor, MI, 1980), 61, 81.

31. See, for example, Mark Selden, *The Yenan Way in Revolutionary China* (Cambridge, Mass., 1971).

32. See, for example, Susan Daruvala, *Zhou Zuoren and an Alternative Chinese Response to Modernity* (Cambridge, Mass., 2000); Poshek Fu, *Passivity, Resistance, and Collaboration: Intellectual Choices in Occupied Shanghai, 1937–1945* (Stanford, 1993).

33. On Wang's decision to collaborate, see John Hunter Boyle, *China and Japan at War, 1937–1945: The Politics of Collaboration* (Stanford, 1972).

34. Hung, *War and Popular Culture*, ch. 4; Charles Laughlin, *Chinese Reportage: The Aesthetics of Historical Experience* (Durham, NC), chs. 4, 5.

35. 'You Taiyuan dao Fengzhen', 269; 'Guitu' [Back on the road] (orig. in *Dikang*, 6 October 1937), in *Huan wo heshan*, 266.

36. *Huan wo heshan*, 6–7.

37. Yeh, 'Progressive Journalism', 186.

38. Odd Arne Westad, *Cold War and Revolution: Soviet-American Rivalry and the Origins of the Chinese Civil War, 1944–1946* (New York, 1993), and *Decisive Encounters: The Chinese Civil War, 1946–1950* (Stanford, 2003).

39. Ding Ling, *The Sun Shines over the Sanggan River* [tr. Yang Xianyi and Gladys Yang] (Beijing, 1984), 310.

40. Neil Diamant, 'Between Martyrdom and Mischief: The Political and Social Predicament of CCP War Widows and Veterans, 1949–66', in Diana Lary and Stephen MacKinnon, *Scars of War: The Impact of Warfare on Modern China* (Vancouver, 2001); Eddy U, 'Professional Degeneration and Political Decay: Shanghai Schoolteachers and the State 1949–1968' (Ph.D. dissertation, University of California, Berkeley, 2001).

41. On architecture and power at Tian'anmen, see Wu Hung, 'Tiananmen Square: A Political History of Monuments', *Representations* 35, Summer 1991.

42. An ironic reversal took place in the 1990s, when Shanghai, now freed by the reform-era CCP to grow again as China's economic powerhouse, entered negotiations with HSBC (the Hongkong Shanghai Banking Corporation) for the latter to take back their old building. In the end, it seems that the excessive rent demanded by the Shanghai government, along with the inadequacy of the old Bund building for the technology demanded by twenty-first-century banking led HSBC to choose a site in the futuristic Pudong district instead. The old Hongkong Bank building is now occupied by the Shanghai Pudong Development Bank.

43. On the Hundred Flowers and its aftermath, see Merle Goldman, 'The Party and the intellectuals', in Roderick MacFarquhar and John K. Fairbank, *Cambridge History of China*, vol. 14, 242–58.

44. On China and Mao's role in the Korean War, see Chen Jian, *China's Road to the Korean War: The Making of the Sino-American Confrontation* (New York, 1994), and Shu Guang Zhang, *Mao's Military Romanticism: China and the Korean War, 1950–1953* (Lawrence, KA, 1995). On PRC ambivalence about 'wars of national liberation', see Peter Van Ness, *Revolution and Chinese Foreign Policy: Peking's Support for Wars of National Liberation* (Berkeley, CA, 1970).

45. Van de Ven, *War and Nationalism*, 258–65.

46. Judith Stacey, *Patriarchy and Socialist Revolution in China* (Berkeley, 1983), 212–16. On the consequences of the famine, see Dali L. Yang, *Calamity and Reform in China: State, Rural Society, and Institutional Change since the Great Leap Famine* (Stanford, CA, 1996).

47. Jasper Becker, *Hungry Ghosts: China's Secret Famine* (London, 1996), 81.

48. Becker, *Hungry Ghosts*, 274.

49. Becker, *Hungry Ghosts*, 135–6.

CHAPTER 6

1. Nien Cheng, *Life and Death in Shanghai* (London, 1986), 96–97.

2. *Chinese Literature* (hereafter *CL*) 1967:1, 3; *CL* 1967:1, 3–4.

3. Schwarcz, *Chinese Enlightenment*, 249.

4. *CL* 1967:1, 29.

5. *CL* 1967:1, 87.

6. *CL* 1967:1, 5.

7. *CL* 1967:1, 11.

8. *CL* 1967:1, 30.

9. *CL* 1967:1, 28, 46.

10. *CL* 1967:1, 44.

11. *CL* 1967:1, 39.

12. *CL* 1967:1, 64.

13. *CL* 1967:1, 69.

14. Mu Xin, *Zou Taofen*, 391.

15. Duara, *Rescuing History from the Nation*, 90.

16. Victor Klemperer, *The Language of the Third Reich: LTI, lingua tertii imperii, a philologist's notebook* (London, 2002).

17. Joan Robinson, *The Cultural Revolution in China* (Harmondsworth, 1969), 27.

18. Robinson, *The Cultural Revolution*, 25.

19. The politics that led to the Cultural Revolution are analysed in meticulous detail in Roderick MacFarquhar, *The Origins of the Cultural Revolution* (3 vols., Oxford, 1974–97).

20. Gordon A. Bennett and Ronald N. Montaperto (eds), *Red Guard: The Political Biography of Dai Hsiao-ai* (London, 1970), 90.

21. Andrew Walder, 'Cultural Revolution Radicalism: Variations on a Stalinist Theme', in William A. Joseph, Christine P. W. Wong, and David Zweig, *New Perspectives on the Cultural Revolution* (Cambridge, Mass., 1991).

22. *Far Eastern Economic Review* (8 September 1966, 443–5), in Michael Schoenhals (ed. and tr.), *China's Cultural Revolution: Not a Dinner Party* (Armonk, NY, 1996), 142–3.

23. Elizabeth J. Perry and Li Xun, *Proletarian Power: Shanghai in the Cultural Revolution* (Boulder, CO, 1997), 150–1.

24. Shanghai Revolutionary Committee, 'Dangqian Shanghai wenhua da geming de xingshi he renwu' [The present form and tasks of the Great Cultural Revolution in Shanghai] (23 February 1967), Song Yianyi et al., *Chinese Cultural Revolution Database* (hereafter *CCR*), (Hong Kong, 2002) Part VI.

25. Bennett and Montaperto, *Red Guard*, 82–3.

26. Bennett and Montaperto, *Red Guard*, 94.

27. Bei Guancheng, 'I saw Chairman Mao!!!' in Schoenhals, *China's Cultural Revolution*, 148–9.

28. Liu Tianzhang, 'As I Watched Zhou Tianxing and Lu Wen Sweep the Floor', in Schoenhals, *China's Cultural Revolution*, 146–7.

29. Nie Yuanzi and eleven others from Peking University, 'Deng Xiaoping shi dangnei zou zibenzhuyi daolu de dangquanpai!!' [Deng Xiaoping is in the clique within the party which is going on the capitalist road!!] (8 November 1966), *CCR*, Part VI.

30. Nie Yuanzi, 'Chedi pipan Liu Shaoqi, Deng Xiaoping; jiang wuchan jieji wenhua geming jinxing daodi' [Repudiate Liu Shaoqi and Deng Xiaoping utterly; carry out the Great Proletarian Cultural Revolution to the end] (27 December 1966), *CCR*, Part VI.

31. 'Interrogation record: Wang Guangmei', and Wu Linquan and Peng Fei, 'Bo Yibo has an attitude problem', in Schoenhals, *China's Cultural Revolution*, 103, 122.

32. Fan Jianchuan, *Yi ge ren de kangzhan: cong yi ge ren de cangpin kan yi chang quan minzu de zhanzheng* [One person's War of Resistance: looking at the whole nation's war from one person's collection] (Beijing, 2000), 105–7.

33. Fan, *Yi ge ren de kangzhan*, 107.

34. 'As we watched them beat him . . .' in Schoenhals, *China's Cultural Revolution*, 166–9.

35. Zheng Yi, *Scarlet Memorial: Tales of Cannibalism in Modern China* (tr. T. P. Sym) (Boulder, CO, 1996), 85.

36. Zheng Yi, *Scarlet Memorial*, 85–7.

37. Richard W. Bodman, 'From History to Allegory to Art: A Personal Search for Interpretation', in Richard W. Bodman and Pin P. Wan (ed. and tr.), *Deathsong of the River: A Reader's Guide to the Chinese TV Series* Heshang, 37.

38. Bodman, 'From History', 37.

39. Merle Goldman, *Sowing the Seeds of Democracy in China: Political Reform in the Deng Xiaoping Era* (Cambridge, Mass., 1994), 339.

40. Lynn White, *Policies of Chaos: The Organizational Causes of Violence in China's Cultural Revolution* (Princeton, 1989), 38–42. This book has an excellent chapter on 'The Cultural Revolution: What it was and why it happened'.

41. This point is made forcefully in Mark Mazower, *Dark Continent: Europe's Twentieth Century* (London, 1998).

42. Duara, *Rescuing History from the Nation*, 107–10.

43. Van de Ven, *War and Nationalism*, ch. 3.

44. ' "Kongzi taolunhui" shi niugui sheshen xiang dang jingong de heihui' [The 'discussion group on Confucius' is a black group of cow demons and snake spirits aimed at attacking the party] (10 January 1967), *CCR*, Part VI.

45. Lee, *Romantic Generation*, 199.

46. Spence, *Gate of Heavenly Peace*, 215.

47. *CL* 1970:7, 64.

48. *CL* 1970:10, 3–40.

49. *CL* 1970:10, 97.

50. *CL* 1970:10, 97.

51. Harriet Evans, ' "Comrade Sisters": Gendered Bodies and Spaces', in Harriet Evans and Stephanie Donald (eds.), *Picturing Power in the People's Republic of China: Posters of the Cultural Revolution* (Lanham, MD, 1999), 66; Emily Honig, 'Maoist Mappings of Gender: Reassessing the Red Guards', in Brownell and Wasserstrom, *Chinese Femininities/Chinese Masculinities*, 255–68.

52. Spence, *Gate of Heavenly Peace*, 168.

53. Harriet Evans, *Women and Sexuality in China since 1949* (Cambridge, UK, 1997), 7–8.

54. 'Report on an Investigation of the Peasant Movement in Hunan' (March 1927), in *Selected Works of Mao Tse-tung*, Vol. 1 (Beijing, 1975), 28.

CHAPTER 7

1. Zhao, *Power of Tiananmen*, 201.
2. John Simpson, *Strange Places, Questionable People* (London, 1999), 315.
3. Xudong Zhang, *Chinese Modernism in the Age of Reforms: Cultural Fever, Avant-Garde Fiction, and the New Chinese Cinema* (Durham, NC, 1997), 1.
4. Deng Xiaoping, *Speeches and Writings* (Oxford: Pergamon Press, 1984), 91. (The interview took place in 1982.)
5. Zhang Xinxin and Sang Ye, *Chinese Profiles* (Beijing, 1986), 117. Translators of *Chinese Profiles* include Geremie Barme, Don J. Cohn, Stephen Fleming, W. J. F. Jenner, Frances Wood, and Gladys Yang.
6. Lu Xinhua, 'The Scar' (tr. Wang Mingjie), in *Prize-Winning Stories from China, 1978–1979* (Beijing: Foreign Languages Press, 1981), 111–12.
7. Laughlin, *Chinese Reportage* gives the history of the genre.
8. Liu Binyan, ed. Perry Link, *People or Monsters? And Other Stories and Reportage from China after Mao* (tr. James V. Feinerman, with Perry Link) (Bloomington: Indiana University Press, 1983), 43–4.
9. Deng, *Speeches and Writings*, 51.
10. Zhang and Sang, *Chinese Profiles*, 333.
11. Xinran, *The Good Women of China* (London, 2002), 5.
12. Shirin Rai, ' "Watering another man's garden": gender, employment, and educational reforms in China', in Shirin Rai, Hilary Pilkington, and Annie Phizacklea (eds.), *Women in the Face of Change: The Soviet Union, Eastern Europe and China* (London, 1992), 34.
13. Zhang and Sang, *Chinese Profiles*, 162, 288.
14. Richard Baum, *Burying Mao: Chinese Politics in the Age of Deng Xiaoping* (Princeton, 1994), 200–1.
15. Zhang and Sang, *Chinese Profiles*, 304–5.
16. Xinran, *Good Women of China*, 40.
17. Daria Berg, *Portraying China's New Women Entrepreneurs: A Reading of Zhang Xin's Fiction* (Durham, UK, 2000), 11.
18. Among the rich writings on Chinese democracy are Suzanne Ogden, *Inklings of Democracy in China* (Cambridge, Mass., 2002) and Andrew Nathan, *Chinese Democracy* (New York, 1985).
19. Zhang, *Chinese Modernism in the Age of Reforms*, 15.
20. Zhang and Sang, *Chinese Profiles*, 354.
21. On the Culture Fever of the 1980s, see Jing Wang, *High Culture Fever: Politics, Aesthetics, and Ideology in Deng's China* (Berkeley, 1996); Xudong Zhang, *Chinese Modernism in the Age of Reforms*; and Chen Fong-ching and Jin Guantao, *From Youthful Manuscripts to River Elegy: The Chinese Popular*

Cultural Movement and Political Transformation 1979–89 (Hong Kong, 1997). Tang Xiaobing, *Chinese Modern: The Heroic and the Quotidian* (Durham, NC, 2000), explores literary connections between the early twentieth century and the reform era.

22. *Reading* [*Dushu*], editions 1987/4 to 1988/3.
23. Don J. Cohn and Jing Qing, 'Introduction', in Bo Yang, *The Ugly Chinaman and the Crisis of Chinese Culture* (ed. and tr. Don J. Cohn and Jing Qing) (London, 1991), xi–xiii.
24. 'Chouluo de Zhongguoren' [The Ugly Chinaman] in Bo Yang, *Chouluo de Zhongguoren* (Hong Kong, 1987), 25.
25. 'Zhongguoren yu jianggang' [The Chinese and the soy paste vat], in Bo Yang, *Chouluo*, 65–6.
26. 'Chouluo de Zhongguoren', 24.
27. I have used the version of the script (referred to hereafter as *Heshang*) which appears in Cui Wenhua (ed.), *Heshang lun* [*Discussions on* Heshang] (Beijing, 1988). *Heshang*, 3.
28. Goldman, *Sowing the Seeds of Democracy in China*, ch. 12.
29. *Heshang*, 31.
30. *Heshang*, 27, 22.
31. *Heshang*, 14.
32. Bodman and Wan, *Deathsong of the River*, 311–27.
33. *Heshang*, 76, 43.
34. *Heshang*, 49, 50.
35. *Heshang*, 76.
36. *Heshang*, 77.
37. On rival May Fourths and conceptions of Chinese democracy, see Schwarcz, 'Strangers No More', in Watson, *Memory, History, and Opposition*.
38. Han Minzhu (pseud. ed.), *Cries for Democracy: Writings and Speeches from the 1989 Chinese Democracy Movement* (Princeton, 1990), 15.
39. Zhao, *Power of Tiananmen*, ch. 8.
40. Han, *Cries*, 17.
41. Han, *Cries*, 136–7.
42. Han, *Cries*, 140.
43. Han, *Cries*, 183.
44. Han, *Cries*, 162, 163, 170.
45. Ian Buruma, *Bad Elements: Chinese Rebels from Beijing to Los Angeles* (London, 2001), 73.
46. Zhang Liang, Andrew J. Nathan, and Perry Link (eds.), *The Tiananmen Papers* (London, 2001), 199–200.
47. Zhao, *Power of Tiananmen*, 199.

48. *Tiananmen Papers*, 371.

49. *Tiananmen Papers*, 379.

50. Frank Pieke, *The Ordinary and the Extraordinary: An Anthropological Study of Chinese Reform and the 1989 People's Movement in Beijing* (London, 1996), 224.

51. Han, *Cries*, 136.

52. Michael Sullivan, 'The 1988–89 Nanjing Anti-African Protests: Racial Nationalism or National Racism?', *The China Quarterly*, 138 (June 1994), 438–57.

53. Frank Dikötter, *Imperfect Conceptions: Medical Knowledge, Birth Defects and Eugenics in China* (London, 1998), especially ch. 4.

CHAPTER 8

1. Kam Louie, 'Sage, Teacher, Businessman: Confucius as a Model Male', in Shiping Hua (ed.), *Chinese Political Culture, 1989–2000* (Armonk, NY, 2001), 34.

2. Geremie Barmé, *Shades of Mao: The Posthumous Cult of the Great Leader* (Armonk, NY, 1996), 3–73.

3. In the 1990s, the idea that the war against Japan had lasted fourteen years (that is, from the invasion of Manchuria in 1931) became widespread among Chinese historians. In Japan, the idea of a 'fifteen-year war' (a different counting of the same period) became widespread at the same time.

4. Joseph Fewsmith and Stanley Rosen, 'The Domestic Context of Chinese Foreign Policy: Does "Public Opinion?" Matter?' in David M. Lampton (ed.), *The Making of Chinese Foreign and Security Policy in the Era of Reform* (Stanford, 2001), 162.

5. On China's role in the UN, see Sally Morphet, 'China as a Permanent Member of the Security Council, October 1971–December 1999', *Security Dialogue*, 31:2 (2000).

6. Allen T. Cheng, 'Professors who set alarm bells ringing in Beijing', *South China Morning Post* (19 May 2003).

7. Geremie Barmé, *In the Red: On Contemporary Chinese Culture* (New York, 1999), 350–1.

8. *Shanghai Star* (31 January 2003).

9. Jonathan Watts, 'Sow flowers, stop spitting – and score high on Beijing's morality index', *The Guardian* (London) (4 September 2003), 16.

10. Summary of article in *China Youth Daily* in CRI Online (http://english.cri.com.cn/english/2002/Nov/79819.htm)

11. Buruma, *Bad Elements*, 58.

12. Buruma, *Bad Elements*, ch. 2.

13. A selection of Wang Hui's work is presented in English in Wang Hui (ed. Theodore Huters), *China's New Order: Society, Politics, and Economy in Transition* (Cambridge, Mass., 2003).

14. Joseph Fewsmith, *China After Tiananmen: The Politics of Transition* (Cambridge, UK, 2001), 122.

15. Fewsmith, *China After Tiananmen*, 154–6.

16. Verna Yu, 'Crusader vows to fight on', *South China Morning Post* (31 July 2003).

17. On Taiwan, see David Shambaugh (ed.), *Contemporary Taiwan* (Oxford, 1998).

18. Ralph Wiley, *Dark Witness: When Black People Should Be Sacrificed (Again)* (New York, 1996), 32.

19. 'Spokesperson on the resolution on China's religious freedom adopted by the European Parliament' (20 February 2001), Ministry of Foreign Affairs, People's Republic of China [www.fmprc.gov.cn/eng/gjhdq/dqzzywt/2633/2637/2638/t15576.htm]

Index